Gardening TODAY

Gardening TODAY

Edited by Lizzie Boyd

WARD LOCK LIMITED · LONDON

First published in Great Britain in 1978
by Ward Lock Limited, 116 Baker Street,
London W1M 2BB, a member of the Pentos Group

House editor: Mia Stewart-Wilson
Layout: Heather Sherratt
Line illustrations: Sue Sharples

Text set in 11/13 VIP Bembo, printed by photolithography,
and bound in Great Britain at The Pitman Press, Bath

British Library Cataloguing in Publication Data

Boyd, Lizzie
Gardening Today.
1. Gardening
I. Title II. Coutts, John
635 SB 453
ISBN 0–7063–5185–1

Contents

Acknowledgments

For use of the colour photographs, the publishers gratefully acknowledge the kind permission of Frank Fawkes (pp. 65, 66, 100, 168 and 201), W. Scott Morrison (pp. 269 and 270) Mia Stewart-Wilson (pp. 99, 134 and 167) and W. J. Unwin Ltd (p. 303). The publishers regret that despite considerable effort, they have been unable to identify the copyright holders of the remaining colour photographs, to whom thanks for their cooperation are extended.

1
Starting a Garden

The ideal garden would be on a gentle south-west-facing slope with deep, rich, slightly acid loam. For most people, however, the location of their work and the size of their pocket determine where and how they will live, and the garden is often low on the list of priorities when choosing a place to live. Most gardening, therefore, involves learning to cope with and improve a less than perfect situation.

The shape of the plot

This is important but easily modified by the use of screens, hedges and borders to divide the garden into various parts of suitable shape. The hardest problem occurs when a house is in the middle of a square plot, as this leaves a narrow uniform belt of garden with little scope for variety and interest. Diagonal views across the garden with a focal point in one corner will make such a garden appear larger than it is.

With the house in one corner it is possible to create longer views and, by screening part of the garden from direct view, to add interest. A long, narrow garden can be oppressive but subdivision into smaller areas and elimination of any lines running along the length of the garden – which would emphasize the narrowness – will improve the appearance of such plots.

Wedge-shaped plots are very common on curves and corners of roads. Plots which widen away from the house are excellent, allowing small-scale treatment of paving and flowers adjacent to the house with expansive views and room for tree planting at a distance. Plots which narrow, sometimes almost to a point, confine the view and are more challenging. The most satisfactory treatment of such sites is to plant densely on either side of the house and at the end of the garden, ideally on a curving line, effectively cutting off the triangle to leave a broad open centre. If the size of the garden permits, informal winding paths can penetrate the planting to simulate 'woodland' walks.

Orientation and topography

These are unalterable factors. South- and west-facing gardens receive full benefit from the sun, but on the coast may be open to Atlantic gales.

North- and east-facing gardens may be heavily shaded and exposed to cold winter winds from the Arctic. It is seldom, however, that a whole garden is shaded all the time so it is desirable to allocate the more open, south-facing parts of the garden to vegetables, greenhouses and lawn with the west-facing corners as sheltered sitting areas for the afternoon and evening. This leaves the north- and east-facing parts for growing ornamental plants and, although this may at first glance seem unsatisfactory, there are many attractive plants which grow in such situations, not least the ferns and other foliage plants.

Topographical aspect is not amenable to such manipulation. Land sloping down to the south and west has a great advantage in absorbing more of the sun's light and heat than flat land, and even a moderate slope can create a climate similar to one further south. In contrast, a north- or east-facing slope will be dark and damp, especially in the winter, and will increase the heating costs of the house quite substantially. Such an aspect should be avoided, therefore, unless it commands exceptionally fine views.

Hill-top sites often have extensive views but are exposed to strong winds which make it difficult to establish plants unless some kind of shelter is provided (*See* Ch. 10). Low-lying sites are more sheltered, unless open valley sides serve to funnel the winds and increase their force, but may have poor soil and air drainage. Poor soil drainage is often obvious and may be countered by draining (*see* Ch. 3), but cold air flows down slopes in the same way as water and will accumulate in hollows, increasing the risk of frost damage. This is especially important to bear in mind when siting fruit trees, where frost damage to the flowers can ruin crops.

Existing features

Permanent and semi-permanent features, be they boundaries or plants, also require consideration. Wholesale clearance of a plot can be much easier than working around plants thought worthy of retention, but a much more satisfactory result ensues from working any existing features into the new plan. Old fruit trees can be brought back into bearing by careful treatment, or simply left as ornaments, with a new orchard planted elsewhere.

Before deciding on a plan it is worth living with the garden for a year – unless, of course, it is completely new – to allow all the plants already there to make their appearance. Only when they have done that can you give your own ideas a chance to consolidate. This time will not be wasted; preliminary clearing can be done and you will probably save much effort in the long term. Land which might otherwise have been deeply dug, for example, will require much less preparation if you decide to use it for lawns or paths rather than borders or vegetable plots.

Clearing the land

Most new gardens require a thorough 'spring cleaning'. All debris should be collected and disposed of. Combustible rubbish may be burned, builders' rubble collected into a pile for later use in path foundations or drainage sumps, and other waste buried deeply or put out for collection by the local authority who will usually remove even large objects for a modest charge. Care must be taken in disposal of cement, tar, paints, oil and similar waste as burial or seepage into soil can permanently affect plants later grown on it.

Dead plants, damaged or dead branches, old tops of herbaceous plants, etc. should also, in the first instance, be burned; subsequently, when cleaning up can be done regularly, much of the material may be clean and soft enough for the compost heap.

Perennial weeds must be completely eradicated. In old gardens and on new housing estates built on farmland which has been neglected for years, there is often a heavy infestation of creeping thistle, bindweed, couch (twitch), ground elder or nettles, and it is futile to attempt to establish a garden until these weeds have been banished. Repeated deep cultivation will weaken the weeds but, if the ground can be allowed to lie fallow, chemical control is usually more effective (*see* Ch. 8).

Old grassland is often infested with wireworms, leather jackets etc. so a garden newly established on old pasture may require fumigation (*see* Ch. 9). The safest chemicals are Jeyes' fluid, bromophos and naphthalene. Formalin can be used on vacant ground, but not near trees and shrubs. There are several more effective chemicals controlling a wide range of soil pests and diseases, but these are suitable for use only by qualified people. However, except in severe infestations regular cultivation will decrease the pest population by bringing them and their grubs to the surface where they will be picked off by birds.

Drainage and levelling

If major alterations to the level of the garden are contemplated this work should be done before anything else, as re-shaping the ground can be very damaging to the surroundings and the cost of re-shaping rises very sharply if there are any obstructions – new paths, lawns or trees – to prevent unrestricted use of machinery. Drainage schemes should also be installed, where necessary, as a first priority (*see* Ch. 3 for details).

Minor changes of level should be carefully considered. If the levelled area is to be used for lawn or borders it will be necessary to remove all the topsoil, level the subsoil as required, then replace the topsoil in a uniform layer. So altering the ground level by a small amount may mean moving large quantities of earth. A less arduous, though more expensive method for re-shaping small gardens is to buy in sufficient good soil to make up the level as required.

Paths, patios and terraces

When the land has been consolidated after levelling you can install the drive, the main paths and sitting areas, but it is advantageous to construct the foundations for these areas and to leave their surfacing until other garden operations are complete. This provides dry, level routes for wheeling heavy materials about and settles the foundations without risk of damaging the finished surface.

Lawns and planting

If the garden is to be completed in a single operation the best procedure is to plant trees first, then shrubs and herbaceous plants and finally to make the lawn. This avoids walking and dropping mud and stones on the lawn during planting operations. If the garden is to develop slowly over the years then it is advisable to grass down all areas not required for immediate planting. Regular mowing produces a healthy lawn, keeps weeds in check, and when the grass is later taken up to give room for borders and beds, the sods can be dug in as an aid to soil improvement or used on the compost heap.

2
The Nature of Soils

Soils are composed of a mixture of mineral particles from weathered rocks, organic materials and air and water. The composition of a soil type depends very much on the rock materials from which it is derived, and while large areas of similar geological formation have broadly similar soil types, the effect of erosion on a hillside often results in the soil at the bottom of the slope being deeper, richer in nutrients and usually more alkaline. Outcrops of different rocks may result in markedly different soils, sometimes with spectacularly different natural vegetation. All soils contain the mineral components of silt and clay, but in varying proportions and their fertility is determined considerably by the presence of organic material and the micro-organisms that inhabit it.

Sand

A sandy soil is hard and gritty to the touch with particles which do not readily stick together even when moist. The particles are loosely packed so that water drains rapidly through the large spaces between them, washing out silts and other nutrients. Sandy soils therefore drain very freely; they are usually acid and poor in nutrients. They dry out quickly in hot weather, but warm up rapidly in spring and are easy and light to cultivate and particularly suitable for early shallow crops.

Silt

Silt is similar in structure to sand, but is composed of finer particles which compact tightly and result in poor drainage. Silt soils are difficult to work and readily form hard pans through which seedlings cannot force their way and there is little air and water for the roots in which to develop. Most so-called silt soils of river estuaries are in fact fine sands which can be made productive by incorporating large amounts of organic manures.

Clay

Clay particles are formed of many layers of material between which are held essential plant nutrients which are gradually released as the clay breaks down. Their chemical structure of sticky particles is such that they retain any nutrients for a long time, making them more readily available than in light sandy soils. The particles are exceedingly fine and swell up when wet so drainage is slow. While some clay is desirable in the soil because of its water-holding capacity, a heavy proportion of clay makes a soil sticky, difficult to work and often waterlogged. However, if drainage is improved and humus dug in to lighten the soil and facilitate root development of plants, clay soils are usually very fertile. They take longer than sandy soils to warm up in spring, but holding water well are therefore more suitable for summer and autumn crops. The structure of clay soils can also be improved by liming and manuring (*see* Ch. 4).

Organic material

The organic matter present in soils is the result of decayed vegetable and animal debris and is constantly being replenished in a fertile soil by the

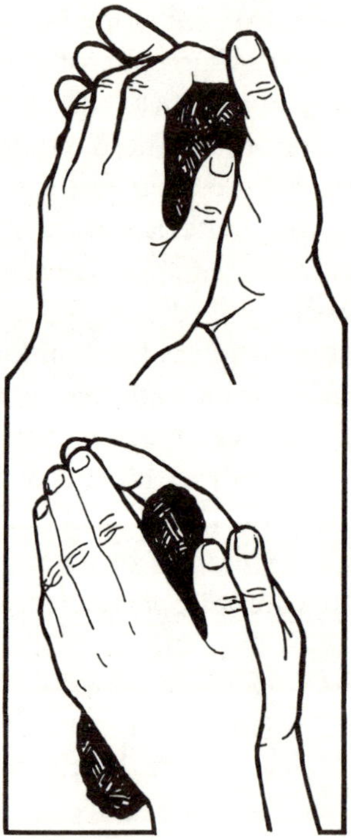

The most important types of soil can be recognized by a manual test when the ground is fairly moist
right above: typical loam can be moulded
right centre: clay can be formed into a sausage shape
below left: light sand runs through the fingers
below centre: loamy sand crumbles
below right: medium sandy loam can be shaped but breaks into medium sized crumbs

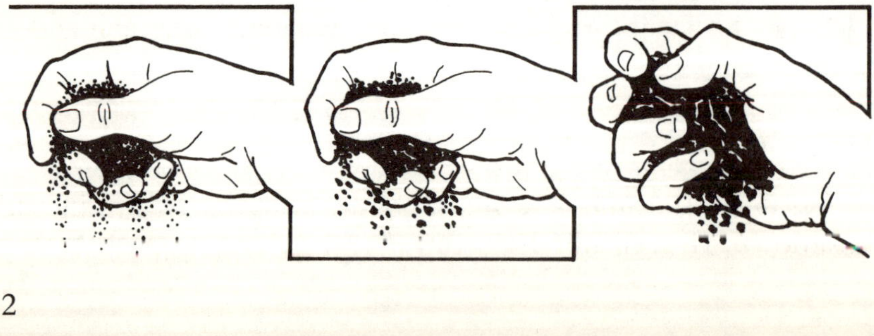

action of micro-organisms and earthworms. Organic matter – or humus – is present in varying degrees in the topsoil but is seldom sufficient for healthy plant growth unless supplied regularly by digging in bulky manures. Partially decayed organic material (humus) acts like a sponge, holding large quantities of water and releasing the necessary nutrients the soil needs. It greatly improves the water-holding capacity of sandy soils and helps to break up compacted clay soils. It, and the organisms which feed on it, also bind the soil particles together into larger crumbs thereby aiding drainage and aeration, so important for root growth as well as for improving the water-holding capacity. Thirdly, the decay of organic material releases plant nutrients, including trace elements, in forms readily available for uptake by plants. As decay proceeds most rapidly when the soil is warm and moist, the presence of sufficient organic material in the soil has the effect of providing a reservoir of plant nutrients which are not washed away by rain but which are released gradually as required by plants.

Soils in their natural state vary in organic material; peaty and leafy woodland soils have the highest proportion, but at the same time they are extremely light and loose and need careful management in order to retain their fertility.

Soil texture and structure

Most soils are mixtures of mineral particles and are seldom pure sand, silt or clay. As the sand fraction provides good drainage and clay provides a reservoir of water and nutrients, so the texture of soil is determined by the relative proportions of sand, silt and clay. A soil with a good balance of all three is neither light nor heavy but has a medium texture; it is known as loam or, if one particle type predominates, as sandy loam or clay loam. It also has a balanced humus content and is the ideal soil for all plant growth.

The swelling and shrinking of soil on wetting and drying, and the action of roots, worms and other natural agencies result in soil particles forming large crumbs which hold water, air and nutrients with large enough pores to provide drainage of excess water. It is important to preserve this soil structure by incorporating bulky manures and by working the soil only at the proper time. Badly timed digging, when the soil is sticky, can damage the structure, as can treading.

3
Drainage and Digging

Plants vary in their soil requirements, and while some will grow, if not thrive, in heavy clay or light sand, the majority give of their best in soil that supplies their immediate needs. It is a thankless task to attempt to alter a soil type to suit a particular type of plant; rhododendrons, for example, and other lime haters will never be happy on an alkaline soil, and many vegetables, especially brassicas, will only do well on acid soil if this is limed annually. The majority of plants, however, are less demanding and will thrive on a neutral or slightly alkaline soil. But irrespective of soil preference it is essential that the soil is both fertile and well-drained; fertility is maintained by cultivation and manuring, and waterlogged or badly drained soil can be improved by artificial drainage.

A system of drainage pipes will rapidly lower the water level in the soil and create a deep, well-drained zone in which plants can grow successfully. Agricultural tile-drains are most frequently used although these are now being superseded by perforated plastic tubing which is lighter and easier to lay. Brushwood drains or French drains (using a trench partially filled with gravel instead of a pipe) are also suitable although less durable.

Sinking drains

There are various ways of laying out drains, according to the configuration of the surface. If the ground has a clay subsoil and a uniform slope, as is the case with most garden plots, it will be sufficient to lay parallel lines of 5 or 7.5cm (2 or 3in) pipes at a distance of 4.5 to 6m (15 to 20ft) apart. Where the land slopes slightly on either side to a depression in the middle, a main drain of 7.5 or 10cm (3 or 4in) pipes should be laid along this depression from the head to the outlet, with lateral drains of 7.5cm (3in) pipes entering the main drain and connected to it by junction-sockets and elbow joints. The layout will depend on the nature of the soil and the contour of the surface, but is most often in a herring-bone pattern. The depth will also depend upon circumstances, but a main drain should lie 0.75 to 1m ($2\frac{1}{2}$ to $3\frac{1}{2}$ft) from the surface, shallowest at the top and deepest at the outlet. Lateral drains should run obliquely into the main drain, not at right angles, with the fall greater where the lateral approaches the main drain than elsewhere. A distance of 4.5 to 6m (15 to 20ft) is sufficient between the feeders to a main drain on clay soils. The fall of a main drain should never be less than 1 in 200.

Laying drain pipes

Before installing drain pipes, V-shaped trenches to the required depth should be taken out and covered with a 20cm (8in) layer of rubble for the water to drain through. Sometimes drain pipes are laid with collars, that is, short pieces of piping connecting the ends of two pipes and keeping them firmly in place. In other cases the pipes are joined together by bands of tempered clay when the upper sides of the pipes should be perforated to let the water percolate through. More often, however, the pipes are simply laid end to end in a straight line, or fitted into the socket on the next; bind the pipes together with clay or cement only at the junctions where the feeders meet the main drain.

Use a straight-edge and a spirit-level to make sure that the pipes are laid truly. This will save clogged or ineffective drains in the future.

Cover the pipes for a few cm (in) with rough porous rubbish, such as broken bricks or old rubble or even brushwood material. This is especially necessary on heavy clay soils. Alternatively lay flat tiles over the drain itself, then set tunnel-shaped half-pipes or bridge-pipes over these, and finally fill in the trench with earth and, without ramming or treading it tight, allow it to settle.

Small garden drainage

The installation of a drainage system in a small garden creates additional problems as there is usually no way in which to dispose of the surplus water. It will usually be necessary to dig a deep rubble-filled sump on the lowest part of the land into which the drains can lead. The sump will need to be about 1.5m (5ft) deep and filled for most of its length with loose rubble or clinkers. However, in most cases paths and drives adequately constructed on a base of hardcore will assist shallow water to escape.

Digging

The main reason for digging is to loosen the soil, incorporate manures and prepare for planting or sowing. On heavy soils digging is best done in the winter, leaving the surface rough and therefore better exposed to the elements; the frost will help to break down large clods into crumbs. Light soils are better dug in spring as the nutrients in the manure are likely to be washed away during the winter if cultivation is carried out earlier. For most purposes it is sufficient to dig the soil to one spade's depth – or spit – and this is particularly true on shallow topsoil. But for some vegetable crops or where deep manuring is necessary to improve the soil, double-digging, that is digging to two depths of the spade, is sometimes carried out. Bastard trenching, which involves digging to three depths of the spade, is hardly ever practised now.

Single digging

Digging with a fork has little effect apart from breaking and turning over the ground and reducing the clods turned up; with a spade the soil can be moved from one position to another. Digging is hard work, but can be eased by using proper tools – lightweight spades and forks for example – and by choosing a handle that is neither too long nor too short for the gardener, the strain on the back is much reduced. Avoid digging for long periods of time and do not try to take out more than a clod 12.5 to 15cm (5 to 6in) wide at a time; always dig to the full depth of the spade and insert the blade as near upright as possible.

First mark the ground out into strips some 3m (10ft) wide; trenches longer than this make it difficult to keep the soil level. Next take out a trench about a spade deep and a spade wide, the full length of the strip. The sides should be cut straight and square and the bottom flat and even; remove the soil from this trench to the far end of the ground to be dug over. Fork the bottom of the trench lightly and spread a layer of manure or compost if the soil needs improving. Now take out another trench of the same size and turn the soil from this into the first trench, leaving clay soil as rough as possible to expose a large surface to the action of the weather during the winter months. Continue this process until all the ground has been dug and the last trench filled with soil from the first.

Try to complete winter digging of clay soil before it becomes too wet; if left too late, the soil may be unworkable so that digging has to be left until early spring and the ground is deprived of the beneficial action of air, rain and frost through the winter. Digging when the soil is very wet does more harm than good; the earth becomes trodden down and compacted, losing all its porosity, which is the very characteristic that digging is meant to increase. While digging, carefully pick out all roots of perennial weeds; vegetable stems and leaves and all annual weeds can be dug in as manure provided they are deeply buried.

Double digging

This is sometimes adopted for deep cultivation and manuring of the part of the vegetable garden intended for peas, beans and other greedy crops. As with single digging, divide the plot into strips and begin by taking out a trench 30cm (12in) deep and wide. Next fork the bottom of the trench to a depth of about 25cm (10in) and mix manure or garden compost into this second spit. Take out the next trench and dig the top spit over the manure and loosened soil in the first trench. Continue in this manner until the whole plot has been deeply dug and manured.

4
Manures and Fertilizers

In order to retain and improve soil fertility and produce maximum crop yields it is necessary to supply plants with nutrients. These are available as inorganic and organic fertilizers, and as bulky organic manures which also add humus to the soil. The necessary elements are nitrogen, phosphorus and potassium, with lesser amounts of calcium, magnesium and iron, and trace elements.

Inorganic fertilizers

These are usually simply chemicals (nitrate of soda, superphosphate, sulphate of potash) each of which supplies only one particular nutrient. They may be mixed at home to produce a balanced fertilizer supplying all three major nutrients or bought ready-mixed as proprietary fertilizers for a variety of purposes, with extra potash for tomatoes and flowers, extra nitrogen for grass, etc. Compound fertilizers usually state on the packet the percentage of each nutrient, ie nitrogen, phosphate and potash, and is usually expressed in figures, 5:5:10 for example, denoting 5 per cent nitrogen, 5 per cent phosphate and 10 per cent potash.

The range of inorganic fertilizers is wide, and they are obtainable in liquid form, as completely soluble powders for rapid effect, or in capsule form for slow, regulated release in the soil. Most inorganic fertilizers are concentrated and quick-acting and should be applied and diluted as directed on the packet. The granules should be kept away from direct contact with soft plant tissues to avoid scorching. Compound fertilizers are also available as foliar feeds; these are applied to the leaves of plants with a watering can, and while they cannot replace the regular feeding programme, they act as a quick boost, resulting in rapid growth and increased yields.

Nitrogen

Apart from mixed fertilizers, the most useful nitrogenous fertilizers are nitrate of soda and sulphate of ammonia; the latter should be applied early in spring at the rate of 50g (2oz) to the sq m (yd). The former is often applied at the rate of 15g (½oz) to the sq m (yd) as a top-dressing during the growing season. Nitrate of potash is also good, but is much more expensive. In well-drained soils certain bacteria exist, especially round the roots of leguminous plants such as peas, beans and clover, which collect nitrates from the air and add them to the soil. Thus it is often possible to furnish a soil with both humus and nitrates by growing a crop of clover and lucerne and digging it in. Nitrogenous fertilizers act very rapidly and growth is often visible a few days later. The plants become noticeably greener and more vigorous. Nitrates must not be added to excess, or rank growth will follow, accompanied by lack of flowers and fruit and susceptibility to attack by fungus.

Phosphorus

This assists the correct development of the plant, its fruit or seed and its roots. The three most common forms of phosphatic fertilizer are superphosphate of lime, bone meal and basic slag. Superphosphate is the quickest acting, whilst basic slag is the cheapest, slowest acting, and longest lasting. It is best applied in autumn. Superphosphate is usually applied just before the plants are mature at the rate of 65g (2½oz) to the sq m (yd) and should be well mixed into the top 10cm (4in) of soil.

Basic slag consists largely of lime, phosphoric acid and various iron oxides. It contains other constituents as well but in small proportions. Its effects are similar to those of superphosphate, but almost twice the quantity is required to produce a given result. It does not succeed mixed with ammonia salts, as it sets free the ammonia and wastes valuable material, but is useful with nitrates. It is most valuable on medium or heavy soils which are deficient in lime, or are too wet and stiff; but to obtain the full advantage the soil must already be fairly well provided with organic matter. As a fertilizer it is good for flowering shrubs, roses, fruit trees, lawns and pastures. It should be applied and forked in during the autumn at the rate of 200g (7½oz) to the sq m (yd).

Phosphates encourage the formation of fibrous roots and earlier development of the plants, and counteract rank, sappy growth caused by excess of nitrogen in the soil. They should be applied every third year.

Potassium

This fertilizer helps the development of sugar and starch in seeds, tubers and fruit, and improves the colour and size of the blooms. The most popular potash fertilizer is sulphate of potash, particularly on heavy soils. It should be applied at the rate of 20g (¾oz) to the sq m (yd) in the spring. A simple way of providing potash for a small plot of ground is to add wood ashes and the ashes from burnt weeds in generous quantities.

Calcium

Calcium is used in building up plant tissues; soils deficient in this chemical produce small, stunted plants. Extreme deficiency is rare, but calcium also has important effects on soil acidity, soil structure and the availability of other nutrients apart from its function as a plant nutrient.

Magnesium and iron

These chemicals are involved in the making and functioning of chlorophyll, the green matter which enables plants to manufacture sugars, using energy from the sun. Plants deficient in magnesium or iron are pale yellow/green. Magnesium is not often deficient, but can be applied as Epsom salts (magnesium sulphate) if necessary. Iron is usually present in soils but becomes unavailable if there is too much lime present. It is therefore necessary to reduce the lime content or to apply the iron in sequestered form which remains available even in the presence of lime.

Trace elements

Other nutrients are also required for healthy plant growth but in such minute amounts that they are referred to as 'trace elements' or 'micro-nutrients'. As these are required only in minute quantities and over-doses result in serious, long-lasting damage to plants, they are not usually applied separately to the soil. They are usually present in sufficient quantities in organic manures and as impurities in fertilizers. If plants are grown in peat and/or sand without soil, addition of trace elements may be required and they are then applied as fritted trace elements which release the nutrients very slowly to reduce the risk of an overdose.

Organic fertilizers

Animal or vegetable refuse, such as dried blood, fish meal, hoof and horn, and bone meal, have appreciable amounts of nutrients, especially nitrogen, often in a form which is only gradually released to plants. Because they are slow-acting they can be used with safety. They also contain trace elements. Advocates of organic gardening use only organic fertilizers, claiming that inorganic fertilizers 'poison the soil'. However, there is no scientific evidence to favour either type.

Bulky organic manures

These include farmyard manures, wool shoddy, spent hops and composted vegetable refuse. They are chiefly humus-forming and have only small amounts of nutrients which are released slowly as the material decomposes. These manures are used mainly for the improving effect which they have on soil structure, but in large amounts they also contribute significant amounts of nutrients, especially trace elements which may be lacking in artificial fertilizers. Some bulky organic materials, especially shoddy and hops, actually use up nitrogen from the soil during decomposition and may depress plant growth temporarily unless an additional nitrogenous fertilizer is applied.

Nutrient cycling

In nature all nutrients are recycled. Leaves fall to the ground, plants eventually die and animals produce excrement and also eventually die. The processes of decay reduce these dead remains to simpler materials which become available again as nutrients for plant growth. In the garden leaves are usually swept away, lawn-mowings are removed and large quantities of vegetables are removed from the vegetable garden to the kitchen so nutrients are gradually but permanently being withdrawn from the soil. Natural recycling can be encouraged in part by consigning all soft vegetable waste, dust from the vacuum cleaner, bonfire ashes and other material of organic origin to a compost heap. Diseased or woody material is best burned, providing more ashes.

The compost heap

Healthy garden waste is ideal for composting and provides the cheapest manure possible. A compost heap is made of 25cm (10in) layers of garden and kitchen waste, with a sprinkling of sulphate of ammonia or a proprietary 'accelerator'. If the material is dry it should be well soaked, and if sulphate of ammonia is used a sprinkling of chalk or powdered lime (not quick-lime) should also be added. Heaps can be any size, but should not be more than 2m (7ft) wide and 1.5m (5ft) high. They soon warm up as decomposition begins and after six to eight weeks should be turned by forking over from one end and turning the outside unrotted material into the centre. After another eight weeks or so, the compost should be well rotted and ready for digging in.

Compost containers and bins, made from wire mesh, wood or heavy polythene, are both unobtrusive and space-saving.

Requirements of different crops and soils

Different crops naturally need different treatment. Thus potatoes and tomatoes, for example, particularly require potash, while leguminous plants, such as peas and beans, and certain roots such as turnips, respond well to the addition of phosphates.

The requirements of each soil can only be discovered after individual consideration, experiment and possibly analysis. But there are some rough rules. Farmyard manure in reasonable quantities improves almost all soils, heavy or light. It is usually unnecessary to add potash to clay soils, and usually necessary to add it to sandy soils. It may also be necessary, in order to liberate the potash in the clay soil, to add lime. Gravelly and sandy soils are nearly always deficient in nitrogen, and are much less retentive of fertilizers. Soils that are peaty, or that have become sour from excessive humus from constant year-by-year manuring with organic manure, can be improved by the addition of quick-lime applied frequently in small doses and dug in at once.

Application of manures and fertilizers

Slow-acting fertilizers, such as bone meal, and manures such as basic slag, farmyard manure and compost, are best applied while the digging is being done in the autumn and early winter. Quicker-acting fertilizers, such as nitrate of soda, sulphate of ammonia, sulphate of potash, must be applied in the spring or when the crops are growing. It is useless to apply quick-acting fertilizers in autumn and winter as the rain would wash away all their properties before the plants were ready to assimilate them. In the same way, slow-acting fertilizers would provide little benefit if applied while the plants were growing. Rates of application are given in the table below.

Application and uses of manures

Showing the soils to which they are most suitable and the time and quantity to apply.

Fertilizer/Manure	Soil to which best suited	When to apply	Rate per sq metre (yd)	Remarks
Ammonia, nitrate of	Any	Growing season	25g (1oz)	Fruit and vegetables.
Ammonia, phosphate of; Ammonia, sulphate of	Clay and chalk	Spring and early summer	25g (1oz)	Cabbage tribe, cucumbers, etc. Never on soil deficient in lime.
Basic slag	Heavy or light	Autumn (heavy) spring (light)	200g (7½oz)	Best for slow-growing plants. Do not use on chalk or sand.
Blood, dried	Any	Growing season	75g (3oz)	Good for flowers and vegetables.
Bone meal	Light	Autumn, early spring	65g (2½oz)	Excellent for lawn, fruit, shrubs and herbaceous plants.
Bones, dissolved	Chalk	Spring or summer as top-dressing	50g (2oz)	Never on soil deficient in lime. Good for all plants.
Farmyard manure	(Horse) heavy (Cow) light	Autumn or winter Spring	A good dressing	All crops.
Fish meal	Light or medium	Autumn and winter	40g (1½oz)	Good for nearly all plants, especially potatoes, turnips, etc.
Hop manure	Clay, chalk, gravel and sand	Autumn	425g (15oz)	Good for all fruit trees, shrubs and herbaceous plants.
Leaf-mould	Heavy clay	Winter or early spring	A good dressing	Adds humus to the soil.

Fertilizer/Manure	Soil to which best suited	When to apply	Rate per sq metre (yd)	Remarks
Lime, nitrate of	Any	Growing season	25g (1oz)	Especially good for cabbages but suitable for all crops.
Lime, sulphate of	Clay or medium	Spring or early summer	175g (6oz)	Fruit and vegetables.
Nitrate of potash	Any	Spring	25g (1oz)	All plants.
Nitrate of soda	Light and dry	Spring or early summer	15g (½oz)	Improves leaf growth in cold weather or after attack by insect pests.
Potash, muriate of	Light and medium	Spring or early summer	40g (1½oz)	Fruit and vegetables.
Potash, phosphate of	Light	Spring or early summer	40g (1½oz)	All flowers and vegetables, and all fruits under glass.
Potash, sulphate of	Light or heavy	Spring or early summer	20g (¾oz)	All flowers; asparagus, carrots, cauliflowers, onions, potatoes.
Poultry manure	Any	Growing crops or autumn	150g (5oz)	All plants, especially root crops.
Salt	Light	Spring or early summer	25g (1oz)	Salt-loving plants such as asparagus, beet, cabbages, celery, leeks, onions, etc.
Seaweed (fresh)	Light	Spring or autumn	A good dressing	All salt-loving plants as above.
Soot	Sandy or light	Summer	A dusting	All young plants.
Superphosphate of lime	Medium or light	Autumn (medium), spring (light)	65g (2½oz)	Never on soil deficient in lime.
Vegetable ashes	Any	Spring	150g (5oz)	Beans, carrots, onions, peas, potatoes, etc.
Vegetable refuse	Medium to light	Winter	A good dressing	Adds humus to the soil.
Wood ashes	Heavy and rich	Autumn or as top-dressing in spring, summer and autumn	150g (5oz)	Excellent for beans, carrots, onions, peas, potatoes and fruit trees.
Wool waste (Shoddy)	Any	Winter	200g (7oz)	Slow-growing crops. Manurial value lasts over three years

Top-dressing the soil

The aim of top-dressing is to enrich the soil and make new food available for the roots.

Most of the organic manures and artificial fertilizers mentioned above may be used as top-dressings; those most generally used for this purpose are bone meal, potash, leaf-mould, old lawn-mowings, nitrate of soda, sulphate of ammonia, superphosphate of lime and wood ashes. For flower beds and borders a dressing of 75 per cent of well-decayed farmyard manure and 25 per cent leaf-mould or other well-rotted vegetable matter is excellent. Rock plants will need an additional 25 per cent of leaf-mould and a good sprinkling of coarse sharp sand; granite or limestone chippings may also be used.

Top-dressings add to the plant food supplied by the manure dug in at planting time and are also useful when it is not feasible to disturb plants by digging manure into the herbaceous border or rock garden. They are usually applied in spring or early summer. The coarser organic manures are generally applied in even layers about 5cm (2in) thick and may be forked into the soil or left on the surface to act as a mulch. Artificial fertilizers are usually very fine in texture and must be well raked in.

Mulching

A top-dressing of an organic manure is known as a mulch and serves several purposes: it supplies plant nutrients, conserves moisture in the soil and suppresses weeds. Farmyard manure, garden compost, straw and peat are all suitable for mulching; lawn-mowings may also be used, but only in a shallow layer as they generate heat, and they should be avoided if they have been treated with a weedkiller. Mulching is usually carried out during May, June and July. It should not be done earlier as it serves as an insulating blanket and will prevent the soil warming up in spring; make sure the soil is thoroughly moistened first.

A dust mulch created by frequent hoeing is sometimes advocated as a substitute for mulching; it may slightly reduce water loss and is effective in controlling weeds, but unlike an applied organic mulch it does not keep the soil surface moist nor enables plant roots to make use of the most fertile part of the soil.

Soil acidity and liming

Calcium has already been mentioned as a plant nutrient, but the amount of calcium in the soil is also the main factor controlling soil acidity. As nutrients are washed out of the soil or taken up by plants and as organic materials decay, the soil becomes more acid. The main sources of calcium (chalk, limestone, quick-lime and hydrated lime) are all alkaline and serve to correct acidity. Soil acidity is indicated by its 'pH' value which can be ascertained by using a soil-testing kit; pH 7 indicates a neutral soil, neither acid nor alkaline, while acid soil has a pH of less than 7 and alkaline soil a pH above 7. Most plants will grow in soil with a pH value of between 6.5 and 7.

If the soil becomes excessively acid, bacterial activity is inhibited, acid leaf-litter may build up on the surface, nitrogen becomes unavailable and some trace elements are released in such quantities that they become damaging to most plants. Clay also separates into tiny particles, causing bad drainage.

In alkaline soils the clay particles group together, improving drainage, and bacterial activity releases nitrogen and other nutrients for use by plants. However, in excessively alkaline soil (a pH reading above 8), phosphate, iron and some trace elements are made unavailable for plant growth.

Lime requirements of different plants and soils

Plants vary in their responses to soil acidity. Most vegetables and the stone fruits require a moderately alkaline soil of pH 7–7.5. Rhododendrons, heathers, turf grasses and many woodland plants flourish only in acid soil (pH 5–6) and become very pale in alkaline soils. The majority of plants are most successful in soil which is slightly acid (pH 6.5).

Sandy soils lose lime and become acid more quickly than do clay soils, while soils rich in organic material have the ability to adjust to wide variations in lime availability without adverse affects on plant growth.

A soil test will determine the pH of the soil and a chart with the kit usually gives recommended rates of liming for different crops and soils. It is usual to lime a third of the vegetable garden each year, whereas among shrubs and flowers lime is only added when unsatisfactory growth is followed by a soil test that indicates excess acidity.

It is easy to correct acidity by liming, but the problems caused by alkalinity are more difficult to overcome. Powdered sulphur or alum may be used on small areas to make the soil more acid, but both are expensive, and have no long-lasting effect. Organic manures, especially the acid types of peat usually sold as rhododendron peat, can be dug in and, when applying fertilizer, care should be taken to select fertilizers with acidic properties. Sulphate of ammonia is an acidic source of nitrogen, but not nitrochalk and nitrate of soda. Nitrate or sulphate of potash are neutral. Phosphate fertilizers are alkaline, but triple superphosphate less so than single superphosphate or basic slag. Magnesium ammonium phosphate is neutral but very expensive.

Gypsum as a soil conditioner

Lime is used to improve soil structure but it cannot do so without simultaneously increasing alkalinity. If it is necessary to improve structure without affecting the soil pH then gypsum (calcium sulphate) can be used. This is a neutral source of calcium and can lighten clay soils in place of lime, providing calcium for plants requiring an acid soil. It is particularly useful as a conditioner on heavily-used lawns.

Growing acid-loving plants on alkaline soils

Soil amendment to reduce alkalinity may take a very long time. Fortunately most plants requiring acid soil have very shallow fibrous roots and, as lime washes down in the soil, these plants can be grown fairly successfully in raised beds of leafy or peaty soil or in deep containers. Soil fertility can be maintained by annual mulching and *light* applications of fertilizer; watering is usually necessary in dry weather. If plants become pale green, indicating lack of iron, this can be corrected with light dressings of iron sulphate at the rate of 15g ($\frac{1}{2}$oz) per sq m (yd), or with a proprietary source of chelated iron which is not rendered unavailable by the soil.

5 Plant Propagation

Plants may be increased from seed or from one of the vegetative methods which include division, layering, cuttings, budding and grafting. When growing plants from home-saved seed some variation in the resulting plants must be expected, especially from hybrid plants. Many annuals, and particularly the F_1 hybrids, have been crossed and selected by the raiser to produce uniform results, and these can only be perpetuated by repeating the original selection. With perennials the variation is even greater, but seed propagation is a simple and inexpensive way of raising a large number of plants; the best can then be selected and the remainder discarded. Plants raised by any of the vegetative methods will have the true characteristics of the parents from which they were taken, provided sucker growths are not used as propagation material.

Propagation by Seed

Storing seeds

Generally speaking, seeds retain full viability for one or two years only in ideal circumstances. Their life, however, may be greatly extended by storage at low temperature and humidity. Therefore, if seed is to be carried over from one season to the next, it should be stored in a dark, cool place at an even temperature and away from moisture. It is best placed in tins with tightly fitting lids, in thoroughly clean glass bottles if kept in the dark, or in wax-proof paper impermeable to moisture. Soft absorbent paper is useless, as the seeds will either dry and shrivel up or, if kept in too moist a place, get damp and rot.

When saving seeds from the garden, do not gather too early; allow enough time for them to ripen. Also do not leave seeds in their pods, as these dry up and draw both moisture and vitality from the seeds.

Sowing seeds

Seed may be sown in the open or under glass. Most can be raised quite satisfactorily in a prepared seed bed out of doors, but small quantities of seed, very fine or very expensive seed and seeds of plants which are not hardy are raised under glass in pots, seed pans or boxes.

Sowing seeds outside

Never sow in a cold, wet soil. Wait until the ground has dried and warmed up sufficiently; it is false economy to sow just on the offchance of getting an extra early crop. Choose dry, calm weather for seed sowing, and if seed can be sown just before a gentle shower, or when the weather is likely to be showery, that is even better. Of course, there is an ideal or optimum time for sowing every different kind of seed, but these are general instructions which apply equally to all seed sowing. The seed bed should be tolerably dry – dry enough to crumble lightly when worked with the hand although pelleted seeds require more moisture in order to soften the clay coats around them. Seeds sown under some form of protection can be sown earlier than in the open.

Site, soil and treatment of seed bed

The seed bed should be situated in light shade and sheltered from the north and east. The soil should be made as fine as possible, first by breaking up the lumps with a fork and then by raking it thoroughly until the earth is well pulverized. It should contain 10 to 20 per cent of sand – this will make it porous and will let the air penetrate freely through it. If the seed bed is inadequately prepared many of the seeds will fall down between the clods and will not germinate; those that do come up may

Preparing the ground for sowing seed in drills. Stretch a garden line tightly from one end of the plot to the other to enable you to keep the drills straight

have their tiny roots parched as there will be no fine soil through which they can work to obtain nourishment and moisture. Too rich a soil should be avoided as the seedlings tend to become tall and straggly, instead of short and sturdy. The bed must be pressed down firmly and left to settle for a few days before sowing. Water thoroughly, if dry, and sow the seed thinly in drills running north and south, if possible, or in broadcast drifts.

Depth to sow

Cover the seeds lightly with fine, sandy soil; the depth of covering depends on the size of the seed. Minute seeds need hardly any covering at all, only a sprinkling of sand; medium-sized seeds must have a covering a little less than 1cm (½in) thick; and large seeds, such as those of the iris or paeony, and also those like the seeds of the anemone and phlox which quite often do not germinate the first year after sowing, can do with 1 to 2.5cm (½ to 1in) of soil over them. Few seeds require deeper covering than 2.5cm (1in). Seeds may be sown slightly deeper out of doors than under glass, as the rain is liable to wash out any with too sparse a covering. A good rule is to cover the seeds with a layer of soil twice their own thickness. Seeds sown in heavy soil should not be placed as deep as those sown in sandy loam, while in sandy soil a covering of nearly twice that given in a heavy soil is usual.

Do not sow the seeds too deep, however, for if the seedlings ever reach the surface at all, they will have used up most of their strength and energy and will make weak, straggly plants. If the soil of the seed bed is very dry it should be watered the night before until moist enough for sowing. After sowing do not tamp the drills down, but firm them lightly with the back of a rake.

Methods of watering

As soon as the seeds have been covered, give them a good watering from a can with a fine rose. Keep the soil uniformly moist but not too wet; over-watering causes the seeds to rot and is the most frequent cause of failure. Strands of black cotton, supported on small sticks, and criss-crossed over the bed help to keep the birds away. If, before sowing, the seeds are treated with a seed dressing the incidence of pests and diseases is much reduced.

Thinning-out and transplanting

In a month or so the seedlings should be about 5cm (2in) high and will be large enough to be handled between finger and thumb for thinning or transplanting. This should always be done at the earliest possible moment. Delay in thinning and transplanting means that the seedlings become drawn-up and weakly; when they are eventually moved the fibrous roots may be torn and the seedlings take much longer to become established. So as not to tear the roots, the seed bed should be watered the evening before the day on which thinning is to be done.

For transplanting, prise the seedlings from the seed bed with a small fork; each seedling can then be lifted without any damage to its roots, and should be planted very firmly, using a small trowel, in a hole just large enough to receive the roots without cramping them or doubling them up. Care must be taken not to leave an air-pocket below the roots or they will soon be parched. Sturdy seedlings should be transplanted about 25cm (10in) apart, smaller ones 15cm (6in) apart, depending on their final size. If the seedlings are to be thinned and not transplanted, pull up the unwanted seedlings between the finger and thumb, pressing a finger of the other hand on the soil to keep the roots of the other seedlings in place. Press back the soil around those seedlings left in the seed bed or they will be likely to die off. If transplanting is done in the evening, the seedlings will have the cool night in which to recover, and will not be so liable to scorching. The nursery bed into which the seedlings are transplanted should have a sunny aspect, should have been well dug and the soil, if poor, will be all the better for having had good, well-rotted manure mixed with the top 7.5cm (3in) of soil. A further dressing of weathered ashes will help to lighten the soil and furnish nourishment for the seedlings.

In dry weather the nursery bed should be well watered the day before, but not made too wet, as the seedlings will not grow in compacted soil. Water the bed again after transplanting has been done, or, even better, transplant in showery weather.

Care of seedlings

In dry weather, the seedlings should be watered (but not when the hot sun is on them) and the bed must be kept well hoed. Tepid water is far better than cold water from the tap or a deep tank, and provided the soil is fairly rich the seedlings should need no feeding until they approach maturity.

In warm and sheltered districts the young plants may be left in the open all winter (annuals will, of course, have attained maturity, flowered and died down), but in colder districts it is safer to winter them in a frame from October onwards. Light, sandy soil and a southerly aspect suit most seedlings best; the frame should be freely ventilated, though excessive damp and hard frosts should be guarded against.

In November of the second season or in March of the third year the plants can be put out in their permanent positions; tender and half-hardy plants should be given some protection during the second winter. Slugs and snails are the great enemy of young seedlings, but slug bait should prove effective.

Sowing seeds under glass

The less hardy plants must be raised under glass, preferably in John Innes seed compost, a proprietary loam or peat seed compost, or a mixture of two-thirds good loam and one-third leaf-mould, together with a good sprinkling of sharp silver sand. Sift the compost through a 6mm (¼in) wire-mesh sieve and the soil for covering the seeds through a sieve which is even finer. Mix the compost thoroughly, press it gently into the pot or box, and make the surface level just below the rim of the pot. Clay and wood seed pans or boxes should be drained by means of crocks or broken pots, 2.5cm (1in) of crocks being enough in a box or pot 12.5cm (5in) deep. Plastic seed pans and pots have more perforations and do not need crocking. Sow seeds thinly in February or March, and water by immersing the pots or pans nearly to their brims, thus allowing the water to soak up from the bottom. Place the seed pans in a frame or greenhouse in moderate but steady heat of 15°C (59°F). Place a sheet of glass over each pot and cover the glass with brown paper or newspaper to keep out the light. Lift the glass every day so that the condensation may be wiped off, or the seeds will be kept too moist. No further water need, as a rule, be given until the seeds have germinated. As soon as the seeds are up (in about three weeks, according to type) remove the glass and paper, and move the boxes nearer to the light. If the box is left some distance from the glass, weak straggling seedlings will result. In warm weather it is wise to water the seedlings in the evening, but in colder weather any watering should be done in the morning or there may be danger of the seedlings damping-off.

Seeds in a frame

The seeds may be sown in a frame, either directly into the soil bed or in pans or boxes as described above. Unless the frame is heated, delay sowing until early spring. The frame should be in a sheltered position, as it is essential to ventilate as much as possible when the weather is sunny and calm.

Pricking-off

When the seedlings are about 5cm (2in) high they should be pricked-off, using a small cleft, wooden label, from 2.5 to 7.5cm (1 to 3in) apart so that the leaves do not touch (strong-growing kinds 15cm (6in) apart). Transplant them into boxes of light sandy soil or a proprietary potting compost and place the boxes near the glass. Insert the wooden label in the soil about 2.5cm (1in) from the seedlings, whose roots may then be gently levered up without damage – never pull seedlings up between finger and thumb, as this will damage the roots. Plant the seedlings so that the first pair of leaves show just above the soil and with the soil pressed firmly down round the roots and stems, though care must be

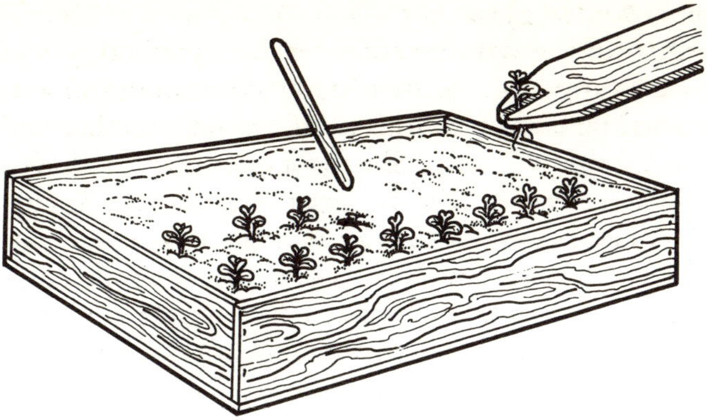

Pricking-off seedlings and transplanting them into a box, using a split wooden label and a small dibber to make the planting holes and for firming the soil.

taken not to injure any part of the seedling. A thin dibber about the size of a pencil can be used to make the planting holes; they should not be made too deep or the roots of the seedlings will not reach the bottom and the air-pockets under them will wither their roots. Do not firm the seedlings by pressing the soil round the stems with the fingers, but use the dibber, inserting it into the soil, in three or four places round the seedlings, about 1cm ($\frac{1}{2}$in) from them, and to the same depth as when preparing the holes. This will firm the soil all round the seedlings, right down to the bottom of the roots; the fingers would only press in the top and the roots would be left loose in the soil. Strongly-growing seedlings can be potted up at once, instead of being pricked-off. In the case of seeds that germinate irregularly, the first batch of seedlings should be pricked-off as soon as they can be handled, and the seed boxes returned to their covering so that the remaining seeds may germinate.

Such treatment is necessary with plants like the anemone, auricula, polyanthus and other primulas. After pricking-off or potting up, keep the seedlings in a close atmosphere and shade from the sun for a few days until they are established in their new pots.

Hardening off and damping-off

In March or April move the seedlings to a cold frame where they are hardened off by gradually allowing them more and more air until they are planted out in a prepared nursery bed in May or at the beginning of June. Annuals will be placed in their flowering position if not sown there.

Half-hardy biennial and perennial seedlings, however, will require protection during the coming winter, and in early October must be lifted, then replanted close together in light sandy soil in boxes, to be stored in the greenhouse in a temperature of about 10°C (50°F), or in a cold frame. Give as much air as possible when the weather is fine and dry to prevent the plants from damping-off. If there are any signs of this, take every opportunity of thoroughly ventilating on dry warm days and water lightly with Cheshunt compound. The following May the biennials should be set out in their flowering positions. Tender perennials will require protection during each winter and will have to be lifted in October and wintered under glass. Check the temperature with a thermometer at night and cover the lights with sacking if frost threatens and remove this again after the frost has cleared the next morning.

Half-hardy perennials or biennials can also be sown in an open seed-bed in May or June and wintered as above. Hardy plants are frequently sown under glass to raise early and sturdy plants for bedding-out in the spring.

Propagation by Division

Division provides a simple means of increasing shrubs and herbaceous plants. Lift a clump carefully with as little disturbance to the roots as possible, and break or cut the crown carefully into smaller pieces; discard the old woody centre and replant each of the divisions taken from the outer sides. The easiest method of dividing tough plants is to thrust two forks back to back vertically into the centre of the crown and lever it apart; some plants can be easily pulled apart while woody and tough crowns may have to be cut with a sharp knife or spade. In this case it is wise to wash the soil off the roots so the growth buds are clearly visible.

Division is best done in October and November for woody plants and spring-flowering herbaceous plants and in March and April for autumn-flowering herbaceous plants. Irises are best divided just after flowering when new roots are forming.

Propagation by Layers

This is an easy method of propagation, usually carried out about July, though it may be done at any season of the year. The aim is to produce roots on one or more of the lower shoots of the plant to be propagated. An upward cut, just below a joint, is made in the layer or shoot; the cut passes from the underside through to the centre of the shoot, and should be from 2.5 to 7.5cm (2 to 3in) in length, according to the size and nature of the plant. The cut or tongue of bark and wood is then wedged open and pegged down into the soil; the more the tongue is kept open when placed in contact with the earth the better the chance of rooting. The shoots chosen for layering should be perfectly healthy and of semi-matured wood. It is usual to layer several shoots at a time, and when the cuts have been made the soil all round the plant should be forked over to a depth of 7.5cm (3in) and the layers pegged down firmly, so that the tongues come well in contact with the soil. Soil is then heaped over the cut portions and kept in place with small stones or wire clips. An addition of coarse sand to the soil (often in the proportion of 50 per cent of its volume) helps the layers to root. Turn the outer end of the shoot, beyond the cut, upwards to check the flow of the sap and tie it to a stake to keep it upright; remove all buds not required to form shoots in the new plant. When the layers have rooted well, sever them from the parent plant, pot up or plant out, preferably in autumn. The layers of soft-wooded plants such as the carnation will usually root in six weeks or so, shrubs like the laurel or hebe will take two or three months to form roots; with hard-wooded shrubs like magnolia or rhododendron, it will be a year or more before the layers can be severed.

Tip layering

This is a still easier method of propagation. The tip of a vigorous shoot is bent down and held in place with a pin or stone in a pot sunk into the ground. When the presence of a strong new growth indicates successful rooting, the new plant can be separated from its parent. This method may be used for blackberries, rambler roses and arching shrubs such as forsythia and winter jasmine, many of which will layer themselves naturally with no help from the gardener.

Some plants, such as strawberries and Michaelmas daisies, produce runners which will layer themselves. These runners may be pegged down after loosening the soil around the plant to assist rooting.

Air layering

Sometimes known as Chinese layering or marcotting, air layering is a useful method for rare and valuable plants which are difficult or impossible to propagate from cuttings, and where ordinary methods of layering are not practicable. Clean young shoots should be chosen and prepared by making an upward cut about 5cm (2in) long at or about the stem centre, between two nodes; alternatively, remove a ring of bark about 1cm (½in) wide. Dust the wound with hormone rooting powder and keep the tongue open by packing moist sphagnum moss between the cut surfaces and all round it to give complete cover. Wrap a polythene sleeve round the moss to prevent its drying out, and take care to seal the ends of the polythene to prevent rain seeping in and saturating the moss. When new roots can be seen penetrating the moss, sever the shoot and pot it up or grow it on in a nursery bed.

Propagation by Cuttings

Cuttings may be taken from various parts of a plant and encouraged to form complete new plants identical in every respect to the parent. Stem cuttings are the most usual, but leaf and root cuttings are also used.

Success of cuttings

Some plants are inherently very difficult to root, and there is no way of distinguishing the easier from the more difficult except by trial and error. Privet is very easy, for example, but its near relative, the lilac, is difficult. Some roses root easily while others, especially hybrid tea roses, are nearly impossible. Most conifers and large trees are difficult to increase from cuttings. In general, cuttings from young, vigorous and healthy plants have the greatest chance of success; hormone rooting powders stimulate root development and considerably increase the chances of rooting difficult plants.

Success depends on keeping the cuttings in good growing condition until they have produced roots and can support themselves. Control of water loss is important, and soft cuttings are usually rooted in a closed propagating case shaded from direct sun and syringed frequently to keep them moist. Prolonged shading weakens the plant and close, humid conditions are ideal for the spread of rotting and damping-off.

Mist propagation

With a mist propagating case cuttings are induced to root more efficiently. The heated case is equipped with water jets automatically controlled and a fine mist is released over the leaves when they begin to flag. Because water loss is almost eliminated, cuttings can be kept in brighter light and can therefore continue to manufacture sugars and other plant foods. When the rooting medium is heated by low voltage electric cables and the tops of the cuttings are kept cool by frequent spraying, the bases are encouraged to develop roots more rapidly. Small mist propagation units are available and render possible the propagation of plants which would previously have been considered difficult. Easily-rooted cuttings, however, can be set in a frame, and most grey-leaved plants, which collapse if kept constantly wet, are preferably rooted in the drier atmosphere of a frame.

Types of stem cuttings

There are three principal types of cuttings: softwood, half-ripe and hardwood cuttings.

Softwood cuttings are prepared from new growths as they emerge in spring and early summer. They usually root readily and rapidly if they are prevented from drying out. This type of cutting is particularly successful with young shoots of lupin, delphinium, chrysanthemum, *Philadelphus* and other plants whose stems become hollow or pithy as they age. Make the cuttings about 5cm (2in) long.

Half-ripe cuttings are prepared from the tips of young shoots as they cease growth and begin to harden in mid to late summer. Being firmer than softwood cuttings and 5 to 10cm (2 to 4in) long they are less likely to collapse, but still require the protection of a closed frame. This method is successfully employed for broad-leaved evergreens such as ilex, berberis and osmanthus and for many of the scale-leaved conifers such as dwarf juniperus, cupressus, chamaecyparis and thuja.

Hardwood cuttings are prepared from deciduous shrubs after leaf-fall in the autumn. As they are not in active growth and are taken when rainfall is usually above average, the hardier types can be rooted in the open ground, preferably after lightening the soil with sharp sand. They are up to 30cm (12in) long and need a longer period than other stem cuttings to produce roots.

Taking stem cuttings

Strong healthy shoots only should be removed from the parent plant with a sharp knife, cutting cleanly just below a node or joint. The length of cuttings varies according to type, but should be long enough for two or three nodes to be inserted in the rooting medium after removal of the lower leaves, leaving at least one leaf pair above the medium. On half-ripe and hardwood cuttings, the strip of bark, known as the heel, at the base of the shoot can be retained as it stimulates rooting.

Trim all cuttings except heel cuttings cleanly just below a node without cutting into this. Remove all leaves from the part of the stem which will be buried but leave the top pairs after removing any flower buds; too much reduction of leaf area lowers the chances of rooting. Then dip the base of the stem in a proprietary rooting powder. Occasionally the cutting is wounded by taking a thin sliver of bark from the basal portion of the cutting to assist the rooting of more difficult subjects.

Compost for cuttings

For hardwood cuttings rooted in trenches outside it is usually sufficient to lighten the garden soil by generous addition of sand (and peat if the soil is heavy) and to sprinkle 1cm (½in) of sand for drainage over the bottom of the trench so that this trickles around the base of the cuttings when they are inserted. It is a good idea to fill in the trench with sloping sides to throw off excess rain during winter; in a dry spring and summer it will probably be necessary to water the cuttings which should have rooted by the autumn when they can be lifted and planted out in their growing quarters.

Under glass it is inadvisable to use garden soil unless this has been adequately sterilized (*see* Ch. 15). A medium of 50 per cent sharp sand and 50 per cent of peat by volume is a good mixture providing enough water-holding capacity, sufficient aeration and enough weight to anchor the cuttings firmly. But it contains no nutrients, so plants should be watered with a liquid fertilizer or transferred to a richer medium soon after rooting. John Innes potting composts which are available with varying strengths of added fertilizers or one of the proprietary peat-based potting composts are recommended. Air in the rooting medium is important; rooting may be improved by setting a number of cuttings around the edge of a pot and plunging this in sand or ashes.

Inserting the cuttings

Cuttings strike more readily when placed at the side of a pot than when inserted in its centre. Usually about seven cuttings can be placed in a 10cm (4in) pot. If they are to be planted directly into a propagating frame or mist unit the cuttings may be packed as closely as their expanded leaves permit to make the greatest use of available space and to help maintain a close, humid atmosphere around the cuttings. No cutting should be set too deeply. As with seeds, the depth depends mainly on the size of the cutting. A good general rule is to set about two-thirds of the length of hardwood cuttings in the soil while with softwood and half-ripe cuttings only one-third or one-half should be inserted. Leaves should not touch the soil; if they do they may cause damping-off. Water well through a fine rose.

When using pots or boxes, it is a good idea to sink these nearly to their brims in ashes, which will keep the soil at an even temperature. Whether the cuttings are covered by sheets of glass, plastic bags, cloches or the lights of a frame, condensation must be wiped off each morning.

Too much light, air, water, heat or cold are all harmful to cuttings freshly inserted under glass. A close equable temperature and a moderate degree of moisture should be maintained until the cuttings have rooted. Without a closed propagation case, these conditions can be achieved with glass or by covering the pots with clear plastic bags suspended above the cuttings over wire hoops or thin canes and tied underneath the pot. Provide light shade if necessary.

Decaying leaves must be removed to avoid any possibility of disease spreading and, if plants are particularly prone to decay, they may be sprayed with captan as a precautionary measure.

Potting-on

Cuttings in a frame or mist unit may produce roots in a few days or they may take several months depending on the variety. Most will root in two or three weeks. When careful lifting reveals that roots have been produced and before the roots are so long that they become entangled with adjacent plants, the cuttings should be moved from the propagating unit and potted-on into single pots or deeper boxes. Cuttings inserted originally in pots may be left undisturbed. Potting-on and hardening off are important for softwood and half-ripe cuttings. It is all too easy to root them then kill them off by exposure to full light and dry air.

Transfer newly-rooted plants to a slightly heavier potting compost with fertilizers added (*see* Compost for cuttings, above) and gradually give increased ventilation and reduce shading by degrees until the young plants are protected only from fierce midday sun. Eventually move the plants to an open cold frame to harden off fully before planting out.

Hardwood cuttings need less attention, but must be watered during dry spells. The cuttings are inserted outside in the autumn and roots should begin to develop during the winter. The leaves will start into growth as usual in spring, and any cuttings which have failed to root will quickly shrivel as they fail to replace water lost from the expanding leaves. Light shade from full sun, shelter from wind and watering during dry periods in the spring greatly increase the survival rate of those cuttings which are barely rooted. A year after insertion the rooted cuttings can be lifted and transplanted to allow the developing plants more room; the leading shoot may be cut back to encourage branching.

Preparation and treatment of root cuttings

Some plants, especially those with fleshy roots, can be propagated by taking pieces of root and stimulating them to produce shoots. The parent plant should be lifted in autumn and the soil carefully shaken off to expose the roots. Cut thick roots, 6mm (¼in) or more, into 5 to 10cm (2 to 4in) lengths, slicing squarely across the top of each cutting, with a slanting cut at the bottom to make it easier to identify top and bottom as shoots will only be produced from the upper end. If cuttings are inserted upside down the new shoots will fail to develop.

Plant the cuttings, square ends uppermost, in pots or deep boxes of potting compost with the top of the cutting about 2.5cm (1in) beneath the surface and keep them in a cold frame. If kept moist they should produce buds and new growth during the spring, but they should be left until the autumn to become established before they are moved to their final positions.

Thin fibrous roots, like those on phlox, need different treatment. Cut them into 5cm (2in) lengths and lay them on potting compost in trays, covered by 1cm (½in) of soil and keep for the winter in a cool greenhouse or frame. When shoots emerge pot up each plant separately and harden off before planting out.

Plants which will grow from root cuttings include quince, raspberry, horseradish, seakale, acanthus, *Anchusa italica*, Japanese anemone, ceratostigma, *Papaver orientale, Phlox paniculata, Primula denticulata* and sumach.

Preparation and treatment of leaf cuttings

Propagation by leaf cuttings is a useful method for plants with succulent or thick spongy leaves and soft veins.

Select a healthy leaf and plant it, stalk downwards with the leaf proper just clear of the soil, in a propagating case in equal parts of sandy loam and leaf-mould or moss peat. Roots will soon form and a young plant will grow from them. Haberlea, ramonda and saintpaulia may be treated like this. In the case of a large and thick leaf, such as *Begonia rex*, the veins on the back may be slit at their junctions. The stalk is planted in the rooting medium and the whole leaf is pinned firmly down, so that it is in close contact with the compost in the propagating case, at a temperature of 21°C (70°F) and given plenty of moisture, though the bed must be well drained and not allowed to become stagnant or the leaves will rot. In a short time plantlets will appear where the veins have been slashed.

The long narrow leaves of sansevieria may be cut into 5cm (2in) sections and sliced in half along either side of the main vein; insert the sections with their cut edges just beneath the compost in 12.5cm (5in) pots; eventually plantlets will develop from each section. The little plants can be removed and potted up as soon as they are large enough to handle.

Achimenes, begonia, gloxinia, haberlea, peperomia, ramonda, saintpaulia, sansevieria and streptocarpus can all be propagated from leaf cuttings. Sansevieria will produce only green plants even if propagated from the variegated form.

Propagation by Grafting

Grafting is a propagation method chiefly practised on a commercial scale for fruit trees, the aim being to join the rootstock of one variety to the scion of another. The purpose of grafting fruit trees is to control vigour of the roots for a given variety or a particular soil type. Ornamental plants are grafted only when they are too difficult or too slow to produce from cuttings or where the roots are prone to suckering. As the graft union often grows into an ugly scar, it is important to graft as low as possible so that the scar is at or below ground level and does not detract from the appearance of the plant.

The uses of grafting

In grafting the branch which is transferred is known as the scion and the tree to which it is attached as the rootstock. The scion becomes parasitic on the stock, and by carefully removing all branches which spring from the stock below the point of union, all the energy produced by the roots is diverted to the scion. It is only possible to graft on to a stock of allied species. Quinces, apples, pears and medlars can all be grafted on to one another, as can plums, peaches, apricots and almonds, but it would be impossible to graft apple on to oak or plum on to willow.

Valuable time is saved by grafting; it might take some fifteen or twenty years before a tree raised from seed would bear fruit, but by grafting fruit might be had in three or four years and by joining rootstocks of known vigour with scions of a choice variety better yields can be predicted.

Grafting is also used to alter the growth habit of a tree. Pears and apples are dwarfed by grafting them on to dwarfing rootstocks, a process that has been developed by the East Malling and Long Ashton research stations. Dwarfed weeping trees are converted into tall standards by attaching a scion from the weeping variety to a tree with a tall upright trunk.

Suitable rootstocks

In the selection of a suitable stock consider not only the readiness with which a union can be effected between the scion and the stock, but also the soil in which the trees are to be grown. For example, in light soil, plums grown on their own roots rarely do well, but when grafted on to peach they usually thrive. *Vice versa*, peaches on their own roots rarely do well in heavy or chalky soils, and may often be made to succeed by grafting them on plum. Research has shown that in some cases the flavour of fruit can be modified by the stock on which the variety is grafted. The performance and development of suitable rootstocks are now so advanced that it is possible to buy grafted fruit trees to suit almost any type of soil.

Development and restoration

Grafting is also occasionally used to improve flowers or fruit from parts of a tree lacking in them. Sometimes it is used to restore an exhausted tree or to bring together on one stock the two sexes of monoecious plants – which bear their male and female flowers on different trees – and so to help their pollination and fruit-bearing qualities.

Time to graft

For a successful union to take it is essential that the cells in the cambium of both scion and stock are in direct contact with each other and that the sap is flowing in both. The best time for grafting is therefore at the end of the dormant season. Under glass the time is somewhat earlier, from January to March, and again from July to September. The operations of budding and grafting are similar in theory but whereas in budding a single bud of the current year's growth is used, in grafting whole branches are used, while their buds are still dormant or nearly so. The time for grafting trees varies with the time of their breaking into leaf, those kinds which bud early being dealt with first. Plums are generally the first to be ready, in late March, then come quinces and pears, followed by cherries and apples in this order; but as the time of leafing varies with certain varieties this order cannot be strictly adhered to. To check whether the stock is ready for grafting, slit the bark and if it is easily raised to expose the polished surface of the wood beneath, the stock is ready. If the bark tends to tear, leave the stock for a week or so longer.

Initial preparations

Grafting needs a certain amount of initial preparation. The stock or tree which is to receive the graft should be headed back towards the end of January. During severe frosts delay cutting back the stock though not for so long that the sap is flowing rapidly. Scions are prepared a month or two earlier (December) so that last year's ripened sap is still in them, to supply life to the severed scion until the union has been effected. Cut the scions from well-ripened, one-year-old wood from healthy trees while the buds are still dormant. Plant the scions in a cool place against a wall or fence where the buds will remain dormant until grafting is carried out. If the weather is so mild that it seems likely to cause movement of the sap, the scions should be pulled up occasionally and left exposed to the air for a little while in order to check growth. The scions should be cut to lengths of three buds at about the same time as the stock is prepared.

The best stocks are from three-year-old plants, planted at least a year before grafting. Remove all side branches, together with the top, and cut down the main stem to just above a bud about 17.5 to 20cm (7 to 8in) above ground level. Where older plants are used as stocks, as in the case of grafting on to mature trees, these should be cut back to 1 to 1.8m (3 to 6ft) from the union, according to the size of the tree. Enough wood should be left to allow for removal of a further portion which will be necessary when the grafting is done. Heading back must be done during dormancy otherwise gumming is likely to result. Stocks to be used as standards should be allowed to grow to the height required.

The time of grafting varies according to the stock used, but make sure that the sap is beginning to rise – it is better to be a little too late than too early. Usually May is the best time for grafting on to mature trees, and March and April for young trees.

The process of grafting

The stock should be grafted or budded as near to the ground as possible. The inner layer of the bark (cambium) is the only portion of the wood which is capable of uniting, and to effect a union this part of the scion and stock must meet and remain in contact. The outer bark of the two portions is removed so that these inner layers touch when the two pieces are pressed together. The union is kept together with raffia and air excluded with grafting wax.

Grafting tools and materials When you are ready for the actual grafting, prepare the stocks and scions and have ready a strong knife for cutting back the stocks, a saw, chisel and mallet, a small knife with a narrow blade for fine operations, raffia or soft string and grafting wax.

Whip and tongue grafting The chosen method of grafting depends largely on the size and conditions of stock and scion. Where the stock is young and about the size of a finger, whip and tongue grafting is most suitable, and for this method the stock must be more advanced in growth than the scion. Prepare the scion from a well-ripened, one-year-old shoot about 15cm (6in) long, with two healthy buds that come on opposite sides of the shoot, one a little higher than the other. Beginning just below the upper bud, make a clean cut through the wood, coming out just below the lower bud. It is essential that there should be a good bud just above the cut at each end. Now, beginning at the top of the cut just under the top bud, cut a hollow curve down in a straight line to the tip of the cut by the lower bud. The bottom of the shoot, in profile, now looks like an inverted J.

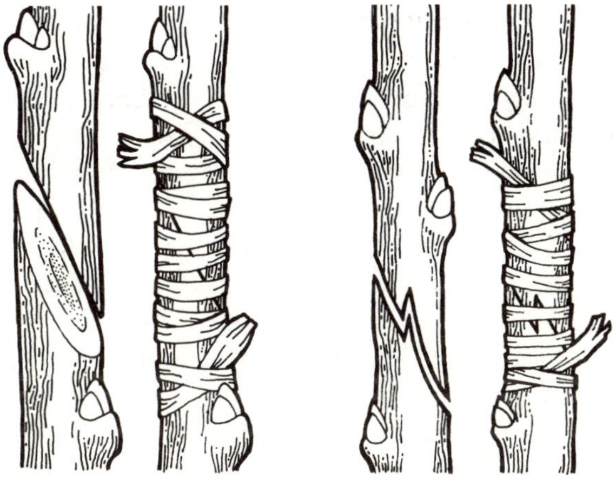

On the left is shown splice grafting, the easiest but least successful method, and on the right is an example of whip and tongue grafting

Having prepared the scion, deal with the stock. This should have been cut back in late January to about 20cm (8in) from the soil. Remove any side growths from the base and selecting a good smooth place about 10cm (4in) above ground level, cut the stock cleanly off just above a healthy bud. The chief function of this bud will be to draw up the sap into the top of the cut parts while they are knitting together, just as the buds on the scion do, but while the latter are allowed to grow and become the upper part of the tree, the former should not be allowed to outlive its usefulness. Allow it to grow two or three leaves and then rub it out. Having cut down the stock, carefully measure the top against the scion, and cut down in a curve to match the curve of the scion. Where the scion has a long J-shaped tail, peel a strip of wood and bark carefully from the side of the stock so that the stock and scion will fit together perfectly when placed together. The tail of the scion will fit on to the peeled strip of the stock, with the cut surfaces of both stock and scion touching closely. If it is impossible to make the bark layers meet on both edges, make them meet perfectly on one. The tail of the scion should not come below the end of the peeled piece of the stock.

When scion and stock fit, make a small upward cut in the tail of the scion to create a thin slip projecting towards the stock. Make an incision in the stock, opposite this slip, to hold stock and scion together while you are tying and sealing with wax. When scion and stock have been joined closely together and the layers of inner bark are fitting neatly, make the union firm by tying it with raffia or soft string. Tie firmly to prevent movements but not so tight as to prevent circulation of the sap beneath the bark. Lastly, seal the whole junction – scion, stock and ligature – with grafting wax and attach a label to the stock, not to the scion.

Splice grafting This method is also used for young stock; it is similar to whip and tongue grafting but simpler as it does not involve cutting out a tongue. On the other hand, a splice graft is less secure and may fail to take if the two cambium layers shift away from each other. Prepare scion and stock as for whip and tongue grafting, making a long slanting cut between two buds on the scion and a corresponding cut on the stock. Press the two cut surfaces firmly together and tie with raffia before sealing the union with wax.

Saddle grafting This method of grafting is used for stocks with the thickness of a broom handle. The scion is of the same thickness as the stock and cut with two tails, the one below the upper bud shorter than that below the lower bud. The whole of the inner part of the wood below the buds is removed, and the scion will now have two tails of unequal length, the shorter one having a bud at the top and the longer one having a bud midway up. Cut the top of the stock at corresponding angles so that the tip will fit between the tails of the scion. Peel a slip to correspond with the long tail of the scion and fit the scion over the stock saddlewise, the long tail fitting its peeled slip, and the top angle of the stock fitting into the top angle of the cross cut. The short tail of the scion will cross the top of the stock and project a little. Cut a slip off the side of the stock to fit this projecting piece of the tail, which is bent down on to it, and the graft is ready for tying and sealing. This system has the advantage that the scion unites on both sides of the stock, and is therefore not so liable to an accidental break during the healing process.

These methods of grafting are both employed for young stocks, but others must be used in the case of mature trees, where the branches are usually too large for either of the systems described – notch or slit grafting and crown or rind grafting.

Notch or slit grafting Notch grafting, although difficult, is used when the diameter of the stock is roughly four times that of the scion. In this method the stock is first cut clean across, and then pointed, wedge-shaped incisions are made in the bark and wood, beginning at the cut edge of the bark and sloping downwards and outwards. The scions are prepared by making sloping cuts on two sides of the wood, making an angle corresponding with that of the wedge-shaped incision in the stock, so that the scion, when fitted into the stock, fills the space closely, the outer layer of the bark of the scion being slightly lower – because thinner – than that of the stock. The best way of doing this is to make the first cut in the stock with a widely-set saw, and then slope the sides of the cut slightly outwards with a sharp knife. The angle of the cut in the stock should not be quite as wide as that of the scion, to hold it tighter in the slit. The scion, when properly shaped, should be set into the cut and hammered lightly down into position with a small wooden mallet. Tie with raffia and seal with wax as already described.

Crown or rind grafting is the most popular and the easiest method of grafting on to mature trees when the stock is comparatively large, especially when renovating old fruit trees. In this system the scion is prepared much as for whip and tongue grafting, but the curve at the top is replaced by a sloping cut above 3.5cm (1½in) in length. The tail should be quite thin.

Cut the stock off cleanly and make a slit in the bark of the same length as the tail of the scion. While the knife is still in the cut, gently press the blade from side to side so as to loosen the bark in the immediate neighbourhood of the cut. Then withdraw the knife and slip the scion between the wood and the bark, pressing it down until the surface left by the cross cut at its head lies on the top of the stock.

Graft from two to four scions on each branch over 10cm (4in) in diameter. The more scions there are the better and more strongly will the sap be drawn up and the quicker and better the stock will heal and effect a union. When the grafts are growing well they should be tied to stakes fastened securely to the branches of the stock.

After-care of grafts

By May the grafts should begin to make new growth; remove the grafting wax so that the binding can be undone before it strangles the new growth.

If the graft is not yet secure replace the binding immediately, but more loosely. Do not seal it with wax again, but support the graft with a stake tied firmly to the stock. Laterals that form on the graft should be pinched out to encourage a good straight single shoot from the graft, and any shoots forming on the stock below the point of grafting must be rubbed off once they have served their purpose in drawing sap up to the graft.

Budding

Budding is another method of improving or altering the nature of a plant's flowers and fruits and is mainly used to propagate roses. It is based on the same principles as grafting but is preferable to the latter as it produces a more perfect union, a proportionately larger surface of the inner bark coming in contact with that of the stock. In budding the scion consists of only one bud with a mere sliver of bark attached.

Time to bud

Choose a spell of showery or dull weather for the operation of budding, as the bark then separates easily from the wood and gives the stocks to be budded a good soaking of water for a day or two before. The best time for budding is between the early part of July and the end of September, and if the buds do not start until the next spring so much the better. New wood of the current year's growth is usually the best for budding on, but young growths up to two or three years may also be used. Fruit trees are best budded in July and August, while roses do best from the middle of July until early in September.

Budding operations

In this operation, unlike grafting, the bud and stock are prepared on the spot, not beforehand. Choose a time when the sap is rising freely in both stock and bud. Select a healthy shoot for cutting the buds. If they are not to be used at once put the shoots in water, or the bark will dry slightly and be more difficult to work. Choose a good half-matured shoot of current year's growth and remove the leaves from it close to the leaf-stalk, leaving only a piece of the latter. If the leaves are left on they will draw out the moisture from the bark and bud, shrinking the bud. Cut the bud out of the wood with a sharp knife, making a curve behind the bud and bringing it out in the centre of a thin strip of bark. Begin the cut about 1cm ($\frac{1}{2}$in) above the bud and finish it at an equal distance below it. Remove any wood behind the bark of this shield by holding the leaf-stalk and bud in one hand and peeling the bark away from the wood with the tip of the knife. Occasionally, and generally when the bud is too forward, the wood will leave a small hole in the bark behind the bud as it pulls away. Such a bud will shrivel and die before it has time to build up new cells; it is of no use for budding and must be replaced with a fresh, less developed bud.

When the bud is ready, deal with the stock. Choose a clean, smooth spot on the stem, and with a budding knife make a cut about 3.5cm ($1\frac{1}{2}$in) long, using just sufficient pressure to pierce the bark without penetrating the wood beneath. At the top of this make a cross cut 1cm ($\frac{1}{2}$in) long and raise the bark on either side of the first cut with the knife. Now insert the 'shield' containing the bud at the cross cut, and gently push it under the bark until the bud is well down below the level of the cross cut. The easiest way to do this is to hold the shield between the finger and thumb of the left hand, by the leaf-stalk, holding the bark open with the knife in

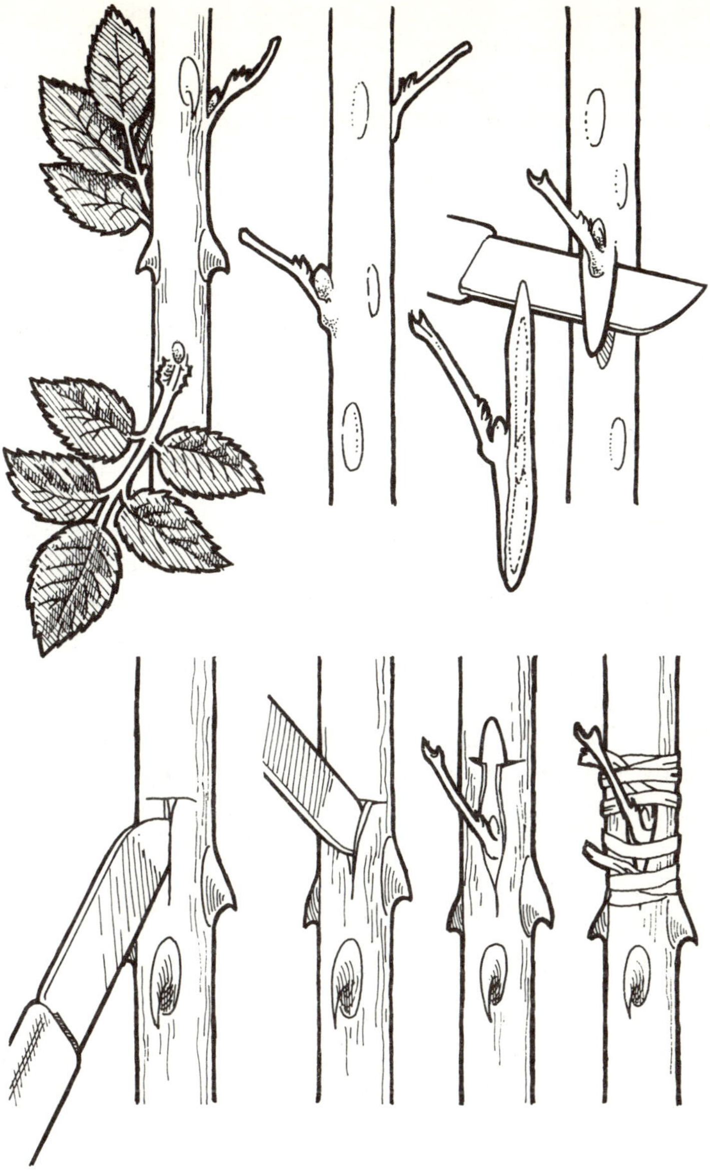

Budding a rose, showing the bud scion being removed from a chosen variety and its insertion into a T-shaped cut on the new rootstock

the other hand. When the bud is well down cut off the projecting tip of the shield exactly on a level with the cross cut in the stock, so that the top of the shield fits inside the bark. Afterwards bind lightly with soft raffia or twine above and below the bud, bringing the lips of the bark of the stock together again over the bud with the binding so that no opening remains between them. Above all, take care that the base of the eye is in close contact with the bark of the stock; success in budding depends on the moist condition of the bud and stock when brought into contact.

Selecting the buds

In selecting buds, particularly for fruit trees, make sure that they are wood buds, from which a shoot will start, and not fruit buds. These are more easily distinguished in some kinds than in others, but as a rule wood buds are more pointed than fruit buds. On some fruit trees, usually in dry seasons, the buds are difficult to peel away from the wood and it is then a good idea to pierce the wood just behind the bud with the point of a knife, so as to cut away from the bud at that point, before beginning to peel it from the wood. The shoots selected for budding, whether for fruit or rose trees, should be plump, firm and well-ripened. Watery shoots or buds are useless.

After budding is complete, leave the stock untouched and do not cut away leaves or any other part until November, when the binding should be slit to allow the stock to grow. At the same time the top of the stem which bears the bud may be cut back to about 7.5cm (3in) above it. When the bud shoots in the spring – or possibly before – reduce this piece to 2.5cm (1in), and cut away all shoots springing from the stock during the summer. In autumn the snag above the bud may be cut away altogether.

When the buds begin to grow they need to be protected from strong winds which might loosen them from the stem. Drive a stake firmly into the ground and tie with strong cord or patent tree ties to the stem of the stock above and below the union; tie the shoot of the young scion firmly to the stake above, protecting it with a padding of soft rags to prevent the bark being injured.

6
Planting, Transplanting and Staking

The planting seasons

The usual time for moving plants is in the dormant season, from late October to March. On all but heavy soils, autumn is the best time for planting deciduous plants. Soon after leaf-fall they are still active, and soil temperatures are high enough to encourage root development. If planted in mid-winter new roots do not develop in cold or wet soil and older roots may begin to decay. Plants moved in early spring may start into leaf before they have had the opportunity to send roots out into the soil, and the extending shoots use resources which might otherwise have been used to produce a stronger root system.

Spring planting is preferable to autumn planting on heavy soils where the plants would spend their first season in cold, wet soil that might prove fatal to the young roots. Spring planting is also the general rule for plants with fleshy roots, such as magnolias, and for plants which are only marginally hardy.

Evergreens are best planted in the autumn while the soil is still warm, but the air temperature low and the plants run less risk of drying out. Spring planting is possible but conifers especially will need overhead spraying to counteract transpiration losses. Evergreens are usually moved with a ball of soil around the roots to reduce the effect of root disturbance. Container-grown shrubs, trees and herbaceous plants can be moved at any time, even when in full leaf and bloom, but avoid planting in frozen or waterlogged soil.

The season for moving herbaceous plants depends on the soil and the plants. Spring-flowering plants are best moved as soon as they have died down in the autumn, except on very heavy soils where careful moving of the plants just after flowering may be more successful. Autumn-flowering plants should be set out in spring while summer-flowering plants may be moved in autumn on light soils or spring on heavy soils. Some plants, such as doronicum pyrethrum and bearded iris which flower in spring or early summer then die back and produce entirely new growth in the summer, are moved most successfully after flowering, before the new roots are established.

Plant half-hardy annuals, tender perennials and other bedding plants set out for the summer only when all danger of frost has passed. This usually means late May in southern England to mid-June in the north and Scotland.

Ground preparation

As long as possible before plants arrive, prepare the ground thoroughly by deep digging and incorporation of well-rotted manure or compost with phosphate and potash fertilizers added. Pick out all perennial weeds and bury annual weeds deeply, then leave the ground to settle. If a whole bed is prepared for planting, firm the soil by treading shortly before planting and when the soil is reasonably dry, and rake level.

Trees and shrubs in particular need thorough preparation, especially where they are being added to an existing planting scheme. Where possible, take out an area 1.2m (4ft) in diameter and dig it to a depth of two spits; loosen the subsoil if necessary, but take care not to bring it up to the surface. Fork in liberal amounts of well-rotted manure or garden compost, mixing it well with the soil. Remember that roots in direct contact with fresh manure may suffer burns. It is inadvisable to make planting holes just large enough for the roots; a pit of well-cultivated soil in an area of otherwise heavy clay will confine the roots almost as firmly as if they were in a pot, and in winter the hole acts as a drainage sump, filling with water and often killing the plant. An area of roughly dug ground with a light application of manure beyond the planting hole is therefore to be recommended.

Do not ignore these initial preparations for planting trees and shrubs. They will occupy the ground for many years to come with no further opportunities for making major improvements to the soil and small specimen plants will get off to a more satisfactory start if provided with good growing conditions.

Lifting plants

When it is necessary to lift plants in the garden to move them to new positions, it is usually a simple matter to dig up the plant carefully by loosening it round the roots with a fork, wheel it to its new situation with as much soil as possible around the root ball and to water it in well. Most plants including young shrubs can be moved successfully at any time of year although the disturbance is obviously less if the move occurs when the plant is not in active growth.

If large shrubs or trees have to be moved, then advanced preparations are called for. It is possible to excavate large root systems by digging away around the plant, but it is easier to root-prune the tree before moving it. Take out a trench about 45cm (1½ft) deep and wide and 60 to 120cm (2 to 4ft) away from the trunk, until the thick anchoring roots are exposed; sever these cleanly and refill the trench. Root-prune in this way round half the tree in autumn and complete the remaining half the following spring; by the autumn the tree will have produced new roots in a more compact root ball, ready for moving.

Lift the tree by digging a trench around the roots and undercutting to form a compact root ball which should be wrapped in strong sacking to keep it intact for the journey to its new position. Plant firmly, setting the tree as deep as in its original position, and provide a firm stake until the roots have taken a firm hold.

Treatment of plants on arrival

There are three ways of dispatching plants from a nursery. Deciduous plants arriving during autumn and winter are usually moved bare-root, that is with the soil shaken off the roots which are then wrapped in straw or other light packing material for dispatch. Most evergreens, including conifers and hollies, are transported with a ball of soil around their roots held in place with sacking or heavy polythene. Plants sold from garden centres are usually grown in containers – flower pots, plastic bags or tin cans and sold in the container in which they have been growing. Such container plants can be planted throughout the year; when inspecting plants it is a good idea to examine such plants carefully to see that they are really container plants and not plants lifted bare-root from a nursery and potted up. In the latter case they are bound to have suffered a check to growth and may never recover.

Bare-root trees and shrubs should be unpacked on arrival if the weather is suitable for planting; trim off any damaged roots and branches and if the plants are at all dry, soak the roots overnight before planting. If plants arrive during frosty or very wet weather they may remain in their loosened wrapping for a week or more without harm, but should be stored in a cool, frost-free shed or garage away from direct light. When prolonged cold or wet spells are obviously going to preclude planting for several weeks it is wise to cover a small area of vacant ground with cloches, straw bales or other protection in anticipation of the arrival of the plants. When the plants do arrive remove the protection and heel the plants in by taking out a shallow trench and lining them out almost horizontally; throw the earth loosely back over the roots and leave until suitable weather occurs.

Balled plants should be unpacked on arrival without disturbing the wrapping of the ball itself and, if they appear dry, immerse the root balls in water for a few hours before draining thoroughly. During unsuitable weather, the plants may be heeled in as bare-root plants, but it is usually satisfactory to keep them moist in a cold greenhouse.

Container-grown plants can be moved at any time of year, but if planting is delayed for any reason, stand them in a sheltered lightly shaded position out of doors and treat them as other pot plants.

Heeling in woody plants while waiting for suitable weather to plant them out. Keep the roots close together and the stems almost horizontal

Planting

Bare-root plants should have their roots carefully disentangled and covered by moist sacking while awaiting planting. Take out a hole wide enough and deep enough to accommodate the roots easily, and leave a slight mound of soil in the centre of the hole. The soil mark on the stem of the plant indicates the correct planting depth. Set the plant on the mound twisting it gently to work soil under the roots and eliminate air spaces. Check the correct depth of planting with a stick, adding or removing soil as necessary. Position the plant so that it shows its best side. If staking is necessary (*see* Staking) insert the stake before planting to avoid damage to the roots and tie the plant loosely to the stake.

Now work the soil in, round and over the roots, trying to keep them in the same position that they held originally; shake the plant gently a few times to help the soil settle around the roots and tread down as planting progresses. When planting is finished, tread the soil and surrounding area firmly, spread any remaining soil round the plant to make a tidy finish and rake lightly to remove footmarks. A shallow depression in the soil may be left round newly-planted trees and shrubs, creating a saucer to facilitate watering; fill the depression with a well-rotted mulch after first watering the plant thoroughly and it will have the best possible start. Before watering and mulching, replace the temporary tie to the stake with a permanent tie.

Balled plants should be set in a flat-bottomed hole, sufficiently wide to work the soil firmly around, under and over the ball, leaving no large air spaces. Remove the wrapping on small plants immediately before planting. On larger plants it is preferable to place the undisturbed root-ball in the hole, release the wrapping material and leave it spread out in the bottom of the hole where it will eventually rot down. Plastic wrappings, however, which will not decay, should not be left in position. Insert the stake, if necessary, beside, not through, the ball, fill in the hole and tread it down firmly, leaving a saucer-shaped depression as described above.

Container-grown plants should be planted with the minimum disturbance, complete with the container if this is decomposable as in peat pots. For trees and shrubs, however, it is essential to remove the container, and if roots have wrapped themselves round and through the base they must be unwound and spread out. On pot-bound plants, with a mat of roots around the soil ball, slit the container from top to bottom in several places before easing it away and spread out the roots as much as possible before planting. If this is not done the main roots will eventually swell into a tight knot, often girdling the stem, and the plant may die or fail to grow satisfactorily or be blown over.

Staking Various types of stakes and supports are used in the garden. Most trees and some shrubs need the support of a stout stake until the roots have established themselves firmly and the trunk has thickened enough to maintain a straight upright position. Poles of chestnut, oak or larch are the most suitable, but sawn timber, 5 to 7.5cm (2 to 3in) square, may also be used. Treat the lower 60cm (2ft) of the stakes with a wood preservative – never use creosote which is harmful to plants.

Set the stake for a tree in the planting hole before planting is complete (*see* Planting above), using a mallet to drive it at least 45cm (18in) into the soil; it should be tall enough to come just below the head of the tree. After planting, tie the tree to the stake, half-way up the stem and near the top. Proprietary plastic or webbing straps with buffers can be used or pads can be made from hessian and wound round the stem several times; secure to the stake with strong tarred string.

Check the ties several times during the year to see if they are rubbing the bark or have been broken by strong winds. Renew the ties as necessary and loosen them as the stem thickens. Remove stake and ties when the tree is mature and established enough to support itself.

Supporting wall plants Self-clinging climbers, such as ivy, will attach themselves to walls and fences without any support, but the majority of climbing plants need some form of support. Trellis, horizontal wires stretched between vine eyes or rigid square-mesh plastic netting are all suitable. Put them in position before planting begins and afterwards tie the plants to the supports with raffia, soft string or plant rings.

Staking perennial and annual plants All plants that grow to a height of about 75cm ($2\frac{1}{2}$ft) and many more of a less robust nature will require staking, otherwise wind and rain will soon break them down.

Strong shoots can be tied individually to bamboo canes, but for bushy clumps it is easier to drive in three or four sticks round the plant and tie string from stick to stick to support the flower stems. The sticks should slope slightly outwards and away from the plant and the string must not be drawn too tight. This is a good method of supporting plants with delicate stems that would be damaged if tied individually to stakes. As an alternative method, a stake may be driven into the ground at the centre of the plant and the chief stems tied loosely to this with string.

The stakes should be hidden as much as possible and be placed behind the stems and foliage. If branches and twigs of hazel or birch, which are the least unsightly, are placed between and round the plants in spring, the stems will soon grow up and hide the supports. Whatever the type of support they should, on an average, be three-quarters of the eventual height of the plant. It must not be forgotten that the plants continue to grow and that further tying and staking will be necessary at intervals. Ring supports of metal or strong plastic on three legs that are pushed into the soil make a neat and quick job of staking plants, such as paeonies.

The tying material varies with the plant and the weather conditions to which it will be subjected. For trees in the open, use tarred cord of a thickness to suit the size of the trees and tie perennial border plants with soft tarred string if it is to last for more than a season. For annuals in the open, for most greenhouse plants and for all tying that need not last for more than a year, raffia or soft string is both suitable and convenient.

Wind the tie securely round the stake and then loop it round the stem tightly enough to hold it in position, but not tightly enough to cut into the bark or stem and allowing for future growth of the branches. Stems should be tied so that they maintain their natural distances apart; if bunched tightly together they will be deprived of a large amount of sun and air.

Where appearance is less important, as with trained fruit trees and bushes, heavy posts of treated timber, metal or concrete are anchored at each end of the row to support horizontal wires strained along the row. Tie the stems or bushes to the wires or allow them to grow through rigid large-mesh netting supported by the posts.

Unobtrusive beds of plants grown for cut flowers are easily supported by driving a stout stake into each of the four corners and running taut string along the rows.

Care after planting Plants from reputable nurseries are well prepared for moving, but some check of growth is inevitable. It is important to inspect plants regularly for the first year or two, and examine the staking. Watering should be thorough and widely distributed to encourage roots to grow out into the surrounding soil. In the first spring after transplanting, young plants may suffer water shortage because the roots have not established themselves sufficiently even if there is adequate water in the soil. Then further watering will only flood the roots and cause more harm. Some protection from drying winds is also advisable, and conifers in particular will benefit from sprays of anti-desiccant solutions to reduce water loss from the leaves.

7 Routine Care of Plants

Pruning

Pruning, which chiefly concerns trees and shrubs, serves to remove dead and diseased wood, to control the shape and size of the plant and to improve its quality, whether this is measured by brighter stems, or better foliage, flowers or fruit. Correct pruning should maintain the natural form of the plant while at the same time letting light and air into the centre of the crown.

All pruning cuts must be made cleanly back to a point of origin, leaving no ugly stubs which will either produce tufts of new shoots or may die back, causing rotting which spreads to the rest of the plant. When cutting back healthy shoots, make the pruning cut just above a bud pointing outwards and at a slanting angle. It is important to understand the growth patterns of various shrubs and the reasons for pruning before setting about the task. For this purpose woody plants may be grouped into five categories.

Flowering on new growth

Many late-summer flowering plants bloom at the tip of their new shoots. In the following year, when the tip has ceased to grow, numerous side shoots grow and these in turn flower at their tips. Such plants soon become twiggy, unproductive and crowded with dead wood. Pruning is done in early spring by cutting all side growth back to a few buds, and removing old stems at ground level. This results in a limited number of stronger shoots with larger and more flowers.

Examples include *Buddleia davidii, Clematis* x *jackmanii, Spiraea* 'Anthony Waterer' and most bush roses. Shrubs which are grown for the colour of their young stems are also pruned in this way, or they may be cut back almost to ground level.

Spring flowering on last year's shoots

Most early spring shrubs produce strong shoots in one year which form flower buds during the following autumn and winter and flower in the spring. Flowered shoots continue to grow although rather weakly with sporadic side shoots. Better flowers are produced on new shoots so pruning is done immediately after flowering, removing all shoots which have flowered and encouraging strong new shoots which will flower the next year. Forsythia, *Ribes sanguineum*, winter jasmine and the early ceanothus are examples.

Summer flowering on new laterals

Many shrubs produce strong shoots in one year which become dormant in winter, then produce numerous short side shoots in spring. These side shoots bear flowers which open in early or mid-summer. Such plants are also pruned after flowering, either by removing older whole branches which have flowered or by trimming back all the side shoots to encourage a fresh crop of flowers next year. Examples include deutzia, weigela, philadelphus and *Buddleia alternifolia*.

Spur-flowering plants

With this type of plant the main shoots extend indefinitely year after year, branching occasionally to produce other long shoots which continue to extend. Most lateral growths, however, are short, consisting of a rosette of leaves which, in the second or third year, will produce flowers.

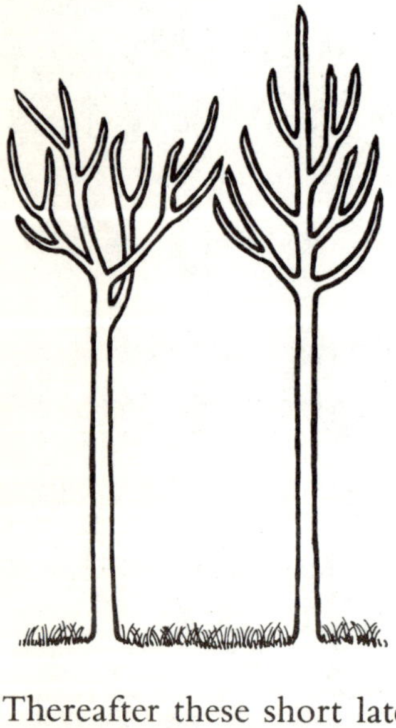

Training of different types of standard trees. The tree on the left has had its leading shoot pinched out to induce branching while the tree on the right with its central leader has been allowed to develop naturally

Thereafter these short laterals, or spurs, continue to flower each year until they are shaded out by the continued growth of the canopy.

There are two methods of pruning this type of shrub. The main shoots can be allowed to develop more or less unhindered, shortening them back to similar side shoots when they outgrow their allotted space, or the majority of stems can be removed at ground level, leaving a skeleton of flowering spurs trained as a cordon, fan, espalier or other artificial form. The second method is most successful if the tree or shrub is not too vigorous, and maintenance pruning is done by removing the growing tips of any long shoots (other than those needed for extension) in July or August, then shortening these shoots back to two or three buds in autumn to encourage new spurs to form.

Most of the ornamental and fruiting *Rosaceae* are of this type, including apple, crab apple, pear, plum, peach and cherry.

Indeterminate flowering plants

A great number of flowering shrubs produce vigorous shoots in the early part of their life. As these branch and rebranch, the growing energy is dissipated into so many growing points that vigorous extension more or less ceases and the plant begins to flower. Growth then continues by the production of one or two short shoots from beneath each terminal flower.

Such plants are usually left to their own devices except for the occasional thinning out and removal of dead or crossing wood. Too hard pruning results in vigorous growth which may not flower for several years. Weak plants on poor soil may flower so freely that they produce less and less growth, eventually flowering themselves to death. These may require some stimulus by pruning, but are more likely to benefit from a generous mulch of well-rotted manure or a spring application of nitrogenous fertilizer.

Examples of this group include lilac, magnolia and rhododendron which while needing no regular pruning should be dead-headed – that is all faded flowers should be removed.

Other garden operations

Herbaceous plants eventually produce crowded masses of thin shoots, and lifting and dividing the clumps then becomes necessary. However, lifting can be delayed with advantage by thinning out crowded clumps in spring leaving only the best-placed and strongest shoots.

Give the herbaceous border an annual spring overhaul, removing all debris, raking in a light dressing of a general fertilizer and staking where necessary. Loosen the soil surface lightly with a fork, cultivator or hoe.

Summer hygiene

The main purpose of tidying up may be to keep the garden neat, but it is also good for the plants. The removal and burning of waste materials does much to stop the diseases and insect pests spreading, and the hoeing and removal of dead shoots after flowering and the picking off of dead flowers and seed-pods while making the beds look tidier also has a useful function. To reproduce its species is the main aim of every plant, and as a rule once this has been ensured the plant ceases to bear more flowers, and in the case of an annual, dies down altogether. For this reason all annuals should have their dead blooms and seed-pods picked off as soon as possible to encourage the production of fresh flowers over an extended period of blooming. Early-flowering herbaceous perennials, such as delphiniums and lupins, should also be dead-headed, but here the whole of the flowered stem should be cut away at ground level; this will often encourage the plants to produce a second crop of bloom in late summer or early autumn.

About mid-summer, or slightly later, border plants will need additional treatment. Many of them will have grown unwieldy and may be suffocating less vigorous plants; these must be trimmed back. Plants of a trailing and creeping nature can be pegged down to head them in the direction they should grow, and to make them cover their allotted space. Early-flowering shrubs may need pruning.

Top-dressing

Top-dressing of beds and borders with a suitable fertilizer provides a valuable stimulus to growth and flowering. In many cases top-dressing can consist of a mulch of well-decayed manure or compost, which will help to conserve moisture and minimize the need of the hoe for control of weeds. Alternatively, fork or rake in the fertilizer before spreading the mulch, making sure the soil is thoroughly moist.

Watering

Fertilizer has no rapid effect in a dry soil, and a mulch applied to dry soil may actually prevent rain from reaching the roots, thus doing more harm than good, so watering in the summer is important.

In the vegetable and fruit garden frequent and regular watering is necessary for rapid growth of vegetables and the swelling of fruits. In the flower garden and on the lawn, watering is a less troublesome task that need not be undertaken until signs of flagging and wilting become apparent. However, all watering must be thorough to moisten the soil properly. A little water over the surface merely chills the soil, and draws roots to the surface where they are quickly scorched, and unless water is given frequently the surface will become compacted and air will be prevented from penetrating to the roots. A thorough watering once a week is far better than a daily sprinkling.

A wide range of equipment is available including static, oscillating or rotating and travelling sprinklers. Most static sprinklers give too heavy and uneven distribution of water, but oscillating sprinklers can be adjusted to water rectangles of various sizes, and rotary sprinklers will water large areas. Travelling sprinklers wind themselves along the hose, which can be laid to follow any required route, among flower beds for example, but they require good water pressure. Perforated hoses, which can be permanently installed, are ideal for vegetable plants, as they release water steadily round the roots without caking the soil or battering the plants. For economy of water, sprinklers should not be used in strong wind or fierce sun as much of the water evaporates at once; trickle hoses laid along rows of vegetables can be operated at any time.

Any fixed sprinkling device requires a licence from the local water authority for its use. A hand-held hose does not require a licence but is assessed separately on the water rates. Where beds are thoroughly forked over, well-watered and mulched immediately with well-rotted manure or decayed garden compost, little watering should be necessary for quite a time, except in very dry weather.

Watering is often neglected with pot-plants and hanging baskets in the open during the summer; a large surface of the soil is exposed to the air and heat so that the compost quickly becomes dry and needs frequent attention, unless the pots are plunged into soil or ashes. Container plants usually need watering once a day during the summer, and in very hot weather hanging baskets may need a thorough watering twice a day. The leaves of evergreens keep much rain from reaching the roots even in winter when other plants receive a good store of moisture. In the same way climbers, shrubs and trees trained on a wall often suffer during the summer unless watered and mulched, as the wall keeps off much rain and prevents the plants from obtaining moisture. Wall shrubs also benefit from syringing of the leaves in hot, dry weather to reduce attacks by red spider mite.

Protection from weather

If the garden is exposed to prevalent winds, plant belts of trees or dense-growing shrubs to break the force, and to protect the plants in the borders. Where the garden is walled or fenced such protection is less vital as the walls, as well as helping to ripen the fruit grown on them, will make an efficient protection against wind. However, while fences and walls break the wind force they also create turbulence in their immediate vicinity, and staking will be necessary for plants growing close to them.

In cold and exposed gardens, herbaceous plants that come into growth early in the spring may need some winter protection. This can consist of bracken, straw or weathered ashes mounded over the crowns, but should be removed as soon as the worst frost is over. For the first few years of their lives, shrubs and trees may also need protection; mats secured to canes or straw packed inside wire mesh can be erected round wall plants and climbers; in the open, make a four-sided framework from canes and sacking or plastic or tie bracken to the canes in 'wigwam' fashion. Any covering should be left open at the top so that rain can enter.

It is advisable to lift the more tender bulbs and perennials in the autumn, box them in dry soil and store them in a dark, frost-free place for the winter. Many choice alpines suffer during winter, not from frost but from excessive dampness; they can easily be protected by panes of glass raised on short sticks over the foliage.

In exposed localities hybrid tea and miniature roses can be protected by a small mound of clean dry straw or bracken heaped round them for a few centimetres (inches) above the ground. The taller roses, standards and half-standards may have dry bracken tied in among their heads. Garden mats are not only useful for tying round tender shrubs, but also for covering frames during hard weather. They may also be tied into a cone shape, and supported on sticks like a 'wigwam' over small plants, or spread over trees trained against walls.

In the early spring protection is needed for the blossoms of early-flowering fruit trees, such as the peach and apricot, while there is still some risk of night frosts. This is best given with muslin or fine netting, but there is a disadvantage in that this frost protection also keeps out pollinating insects.

Most plants in the greenhouse need shading from the sun during the summer months; Chapter 15 gives instructions on this.

Flowers, such as chrysanthemum, dahlia, gladiolus and sweet pea, grown for exhibition purposes, can be protected from sun, wind and insect damage with paper bags tied over the blooms once these are well-developed.

Other routine measures include staking (Ch. 6) and the control of weeds, pests and diseases (Chs. 8 and 9).

8
Weed Control

Weeding is probably the most time-consuming and least enjoyable of all gardening tasks. However, the removal of weeds is essential for they not only compete with cultivated plants for room, soil nutrients and water, but are also in many cases host plants to pests and diseases. A wide range of chemicals are available to combat weeds effectively, although it is both safer and less expensive to eradicate weeds by regular hoeing or forking. But weedkillers are extremely useful on uncultivated ground.

Herbicides

A herbicide is a plant-killer not merely a weedkiller, and great care must be taken in the selection and application of the correct type to avoid damage to cultivated plants. All weedkillers are poisonous and should be kept out of the reach of children; they should never be decanted into other containers or used near pets. Some are also toxic to fish in ornamental pools. Although herbicides are extensively used in the commercial growing of crops, they are less useful in small areas of mixed dense planting as in most gardens, and some persistent weeds develop resistance to a given chemical so that repeated doses must be given, or a more effective chemical chosen.

Where possible, the use of weedkillers should be restricted to neglected ground or hard-surfaced areas, and weed control among ornamental plant and food crops carried out by cultural means.

The Dutch hoe

This is one of the most useful pieces of equipment in small gardens. Used regularly it prevents annual weed growth and eventually weakens perennial weeds. Push the hoe along slightly below the soil surface so that the roots of the weeds are cut off; the tops will quickly wilt and die. Attempts to dig deeply with the hoe and to turn the soil are not only much more tiring, but are also less effective as the weeds are merely pushed about and will quickly re-establish themselves. Weed seeds brought to the surface in any disturbance may merely exacerbate the problem. Large weeds which have been missed by the hoe should be pulled up by hand or dug up before they have a chance to set seed;

pernicious perennial weeds not eradicated during deep cultivation should be dug out before they spread.

An annual mulch, especially round shallow-rooted plants, will help to smother emerging weeds. When forking over beds in spring, try to remove as many weeds as possible, including all broken root pieces.

New ground brought into cultivation should be deeply dug and all roots and rhizomes of perennial weeds removed. It is a good idea to grow a temporary crop such as grass or potatoes to ensure the ground is free of perennial weeds before planting permanent shrubs or fruit trees. Whether manual or chemical means are used to control weeds, their eradication is easier on vacant ground than among ornamental plants. Hedges, paths and odd corners should be kept clean and free of weeds to remove potential sources of pests and diseases.

A combination of regular good cultivation and applications of chemical herbicides should be effective in weed control. The more useful weedkillers are described below. They are usually sold under proprietary names, but by law the active constituents must be described on the packet. Preparations bearing the letter 'A' surmounted by a crown indicates the approval for garden use by the Ministry of Agriculture.

There are three main types of weedkillers: contact, soil-acting and translocated.

Contact weedkillers

These non-selective weedkillers act by killing any soft vegetable material with which they come in contact. Paraquat and diquat are the most widely used, separately or in mixtures. *Paraquat is exceedingly poisonous and must be handled with great care.* Both chemicals are rendered harmless on contact with the soil and are therefore most suitable sprayed on annual weeds to destroy the tops either before crop seedlings emerge or among woody plants. But although woody stems are generally resistant to paraquat/diquat there is a possibility of injuring thin-barked trees and shrubs sprayed in the spring. Paraquat may be sprayed on herbaceous borders in winter, before new growth emerges, to control annual weeds; but be careful not to spray early emerging shoots of delphinium and a few others. As with all types of weedkillers, do not spray in windy weather or when children or pets are around.

Soil-acting weedkillers

These total weedkillers are taken up by the roots and kill all plant growth. Some chemicals also effectively sterilize the soil, eliminating some pests and diseases, but the ground treated remains unusable for up to a year. Sodium chlorate, chloropicrin, carbon disulphide and DNOC are examples. All are dangerous chemicals.

Other total weedkillers remain in the surface layers of soil where they kill weed seedlings as these germinate without damaging deeper rooted plants. Simazine and propachlor are of considerable use. Both are effective in treating perennial and annual weeds and persist in the soil for some time, simazine for several months. They may be used alternately to prevent a build-up of weeds resistant to one or the other.

Simazine may be used at relatively high doses to keep drives and other paved areas free of weeds for a year or more. At lower rates it controls most annual weeds among a wide range of established plants including roses, most shrubs and fruit trees if it is applied early. It will not control large annual weeds but these may be burned off using paraquat.

Dichlobenil is another useful chemical in this category. Unlike simazine it will control established perennial weeds such as ground elder among roses, fruit trees and shrubs if applied in early spring. It is produced in granular form and persists in the soil for several months.

Soil treated with total, soil-acting weedkillers should not be cultivated as this would interfere with the activity of the weedkiller and mix it further into the soil where it could be damaging.

Translocated weedkillers

These are selective weedkillers, often known as hormone weedkillers. They are sprayed on leaves and absorbed in the stems without damaging nearby plants. They are invaluable for controlling broad-leaved, deep-rooted perennial weeds without damaging the soil or nearby plants. Selective weedkillers are most effective when applied to plants growing actively (in moist warm weather) in late summer and in autumn for grass weeds. Dalapon is especially effective at controlling couch grass and other perennial grasses among established fruit trees and shrubs. If applied to control couch grass in uncultivated soil, allow at least three months to elapse before planting or sowing.

The chemicals 2,4-D and MCPA and related materials control broad-leaved weeds in grass and are widely used as lawn weedkillers. 2,4-D may also be used at twice the normal strength for carefully painting on to bindweed foliage to weaken and eventually kill the weed without harming the plant round which it is climbing. 2,4,5-T is a more potent chemical used for killing ivy, brambles, scrub and tree trunks on waste ground. All these materials drift easily on a slight breeze, persist on sprayed materials and in sprayers and can cause widespread damage if used carelessly.

The chemical mecoprop is used to treat clover and other creeping lawn weeds and should be applied in spring when growth is well advanced and followed by a good lawn fertilizer. Lawn mosses can be difficult to eradicate; they should never be raked out as this merely spreads the moss. Lawn sands will check their growth, and mercurous chloride will give some temporary control.

9
Pests and Diseases

The amount of damage to garden crops caused by diseases and pests can be very considerable. Every gardener needs some knowledge of how to identify them and how to treat plants affected by them.

Many insects, mites and other animals are beneficial and these should be carefully preserved. Ladybirds, lacewings, hover flies, centipedes and some of the ground beetles live on other insects. Shrewmice and hedgehogs are also helpful and birds can do more good than harm, if seedlings and fruiting crops are protected by netting or cotton or suitable bird-scarers. Regular careful inspection of plants and localized spraying in the early stages of a pest outbreak will limit the damage to plants and to the natural predators and parasites which keep pests in check in normal circumstances. Blanket spraying of large areas when pests have reached serious levels may do more harm to the natural controls than to the pests. After a temporary lull the pest will return in force causing still greater damage and necessitating further expensive sprays.

The words 'diseases' and 'pests' are used here in their broadest sense. Diseases may be divided into two main groups, those of a physiological character due to poor growing conditions, bad hygiene or lack of some essential plant food, and those caused by parasitic agents such as fungi, bacteria or viruses. The second group is the more important and the organisms concerned are among the simplest forms of vegetable life, minute or microscopic, with the viruses beyond microscopic recognition. Fungi may live on or inside the plant and many of them go through well-defined phases of development, finishing in a fruiting stage which produces spores that spread the disease further. Bacteria multiply by simple cell division and, like the viruses, are usually spread through some intermediary such as a sucking insect, the gardener's hands, boots or tools, by taking cuttings or dividing the roots of an infected plant, or less often by using infected seed.

Among pests, the gardener includes all those animals which attack plants: insects, mites, slugs, snails, birds and so on. The largest group of pests is formed by insects, most of which develop in four stages: egg, larva or grub, pupa or chrysalis, and adult. The grub stage is generally the most damaging for it is then that the insect needs the most food, and the adult stage is usually the most infective when the females seek new quarters for egg laying. Many insects produce more than one generation a year and some, like aphids, produce living young as well as eggs.

From the gardener's point of view, insects are of two kinds, those that bite and eat the tissues of the plant and those that pierce the tissues with their tongues and suck the sap. The first are usually controlled by applying a poison on to their food, the second by applying a toxic substance to the insects themselves or, in greenhouses, by using a fumigant. A sucking insect cannot be controlled by using a spray or dust designed to act only as a surface poison.

Modern research has given an effective answer to pest and disease control in all but a few cases. Some of the methods which are highly successful on a commercial scale are, however, unsuitable for private gardens, and the chemicals are not available to the amateur gardener. With some you have to wear special protective clothing and a respirator, and others may damage nearby crops if the spray drifts in the wind. Such remedies are usually safe on farms and market gardens, but may be extremely dangerous in a residential area with children and domestic pets, where fruit, flowers and vegetables are grown together in a small area and where there is always the risk of causing damage to plants in a neighbour's garden. For these reasons, only the safest of the effective treatments are recommended here, but even so, this involves the use of several poisonous or harmful substances and, like weedkillers, all pesticides and insecticides should be regarded as dangerous and stored out of the reach of children.

Pay particular attention to the time required to elapse between spraying and harvesting of edible crops to avoid poisonous residues. The mixtures recommended can be made up by the gardener or bought in convenient sizes under various proprietary names. In addition, many other preparations are available. They are carefully manufactured and tested and can be used with confidence. But since different active principles may be used and the strengths of the concentrate vary, it is important that the manufacturer's instructions are properly carried out.

Pests may quickly become resistant to some chemicals if these are used repeatedly, and this resistance may develop to related chemicals. It is, therefore, sensible to spray as little as necessary and to vary the chemical used from season to season, preventing the build-up of resistant strains.

Spraying and dusting equipment

Even the smallest garden will require some form of equipment for applying spray fluids or dusts, and manufacturers offer a very wide choice.

For large gardens and fruit orchards a knapsack-type of sprayer which is strapped to the shoulders and has its own 'one-hand' pump, and a flexible hose and sprayer is perhaps the most suitable. Smaller machines of the stirrup-pump type are available in many forms, and for the small garden there are various types of syringes and atomizers which blow the fluid out as a misty spray.

Dusting machines are smaller and lighter. The larger kinds are generally carried on the shoulder and have a 'one-hand' bellows and a flexible spout which can be directed up to a tree or down to a ground-level crop. For small-scale work there are many kinds of hand puffers, some of them being incorporated in the container bought from the shop.

But whatever method is used the main aim must be to cover the whole plant thoroughly, including the undersides of the leaves. This can best be done by putting on the spray or the dust in the finest particles possible, and for this reason it is important to buy good quality dusts which use a very fine base powder as a carrier or to add a spreading agent to the fluids and use a fine nozzle on the sprayer. The work should be carried out on calm, dry days and dusting should preferably be done in the early morning or evening when the normal dampness on the leaves will help the dust to cling. Once the spray or dust has dried on, only heavy rain will wash it off. Dusts are washed off more easily and therefore have to be applied more frequently than sprays, but the job is lighter and quicker.

Essential precautions

There is no short cut to the control of diseases and pests and since most of them appear at different times of the season on a wide variety of crops and develop in various ways with their most vulnerable stages occurring at different times there is, as yet, no cure-all or once-for-all magic available. But some chemicals combine insecticides and fungicides, and most will control more than one kind of pest. With the development of systemic pesticides and fungicides, where the chemical is absorbed in the plant sap, longer control is possible with a single spraying, and the new selective pesticides eliminate pests only, not the natural predators. Some soil fumigants will control many soil insects as well as fungi.

In the average garden where fruit, flowers, shrubs and vegetables are generally grown close to each other, the control of diseases and pests is not always a straightforward job and certain fundamental precautions are necessary.

1. Winter-washes, eg tar oils, must be used only in the dormant period and should not be applied to fruit trees if leafy vegetables or herbaceous plants are growing underneath. Instead, spray with nicotine in spring.
2. Fruit and ornamental trees or shrubs should never be sprayed with an insecticide while the blossom is open because of the danger to bees and other pollinating insects.

Azaleas and rhododendrons bring a wonderful display of early colour, but will only thrive on acid soils

A carefully planned vegetable garden. The path is wide enough to take a wheelbarrow, and the greenhouse is conveniently placed

3. Persistent and systemic insecticides must never be applied to a food crop nearing harvesting time.
4. Insecticides containing BHC (benzene hexachloride) should not be applied to cucumbers, melons and marrows or vines or as a seed-dressing to root vegetables.
5. Derris should not be used where it may contaminate a stream or ornamental pond containing fish.
6. Boxes or sheds used for storing fruit or vegetables should be cleaned every year with hot water and soda and not with any disinfectant which may affect the flavour of the stored produce.

Fumigants for the greenhouse

Fumigation is the most convenient way of controlling the more serious pests and diseases in greenhouses, particularly red spider and white fly. Various substances are used, the active principles being nicotine, hydrocyanic acid gas, azobenzene, tetrachlorethane or sulphur. They can all be bought as proprietary articles, many of them in the form of smokes. But as most of them are very poisonous the maker's instructions must be followed precisely and on no account should a greenhouse or conservatory leading into a house be fumigated in this way.

The best time to do the job is in the evening when the plants are dry. Tender plants and those in full flower should be removed and treated separately. The greenhouse must be made as airtight as possible and the work done quickly, starting from the far end, and moving towards the door. When finished, the door should be locked. In the morning when the door is opened plenty of time must be allowed before going inside.

Soil fumigants

A different type of fumigation is occasionally used in the open. It is rarely necessary in well-managed gardens, but may be the best way of dealing with heavy infestations of leather jackets and wireworms which often occur when old, rough turf or neglected land is broken up. Naphthalene is used in powdered form and raked in, and as it does not harm growing plants (except very young seedlings) it can be used at any time of the year. Formaldehyde is used as a liquid, but as it is harmful to plants when freshly applied, it should only be used when the land is uncropped. Formaldehyde will also control a number of soil fungi.

Soil sterilization

In greenhouses where plants are grown in beds or borders, the soil may become infected with certain serious root diseases or pests like eelworms. It must then either be replaced with fresh clean soil or sterilized. The best sterilization is by steaming, but in a private garden the second best is to burn sulphur; the fumes are poisonous, and the greenhouse should first be emptied of all plants. After sterilizing the house should be well aired for ten to fourteen days.

Small quantities of soil for potting can be sterilized at home in a special soil sterilizer or by baking or steaming. Thin layers can be placed on a shovel held over a fire until the soil is just too hot to hold. It must not be overbaked. Alternatively, a bucketful of soil can be suspended for one hour in a large pan of boiling water so that the steam envelops it. The pan must be covered over and no water allowed to get into the bucket.

Essential hygiene

Plants that are well grown and well managed are much less liable to be attacked by diseases or pests than those which are struggling in their surroundings. But even the strongest are by no means immune and everything possible must be done to prevent trouble. General tidiness helps to remove potential sources of infection. Weeds should be kept down, hedges trimmed and cleared of rubbish at their base, and boxes, pots, stakes, etc, kept clean and stacked tidily in a shed or outhouse.

Very often, the prompt removal and burning of an attacked shoot or plant will prevent any further spread, and sometimes it may pay to scrap an unhealthy crop entirely and buy in fresh, clean plants or follow with a different crop altogether. Broken branches on trees and shrubs or accidental wounds should be pared off smoothly and covered with a wound sealing paint, and as soon as flowers or vegetables are finished the remnants should be taken up and composted. Anything showing signs of rotting, such as rotten fruit or slimy growth, should be burned.

List of Pests and Diseases

Ants

Ants do not attack plants themselves but cause damage by helping to spread aphids, which they often 'nurse' for the honeydew, and they may tunnel among the roots of young seedlings.

Treatment Destroy the nests with boiling water, liquid derris, paraffin, or a proprietary ant killer. If you cannot find the nest, sprinkle a little sugar about; the ants will carry this away to their homes.

Aphids

These are the well-known greenfly or blackfly, which attack a wide range of both outdoor and greenhouse plants. They may be black, green, reddish, almost white or bluish. There are several generations a year, with or without wings. They feed by sucking the sap and in so doing frequently spread virus diseases. They occur on the roots of some plants, such as lettuces and brassicas, as well as above ground. Most of them exude a sticky honeydew on which sooty moulds frequently grow,

further spoiling the appearance of the plant. The woolly aphids, commonly seen on apple trees, produces a white fluffy covering.
Symptoms Attacks generally start on the undersides of the leaves or tips of the shoots. Curling and malformation follow, making spraying difficult. Prompt attention is therefore essential.
Treatment Spray or dust with nicotine, derris, malathion or pirimicarb. Several applications may be necessary. On fruit trees the routine winter-washing should not be missed, and in greenhouses carry out an annual fumigation.

Apple blossom weevil
A dark-coloured weevil about 6mm ($\frac{1}{4}$in) long, covered with greyish hairs and with a yellowish V-shaped mark across the wing cases. The insect has a long snout which the female uses to bore a hole in the flower bud ready for laying an egg. Usually only one egg is laid in each bud. Pears, quinces and medlars are sometimes attacked, but apples are the most susceptible.
Symptoms When the grub hatches it feeds on the growing flower which wilts, turns brown and fails to develop a fruit. The brown petals form a 'cap' under which a grub is usually found.
Treatment Spray with BHC or fenitrothion just before buds begin to burst, or dust with a 5 per cent BHC dust when the flower buds are breaking and again just before bursting. An alternative method is to tie bands of sacking or corrugated paper around the trunks in June, to trap the egg-laying females. Remove and burn the bands in October.

Apple sawfly
The adult insect is about 8mm ($\frac{1}{3}$in) long, black, with legs and underside yellowish red. It appears at blossom time, laying its eggs, one to a flower. The grub is creamy white with a black head which later becomes brown.
Symptoms The grub tunnels into the developing fruit which often shows the tunnelling as a ribbon-like scar. By June the attacked fruits show a hole from which a dirty brown mess exudes. Onc grub may attack several fruits. When fully fed it drops to the ground and pupates in the soil.
Treatment In small gardens, affected fruits should be picked or gathered up and burned. On a larger scale spray with BHC, fenitrothion or dimethoate at petal fall or within the next few days.
Note Damage done by apple sawfly must be distinguished from that of codling moth (which *see*) because control measures are different.

Apple and pear scab
Two species of fungi are responsible, each confined to its own host. Infection can occur at any time during the growing season, the winter stage being passed under the bark or on fallen leaves.

Symptoms As the leaves develop, dark olive-green patches appear and later become brownish or black. Blister-like swellings and cracks occur on the shoots. Later the fruits are infected, the skin becoming cracked or covered with scattered dark or black spots.
Treatment Diseased material should be collected and burned, and the trees sprayed with lime-sulphur (except sulphur-shy varieties), benomyl or captan. Spray at fortnightly intervals from the time the flower buds are visible and until after petal fall, or until July if necessary.

Apple sucker
Small flattened yellowish insect which is often seen around the young leaves and blossoms. They exude a sticky fluid and white waxy threads. Later they become green and when adult have wings. Small, oval, creamy eggs are laid in the autumn on the fruit spurs.
Symptoms Flower buds die or fail to set fruit. A badly-attacked tree looks as though it has been damaged by frost.
Treatment The best control is routine winter-washing. If this has been missed, spray in spring just before the blossoms burst, with nicotine, malathion or BHC.

Armillaria mellea
Often called honey fungus or bootlace fungus, this disease attacks a wide range of trees and shrubs and occasionally some herbaceous plants; it may cause serious losses. It normally lives on the dead wood of old stumps or roots and sends out underground, black, shiny, cord-like strands or boot-laces to infect healthy trees, even some distance away.
Symptoms The first signs are usually wilting and dying leaves, followed by decay of the trunk or main stem at ground level where the fungus shows as white sheets or fan-like growths under the bark. In the autumn the toadstool stage may appear in the form of honey-coloured caps with brown scales and yellowish stems.
Treatment The only remedy is to dig up and burn affected material, taking care to pick out all the roots and old stumps or stakes. In a hedge, the trees adjoining the affected areas, though apparently healthy, should also be dug up. Dress the soil heavily with lime and dig deeply, or if practicable, replace with fresh soil or soil treated with a 2 per cent solution of formalin. Fruit trees and bushes, ornamental and hedge trees, particularly privet, are all liable to attack. Armillatox or dazomet, proprietary materials, have some chance of preventing the spread of fungus if applied as a soil drench.

Asparagus beetle
The beetle is about 3mm ($\frac{1}{8}$in) long and has a greenish-black head and

orange wings with black bars. The eggs are greenish-black and laid in rows on the shoots of asparagus.
Symptoms The beetles eat the buds and later the grubs feed on the foliage.
Treatment Spray or dust with derris or pyrethrum. After cutting is finished, malathion can be used. As the beetles hibernate in old stems or surrounding rubbish, the beds and the garden around must be kept tidy.

Bacterial rots
Most of the common bacterial diseases cause varying forms of wet or slimy rot. The first sign is a sudden wilting, and at this stage discoloured tissues are usually seen if the affected part is cut across. Many herbaceous plants and vegetables are attacked, especially potatoes (blackleg), cucumbers under glass (wilt), tomatoes, rhubarb (crown rot), French beans (halo blight), carrots, onions, iris and other bulbs. The drier forms of bacterial diseases produce typical cankers on trees and shrubs (*see* Die-back) or gall on the roots of fruit and other trees, roses and certain root vegetables, such as beetroot (crown gall).
Treatment The only method is to dig up and burn infected plants. After completing the work, disinfect hands and any tools in a 2 per cent formalin solution.

Bean weevil
The beetle is about 6mm (¼in) long, yellowish-brown, with striped wing cases. They attack peas as well as beans, but are usually only serious on seedling plants.
Symptoms The beetles eat circular patches from the edges of leaves.
Treatment Practise good cultivation and manuring to help the crop grow away quickly in cold slow-growing weather; spray or dust the plants with BHC or spray with fenitrothion.

Beet fly
A greyish-black fly about 8mm (⅓in) long, which lays its eggs under the leaves of beetroot in the seedling or young stages.
Symptoms Pale blotches appear on the leaves caused by the grubs burrowing between the surfaces. The plants wither and may die.
Treatment Hoe regularly and top-dress with nitrate of soda.

Black currant gall mite
This is a widespread, minute insect, just too small to be visible. Its main host is black currants, but red and white currants and gooseberries are occasionally attacked.
Symptoms The mites live in the buds which swell to about twice their size and fail to open normally. In the following spring, the infested buds

dry up and die and the mites move on to fresh buds. The mites also spread the disease known as reversion (which *see*).
Treatment On a small scale, hand-picking of all infested buds, if done in good time, will reduce attacks, but the best control is by spraying with a 1 per cent lime-sulphur solution just before the flowers open and again three weeks later. Some scorching may result and the crop be reduced, but in the following year spraying should be unnecessary and a full crop should be obtained. In severe cases, dig up and burn the bushes and replace them with healthy, virus-free stock.

Black spot
Roses may sometimes be seriously affected by this disease though some varieties are more resistant than others.
Symptoms Black spots or blotches appear on the leaves and sometimes on the shoots.
Treatment Spray with benomyl, captan or maneb. Remove and burn affected shoots and all fallen leaves, and spray the bushes with a foliar feed to encourage vigour.

Blossom wilt
The many separate strains of this disease affect cherries, plums, apricots, peaches, pears and apples. They are closely related to the fungi causing wither tip in plums and brown rot, and their severity varies from year to year. The most important is blossom wilt of apples.
Symptoms The fungus enters the flowers and soon the surrounding leaves wilt and droop. Fruiting spurs become infected and may be killed. In bad attacks the disease may spread along the whole shoot. Spores develop on the infected areas and spread the disease.
Treatment Cut out and burn all infected parts, cutting back to sound healthy wood. Routine spraying with a winter-wash and lime-sulphur also has some control, but benomyl is more effective.

Botrytis
This fungus disease is better known as grey mould; it affects a large number of outdoor plants, especially lettuce, but is particularly troublesome on fruit, flowers and vegetables grown under glass.
Symptoms A greyish velvety mould develops on the leaves and stems.
Treatment Remove and burn infected material. Give ample ventilation and reduce humidity. Benomyl, captan, thiram and zineb are effective. In severe cases, fumigate the greenhouse.

Brown rot
Different species and strains of the fungus causing blossom wilt also attack the crops of all tree fruits.

Symptoms Whitish, yellow or grey pustules show in rings on the fruits. Infected fruits drop off or shrivel and remain on the trees as 'mummied' fruits, to act as a source of infection next year. The disease also occurs among apples in store, the fruits showing characteristic rotting.

Treatment Collect and destroy all rotten fruit and cut out and burn all diseased shoots. Spray with thiophanate-methyl. Examine fruit in store regularly every two or three weeks.

Bulb mite

These small, round, shiny, yellowish mites often occur as a secondary pest, attacking hyacinths, lilies, narcissi and tulips which have first been damaged in some other way.

Symptoms The mites swarm between the scales of the bulbs either in store or when growing, often causing serious rotting of the bulbs and twisted leaves.

Treatment Burn badly infested bulbs and where possible immerse all others in hot water kept at 43°C (110°F) for one hour. All bulbs must be carefully handled to avoid damage.

Cabbage caterpillar

These are the well-known larvae of the cabbage white butterflies and the cabbage moth. They are found on all brassicas and are common on nasturtiums (*Tropaeolum*).

Symptoms The eggs are laid on the leaves, and the caterpillars not only eat the leaves but also spoil the crop with their excreta.

Treatment Early action is essential before the caterpillars get into the hearts. Pick off and crush the eggs and larvae by hand or spray the plants with malathion, BHC, derris or dimethoate. (Nicotine should not be used near harvest time.)

Cabbage root fly

This is a serious pest of all brassicas, especially cabbage and cauliflower. The fly is ash-grey, about 6mm ($\frac{1}{4}$in) long and like a small house-fly. There are two or three generations a year.

Symptoms Attacked plants look pale and stop growing. The leaves flag. If the plant is taken up, white, legless maggots about 8mm ($\frac{1}{3}$in) long will be found around the root or inside. The root may be partly eaten or tunnelled, or almost severed.

Treatment Sprinkle bromophos round the stem of each plant in a ring about 2.5cm (1in) wide. Water in later-planted crops with a solution of diazinon or trichlorphon.

Cabbage white fly

In warm sheltered gardens a small white fly often occurs on brassica

crops, the eggs and larvae being found on the undersides of the leaves. Usually no harm is done, except when the larvae get into the hearts.
Treatment Spraying is rarely satisfactory as it is difficult to reach the flies, but some control may be obtained with BHC or malathion. Generally good control can be obtained by pulling off and burning the lower leaves. Burn all stumps from an infested crop.

Canker

The word canker is loosely used to cover any kind of wound surrounded by swollen bark or callus. It may be caused by mechanical injury when the wound usually heals naturally or by certain fungi or woolly aphids. Cankers due to fungi occur on cabbages and turnips and on fruit trees, principally apples and pears. The so-called canker of parsnips is a physiological disorder common on wet soils deficient in lime.
Symptoms Small depressed areas occur in the bark and extend to form a ragged wound which often encircles the branch or twig. Whitish pustules appear followed by small round, red bodies.
Treatment As the fungus enters through wounds, any breakages in the branches and cut surfaces made by pruning should be coated with a proprietary canker paint or grafting wax. Insects, especially woolly aphids, must be kept down. Poor growing conditions, such as bad drainage, appear to aggravate the disease, especially on apples.

Where the infected branches are small they should be cut well back to healthy wood. On large branches, cut out infected areas and seal the wounds. Badly attacked trees should be dug up and all infected material burned.

Capsid bugs

Several species of capsids, all about 8mm ($\frac{1}{3}$in) long but varying in colour from green to reddish-brown, attack many garden plants.
Symptoms In most cases rusty-looking pin-prick holes appear on the leaves. On apples, rough scars also appear on the surface of the fruit. Frequently the growing point of a plant is damaged and poor or malformed growth follows.
Treatment Spray or dust with BHC, nicotine, malathion or diazinon, covering also the soil round the plants as the capsids are very active and usually drop off the plants when disturbed. On fruit trees winter spraying will help by controlling the egg stage.

Carrot fly

A shiny, greenish-black fly about 8mm ($\frac{1}{3}$in) long, with yellowish legs appears in May and again in August when the second generation occurs. It lays its eggs on or near carrots
Symptoms The foliage wilts and turns reddish in colour. A lifted root

will show a number of small colourless maggots burrowing into the flesh.

Treatment In badly-infested areas the crop should not be sown before the end of May. This will avoid the first generation. Seed should be sown thinly so as to avoid or reduce thinning out which bruises the seedlings and sets free the smell of carrots which attracts the flies. Burn any thinnings. Bromophos sprinkled along the rows at fortnightly intervals to the end of June, or watering with diazinon or trichlorphon two or times will act as repellants.

Celery beetle

A small steel-blue beetle about 8mm ($\frac{1}{3}$in) long, which normally feeds on weeds, may attack celery and occasionally carrots and parsnips during July and August.

Symptoms The leaves and the stems are eaten.

Treatment Dust with derris.

Celery fly – *See* Leaf-miners.

Centipedes – *See* Millepedes.

Chafer beetles

There are four species. The adults vary from 12 to 25mm ($\frac{1}{2}$ to 1in) long. All have hard brownish wing-cases except the rose chafer which is green. The beetles feed on the leaves of many trees and shrubs, and the fleshy, white, curved, brown-headed grubs feed on the roots.

Symptoms The plant suddenly wilts and on being dug up a grub is often found having eaten right through the root.

Treatment Pick off the grubs whenever possible or dust or spray the soil with BHC. Deep cultivation helps in bringing the grubs to the surface where they will be picked up by birds.

Cherry sawfly – *See* Slugworms.

Chocolate spot

Occasionally this disease is serious on broad beans, if the season is wet.

Symptoms Chocolate-coloured spots appear on the leaves and sometimes on the stems and pods. The flowers may fall.

Treatment Top-dress with sulphate of potash or lime the soil; burn the haulm after harvesting. In severe attacks, spray with a copper fungicide.

Chrysanthemum midge

A small brownish fly, about 2mm ($\frac{1}{10}$in) long, with a red abdomen, may attack chrysanthemums in greenhouses where it breeds all the year

round. Occasionally in dry summers it may be found out of doors.
Symptoms The larvae burrow into the leaves or shoots and as they grow cause cone-shaped swellings which lead to malformation of the buds and flowers.
Treatment Remove galls and spray every week with nicotine or BHC.

Club root
Sometimes called finger and toe, this is a common and generally well-known disease, favoured by an acid condition of the soil. The cabbage family, turnips, swedes and radishes are the most important of the susceptible crops, but any cruciferous plant is liable to attack. Many weeds such as charlock and shepherd's purse can also become infected and occasionally the disease is found on wallflowers, stocks, etc.
Symptoms The plants look stunted and unhealthy. Swellings of various shapes occur on the roots or on the stems at ground level, later becoming slimy as they decay. If cut through the swelling is solid and often has a marbled appearance, different from the swelling caused by gall weevils which is hollow and usually has a maggot inside.
Treatment Improve drainage on waterlogged soil, and keep up the lime content of the soil by regular dressings; space susceptible crops as far apart as possible in the rotation. In severe cases dip plants in a paste of calomel before planting out or sterilize the soil with dazomet.

Codling moth
The moth is brown-grey with a coppery tip to the wings. Eggs are laid in June and July and the grub enters the fruit through the side or the eye, and burrows into the core. Apples are most generally attacked, but pears, quince and walnut may occasionally suffer.
Symptoms When fully fed the larva burrows its way out of the fruit which may stay on the tree or fall. It leaves a characteristic hole with no 'frass' showing.
Treatment As the larva hibernates in cracks in the bark or in rubbish such as dead leaves on the ground, general tidiness is essential. Trees with rough, moss-covered bark should be sprayed with tar oil in winter. In bad attacks, spray the blossoms about fourteen days after petal fall with malathion or fenitrothion and repeat three weeks later.
Note Codling moth should be compared with apple sawfly. Codling moth occurs later and its grub has eight pairs of legs while that of the sawfly has ten. Fruits attacked by codling moth do not show frass exuding from the hole in the flesh and if cut across the destroyed part will be mainly in the centre round the core.

Coral spot
The disease attacks a wide range of ornamental, forest and fruit trees and

shrubs. It is particularly common on red currants, and often enters through wounds or breakage of branches.
Symptoms Branches often wilt suddenly and die. When the wood is dead, pink and red pustules appear. These are full of spores which are later released and so spread infection.
Treatment All wilting and dead branches should be cut out as soon as possible and burned. Cuts should be painted with mercuric oxide or other wound sealer. As the fungus can also live on dead twigs, or old stakes and posts, tidiness in the garden is essential.

Cuckoo spit
The small, pale greenish-yellow larva of the frog-hopper attacks many plants, especially herbaceous plants, sucking the sap and surrounding itself with a white froth. Not usually serious.
Symptoms The froth is generally seen towards the top of the shoots.
Treatment Spray forcibly with nicotine, BHC or malathion.

Currant moths
The currant clearwing and the currant shoot borer are two moths which sometimes cause appreciable loss but are generally of little importance. The life histories are different but the caterpillars of both tunnel into the young shoots causing them to wilt and die.
Treatment Cut off and burn infested shoots.

Cutworms or surface caterpillars
This heading covers the caterpillars of several different moths. They are mostly grey to black and generally feed at night on a wide range of plants.
Symptoms Seedlings and young plants suddenly wilt and are found to be eaten at or just below ground level.
Treatment Collect the caterpillars to be found round wilted plants; treat seed drills with a dressing or work bromophos or BHC dust into soil.

Damping-off
Several different fungi are responsible, and a wide range of plants in the seedling stage may be affected.
Symptoms The fungi attack the seedlings at ground level and a sudden collapse of the stems follows.
Treatment Good growing and general hygiene are essential. Under glass give ample ventilation and avoid excessive moisture. Seeds should be sown in sterilized compost and watered with Cheshunt compound, captan or zineb.

Deficiency diseases
This term is used to cover a wide range of non-parasitic disorders due to

the lack of any one essential plant food leading to unnatural or malformed growth. Among the most common are:

Leaf-scorch. Many trees and shrubs may show dry, yellow to reddish-brown leaves due to lack of potash.

Blotchy ripening in tomatoes may be due to lack of potash or less commonly of nitrogen.

Brown heart of turnips and swedes due to lack of boron may cause the roots to be tough and bitter after being cooked. Beetroot may suffer in a similar way.

Chlorosis or patchiness in the leaves may be due to lack of lime or iron.

Whiptail of cauliflowers may be due to lack of molybdenum causing the young plants to go blind and show malformed leaves.

Treatment A proper system of manuring must be carried out. The trace elements, such as boron, are required only in minute quantities and are best applied in the form of good farmyard manure and organic fertilizers, such as hoof and horn, dried blood and bone meal.

Die-back

This term is used to describe various kinds of sudden die-back in the young shoots of many trees and shrubs. This may be due to poor soil or cultivation or caused by certain bacteria and fungi. The effects often resemble those of canker.

Treatment Cut out and burn affected shoots and branches.

Downy mildew – *See* Mildew.

Dry rot of potatoes

The early varieties are the more susceptible, and the disease is most noticeable during the storage period.

Symptoms Infected tubers shrink and shrivel, the sunken areas showing white or pinkish pustules.

Treatment All tubers in store should be examined regularly and infected ones removed and burned. Suspected tubers should never be used for seed as the rot is progressive and will lead to misses in the rows. Potatoes should always be handled carefully as infection easily enters through wounds.

Earthworms

Earthworms are entirely beneficial. Their burrowing helps to drain and aerate the soil, and they pull down large quantities of decaying vegetable matter for their food. But their cases can sometimes spoil the appearance of a lawn or interfere with games.

Treatment Regular brushing is generally sufficient, but where large numbers are present the lawn should be dressed with a proprietary worm-killer or potassium permangate at 20g (¾oz) to 4 litres (1 gal.) of water for every square metre (yd). Poisons such as copper sulphate should be avoided as the dead worms will be poisonous to birds or poultry. Chlordane may be used on lawns only. (*See also* Chapter 12.)

Earwigs

Earwigs feed at night and hide during the day under leaves, in canes, boxes or rubbish. They are generally most troublesome on greenhouse plants, but also attack many plants grown out of doors.

Symptoms The leaves show holes and eaten areas and the flowers become ragged or malformed.

Treatment All dead leaves and rubbish should be cleared up and the plants sprayed or dusted with BHC. Large numbers of earwigs may be trapped in pieces of sacking or crumpled paper or in plant pots loosely stuffed with straw and set up on canes.

Eelworms

There are many different species and strains of eelworms and several of them cause serious damage to cultivated plants. Generally speaking, they keep to their own host-plants or groups of plants, and if in the course of rotational cropping these are not grown in the infested soil the eelworms can still exist as dormant cysts for a few years. All species are minute, the largest being just visible to the naked eye. They can live within the plant tissue or encysted in the soil, so that they are easily and quickly spread.

Symptoms The stem and bulb eelworm causes stunted, malformed growth in a large number of herbaceous and bulbous plants. The leaves are often narrow and twisted and the stems split or wiry-looking. The leaf blotch eelworm causes brown or black areas in the leaves of many greenhouse plants, including ferns, and a related species causes similar and often very serious damage to chrysanthemums which generally also show malformed flowers. The root-knot eelworm causes galls on the roots of many plants, particularly tomatoes, cucumbers and flowers grown in greenhouses. In bad attacks the whole root system is affected, the plant wilts and may even die. Another species attacks the buds of currants and yet another may be extremely serious on potatoes by stunting the growth so much that little or no crop is obtained. In this case the females can often be seen as minute whitish to brownish spherical bodies on the roots or tubers.

Treatment Chemicals for control of eelworms are not available to amateur gardeners. All plants bought in should be purchased from reliable sources. Susceptible crops should not be planted in infested soil for three to five years, and infected stock should not be propagated; in the vegetable garden practise a long rotation and follow it strictly. Sterilize greenhouse borders.

Flea beetles
Several species of small, black or blue-black beetles about 2mm ($\frac{1}{10}$in) long, with yellowish stripes on the wing-cases, attack many plants especially the cabbage family, turnips, beetroot and several herbaceous plants. They are most destructive to seedlings.
Symptoms The leaves show small holes as well as eaten areas. The plants look blue.
Treatment As the beetles hibernate in rubbish, hedges, etc, a clean, tidy garden is essential. Dust the seed drills with a dressing, and spray or dust seedlings with derris or BHC once a fortnight for as long as necessary.

Gooseberry sawfly
This is a common pest which may be very destructive if not controlled in the early stages. It occasionally also attacks currants. The fly is typical of many sawflies, black and yellowish in colour and 1cm ($\frac{1}{2}$in) long. The caterpillars are green at first with black spots. Later the spots disappear and small orange-coloured areas develop at both ends. There are generally three generations a year.
Symptoms The caterpillars feed on the leaves and shoots and if unchecked may strip a whole bush of its foliage.
Treatment Spray or dust with derris, fenitrothion or malathion in spring. On a small scale the caterpillars can be picked off by hand.
Note It is important to distinguish the caterpillars of this sawfly from those of the magpie moth which are black, white and yellow, for although the control measures are the same, there is only one generation of magpie moths a year, whereas the sawflies will continue to demand attention.

Grease banding – *See* Winter moth.

Greenfly – *See* Aphids.

Greenhouse white fly
This white waxy-looking fly less than 1mm ($\frac{1}{25}$in) long attacks many greenhouse plants. It is distinct from the cabbage white fly and cannot survive the winter out of doors.
Symptoms The larvae suck the sap, causing the leaves to lose colour and look spotted. The flies fly off readily when disturbed.
Treatment Fumigate the greenhouse with dichlorvos or BHC. Alternatively establish a tiny parasitic wasp to control white fly less dramatically, but more safely and effectively in the long term. The wasp must be protected from all chemical sprays.

Grey mould – *See* Botrytis.

Honey fungus – *See* Armillaria.

Lackey moth
Although always present, especially in the south, these yellowish to reddish-brown moths with a wing-span of 3.5cm ($1\frac{1}{2}$in) do little harm unless they assume epidemic proportions. Most kinds of fruit trees and several kinds of forest and ornamental trees are attacked.
Symptoms The eggs, which are easily seen, are laid on young shoots in the form of a bracelet made up of 100–150 eggs. When hatched, the caterpillars keep together spinning a web to form a tent in which they live. As they eat the foliage they move on, spinning another tent. The caterpillars are bluish-grey with white and orange stripes.
Treatment The best control is to break up the tents and destroy the caterpillars by hand. Sprays of BHC must be done early to be effective. In winter, cut off and destroy the egg bracelets.

Leaf galls
Many different kinds of galls and swellings may often be seen on the leaves of a number of ornamental trees and shrubs. They are caused by various species of gall-wasps, gall-midges and gall-mites, but only very rarely does any harm result.
Treatment If a young valuable tree is seriously attacked by gall-wasps or gall-midges, spray with nicotine. If the galls are caused by gall-mites spray with 5 per cent lime-sulphur.

Leaf-miners
The larvae of many different species of moths, weevils and flies are loosely but conveniently classed as leaf-miners. They attack a wide range of plants, among them apples, roses, shrubs, herbaceous plants and vegetables. Chrysanthemum, lilac, cineraria, azalea, holly, privet, celery and beetroot are probably the most important.
Symptoms The larvae live on the inner tissue of the leaf between the upper and lower surfaces, making characteristic tunnels or mines as they move along.
Treatment Weeds must be kept down since many of them can act as host plants. On a small scale the larvae can be crushed in their mines with the finger and thumb or affected leaves can be picked off and burned. Apply quick-acting top-dressings to help vegetable crops along or dust the soil with BHC or diazinon to repel the egg-laying adults. On a larger scale or when the attack is severe spray with nicotine or BHC.

Leaf mould of tomatoes
This fungus disease often causes severe losses in tomatoes under glass. It is rarely seen on the outdoor crop.

Symptoms Yellowish spots which later take on a purplish-brown tinge appear on the leaves in June or July. On the undersides a grey mould appears. The affected parts dry out and the leaves shrivel or die.
Treatment The atmosphere must not get too warm or too humid. Give plenty of ventilation and increase this as soon as the disease appears. Stop overhead spraying and reduce watering. Strip off lower leaves. If necessary use a colloidal copper spray, zineb or maneb at intervals of ten to fourteen days. At the end of the season disinfect the house with formalin or fumigate with sulphur. Resistant varieties are readily obtainable.

Leaf roller – *See* Slugworms and Tortrix moths.

Leaf spots
Several different fungi attack different crops, including many herbaceous plants, but the disease is not generally serious. Celery and chrysanthemums are perhaps the most important.
Symptoms Brown, round spots appear on the leaves and occasionally on the stems.
Treatment With most plants good growing is generally a sufficient control. In severe attacks spray with Bordeaux mixture. With celery the disease is carried in the seed, and care should be taken to buy certified seed from a reputable source.

Leather jackets
These are the well-known dirty-brown or greyish-black legless grubs of the daddy longlegs or crane flies. They have a tough, leathery skin, are about 2.5 to 3.5cm (1 to 1½in) long, and feed on the roots of a wide range of plants.
Symptoms The plant suddenly wilts and if dug up a grub can often be found or it may have moved on to the next plant.
Treatment General cleanliness and regular hoeing is normally sufficient. Bad attacks often follow the breaking up of old or neglected turf when BHC or bromophos can be watered into the soil.

Leopard moth
The wings are white with bluish-black spots and have a span of 6cm (2½in). The moths appear in June and July and lay eggs on fruit trees, especially apples, and many ornamental and forest trees. The caterpillars are yellowish-white with black spots and grow to 5cm (2in) long. They tunnel into the shoots and branches where they stay for two or three years.
Symptoms The foliage turns yellow and wilts and on young trees sawdust or frass may be seen. The tunnels may be seen when infested branches are cut open.

Treatment Cut out and burn infested branches or work BHC dust into the tunnels. In severe attacks it may be necessary to dig up and burn the whole tree.

Magpie moth

The caterpillars of this well-known black, white and yellow moth feed on the leaves of currants, gooseberries, laurels, apricots, nuts and other plants and if neglected may cause serious defoliation. There is one generation a year beginning in July or August when the eggs are laid.

Symptoms The caterpillars are at first small and black. They feed until the autumn, then hibernate on bark or dead leaves and emerge again in the spring when they feed on the young growth, become much larger and black and white with a yellow stripe. They pupate generally on the tree and the moth emerges in July.

Treatment As soon as the caterpillars are seen, spray or dust with derris, BHC or malathion. On a small scale pick off the caterpillars by hand.

Mealy bugs

These small, scale-like insects have a white, waxy covering, are fairly active and breed throughout the year. They occur principally in greenhouses, especially on vines, but are also found out of doors on ribes, ceanothus, robinia, laburnum and less commonly on other shrubs. They feed by sucking the sap and may occur on the roots as well as the foliage.

Treatment Spray regularly with nicotine, malathion or dimethoate. In addition fumigate greenhouses with dichlorvos or tecnazene at the end of the season.

Mildew

The mildews which occur on a great number of trees, shrubs and plants can be broadly divided into two types: the powdery mildews where the fungi live on the surface of the foliage, spoiling the appearance rather than causing harm, and the downy mildews, which are more deep-seated, live within the tissues and as a rule are far more serious. Powdery mildews are found on roses, vines, apples, gooseberries, marrows, turnips, strawberries, chrysanthemums, asters, calendulas and many other plants. Downy mildews appear on brassica seedlings, lettuce, onions, spinach, vines, wallflowers, stocks, etc.

Symptoms The powdery mildews generally produce a whitish to greyish powdery effect on the foliage while the downy mildews cause yellowish patches on the leaves often with a greyish or purplish downy growth on the underside.

Treatment For powdery mildews spray with sulphur, benomyl or dinocap and remove any badly-infected shoots. For downy mildews remove all infected plants and shoots and spray with Bordeaux mixture or dust with a copper-lime dust or zineb. In both cases, avoid overcrowding and under glass give ample ventilation and reduce humidity. Fumigate the house with dinocap.

Millepedes
Millepedes attack the leaves of seedlings and the roots of a large number of plants and frequently eat into bulbs. They often extend the damage caused by wounds or other insects and generally set up decay. (They must be distinguished from centipedes which are beneficial. Centipedes are flat in appearance, have one pair of legs to each body segment and are very active; millepedes have two pairs of legs to each segment, are more rounded and usually curl up when disturbed.)
Treatment Regular hoeing and good cultivation is generally sufficient. In bad attacks dress the soil or seedlings with BHC dust. Large numbers may be trapped in pieces of potato or carrot buried in the soil. These baits should be marked and examined every few days.

Mosquitoes
Mosquitoes, particularly the blood-sucking females, are a pest of the gardener and not of the plants he grows. In some gardens where there are ponds, streams or exposed water and liquid-manure tanks they can be a great nuisance. The larvae, sometimes called wrigglers, live and feed in the water, continually rising to the surface to breathe through their tails.
Treatment Fish in ponds will readily eat all the eggs and larvae they can reach, and they should be helped by preventing plants from spreading over the surface of the water and providing hiding-places for the pest. BHC should be used only on the water when there is no danger of its coming into contact with fish as it is toxic.

Mushroom flies
Several species of small black flies about 6mm (¼in) long, which normally live on decaying vegetable matter, will attack mushrooms.
Symptoms The larvae eat into the stems and cause decay.
Treatment Doors and ventilators should be screened with fine gauze or muslin and the beds sprayed or dusted with derris or pyrethrum. In severe attacks it may be necessary to fumigate with hydrocyanic acid gas.

Mushroom mites
Several species of mites often occur on mushroom beds, usually introduced in the manure. Slow-moving grey or white mites are the most harmful, but they have their own enemies – the more active brown mites which are therefore beneficial.
Symptoms The mites tunnel into the stalks and caps and the mushrooms turn brown.

Treatment Fumigation is of doubtful value. Derris dust gives some control but the best method is to clean the shed and equipment thoroughly with boiling water.

Mushroom moulds

The white plaster mould may appear as a whitish powder on the surface of the bed at spawning time and the brown plaster mould may occur on the compost as a white fluff which later turns brown. Both these fungi rob the crop of its nutriment but neither is usually serious, and good growing is normally a sufficient control.

But there is another white mould or mycogone which grows vigorously, completely covering the mushrooms and ruining the crop. The only control is to remove and burn all infected material and when the crop is finished to disinfect the house, boxes and trays with a formalin solution.

Narcissus flies

There are three kinds: the large narcissus fly which confines its attacks to narcissi (which include daffodils) and two smaller ones, known as small bulb flies, which may also attack other bulbs and occasionally some of the root vegetables.

The large fly resembles a small bumble bee. It lays eggs in May and June singly on or near a bulb. The larva burrows in and eats out the centre of the bulb. The small flies appear earlier, are more like hover flies and lay several eggs on each bulb.

Symptoms Bulbs which show weak or distorted growth in spring should be lifted. If soft they will probably contain the larva or chrysalis of the large fly or if rotten they may show the presence of the small flies. At planting time press the bulbs gently: those which feel soft and springy may contain the hibernating larva of the large fly and should be discarded.

Treatment Discard all suspicious bulbs. In bad attacks, dust with BHC every fortnight from the end of April until the end of June. Close up holes near the bulbs to prevent entry by the flies. Where possible suspected stocks can be given hot-water treatment before planting: immerse for one hour in water kept at 43°C (110°F).

Onion fly

A small grey fly with black and brown markings, resembling a housefly, may attack onions, leeks and shallots from spring onwards. The eggs are laid on the young leaves and stems. There are three generations.

Symptoms Dirty-white maggots about 8mm ($\frac{1}{3}$in) long burrow into the bulb. The leaves and stems turn yellow, seedlings may be killed and the bulbs begin to rot.

Treatment Remove and burn infected plants, taking care not to leave any maggots in the soil. Dust the drills with calomel and grow the next crop as far away from the site as possible or water the plants with a solution of trichlorphon.

Onion smut

Onions, leeks, shallots and chives are attacked in the seedling stages and serious losses may occur. The disease is not general.
Symptoms Dark, greyish stripes occur on leaves, which begin to wilt.
Treatment Burn infected plants. Susceptible crops should not be grown on the same site, as infection remains in the soil for many years.

Pea moth

A grey-brown moth about 6mm (¼in) long may be seen fluttering over the crop from mid-June to mid-August.
Symptoms The caterpillars eat into the pods and feed on the developing peas, causing the well known maggoty peas.
Treatment Regular hoeing will destroy many of the larvae which, when fully fed, leave the plant to pupate in the soil. In bad areas damage can be largely avoided by sowing only early and late crops and missing out mid-season varieties. Spraying with formothion gives partial control.

Pea weevil – *See* Bean weevil.

Peach leaf curl

Sometimes called peach leaf blister, this disease is caused by a fungus which attacks peaches, nectarines, almonds and occasionally other species of *Prunus*.
Symptoms The leaves become swollen, curled or malformed, look blistered and change to a reddish colour. The flowers and fruits may sometimes be affected.
Treatment Spray with lime-sulphur or Bordeaux mixture before leaf fall, again in February or March as soon as the buds begin to swell, and a fortnight later. Pick up and burn fallen leaves.

Pear leaf blister mite

This may be a troublesome pest in the south of the country especially on cordons or trees trained against a wall. Apples, cotoneaster, rowan and some other trees may also be attacked. The mite is microscopic, hibernates at the base of a bud and begins to feed as the new growth develops. There are several generations a year.
Symptoms The mite burrows into the leaf, causing green or reddish blisters, which later turn brown or black. Young fruits and stalks may also be attacked.

Treatment Spray with 5 per cent lime-sulphur just before the buds open (usually in March). Slight attacks can be controlled by the early removal and burning of affected leaves.

Pear midge

The minute black adults, typical of midges, lay their eggs at blossom time. The maggots burrow into the developing fruits. Mid-season varieties suffer most.

Symptoms Attacked fruitlets have a flattened appearance. Most of them fall to the ground. If cut open they generally show the maggots inside.

Treatment As the maggots pupate in the soil regular hoeing will destroy most of them. All infested fruits should be collected and burned. Alternatively, spray the soil in winter with tar-oil wash, covering an area a little greater than the spread of the tree.

Physiological disorders

Poor conditions, lack of air or water, unsuitable temperatures in greenhouses or an abnormal climate out of doors will produce certain well-recognized disorders in many plants. None of them is infectious.

Tomatoes seem particularly subject: irregular water and excess of nitrogen often cause a premature blossom drop, and too much heat and humidity may cause a blister-like oedema on the leaves and sometimes on the fruit. Potato tubers may show various forms of cracking or malformation, generally due to excessive moisture after a dry spell, or the flesh may show a discoloration which is probably caused by lack of humus. Many fruits may suffer from sun-scald, causing discoloration of the skin or glassy patches. Apples are subject to various kinds of breakdown, particularly in store, one of the commonest being bitter-pit, which causes spongy brown spots in the flesh.

Treatment Improve hygiene and growing conditions, paying particular attention to soil improvement, mulching, feeding and watering, and wider spacing of the plants.

Potato blight

This disease may cause serious losses among potatoes and outdoor tomatoes, especially in warm, moist summers when infection spreads rapidly. The damage done to the leaves prevents a normal crop being produced.

Symptoms Patches appear on the leaves, generally near the edges at first. They are brown to black on top and greyish underneath. In potatoes the spores may be washed down through the soil to the tubers and cause a brownish colour on the flesh under the skin. The infected tubers may rot in store and affect sound tubers. In tomatoes the fruits show dark brown and marbled spots; they shrivel, crack and rot before maturity.

Treatment Immediately the first sign is seen the crop must be sprayed with Bordeaux mixture, or a proprietary copper spray, maneb or zineb. The spraying must be repeated every fortnight as necessary. Earth up potatoes well. Dusts may also be used (as often as once a week in a wet season). When lifting the potatoes the haulm should first be cut and burned and only sound tubers should be put into store and none saved for seed.

Potato scab

There are two forms of scab caused by different fungi, common scab and powdery scab.

Symptoms Common scab causes rough, dry, scabby patches on the skin of potatoes. Sometimes the patches are deep and sunken, but generally they are only skin deep and are removed in peeling. The seriousness of the disease is that it spoils the appearance of the crop.

Powdery scab also causes scabby areas which at first resemble raised swellings and later break to release a powdery mass of spores. It is the more serious but less common of the two.

Treatment Common scab is worst on dry, gravelly or overlimed soils and can be reduced by good dressings of farmyard manure or compost. Lime should never be applied to a potato crop.

For powdery scab the best remedy is to space the crop as far apart as possible in the rotation. Tubers from an infected crop should not be stored or saved for seed.

Raspberry beetle

The beetles are about 3cm (1⅙in) long, golden-brown to greyish-brown. They attack the buds and flowers and the yellowish larvae burrow into the fruits, causing maggoty raspberries. Loganberries and blackberries are also attacked. Severe infestation will render the crop useless and even slight attacks will spoil the appearance of the fruit.

Symptoms These are not generally noticed until the grubs are found inside the ripe fruit. Eradication is then impossible, but the warning is given that control measures will be essential for the following crop.

Treatment Spray or dust with derris, malathion or fenitrothion ten days after flowering and again a fortnight later.

Raspberry fungus diseases

Several different fungi attack raspberries. The leaves may suffer from rust or mildew and the canes from several forms of spotting or wilting. As a rule none of these is serious, and good growing, removal of infected canes, tidiness and the avoidance of overcrowding keep the crop healthy. Always buy virus-free stock and control aphids which cause the disease to spread.

Raspberry moth

The moth is dark purplish-brown, small, with a wing-span of 6mm ($\frac{1}{4}$in). The eggs are laid on the flowers in June and for a time the tiny larvae live inside the plug of the fruit but they do no harm. They leave the fruit to hibernate and the following spring crawl up the canes and enter the shoots, tunnelling inside. They are then pink to red.

Symptoms The new shoots begin to wither and die. If cut open, the caterpillars may be found.

Treatment Cut out and burn wilted canes and keep the bed tidy and regularly hoed. In severe attacks spray the canes with malathion.

Red spider mites

Three species are of importance to gardeners, the greenhouse red spider which attacks a wide range of greenhouse plants, including fruits like grapes and peaches, the fruit tree red spider found on fruit trees growing out of doors, and the gooseberry red spider which not only attacks gooseberries but also many alpine plants in the open and under glass. In hot, dry summers other outdoor plants may also be attacked. The mites are small, just visible, and are usually greenish-grey to pale red, becoming more red as they mature. They generally feed on the underside of the leaves, sucking the sap, and often spin a fine webbing which acts as a protection.

Symptoms Attacked leaves lose their fresh green colour and look dry. Later they take on a rusty colour with a silvery effect and begin to fall. The mites and their webs may be seen on the undersides.

Treatment Spray outdoor trees with a DNOC/petroleum wash in winter or with malathion, dimethoate or derris immediately after flowering. Fumigate greenhouses with dinocap, but spray tender-leaved plants with nicotine or malathion.

Syringing foliage, especially against walls and in greenhouses where humidity is likely to be low, will reduce the possibility of attack. Predatory mites have been used very successfully to control red spider mites in greenhouses. They are most effective at high temperatures but must be protected against insecticide sprays.

Reversion

This is a serious virus disease of black currants. As infection spreads in the bush the blossoms become affected and the crop is progressively reduced. The disease is spread by the black currant gall mite and possibly by aphids and capsid bugs. It can also be carried on pruning knives.

Symptoms The leaves become smaller and narrower and the marginal teeth and main veins become fewer. A healthy leaf has five to eight veins on each side of the main (middle) vein, a reverted leaf has less than five. These symptoms are only reliable if seen during June on strong-growing

shoots. They can also arise from mechanical or other damage, but in such cases later growth quickly becomes normal.
Treament Once infected a bush cannot be cured. The only safe course is to dig up and replant with healthy stock, certified as free of the virus. Cuttings should never be taken from an apparently healthy branch on a bush which also shows one or more infected branches.

Rhododendron bug
The adult is about 4mm ($\frac{1}{6}$in) long, shiny and black with netted wings. The eggs are laid on the lower surface of the leaves in late summer and the larvae hatch in the following spring.
Symptoms The leaves become spotted with rusty-looking spots on the underside and mottled on the upper surface.
Treatment Spray the undersides of the leaves with BHC, malathion, derris or nicotine about mid-June and again three to four weeks later. After bad attacks carefully cut back all shoots in March. These should be burned to destroy the eggs which are generally laid on the top leaves.

Rhododendron white fly
The small white mealy fly may be seen in June and July on the undersides of the leaves. Eggs are laid on the leaves and the larvae feed until the following spring.
Symptoms The larvae excrete honeydew which falls on to the leaves below. These become black owing to the growth of a sooty mould. Where flies are suspected, shaking the branches may dislodge the flies which at once fly upwards but quickly resettle.
Treatment Spray or dust with nicotine in September and April, taking care to cover the undersides of the leaves. In bad attacks prune hard in March.

Rose sawfly – *See* Slugworms.

Rusts
Several different species of fungi cause rusts on the foliage of a number of plants. The most important are roses, antirrhinums, asparagus, carnations under glass, chrysanthemums, hollyhocks and mint.
Symptoms Small brown, reddish or orange-coloured spots occur, often giving a dry, rusty appearance. The spots contain the spores which may sometimes be released as a dust when the plant is shaken. Defoliation and death of the plant may follow.
Treatment General hygiene and good, careful growing are usually a sufficient control on chrysanthemums, carnations and hollyhocks, especially if the first leaves to be attacked are removed and burned. Dust asparagus with sulphur and grow resistant varieties of antirrhinum.

Destroy infected beds of mint and replace with healthy stock, although a partial control can be obtained by burning off the bed with straw in the autumn. Rose rust is rare, occurring only in very hot summers. Mild attacks may be controlled with maneb or zineb, but it is safer to burn infected leaves.

Scale insects

There are several different species, varying in colour and shape, but all are what may be called stationary pests. When young the larvae move about on the host plant, but later they develop a protective covering (which may be hard or soft) under which they live by sucking the sap from the plant. Some species attack outdoor plants, including fruit trees, forest trees and ornamental trees and shrubs, the most important being apples, beech, ceanothus, cotoneaster, yew, peach, currant, ivy, holly, camellias, etc. Others are found on a wide range of greenhouse plants, particularly vines, figs, ferns, orchids and palms. In large numbers, scale insects can be very serious.

Symptoms The stationary oval to round scale appears to be stuck on to the plant. Many species excrete a honeydew which falls on to other leaves and often becomes covered with a sooty mould. Ants are frequently present, attracted by the honeydew.

Treatment Tender plants should be sprayed with nicotine, malathion or a systemic insecticide. Single scales can be prised off with a pointed stick or can be wiped off with a cloth dipped in soapy water. In more serious cases spray deciduous trees with tar oil in winter. Fumigate greenhouses with dichlorvos when possible.

Silver leaf

This disease is due to a fungus which invades the branches of trees and interferes with the normal growth of the leaves by allowing air to enter between the top and bottom surfaces. This produces the characteristic silvery or leaden sheen. It is a serious disease of plums, but also occurs on apples, poplars, Portugal laurel, cherries, various thorns and peaches.

Symptoms In addition to the silvering of the leaves, dead branches are usually present. On the dead wood the fruiting stage of the fungus may be seen in the form of purplish crusts several centimetres (inches) long or as bracket-shaped projections up to 2.5cm (1in) wide.

Treatment Since infection can only come from the spores in the fruiting bodies, all dead wood must be cut out and burned. This should be done early in the summer when natural healing takes place most readily, but as a precaution paint all pruning cuts with a protective paint. The fruiting bodies also occur on wooden posts or stakes which should not therefore be left lying about. As the spores can only enter through wounds any broken branches should be cut clean and all pruning wounds sealed.

Slugworms or sawflies

The name is given to a large group of sawflies, the larvae of which resemble small slugs, although they are usually white when young and become dark-green to black later, and have ten pairs of legs which is a characteristic of all sawflies. The most important species are those which attack cherries and pears, various shrubs and roses. The adult flies are generally dark in colour, about 8mm (⅓in) long, appearing in May and June and again in August when a second generation occurs.

Symptoms The slugworms feed on the leaves, often eating the upper surface completely away. Some roll the leaves into a rough cylinder and others, particularly the rose shoot-borer, burrow down the stem.

Treatment Since most sawflies pupate in the soil, good and continuous cultivation helps to reduce numbers considerably. In severe attacks spray with BHC or nicotine, derris, malathion or fenitrothion.

Slugs and snails

Enormous damage is done by slugs and snails, much of it never visible. Some species feed at or above ground level, others below. Most of the feeding is done at night or on moist warm evenings and whole rows of germinating seedlings may be eaten off in a very short time. Slugs feed all the year round, snails hibernate generally in groups, especially in rockeries. Their presence is detected by their silvery trails.

Treatment Continual attention is necessary and methiocarb or metaldehyde slug baits should be put down; a bait can be made up at home using 25g (1oz) metaldehyde to 1.5kg (3lb) of bran; dot this about in small heaps about 30cm (12in) apart.

Small ermine moths

The caterpillars of several species of ermine moths feed on the foliage of apples, hawthorn and spindle. Other fruit trees and shrubs are less commonly attacked.

Symptoms From May to July greyish caterpillars up to 1cm (½in) long, with black spots, may be seen eating the leaves and living in webs spun between the leaves or twigs.

Treatment Spray with derris or malathion. Tar-oil washes may be used in winter on deciduous trees.

Storage rots

Not all forms of rotting which occur among fruit, vegetables, bulbs or roots in store are necessarily serious, apart from the loss they cause. But those due to fungi and bacteria must be regarded very differently because they are generally infectious, may spread very quickly and contaminate the store.

Treatment Stores must be kept clean and should be washed down every year with boiling water and soda or a weak disinfectant solution. Examine crops in store regularly. In bad cases clean the store with formalin, but other disinfectants with characteristic odours should be avoided as many fruits and vegetables will become tainted.

Thrips

Small black flies about 1.2mm ($\frac{1}{15}$in) long are often seen on many plants both out of doors and in greenhouses. As a rule they appear to do little serious damage outside, but they act as carriers of certain virus diseases. In greenhouses they may become a serious pest of many flowering plants. They breed more or less continuously.

Symptoms Thrips feed by scraping away the surface tissue and sucking the sap, causing mottled, spotted areas. In greenhouses, flowers of carnations, cyclamen and many other plants may become distorted.

Treatment Spray with malathion, BHC or derris when damage is first noticed; fumigate with dichlorvos.

Tortrix moths

There are a number of species which attack a wide range of plants in various ways. The larvae appear in spring, most of them active and having the characteristic of wriggling backwards when disturbed or hanging from the leaf by a thread.

Symptoms The larvae feed on the leaves, shoots or buds, most of them rolling or spinning the leaves together. They are very common on oak trees. In apples the surface of the fruit is also scarred, in some herbaceous plants the flowers may be eaten, and in some shrubs the centre of the shoots may be eaten out.

Treatment Pick off and crush the larvae in the rolled leaves. In severe attacks spray forcibly with BHC, trichlorphon or derris as soon as damage is seen – in the case of apples a few days before the blossom opens. (*See also* Codling moth and Pea moth which belong to the *Tortricidae*.)

Tulip fire

This can be a very serious fungus disease of tulips. It is generally worst in cold, wet seasons.

Symptoms Specks and streaks occur on the leaves and flowers and the tips of the leaves become brown and scorched.

Treatment Lift the bulbs every year and destroy all unsound ones. Dust the remaining bulbs with quintozene before planting in a fresh site, and spray the emerging leaves with benomyl and repeat every ten days until flowering.

Turnip flea beetle or Turnip fly – *See* Flea beetles.

Virus diseases

This group of diseases attacks a great number of plants. All are carried in the sap and so are frequently spread by sucking insects or other means of contact. Many have been proved to be highly infectious.

Symptoms The general symptoms are an unhealthy or stunted appearance about the plant. Growth is frequently checked and there may be malformation of the foliage or bad colour. In some cases parts of the foliage may dry up and die.

The most common types are as follows:

Mosaic. Many plants are attacked, showing a mottling or spotting of the leaves. Raspberries, potatoes, dahlias, marrows, cucumbers and lettuce are all susceptible.

Leaf-roll is often found in potatoes. The lower leaves curl upwards and feel dry and papery. The plant looks stunted and spiky.

Strawberries suffer from several virus diseases which cause a yellowing of the edges of the leaves, a crinkling or the production of many small leaves and few if any flowering stems instead of normal growth.

The breaking of tulips is due to infection by virus.

Treatment The greatest control is effected by keeping down insects, especially aphids, and by buying only healthy, certified stocks of plants from reliable sources. Seed, including seed potatoes, cuttings or any other form of propagating material should never be used from an infected crop. Burn infected plants as soon as they are discovered.

Wasps

Most wasps are minute and many are beneficial as they feed on garden pests. Large wasps devour aphids and other soft-bodied insects, but they will also attack ripening fruit, causing serious losses. Wasp nests around buildings also invite danger of painful stings.

Treatment Wall fruit and greenhouses may be netted with fine muslin for short periods when fruit is ripening. A simple trap can be made by fixing a funnel into the neck of a large jar containing a syrupy mixture of jam and water in a shallow layer over the base. Wasps crawl down the funnel but try unsuccessfully to escape by crawling up the side of the jar. If the nest can be located, derris can be used to destroy it although this may take some time to be effective, and it is better to use a proprietary wasp powder.

Waterplant pests

Some of the plants grown in ornamental pools, particularly water lilies, may be attacked by aphids and the larvae of the water lily beetle.

Symptoms The water moth larva is a caterpillar living in a tubular case; it feeds on the submerged part of the plant. The water lily beetle is brown and feeds on the leaves and petals.

Treatment None of the usual sprays containing derris or BHC can be used because of the risk of poisoning fish. The best plan is to help the fish reach the insects by syringing the plant forcibly to knock the insects into the water or by submerging the whole plant for a day at intervals until the beetles are dislodged.

Weevils

Weevils are a type of beetle distinguished by their snout-like heads and legless grubs. There are several important species varying from brown to black, most of them about 1cm ($\frac{1}{2}$in) long. The adults generally hide by day and feed at night, eating the leaves of many trees, bushes and plants while the grubs live on the roots. The bark of young trees is often attacked.

The vine weevil may become a serious pest both out of doors and under glass, especially to alpines and plants in pots.

Symptoms In addition to the visible damage the plants may also show poor colour and look unhealthy. The grubs may often be seen on the roots of pot plants if the plants are knocked out of their pots.

Treatment The adults may be trapped in small heaps of rolled leaves, pieces of sacking or corrugated paper. Pick off and destroy the grubs from the roots of pot plants and repot in sterilized soil after dusting or spraying with BHC.

White fly – *See* Greenhouse white fly.

Wilts

Various forms of wilts occur on a number of plants grown out of doors and under glass. Many of them are due to fungi which generally cause a sudden collapse of the plant.

Treatment In the open change the crops and introduce a long rotation programme in the vegetable garden. Under glass, sterilize the soil or replace with fresh clean soil.

Winter moths

Three different species of moths give rise to caterpillars which attack fruit trees, especially peaches and plums, and many ornamental trees and shrubs. The caterpillars move with a characteristic looping movement.

Symptoms The caterpillars hatch in spring and can be seen feeding on the buds and young leaves. In June they let themselves down on a silken thread to pupate in the soil.

Treatment As the females are wingless and crawl up the trees to lay their eggs, many can be trapped by grease bands. These can be made from grease-proof paper, 15cm (6in) wide, put round the trunk as high as possible, both the top and bottom edges of the paper being tied with string; smear the paper with a proprietary brand of grease. Alternatively, spray with derris, malathion or trichlorphon as the buds open in spring.

Wireworms

These are the shiny, yellowish-brown grubs found in many soils, particularly where turf has been newly broken up. They are the larvae of the click beetle, which are brown to black, 1cm ($\frac{1}{2}$in) long, and often jump with a click when disturbed. Wireworms take up to five years to reach maturity and are then about 18mm ($\frac{3}{4}$in) long. They feed voraciously on the roots of most plants and burrow into bulbs, potatoes and other roots, and occasionally into the stems of tomatoes and chrysanthemums.

Symptoms Seedlings and young plants wilt and die and when dug up often show the grub round the roots. Larger, stronger plants generally show less visible signs of attack, and on tuberous or bulbous plants and root vegetables, the presence of wireworms may not be suspected until the roots are lifted.

Treatment Thorough cultivation and tidiness are important. Pick up and crush the grubs whenever they are seen or trap them in pieces of potato or carrot put into the soil on pointed sticks. Dust the soil round susceptible plants with BHC or bromophos.

Wither tip – *See* Blossom wilt.

Woodlice

Though living principally on decaying vegetable matter in damp places, woodlice will often attack plants especially in frames and greenhouses. They feed at night and hide during the day.

Treatment Clear all rubbish away. In bad attacks, trap the woodlice in potatoes or orange peel or dust the hiding places with BHC.

Principal uses of insecticides and fungicides

Preparation	Formulation	Uses
Benomyl (benlate)	Systemic fungicide; spray	Botrytis, powdery mildew, leaf spot, black spot
BHC	Persistent insecticide; available as dusts, sprays and fumigants	Aphids, caterpillars, weevils, capsids, sawflies, codling moths, leaf-miners, red spider mites, wireworms. Do not use on open blossom or vegetable root crops
Bordeaux mixture	Fungicide compounded of copper sulphate and hydrated lime. Spray or dust form, harmful to fish	Downy mildew, wilt and canker, potato and tomato wilt and scab

Preparation	Formulation	Uses
Bromophos	Contact insecticide, only available in granular form	Soil pests, such as cabbage root and carrot flies, cutworms and wireworms
Calomel (mercurous chloride)	Poisonous insecticide. Sold as 4 per cent dusts and 20 per cent soluble powders	Root flies; club root disease
Captan	Fungicide, obtainable as powders or in wettable form. Harmful to fish	Black spot, leaf spot, apple scab, botrytis, damping-off
Carbaryl	Insecticide, available in dust or spray forms	Caterpillars, capsid bugs, earwigs, lawn earthworms
Cheshunt compound	Fungicide compounded of copper sulphate and ammonium carbonate	Damping-off; some soil-borne diseases
Chlordane	Persistent, strong insecticide; spray form	Ants and earthworms in lawns
Copper	Fungicide available in powder or liquid form. Harmful to animals	Use as an alternative to Bordeaux mixture
Derris	One of the safest insecticides; available as dusts or sprays. Toxic to fish	Aphids, caterpillars, flea-beetles, thrips, red spider mites; non-poisonous alternative to nicotine
Diazinon	Fairly persistent insecticide; spray form only	Aphids, capsid bugs, leaf-miners, mealy bugs, scale insects, thrips
Dichlorvos	Greenhouse fumigant, in impregnated strips	Aphids, thrips, white flies, red spider mites
Dimethoate	Systemic insecticide, as sprays or soluble for soil-drenching	Aphids, leaf-hoppers, scale insects, red spider mites
Dinocap	Fungicide, available as soluble powders, liquids or smokes for greenhouse fumigation	Powdery mildew. Toxic to fish, and sometimes inflammable. Mixed with captan controls mildew on roses
DNOC	Insecticide in spray form for winter-washing	Capsid bug and red spider mite eggs; use in winter only
Fenitrothion	Contact insecticide; spray form	Aphids, capsid bugs, codling moths, caterpillars
Formaldehyde	Sterilizing compound; poisonous	Disinfection of greenhouses, soil-borne fungi; do not use near plants
Formothion	Systemic insecticide; spray or liquid form	Control similar to dimethoate

Preparation	Formulation	Uses
Lime-sulphur	Pesticide and fungicide; spray form	Apple and pear scab, peach leaf curl, powdery mildew, red spider mites. Do not use on sulphur-shy varieties
Malathion	Non-persistent, general, safe insecticide; available in dust, spray and aerosol forms	Aphids, leaf-hoppers, caterpillars, capsid and mealy bugs, thrips, white flies, etc.
Maneb	Fungicide; soluble powder	Black spot, blight, rust, leaf mould
Menazon	Systemic insecticide, in a mixture with BHC	Aphids
Metaldehyde	Pesticide; as sprays or pellets	Slugs and snails
Methiocarb	Pesticide	Slug and snail baits
Nicotine	Poisonous insecticide and fungicide, available as spray or fumigant	Aphids, capsid bugs, thrips, leaf-miners, leaf-hoppers, insects and young caterpillars
Oxydemeton-methyl	Systemic insecticide, poisonous and persistent; aerosol form	Aphids, red spider mites
Pirimicarb	Contact insecticide, non-persistent; spray form	Very effective against aphids, also caterpillars, leaf-miners, white flies
Pyrethrum	Non-persistent insecticide; spray or aerosol form	Safely used against aphids and white flies
Quintozene	Fungicide; dust or soluble powder	Bulb diseases
Sulphur	Fungicide in various formulations	Powdery mildew, apple scab, leaf mould. Do not use on sulphur-shy varieties
Tar oil	Spray insecticide for winter-washes	Eggs of aphids, winter moths, red spider mites, scale insects, apple suckers. Use in dormant season only
Tecnazene	Smoke fungicide for greenhouse use	Grey mould; some insect pests
Thiram	Fungicide; spray form	Botrytis, downy mildew, rust, scab, tulip fire
Trichlorphon	Non-persistent insecticide; spray form	Caterpillars, leaf-miners, earwigs
Zineb	Fungicide; available as soluble powder	General application for many diseases of ornamental plants and food crops

Inula, or fleabane, is a hardy perennial useful for sunny borders or for a semi-wild garden

A formal planting with graded heights. In the front, border carnations; behind artemisia and delphiniums

10
Hedges, Fences and Walls

Hedges play an important role in most gardens, so it is wise to give some thought to siting and methods of planting and to the type of plants that will form the hedge. The ubiquitous privet and laurel hedges have given way to more attractive hedge subjects, such as the deciduous beech, hornbeam, cherry and plum, and to flowering hedges of roses, fuchsias and forsythia which vie in popularity with evergreen hedges of box, cypress, *Lonicera nitida*, oak, holly, thuja and yew.

Situations and purpose

Whether the hedge is required as a boundary marker, shelter from the wind, as a screen or a barrier or purely as an ornament, are points which must be considered, and shrubs suited to the soil and aspect should be chosen accordingly. Evergreens like holly, laurel or yew and leafy, quick-growing deciduous shrubs like the elder or privet, are excellent for shelter from cold winds. As a screen, chamaecyparis, cypress, holly, laurel, *Lonicera nitida*, thuja and yew are undoubtedly the best. For flowering hedges choose between such shrubs as *Berberis* x *stenophylla* and *B. darwinii*, guelder rose, gorse, lilac, *Viburnum tinus* or floribunda roses. Impenetrable hedge barriers are provided by beech, hornbeam, myrobalan plum or quickthorn.

Factors to consider

Not all plants suit all climates, situations and soil, and although there are many ornamental plants and shrubs that will make good hedges, not all will choose to flourish where we wish our hedges to grow. They must, for a start, be able to withstand quite severe pruning in order to maintain the desired height and shape of the hedge. Most hedges, especially those cut with shears or clippers, should be shaped upwards so that the top is narrower than the bottom; in this way the lower part is not overshadowed by the upper and is kept thick. With general good cultivation and trimming, most hedges will last for many years.

Flowering shrubs

Many flowering shrubs make excellent hedges. The best of these include

Berberis darwinii, *B.* x *stenophylla*, flowering currant, *Chaenomeles speciosa*, gorse, guelder rose, lilac, and the shrubby honeysuckle. The hedge need not necessarily be composed entirely of one species; a very ornamental hedge, sections of which will be in blossom almost the entire year through if plants are carefully selected, can be made up of various species of flowering shrubs. Evergreens may be interspersed among the flowering shrubs, and the hedge will be all the firmer if a thorn or a cherry plum is inserted fairly frequently as a stiffener. The sweet briar and floribunda rose 'Queen Elizabeth' make splendid hedges.

Methods of planting

Bear in mind that a hedge, once planted, is usually in position for many years, and that if it is to do well every care should be taken in its planting. Take out a strip of ground 90cm (3ft) wide and as long as required for the hedge to be planted and dig it to a depth of at least 60cm (2ft). Fork in garden compost, leaf-mould or well decayed manure. Most hedge shrubs are best planted when 60 to 90cm (2 to 3ft) in height, they will establish themselves more readily, are easier to train and are also cheaper. The larger the shrub the more care is necessary in planting. With the exception of the quicker or larger-growing shrubs, such as the evergreen oak or cupressus, most hedge shrubs are best planted out 45 to 60cm (1½ to 2ft) apart; if a very thick hedge is required two rows may be planted about 1.5m (5ft) apart, the plants being spaced as before in the rows, but staggered so that the plants in the first row coincide with the gaps in the second.

Shorten long tap roots before planting, and to ensure bushy plants trim deciduous plants back by up to half in the first spring after planting when the buds begin to swell. Evergreens are best cut back at planting time. Water well after putting the shrubs in, and once a week in dry weather, until the roots are established. Should a very dry season follow, syringe the foliage of evergreens every evening if the plants do not appear to be thriving. In late April or early May, during its first year, the hedge should be well watered and then mulched with a 5 to 7.5cm (2 to 3in) layer of well-decayed manure or well-rotted leaf-mould. Severe frosts during the first winter after planting will probably raise the bushes from the soil and newly-planted shrubs should be firmed back with the foot.

Care of hedges

Most hedges are best trimmed twice a year, in May and again in August or September; few shrubs will make much growth after a late summer trimming and will remain tidy all winter. All hedges, especially evergreens, are best trained and pruned to a pyramid shape, being widest at the bottom. Even a formal square-cut hedge should not be wider at the top. Informal hedges, especially of deciduous flowering shrubs can be allowed to grow naturally, with only an occasional trimming back of straggly shoots.

Prune hollies and laurels and other broad-leaved shrubs with secateurs to avoid cutting the leaves in half. Privet, box, thorn and all small-leaved shrubs may be clipped with garden shears or mechanical hedge-cutters.

In winter thoroughly clean the bottom of the hedge and the soil round it; cut out all dead wood and any brambles and climbers and remove all weeds. Where insect pests and disease have been prevalent, spray the hedge with a suitable solution; choose a calm, frost-free day for this.

Although hedges are delightful features of the garden and a useful form of screen or barrier, think carefully before planting one in a small garden. They take up a great deal of room, keep sun and air from other plants and deplete the soil of nutrients.

Types of fences

Fences may be constructed of various materials and in many different patterns. Whatever the type, a fence must be properly supported to withstand the force of winds. Square-sawn timber posts are suitable for most gardens, but in exposed situations concrete posts are better. Space the posts at intervals of about 3m (10ft) and sink the bottom 45cm (1½ft) into holes in the ground and pack them firmly with rubble and pieces of brick; on heavy, wet soil it is a good idea to bolt the wooden posts to concrete supports set in concrete. Treat the part of the posts to go in the ground with creosote or wood preservative. By law no fence facing a main road or highway may exceed 2m (7ft) in height and it should be sited on the boundary line with the posts on the owner's side of land.

Close-boarded wooden fencing This type is strong and will last for a long time. Teak and oak are the most durable, but both are hard and difficult to work as well as being expensive; fir, larch, pine and deal boarding are commonly used. They are nailed to horizontal cross-beams let into the post supports. Treat the panels with a wood preservative, not creosote which is harmful to plants.

Interwoven fence panels are available in ready-made sections, usually of about 1.8m (6ft) each; they are light and easy to erect though less durable than close-boarded fencing. Shorter sections (90cm, (3ft)) are ideal for surmounting with trellis work against which to grow climbers.

Wattle hurdles These make effective and attractive fences, are, easy to set up and comparatively cheap.

Split chestnut fencing in which the palings are wired together with strong strands of wire so that there is an interval of about 7.5cm (3in) between each, makes an efficient and economical fencing. Although it gives little shelter and no privacy, it forms a useful boundary fence and gives good protection to a newly planted hedge or windbreak of trees.

Rustic fences are more often used as a screen or pergola to separate one part of a garden from another than as a boundary fence. They can be made of hazel, larch, spruce or any soft wood. They should be fairly substantial if they are to maintain their shape, especially if roses or other climbers are to be trained over them. Numerous designs are possible – lattice or trellis patterns – built within supporting bars at least 10cm (4in) in diameter. The bars should be slightly notched, one into another, where they cross, so that they have a better bearing against one another and a firmer holding than round stocks nailed together without notching.

Wire netting There are several patterns and sizes of this type of temporary fence which is no use as a windbreak. However, it can be put up while a hedge is making growth.

Garden walls

A substantial garden wall adds much to a garden. Ideally, walls should be of the same brick or stone as the house but its surface may be enlivened with raised patterns or openwork panels. Coursed walls of brick or stone are difficult to construct on sloping ground as the courses must remain horizontal, resulting in great changes in height or a frequent stepping of the top.

Walls trap heat from the sun, make an ideal background for plants, both ornamental and trained fruit and give great privacy without competing with near-by plants in the way hedges do. However, they divert the wind rather than absorbing and filtering its energy and can cause damaging eddies. Where shelter from wind is of primary importance a hedge is more effective.

Walls are a great deal more expensive than hedges in the first instance but their effect is immediate and, if well constructed, they should require no regular maintenance for many years. Because they offer a large flat surface to the wind, garden walls must be solidly constructed with adequate foundations, a minimum thickness of 22.5cm (9in) and supporting buttresses. A serpentine wall has additional strength by virtue of its wavy shape and need be no thicker than 12.5cm (5in). Height will vary according to the size of the garden, but 2m (7ft) is an ideal height for a screen wall.

Large old gardens often have separate walled enclosures for the cultivation of fruits and vegetables. Such kitchen gardens form very attractive features and can be adapted on a smaller scale for the average garden: trained fruits such as peaches and nectarines, figs and grapes thrive against south-facing walls, pears on west-facing walls, and morello cherry, late plum or trained red currants on north-facing walls. East-facing walls create frost problems and late-flowering apples are the most suitable. There are also flowering shrubs and climbers for walls of any aspect.

Dry walls These are attractive internal features in even small gardens and offer an ideal situation for growing many alpines and other plants requiring free drainage. Because they are a blend of formality and informality they are usually more attractive in small gardens than sprawling rockeries which are often out of scale and proportion.

The dry wall may be constructed either as a retaining wall where changes in level are necessary or as a low free-standing feature with a double wall containing a raised bed of soil, when the top of the wall can be planted with low and trailing alpines. If additional height is wanted plant a hedge or border of rosemary, cistus, lavender or other low shrubs that thrive in an elevated situation along the top.

A dry wall is built of stones, usually sandstone or limestone, from 5 to 20cm (2 to 8in) thick, of any size within reason, but usually about 90cm (3ft) high and slightly less wide, rectangular and more or less untrimmed. Stones are better than bricks as they provide cooler and moister root runs for the plants. They should be bonded or laid in layers, each bedded in about 5cm (2in) of good loam, so that the gaps in each row are staggered between the gaps in the row below and above. This structure serves to keep the wall secure and firm. The stones are best when their upper surfaces are flat, or even cupped, and when placed in position, especially on a retaining wall, they should incline slightly backwards so that they are lower at the back than at the front; the rain will then be collected and drained into the soil at the back of the wall to provide moisture for the roots. Do not use cement, but ram earth firmly into the crevices between the stones, sufficient soil being used to keep the stones about 5cm (2in) apart, vertically. This soil must be rammed well into the back of the wall so that there is soil from the very front to the earth supporting the wall at the back. Firm the soil well after each row of stones has been laid, leaving no air pockets in the crevices where roots will quickly dry up.

Erecting a dry wall

A mixture of good loam, decayed farmyard manure and leaf-mould makes the best compost for the wall garden. The first essential is to make a good foundation for the wall. This should be about 25cm (10in) deep and a shade wider than the base of wall. Ram the soil well down until a solid foundation is provided. Now lay the first layer of stones, using the largest available, and place them so that their upper sides form one straight horizontal line. If the stones are of moderate size, the gaps left laterally between them may be about 7.5cm (3in), the smaller the stones the smaller the gaps between them. Next pack the crevices between the stones tightly with the chosen compost. Place the next layer of stone, properly bonded in the manner already explained on the compost, and repeat the process until the wall has reached the required height. If a stone is occasionally inserted lengthways from back to front, the wall will be more secure. Do not build the wall exactly vertical but let the top incline slightly back at an angle of about 1 in 6: in a wall 1.2m (4ft) high the base will project 20cm (8in) further forward than the top. The top of the wall is best left flat so that the rain can soak through to the roots beneath.

How and when to plant

It is easiest to plant the wall as it is constructed; the roots can then be spread out as they should be and well covered with soil before the next course of stones is laid. In this way larger plants can be used than when planting is done after the wall is completed. March and April, when root growth is vigorous, are the best months in which to construct and plant a wall garden. Seed may be sown in the crevices; at the same time mix the seeds with a little well-sieved moist sandy soil and press it into the chinks in the wall. A small piece of moss inserted into the crevices will keep the seed moist, aid germination and prevent it from being dislodged.

Plants for sun and shade

The great majority of the plants given in the list below as suitable for a wall garden thrive best in full sun. A wall garden situated in the shade, however, can be made anything but drab and uninteresting by choosing plants from a wide range of shade-lovers, and for cool positions do not overlook such hardy ferns as asplenium, polypodium or scolopendrium.

When planting insert the plants with their roots well spread out so that they penetrate well into the soil at the back of the wall. A little well-rotted farmyard manure or peat packed round the roots will prove beneficial. Never set a plant at the *top* of a vertical joint between the stones where the roots would be likely to dry up, but plant it in the crevice just above the centre of a stone.

Ram about 15cm (6in) of compost firmly down on the top of the wall and place large stones at intervals; they will help to keep the soil in place and will provide moist, cool sites for the roots of such plants as rock roses, wallflowers, geraniums, snapdragons, sedums and saxifrages – all ideal plants with which to crown the wall garden.

Selection of Plants for a Dry Wall

Note – For cultural details and for colour, height, and time of flowering, *see* the alphabetic list of Ornamental Plants and Trees, Ch. 23.

**Acaena buchananii* and *A. microphylla*
Acantholimon glumaceum
Achillea species
Aethionema x 'Warley Rose'
Alyssum alpestre, A. saxatile
Androsace lanuginosa and vars.
Antirrhinum (various)
Aquilegia species
Arabis albida 'Flore Pleno' and *A. androsacea*
**Arenaria balearica*

Armeria maritima
Asperula suberosa
Aubrieta deltoidea vars.
Campanula caespitosa
  C. portenschlagiana
Cerastium tomentosum
Cheiranthus (wallflower)
**Corydalis lutea*
Dianthus alpinus
Dianthus deltoides, D. plumarius
Draba rigida
Dryas octopetala
Erigeron karvinskianus
Erinus alpinus
Erodium chamaedryoides 'Roseum'
Genista lydia
Gypsophila repens
Hebe vars.
Helianthemum vars.
Hypericum fragile and
  H. polyphyllum
Iberis sempervirens
Juniperus communis and
  J. horizontalis vars.
Leontopodium alpinum
Lewisia species
Linaria alpina
Linum arboreum and
L. perenne alpinum
Morisia monanthos (hypogaea)
Nepeta x *faassenii*
Onosma albo-roseum
Penstemon menziesii, P. scouleri
Phlox amoena, P. subulata vars.
Polygonum affine
**Primula allionii, P. auricula*
  and *P. minima*
**Ramonda myconi*
Santolina chamaecyparissus
Saponaria caespitosa and
  S. ocymoides
**Saxifraga* species
Sedum species
Sempervivum species
Silene acaulis and
  S. schafta
Teucrium polium
Thymus serpyllum 'Coccineus'
Zauschneria californica

* Plants suitable for growing in the shade.

11
Paths and Paving

Paths and paved areas – patios, terraces and courtyards – are important features in the garden serving not only as a means of communication from one part of the garden to another or as sitting areas, but are also the permanent framework of the garden's design. The essential features of good paving are that it should harmonize with the rest of the garden, and afford a flat, non-slippery walking surface in wet weather. Concrete, ashes and asphalt are sometimes used for paths but in general the three most suitable surfaces are gravel, bricks and paving stones, made of real stone or concrete.

It will be sufficient to describe the construction of gravel, paving stone and grass surfaces. Apart from the different materials used, ash, brick, concrete or asphalt, paths are made like gravel paths.

Paved areas are constructed in the same way as crazy paved paths, but particular attention should be paid to sloping the paving gently away from the house and to dispersing or trapping the water running off the surface during rain.

Width of paths

A path should never be less than 60cm (2ft) in width, even if it is of secondary importance. A good average width is 1.2m (4ft); this allows for the easy passage of the barrow and other garden machinery and for two people to walk side by side. Entrance drives and tracks which must bear motor traffic should be at least 2.5m (8ft) wide, and preferably considerably more.

Paths and drainage

If the path is carefully designed and constructed it will last for many years, and will not only serve its purpose as a means of access, but will also be a great help in draining the garden.

Whether it will be necessary to lay a pipe-drain or not depends on the nature of the soil and the lie of the land. In light, porous soils the rough stones, bricks or clinkers used as a foundation will provide enough drainage, but in heavy, retentive clays a pipe-drain may be advisable; this may run directly below the centre of the path, or on either side of the path; on the lower side when the path is on a side slope, and always at the lowest point below the clinker or brick foundation and resting on a firm base. Where there is any doubt as to the porosity of the soil, always lay a drain. A single drain down the centre or down one side will be adequate for ordinary paths of 1.2m (4ft) in width, but paths wider than this and drives should have drains down each side. The pipes used for draining should be 7.5 to 10cm (3 to 4in) in diameter and must be laid from 45 to 60cm (1½ to 2ft) deep, according to the nature of the soil and the width of the path. The drains should slope gently towards the outlet, which may be into a garden main drain or into a ditch or pond. Once the pipes are in position, cover them with 30 to 37.5cm (12 to 15in) of broken bricks or rough stones through which the water can trickle.

Path foundations

The purpose of this is to provide a solid, but still porous, substratum, which will give enough support to the materials of which the surface of the walk is made, and yet allow water on the path to pass rapidly away.

Gravel paths

Although gravel paths are the cheapest and easiest to install they are sticky and slippery in wet weather, and as the material does not keep its level it needs frequent raking and repeated weed control. To construct the path, mark out the course of the path with stakes, and remove the surface soil to a depth of 15 to 25cm (6 to 10in); the wider the path the deeper the excavations necessary. The nature of the soil also affects the depth of excavation necessary; in heavy clay at least 22.5cm (9in) should be removed, in light soil 15cm (6in) will be enough.

At the time of excavation take great care to eradicate all perennial weeds, especially those with long creeping roots, from the soil at the bottom and sides of the path. If this is not done, all kinds of weeds will soon make their appearance through the new path, and will be difficult to get rid of. Weedkiller *will* kill these perennial weeds, but it takes several applications of a total and persistent chemical to effect a thorough clearance.

Fill from one-third to one-half the depth with rough stones, broken bricks, clinkers or any coarse, hard rubbish that can be gathered together; fill the greater part of the remainder with coarse gravel or shingle which can be mixed with a little earth to give substance. Finally cover with gravel to the depth of 5 or 7.5cm (2 or 3in); rake this level and roll it repeatedly with a heavy garden roller until the path can be marked by wooden pegs driven in to the right depth. Allow the path to set for a few days before using it and then fill up any hollows with more gravel and roll again. Beach gravel is not really suitable as it does not bind and always remains loose. If, however, it must be used, mix a quarter-part of clean dry clay with the gravel before it is laid; when moistened the mixture will bind well. If the ground is of a loose porous character, or wet and marshy, unable to give a solid basis to the pathway, make the trench deeper, and lay brushwood at the bottom before throwing in the rubble.

Gutters and drainage

If you want a solid facing to a garden path so that it is impervious to rain, the surface of the walk should be rounded – slightly higher in the centre and sloping gently down on either side. The water will escape into the earth or turf with which the walk is bordered, or gutters may be constructed to carry the water to a tank in some part of the garden. The gutters may either be moulded in the material of which the path is made or they may be constructed below the surface, like a drain, and hidden from view. In this case catch-pits with iron gratings should be made on each side of the path about 9m (30ft) apart. However, these gratings should not run straight into the drains, as the sand soon chokes them up. Make a well, formed of brick, 30 to 45cm (1 or 1½ft) square and deep enough to leave a space of similar depth (for a 1.2m (4ft) path) below the level of the drain, which should be directly below the lower edge of the grating and at the top of the pit.

The main drain, into which these side drains empty, usually runs down the centre of the path beneath the hard core.

Where the path lies on a steep slope, a heavy shower of rain may soon cause havoc with the gravel, the surface water rushing down and ploughing great furrows in the path. This can be prevented by constructing brick, tile, or cement gutters, 15 to 30cm (6 to 12in) wide, down both sides of the path, and by inserting catch-pits at regular intervals to carry away the water.

Large bricks or pieces of rock placed in the gutter just below the catch-pits will do much to impede the rush of water, and will enable the drains to carry it off more easily.

Another way of getting over this washing-out trouble is to mix cement with the gravel when laying it down in the proportion of six parts of gravel to one of cement. Add water and mix to the consistency of a thick paste, then immediately lay the mixture down over the path, flatten with the back of the spade, level off with a lath of wood or with the back of a rake, and allow it to set thoroughly.

Paving slabs and crazy paving

There is a wide range of paving slabs available in a variety of shapes, sizes, colours and textures from natural stone to cement blocks, simulating stones and made in moulded blocks. Paving slabs can be attractively combined with other types of paving materials, bricks or gravel, granite setts or cobbles, to create distinctive patterns, but take care to make the design uniform and uncluttered. Broken paving stones are often available at low cost from local authorities and the larger pieces are ideal for crazy paving.

All paving must be well and evenly laid, otherwise it is unpleasant to walk on and will give trouble by the loosening and rising of the stones. In the initial stage the procedure is the same as for a gravel path: the foundation of large stones or broken rubble is laid down in the same way, but need not be quite so deep, nor does the layer of clinkers or smaller stones need so much depth. The aim is to provide a sound and level surface for the paving, and a straight-edge and spirit-level are essential for this. The foundations must be rammed and rolled absolutely firm; if there is the slightest chance of any settlement in the base, as may happen in clay, put down a 2.5cm (1in) layer of concrete in which to lay the paving. If concrete is not used, spread a 5cm (2in) layer of sand or ashes over the hard core; make this quite level and then lay down the paving, fitting the pieces carefully together so that small pieces are not required, as these always tend to work loose. No crevices of much more than 2.5cm (1in) in width should be left between the stones or the path will be uncomfortable to walk on and will not remain firm.

An almost dry mix of 1 part cement to 6 parts coarse sand provides a good base as the slabs can be pushed in or slightly raised to keep a level surface and the mortar then sets hard to hold them in place. Alternatively, use a ready-mixed concrete base. Finally brush a dry mortar mix into the joints with a soft broom, syringe lightly to dampen the surface and, when this has set, syringe more heavily to moisten the whole mixture. On larger paved areas, patios and terraces, leave some cracks and crevices and fill them with sandy loam, so that rock plants such as saxifrages, thymes and other creepers and trailers may be planted. (*See* The paved garden below.)

The paved garden

You may want to establish low-growing plants in crevices between paving to soften its appearance. On paths any planting should be limited to the path margins.

A number of dwarf, often scented plants are ideal for growing among paving, partly to relieve the severity of the flat surface and partly to perfume the air when lightly trodden on. On patios and terraces take care to position the plants out of the paths of continuous traffic or garden furniture.

It is also feasible to construct a paved garden entirely for growing choice or interesting alpines, perhaps accented simply with a stone seat; such a paved garden could be set in a checkerboard pattern of paving slabs alternating with group plantings.

If rock work of any kind forms the boundary to the path or the paved garden, allow the plants covering it to encroach a little way and spill over on to the flagstones. This will soften the harsh effect and gives a more natural outline.

Most of the stones used should not be less than about 25cm (10in) in diameter or the paving will have a patchy appearance. Stones rectangular in shape are best for paths, but for square, circular or oval paved areas the flags may be of any shape and size provided they are irregular.

Selection of Plants for Paved Areas

**Acaena buchananii, A. microphylla*
Achillea chrysocoma, A. rupestris, A. tomentosa
Alyssum montanum
Arabis albida 'Flore Pleno'
Arenaria balearica, A. purpurascens
Armeria maritima
Aubrieta deltoides vars.
Calamintha alpina
*Campanula caespitosa, C. cochleariifolia, C. garganica, *C. portenschlagiana*
Dianthus deltoides vars.
Draba rigida
Dryas octopetala
Erinus alpinus vars.
Erodium reichardii
Globularia cordifolia
Gypsophila cerastioides, G. repens
Hebe vars.
Helianthemum vars.
Herniaria glabra
Hypericum olympicum, H. reptans
Iberis saxatilis and *ns*
I. sempervirens
Juniperus communis 'Compressa', *J. procumbens* 'Nana'
Linaria alpina
**Mazus pumilio, M. radicans*
**Mentha requienii*
**Mimulus* hybrids
Minuartia laricifolia
Morisia monanthos (hypogaea)
Oxalis enneaphylla 'Rosea' and *O. megallanica*
Paronychia kapela serpyllifolia
Penstemon menziesii
Phlox douglasii
Pinus mugo and vars.
Potentilla alba, P. tabernaemontana and *P.* x *tonguei*
Saponaria ocymoides 'Compacta'
**Saxifraga* species and vars.
Sedum acre and vars., *S. album, S. anglicum*
Sempervivum species and hybrids
Silene acaulis
Thymus drucei vars., *T. serpyllum*
Vinca minor 'Bowles' Variety'
**Viola cornuta* and hybrids

* Plants suitable for growing in semi-shade.

Grass walks

Grass walks running between borders are attractive; they are not suitable as replacements for hard-surface paths used to move garden machinery. They should never be less than 60cm (2ft) in width or they are difficult to mow and ideally should be more than 1.8m (6ft) wide; the wider they are, within reason, the more imposing they will be. Where there is likely to be much traffic on grass walks lay foundations and drainage as for gravel paths; it is satisfactory to make good gravel walks for general traffic, and to keep closely cut grass walks for meandering round the garden.

A good compromise can be made by sinking a single row of flagstones or sawn logs either edge to edge or some 60cm (2ft) apart level with the surface of the turf. This makes the walk more useful and will also, in many cases, add to its charm. Even more useful, because the borders can be approached in wet weather, will be two paved walks, 45 to 60cm (1½ to 2ft) wide, one down each side of the grass way.

In newly laid-out gardens the grass walks are usually formed from the existing turf, and it is surprising what consistent weeding, rolling and mowing will do. Where, however, the walks are to be seeded, choose a variety of seed that will stand much wear. If you use a barrow on turf walks in winter, lay down boards to prevent the wheels from sinking into and ruining the turf.

For details on the upkeep of grass walks, *see* Ch. 12, The Lawn.

Types of edging

Edgings to paths, lawns and borders can be divided into two sorts, formal and informal. Formal edgings include stone, bricks and wood, grass verges and miniature hedges of box, lavender and rosemary. Edgings made of plants (*see* list over) are informal. Where suitable stones can be obtained the most interesting borders are made of irregular blocks of stone, bedded in cement if large, with alpines growing between and over them. The stones should never project more than 15cm (6in) from the border.

Bricks make excellent border edgings, but they must be of a good hard variety; those that crumble under frost, when lying in the damp ground, are worse than useless and soon become ragged and ugly. Lay the bricks on edge, with one of the shorter sides in the ground, and sloping slightly inwards towards the border and away from the path. If they are set vertically, or incline outwards over the path, they are likely to be damaged by the barrow or roller.

Bury nearly half the brick in the soil, or set in a 5cm (2in) layer of concrete, when only one-third of the brick need be below the surface level.

Concrete makes an easily constructed if dull edging. Set up two boards of wood 1 to 2.5cm (½ to 1in) in thickness, 30cm (1ft) high, and of any length, 10cm (4in) apart, with 15cm (6in) of their height covered by the soil. Excavate the soil between them to the full 30cm (1ft) depth of the boards, which are held firm and upright by two stout pegs driven into the soil on the outer sides and nailed into the board. Lay a series of boards of similar size in line, where the edging is required. Mix the concrete and fill up the space between the boards, making the top flat and neat with a

trowel. When the concrete has set, after four to five days, remove the boards and a neat permanent edging will remain. An iron rod is often laid in the centre of the concrete edging during construction to reinforce it.
Wood edgings are neat and last a considerable time if painted with a wood preservative. They should be made of planks 2.5cm (1in) thick and 15 to 22.5cm (6 to 9in) wide. Bury about half the width in the soil and keep them firm and upright with strong wooden pegs, about 5cm (2in) in length, driven in on the border side until they are flush with the top of the board. Drive the pegs in about every metre (yard) and fix them to the planks with long galvanized iron nails.
Grass edgings entail a good deal of labour if they are to be kept neatly cut and trimmed, and they are out of place in small gardens. Narrow verges emphasize the narrowness of paths and borders which they divide and are useless unless they are planned on a grand scale. In small gardens it is better to use the space to widen the border.

Edging Plants

For details as to colour, height, season of flowering and culture, *see* the alphabetic list of Ornamental Plants and Trees, Ch. 23.

Achillea umbellata (H.P.)
Ageratum houstonianum (H.H.A.)
Alyssum saxatile (H.P.)
Antirrhinum (dwarf vars.) (H.A.)
Arabis albida 'Flore Pleno' (H.P.)
Aubrieta deltoidea vars. (H.P.)
Bellis perennis vars. (daisy) (H.P.)
Campanula (dwarf species) (H.P.)
Cerastium biebersteinii (H.P.)
Cheiranthus x *allionii* (Siberian wallflower) (H.P.)
Dianthus deltoides and modern pink vars. (H.P.)
Dianthus chinensis hybrids (H.P.)
Dryas octopetala (H.P.)
Erica carnea vars., *E. cinerea* vars. (H.S.)
Genista pilosa (H.S.)
Geranium dalmaticum (H.P.)
Geum (dwarf species) (H.P.)
Gypsophila repens (H.P.)
Hypericum olympicum (H.S.)
Iberis sempervirens (H.P.)
Lavandula spica (H.S.)
Lobelia erinus vars. (H.H.A.)
Lysimachia nummularia (creeping Jenny) (H.P.)
Malcolmia maritima (Virginia stock) (H.A.)
Myosotis alpestris, M. rupicola (forget-me-not) (H.P.)
Phlox subulata vars. (H.P.)
Primula vulgaris vars. (polyanthus) (H.P.)
Primula juliae hybrids (H.P.)
Salvia horminum vars. (H.H.A.)
Saponaria ocymoides (H.P.)
Saxifraga (dwarf vars.) (H.P.)
Silene pendula 'Compacta' (H.A.)
Tagetes (dwarf) (H.H.A.)

H.A. = hardy annual; H.H.A. = half hardy annual;
H.P. – hardy perennial; H.S. – hardy shrub.

12
The Lawn

A lawn is a collection of living breathing plants requiring the same care and maintenance to keep it in good condition, if not more than herbaceous borders, shrub borders and flower beds. Just as the varied plants in a border have different habits – the tight crowns of phlox, the wandering Michaelmas daisy and the long-lived paeony, for example – so there are many different grasses. But instead of allowing coarser grass plants to form the green carpet, a velvety-rich lawn can only be obtained by thorough soil preparation, regular mowing, feeding, aerating and raking to give good lawn grasses a strong foothold and eliminate coarser grasses and weeds.

Selecting the site
The best lawn grasses thrive on light, slightly acid soil in open sunny situations away from the shade of buildings or trees. It is possible to choose grasses for any soil or situation but the nearer these conditions, the better will be the quality of the grass. On clay soils, coarse, tussocky grasses predominate and worms are especially troublesome; in shade the grass grows soft and weak, mosses encroach and close mowing will seriously weaken the lawn.

Levelling
It is more than likely that it will be necessary to level the site for the lawn; and it is essential for a tennis lawn. Begin levelling as early as possible so that the land has ample time to settle before sowing or turfing is done. Unless the soil is very porous a lawn should not be dead level, or the water may have difficulty in running off after rain. Where levelling is extensive, be careful to preserve the topsoil by setting it to one side at the outset of the operation.

Drainage
Deep drainage is not necessary but it is vital for water to drain rapidly from the surface. If surface drainage is slow, the grass is easily damaged in wet periods, and the slippery surface is unpleasant to walk on. On heavy clay pipe-drains are usually necessary and where regular hard wear is anticipated, as on tennis courts and sports fields, it may be necessary to

place a 10cm (4in) layer of ashes or coarse grit beneath a 15 to 22.5cm (6 to 9in) layer of topsoil. (*See also* the section on Grass paths, Ch. 11.)

On most soils and when the lawn is to be mainly ornamental with perhaps one dry path to take any traffic in the winter, it is sufficient to work generous quantities of sand, weathered ashes or crushed clinker into the topsoil during cultivation.

Treatment of the soil

The topsoil need not be especially rich but it should be even in depth to avoid a patchy lawn. Heavy soil should be lightened as described above, and very light soils should have a liberal dressing of well-rotted manure worked into the top spit. Except on heavy soil, deep cultivation is undesirable as it creates a puffy soil which settles unevenly.

Dig the soil to a depth of a single spit, working in at the same time any soil improvers as well as a heavy dressing of phosphatic fertilizer. Take care to remove all traces of annual and perennial weeds. Firm the soil by treading (*not* when wet), rake level, firm and rake again until a firm, level and stone-free surface is obtained. If digging is done in the autumn, leave the ground to settle over winter and carry out fertilizing, levelling and raking in spring.

If the ground can be left for two to three weeks, many weed seeds brought to the surface will germinate and can be hoed off or sprayed with a non-persistent weedkiller before seeding or turfing is done.

Turf or seed

Lawns made from turf are expensive but provide a surface which can be used almost immediately. There is little point in buying anything but good quality turf grown especially for lawns; rough pasture contains a mixture of coarse, tussocky grasses and weeds, with uneven turf which after mowing will quickly fade and leave a patchy, weedy and moss-infested lawn.

Seed is much less expensive, although it always pays to buy the better quality mixtures. It takes a full year to establish a lawn from seed, but apart from money saving, there is a great advantage in being able to select seed to suit a particular situation and purpose. Several seed mixtures are available for good smooth looks, hard wear, light shade, heavy soil and playing areas. Most seed mixtures will include New Zealand bent and Chewing's fescue, usually with a proportion of smooth-stalked meadow grass which is slow to establish but hard-wearing. Rye grass is large seeded, so mixtures with rye grass should be sown at heavier rates than the more expensive mixtures. It is a hard-wearing grass, suitable for rough wear and playing areas, but it needs adequate fertilizer and frequent mowing to keep it in good condition. Soft meadow grass tolerates shade but does not stand up to hard wear or close mowing.

Most seed sold commercially has been treated with a bird repellent. Check that this had been done, otherwise it will be necessary to protect the sown area and even then some losses must be anticipated.

Sowing grass seed

Seed can be sown early in April or about the end of August or the beginning of September. Spring-sown seed will take between a fortnight and three weeks to germinate, but in autumn – the better time to sow – the soil is warm and the seed may be expected to show above the ground in a week or ten days. Sowings can be made throughout the summer, but considerable damage may be caused to the young grass in dry spells unless irrigation is available.

Sow seed on a day when there is no wind and when the soil is dry and crumbles easily through the rake. Spread the seed very evenly making two sowings at right angles to each other. This is most easily done by marking the lawn out into 1m (yd) squares, then mix the seed with twice its quantity of fine soil, and divide it into as many portions as there are squares so that each square receives an equal amount. Alternatively, spread the seed through a fertilizer distributor or mechanical seed sower.

If fine seed is sown in good soil, as little as 15g (½oz) seed per sq m (yd) is sufficient. In less ideal conditions and with mixtures including rye grass the rate should be increased to 25 to 50g (1 to 2oz). Heavier sowings are wasteful as they encourage damping-off, and quick-germinating grasses tend to smother the finer grasses which germinate more slowly.

Care after sowing

Rake very lightly, just covering the seed with 6mm (¼in) of finely sifted soil and afterwards roll the ground, lengthways and across. To protect the seeds from birds criss-cross black cotton on short sticks, or spread netting fixed to small twigs over the seeded surface. As soon as the grass is 2.5cm (1in) or so high, roll it lightly in fine dry weather. When it has grown to a height of 5cm (2in) give the grass its first mowing and remove any weeds.

Use a sharp, well-adjusted mower with the blades set high to avoid pulling the grass seedlings out of the ground. After three to four very light mowings, the mowing height may be gradually reduced to 2.5 to 5cm (1 to 2in). If this height can be maintained for the first season a much better root system will be formed than if the mowing height is rapidly dropped to the usual 12 to 20mm (½ to ¾in).

The turf lawn

Choose turves that have a fine texture and are moderately weed-free. Turves of coarse grass and full of weeds will bring trouble later and never make a good lawn.

Turves can be laid in fine weather in spring or autumn, but autumn is generally the better season. In spring, do not lay later than April, otherwise they are likely to suffer from drought. Soil preparation is as described for seeded lawns above. Immediately before the turves are laid loosen the top 12mm (½in) of soil so that the grass roots can work into it and bind the turf to the soil. The turves are usually delivered in strips 90cm (3ft) long, 30cm (1ft) wide and about 3.5cm (1½in) thick. They are easily torn and need careful handling to make the lawn level and even.

If you are not going to lay turves immediately stack them in a sheltered position out of the sun. They should not, however, be stacked for longer than is necessary, and should be laid down while the grass is still green and bright in colour. When put down they should be fitted very close together, laid in straight lines across the prepared bed and staggered as bricks in a wall so that the junction between two in one row comes opposite the middle of a turf in the rows before and after it. Brush finely sifted soil or fine sharp sand in to fill the crevices and water the turf well at once.

Although the grass appears to be established immediately, it takes some time to root down into the soil. Autumn-laid turves may need a light mowing two weeks after laying to even up the grass and can then be left until spring unless the winter is exceptionally mild. Turf laid in spring should be left for two weeks or more before mowing with the blades set as high as possible; then mowing should be frequent but light for the first season as in the case of lawns grown from seed. If the mower is not fitted with a roller, give a light rolling after each mowing during the first season.

Care of established lawns

In the autumn sweep the lawn well and rake it to drag out all weeds, leaves and dead grass. Then roll it with a spiked roller, or thrust the prongs of a garden fork perpendicularly into the turf to a depth of 15cm (6in) to aerate it and help to surface-drain it through the winter. The holes made by the fork should not be more than 7.5 to 10cm (3 to 4in) apart, and should stud the whole surface of the lawn. If the grass, from the nature of the soil, is inclined to grow rank and coarse, it can be improved by a good dressing in spring of clean sharp sand all over it; if, on the other hand, it has a tendency to scald and burn up, it will benefit from a dressing of equal parts of leaf-mould and fibrous loam together with a sprinkling of fine horn-meal, or a proprietary lawn fertilizer. About a week later, apply a selective lawn weedkiller to deal with any emerging weeds; deep-rooted weeds may have to be dug out.

Methods of mowing

Mowing is one of the most important factors controlling the quality of a lawn. Ideally mowing should be done frequently (at least once each week in summer), removing very little grass each time. Infrequent mowing, taking off most of the grass every month or so, is not only a strain on the mower and its operator, but also results in a poor, thin and patchy lawn. Mowing too closely restricts root growth and makes the lawn susceptible to drought.

The exact times of the year to start and end mowing might vary with seasons but as a general rule mowing is necessary from March until about the middle of November. The lawn should be well swept before the first mowing of the season to clear it of all stones, twigs and worm casts that might damage the machine. Begin mowing as soon as the ground will stand it, and the grass, unless newly sown, should not be allowed to grow so long that the first cutting has to be by the scythe. In spring and autumn it should be sufficient to mow the lawn once every ten days; in summer it will be necessary once a week and even twice a week when the weather is warm and showery. In very hot, dry weather, raise the blades and leave off the box so that the cut grass may act as a mulch to the roots. If during a mild winter the grass starts growing and reaches a height of over 5cm (2in) run the mower over it if the ground is firm enough, otherwise the grass will become thin and straggly.

The two most often used types of lawn-mower are the cylinder and rotary types. The cylinder mower, which may be hand- or motor-operated, has six or more blades cutting with a scissor-like action against a sole-plate. This produces a fine, even surface with stripes of dark and light green, but the mower will not handle long or wet grass and is easily damaged by stones or twigs.

The rotary mower, motor-driven only, has two or four blades on a horizontal disc which rotates at high speed, chopping off the grass. It produces a less even finish but is suitable for rougher grass. If used frequently the rotary mower will provide a finish satisfactory for most garden lawns.

The roller and its use

Great mistakes are made in rolling, and lawns otherwise in excellent condition are often ruined through ignorance of the proper methods of doing this. Rolling is intended to keep the surface even and to spread the roots of the grass, but it is *not* meant to and cannot make the lawn level. Where there is a hollow or a hump in the lawn, cut through the grass and fold the turves back, then add or remove the soil below until the correct level is reached. Replace the turves. Never use a heavy roller in wet weather; if the ground is rolled when wet and sodden, a hard crust is formed on the surface, surface-drainage is impeded and the air is prevented from reaching the roots of the grass.

Use the roller when the lawn is on the dry side, and not directly after rain; two rollings with a light roller are far more beneficial than one with a heavy roller. The roller should never be used directly after frost; allow the turf to become thoroughly thawed out before either rolling it or even walking on the grass. Except on sports grounds and for settling of newly laid lawns, the mower provides sufficient firming of the grass surface and rolling is rarely necessary.

Care of edgings

These should be kept neat and cut regularly with the edging shears; if they are neglected an edging iron has to be used. This is hard to manipulate, however, and often results in ragged and uneven edges. During the summer edgings may be trodden down in places. Drive a spade under them, to raise them to the correct level, in the autumn as soon as the ground becomes softer.

When trimming a lawn with an edging iron use a straight plank as a firm edge along which to guide the blade

Feeding the lawn

If the mowings are left to lie and rot down on the lawn, there should be little need for fertilizer. More often, however, grass is cut regularly and closely, and the cuttings removed from the lawn, gradually impoverishing it. The grass becomes weak and gives place to moss, lichen and weeds.

To keep a lawn healthy it needs regular feeding during spring and summer. An application of 15g (½oz) of sulphate of ammonia per square metre (yd) in April and again in June will stimulate the grass and 50g (2oz) of a general fertilizer in September will balance this growth with healthy root development. Occasional dressings of Epsom salts at 15 to 25g (½ to 1oz) per sq m (yd) imparts a deep green colour to the lawn when a special effect is required, but this should not be done more than once a year. Proprietary fertilizer mixtures are also available, some of which

A fertilizer spreader enables you to spread fertilizer and lawn sand evenly and economically over a grass area

also incorporate weedkillers; these should be used according to the maker's instructions.

Frequent small applications of fertilizer, watering and regular light mowing should create a smooth, even and weed-free lawn. If the soil surface becomes caked and flakes off, this may indicate lime deficiency which should be corrected, but on the other hand, excess liming will ruin a lawn very quickly. Gypsum at 50g (2oz) per sq m (yd) may be used more safely.

A top-dressing of loam, peat or manure may be brushed into the lawn after spiking to stimulate root activity and maintain soil structure. If farmyard manure is used as a dressing it should be well decayed, finely sieved, and not applied too thickly or it will smother and kill the fine grass. Mix with twice its bulk of finely sieved sterilized loam and apply in early spring. Brush off any excess as growth begins in March or April.

Watering

Water should never be applied unless necessary. Although established lawns use up a lot of water they can withstand drought for quite a long time. Once begun, watering will have to be continued at least once a week as long as the dry weather lasts. Watering seems to encourage the increase of weeds and clover rather than grass. Brown, scorched and apparently dead grass recovers remarkably quickly after a shower or two of rain, and as the weeds do not make so quick a recovery, many lawns benefit from a drought. If the drought becomes serious and the topsoil is thin and sandy, watering will be essential, and must then be applied liberally with a garden hose or sprinkler. The ideal way is to water through a fine spray over a long period so that it can permeate several centimetres (inches) into the ground, rather than to flood the area in a short time by using a coarse nozzle, for then the water soon runs off and is of little value to the grass. When mowing during dry periods, run the machine over the grass the day after watering and leave the grass-box off so that the cut grass forms a mulch which will preserve the moisture at the roots.

Weeds and weeding

Small patches of weeds may be removed by hand especially on newly-seeded lawns. Chemical weed control, however, is very much easier. There are two types.

Lawn sand is a mixture of sulphate of ammonia (3 parts by volume), sulphate of iron (1 part) and sharp sand (20 parts). Applied to the lawn in moist conditions it settles on rosette weeds such as daisies and dandelions and scorches them badly. It filters down among the more upright grass stems without causing damage and, when washed into the soil, acts as a stimulant encouraging the grasses to smother any remaining weeds.

Hormone weedkillers, containing 2,4-D, MCPA or similar selective herbicides, cause gross distortion and death of broad-leaved weeds without harming grasses if they are applied at the correct rates. They are most effective if applied when the grass is actively growing, and they must be applied on calm days only as any slight breeze will carry the spray to near-by borders causing damage to other plants. Light infestations can be dealt with by treating the individual weeds.

A lawn riddled with moss and weeds is indicative of bad management, and effective control of weeds cannot be expected until the fault is corrected, whether this is caused by bad drainage, incorrect mowing, insufficient fertilizer treatment or excessive rolling.

Removing worms

Although worms are welcome elsewhere in the garden, they are regarded as a nuisance on lawns where they throw up worm casts which damage mowers and create slippery bare patches through which weeds can invade the lawn.

Worms can be expelled from the lawn by using potassium permanganate or mowrah meal or they can be killed below ground by using chlordane. This is a very poisonous, very long-lasting chemical for use only on lawns.

Worms are especially troublesome on alkaline soils so regular use of such acid fertilizers as sulphate of ammonia will discourage them. There is a price to pay for a worm-free lawn, however, as the acid conditions and absence of worms may cause an accumulation of undecayed grass clippings unless these are removed by vigorous raking.

Where worms are a minor problem, therefore, it is best to tolerate them and disperse their casts with a broom before mowing.

13
The Vegetable Garden

If you can, make your vegetable garden rectangular; it will be far more satisfactory and economical to run. One straight, solid path is convenient, but paths between beds need only be earth tramped firm; the vegetable plot should be well drained, sunny and sheltered. In the shadier parts of the garden vegetables that do not need a lot of sun, such as rhubarb, seakale, kale and some salad vegetables, can be accommodated. The pulses, potatoes and cabbages require more sun, and it is a safe rule that where cabbages will grow to perfection almost any vegetable will do well. The sides of any walls which face east, south and west can have borders at their base in which fruit trees and bushes may be grown; these positions are also ideal for seed beds and frames. The width of borders depends on the amount of sunlight and while none should be so wide that cultivation is difficult, those which get most sun may be wider than those whose aspect is less sunny. A bed in the vegetable garden can be devoted to herbs, or since so many are beautiful in form and sweet smelling, the herb garden can be placed near the house if the situation is suitable.

Soil sterilization and fumigation

Land newly brought under cultivation is often infested with wireworms, leather jackets and other soil pests, and deep cultivation and treatment of the soil will be necessary before satisfactory crops can be obtained.

Most of these pests will be present in the soil in autumn, both those that live in the earth all the year round and those that descend from plants and trees to pass the winter in the soil.

For this reason soil sterilization is chiefly practised in the autumn or early winter when the soil will have time to recover from the harmful effects of chemicals before spring sowing and planting take place.

Soil sterilization is only practicable in the greenhouse although small areas outdoors can also be treated to combat disease organisms. The chemicals used are generally a 2½ per cent solution of cresylic acid or a 2 per cent formalin solution. Water the soil thoroughly and cover it with damp sacking for two days; allow at least one month for the poisonous gases to vaporize before sowing or planting. Fumigation is often a more satisfactory means of destroying greenhouse pests and diseases. The easiest method is to use the various fumigants known as smoke bombs. The house should be cleared of all plants and made as airtight as possible. Use the manufacturer's instruction in regard to the number of bombs for the capacity of the house.

Crop rotation

With the exceptions of a few perennial vegetables, such as asparagus and globe artichoke, it is always a good plan to vary the crops grown in any given plot, never growing the same kind on it for two seasons running. Each crop takes out of the soil certain elements and leaves it enriched by others. Leguminous crops for example, such as peas, are able to extract nitrogen from the air, and besides using a part of it themselves, leave the soil richer in nitrogenous constituents than before. The nitrogen is stored in nodules in the roots which should always be left in the soil. Follow legumes with plants such as the onion, which demand a good supply of nitrogen in the soil ready for their use. It is a good rough rule that tuberous- or bulbous-rooted plants should come after fibrous-rooted ones, and *vice versa*. Crops so similar in habit and nature as cabbages, broccoli, sprouts and kale should not follow one another. Plants with shallow roots like the pea, lettuce and cabbage should be grown alternately with deep-rooted plants like beet, carrot or parsnip. The soil for root-crops should never be freshly manured but follow in a plot that was manured the previous season for another crop. Root crops grown in freshly manured soil tend to produced forked or split roots. Related crops usually suffer from the same diseases; this is another reason for a rotation plan as contaminated soil would be likely to infect a plant of similar kind.

To save time, work out a rotation plan well before the planting time. The following table, showing a strip of land divided into three plots, with a rotation on each covering three years, is a useful guide. It can be extended to a four-year rotation plan, but for the average garden, the three-year plan is adequate. For a family of four to be self-sufficient with vegetables throughout the year, a plot of about 250 sq m (300 sq yd) will be necessary.

Three year rotation plan

Plot	1st Year	2nd Year	3rd Year
A	Brassicas	Root crops	Leguminous crops
B	Root crops	Leguminous crops	Brassicas
C	Leguminous crops	Brassicas	Root crops

Succession of crops

Space is valuable, and it is therefore essential to plant another crop as soon as the previous one has been cleared. The chief crops that are over early and allow a second cropping are early turnips, onions, winter and spring cabbages, early potatoes and early peas. Crops that mature quickly and are suitable as a second crop include summer spinach, lettuce, onions, carrots, turnips, cabbages or broccoli for use the following spring. In selecting these crops, give consideration to the correct rotation of crops.

Catch-crops

These are fast-maturing crops that may be planted between the rows of slower-growing vegetables or even in rows between individual plants. Before the main crop has matured and taken up its full space these catch-crops will have matured and been cleared. Suitable catch-crops are shown in the table on p. 154.

When to sow

On fairly dry soil, in a warm situation, sowing in the open may begin about the end of February – a few early peas, early beans, early carrots and lettuce. Alternatively, make the first early sowing under cloches. In March parsnips, onions, beets, turnips and more peas, beans and carrots may be sown. For a succession of vegetables throughout the year with no gluts at one time and scarcity at another, sow the seeds of most vegetables in half or less rows at intervals of two or three weeks so that they will crop successively over a longer period. In the north and in heavy soils, delay sowing until the ground has warmed up and can be broken into a fine tilth.

Always sow in drills, not broadcast, so that the hoe can be used between the rows.

Sow thinly, but evenly, or with larger seeds such as beetroot and beans sow in stations of two or three seeds at final spacings, and later thin the seedlings at each station to the strongest. Pelleted seeds make sowing much easier as the large seeds can be spaced at the correct distances eliminating the need for thinning. It is, however, important that the seed drills are moist and kept moist during germination so that the clay-coating round the seeds can break down.

Thinning and planting-out Where crops are sown thinly, little thinning should be necessary, but as soon as the plants can be handled, thin out to the distances advised for each vegetable. Remove the thinnings to the compost heap so as not to attract insect pests. Firm the soil round the remaining seedlings and if necessary water with a fine spray.

Watering

Seedlings Late in April and early in May while many seedlings are still tender there is often a spell of hot, dry weather that will scorch many of the seedlings unless they are watered. Use the hoe among the seedlings after watering to help keep the earth moist and let the air into the ground.

It is almost always essential to water transplanted seedlings thoroughly to make the soil firm about their roots.

Established plants Crops whose roots spread out near the surface of the soil and do not go down very deeply will need liberal watering at least once a week and more frequently during a dry spring and summer; lettuce is a good example of this type of plant.

There are several other crops which, in spite of the fact that their roots run down fairly deeply, need copious supplies of water in dry weather; beans, peas and celery are examples.

On the other hand, root crops and many plants of the cabbage family, provided they are planted in deeply dug, well-worked soil, will rarely need watering or mulching, even in the driest seasons.

Mulching vegetables with sheets of black polythene round individual plants is one way of conserving soil moisture and suppressing weeds. This method is also suitable for bushes or small trees

Blanching

Several vegetables need blanching to make them tender, to prevent the development of the green colouring matter and to reduce bitterness – celery, leeks, seakale, cardoons, chicory and endive. The first two of these are blanched by earthing-up. Seakale and chicory are blanched under pots from which light is excluded and for endive a large tile or slate is placed over each mature plant; this will exclude all light and blanch the endive in a few days.

Cultivation of Vegetables

Artichokes

Chinese artichokes require space and a well-drained, well manured, deeply dug soil. Plant the tubers in March in drills 10cm (4in) deep, allowing 25cm (10in) between the plants in the rows and 45cm (1½ft) between the rows. Hoe regularly between the rows and in early July give a liberal top-dressing of manure. During July and August water freely if the weather is dry. In light soil the tubers may remain in the ground through the winter, and be dug up as required. Or lift them about the middle of November and store in boxes of sand or fine soil.

Globe artichoke Choose an open, sunny site, in well-drained soil. Dig and manure the ground in the autumn, and plant out about the beginning of April. The best method of propagation is by root division or suckers, as seed cannot be relied on to come true. Discard the plants when three or four years old, but keep a crop going by replanting offsets each year. Pick the flower-heads when about half-grown and closed. Liberal watering and mulching, and, if necessary, staking, are the principal parts of summer treatment. At the approach of winter bank some ashes or sand round the plant, and before frosts are expected cover the crown with straw or leaves. About the middle of March remove the covering and lightly fork the soil between the plants before raking in a general fertilizer.

Varieties 'Gros Vert de Laon', 'Green Globe'.

Jerusalem artichoke does best in a light soil, deeply dug, and in an open situation. Plant the tubers early in March in drills 10cm (4in) deep, allowing 30cm (1ft) between the tubers, and 90cm (3ft) between the drills. In very heavy soil it is better to plant just below the surface and to mix plenty of ashes with the soil.

Storing Cut the leaves down early in November; the tubers may be left in the ground through the winter and lifted as required.

Varieties Good varieties are 'Fuseau' and 'New White'.

Asparagus

Soil and site On clay soils the cultivation of asparagus is somewhat difficult, though even here, by throwing up the soil into ridges, placing broken bricks and rubble for drainage, by the addition of garden compost and leaf-mould, and by surface manuring, asparagus of good quality can still be raised. Where the soil is sandy and the natural drainage is good, everyone may easily grow this excellent vegetable with a little care and attention. Choose a warm situation, preferably with a southern aspect and give protection from prevailing winds. Dig all types of soil deeply, and on heavy soils manure only the top spit or so of soil so as to keep the roots near the surface. On medium and light soil dig in plenty of decayed farmyard manure, preferably to a depth of 60cm (2ft) or more.

Planting After the ground has been forked over and levelled in spring, take out trenches about 20cm (8in) deep and allow 30cm (1ft) between each of three rows and 75cm (2½ft) between the next block of three rows. Plant strong, one-year-old crowns in April, setting them 30cm (1ft) apart. Cover the crowns with 7.5cm (3in) of soil and water well after planting if the weather is dry. Throughout the summer gradually fill up the trenches at the time of hoeing to keep the surface free of weeds. Do

not grow any other crop between the plants. About the end of October spread a mulch of stable manure or well-rotted compost as top-dressing and at the same time cut the ferny foliage down to ground level. In spring each year, apply a general fertilizer. Leave the crowns to build up during the second year and carry out the routine programme. In the spring of the third year draw a ridge over the crowns to blanch the stems and begin cutting in May. Cut the stems when they are about 10cm (4in) above ground. Cut down all stems well below soil level in autumn.
Varieties 'Argenteuil Early' and 'Connover's Colossal'.

Aubergines
Also known as egg plant, this vegetable is becoming increasingly popular and can be grown satisfactorily in Britain if a little trouble is taken in the initial stages.
Soil and site Aubergines need a rich loamy soil, liberally enriched with well-rotted manure. In April fork fine compost or peat into the topsoil and rake in bone meal at the rate of 125g (4oz) per sq. m (yd).
Sowing Sow seed in a warm greenhouse in February, setting three seeds to a 7.5cm (3in) pot, later thinning the seedlings to the strongest in each pot. In May harden off the young plants in a cold frame and towards the third week of June plant them out in the prepared bed, allowing 45cm ($1\frac{1}{2}$ft) from plant to plant. Pinch out the growing point and allow only six fruits to set on each plant. Harvest aubergines when they are about 10cm (4in) long.
Varieties 'Long Purple' and 'Moneymaker'.

Beans, Broad
Soil Broad beans prefer a deep, somewhat heavy soil, which should be deeply dug and moderately heavily manured in the autumn before sowing.
Sowing The earliest sowing may be made in a warm and sheltered situation at the end of October or early in November. Sow seed in the open for a main crop in February and March, under cloches if necessary, with successional sowings until May. Allow 20cm (8in) between the seeds, 20cm (8in) between the rows and 60cm (2ft) between the double rows. A little earth drawn up to the roots when the seedlings are 10cm (4in) high induces them to put out fresh roots. When the first flowers have set, pinch off the top of the stems to encourage the growth of pods. Remove all laterals as they appear. Pinching back also discourages blackflies which can be serious pests of broad beans; it is a good idea to spray the plants with derris or malathion.
Varieties Earliest crop 'Aquadulce', 'Green Longpod', 'Masterpiece'; Main crop 'Imperial Green Windsor', 'Imperial White Windsor', 'Masterpiece Green Longpod'.

Dwarf broad beans grow some 30 to 45cm (12 to 18in) high, are bushy in form and occupy no more space than the tall varieties. The 'Sutton' and 'Dwarf White Fan' are popular varieties.

Beans, French or Kidney

Soil Dwarf kidney beans or French beans like a deep, rich soil, which should be deeply dug and manured in the autumn. They need an open, sunny situation.

Sowing By sowing partly in the open and partly under glass, French beans can be harvested practically every month of the year. In the open, make the first sowing by a south wall about the middle of April, sheltering the young plants as soon as they come up with a little loose straw. Make the main outdoor sowing in early May, and continue sowing a few seeds at weekly intervals right until the beginning of July. Sow the seeds 15cm (6in) apart in drills 5cm (2in) deep and allow 60 to 90cm (2 to 3ft) between the rows.

Thinning and transplanting When the young plants appear, thin or transplant them to leave at least 25cm (10in) from plant to plant in the rows. Gather the pods before the seeds are formed and the period of cropping will be prolonged if the pods are picked as soon as they are large enough; never let them reach more than 10cm (4in).

Varieties 'Canadian Wonder', 'Earligreen', 'Chevrier Vert', 'Sprite', 'The Prince'.

Beans, Haricot

These are grown in the same manner as French beans, but the pods are left on the plants until the autumn, dried and stored for winter use.

Sowing Sow the seeds in mid to late April, 5cm (2in) deep and 15cm (6in) apart, with 45cm (1½ft) between the rows. Support the plants with twiggy sticks and cover them with cloches in early autumn to help the pods to ripen. When the beans are ready, pull up the plants and hang them upside down in an airy shed to dry off. Remove the white beans and store as other dried pulses.

Varieties 'Chevrier Vert' and 'Comtesse de Chambord'.

Beans, Runner

Soil Runner beans do best in a deep, moderately water-retentive soil, which has been well manured and deeply dug in the autumn.

Sowing Sow the earliest seed in a sheltered situation about the middle of May. Successional crops may be obtained by sowing in the open until the middle of June. Sow in drills 5cm (2in) deep, 12.5cm (5in) being allowed from seed to seed in the rows and 1m (3ft) from row to row. Water liberally in hot weather and syringe to aid pollination. A weekly dose of liquid manure as soon as the pods have set will increase the crop.

Training As soon as the plants have formed their first leaves, provide them with tall poles, firmly set in the ground; train the beans along the poles in double rows or in maypole fashion. Put down baits to keep away slugs. Pick the pods as soon as they are ready.
Varieties 'Achievement', 'Enorma', 'Kelvedon Marvel', 'Prizewinner', 'Scarlet Emperor'.

Beetroot
Soil The soil should be deep and of medium texture. No manure should be added before sowing, but ideally let the beet follow a crop, preferably leeks, for which the ground has been heavily manured.
Sowing For early use sow the globe-rooted kind, of which 'Boltardy', 'Burpee's Golden' and 'The Globe' are good varieties, about the first week in April, in a warm bed in the open, in drills 37.5cm (15in) apart and 2.5cm (1in) deep. Firm the soil after sowing, and later thin the young plants to about 20cm (8in) apart. Dust the young shoots with lime to protect them from the birds. The globe-rooted kinds may also be used for later supplies, where the soil is too poor or shallow for the long-rooted kind. Where the soil is suitable, however, the long-rooted kind are preferable for all but the earliest crops. Sow in May as for the globe-rooted varieties. Good long-rooted kinds include 'Detroit', 'Cheltenham Green Top' and 'Long Blood Red'.
Storing Any roots that remain in the ground should be lifted before the middle of October; twist off the leaves and carefully dry the roots, without breaking the skin. Pack in dry sand in a cool but frost-free place. If carefully and periodically looked over the roots will remain in good condition until the following April.

Brussels sprouts
Soil Brussels sprouts require a deeply dug and previously heavily manured soil, well-trodden before planting.
Sowing Sow the seed in a warm sheltered place, in drills about 1cm (½in) deep, and about 15cm (6in) apart, at the end of February or the beginning of March. Cover the surface with cloches or straw until the plants are well up.
Planting out Late in April move the young plants either to their permanent quarters, or to a nursery bed, about 20cm (8in) apart; for later transplanting, allow 90cm (3ft) either way between the plants. Water well after transplanting. For very early supplies seed may also be sown very thinly early in September, the young plants being moved to their permanent quarters the following April, having been transplanted in October. For a later supply seed may be sown in rather rich soil about the end of April. If the plants are developing too quickly a few of the leaves may be cropped back to stumps in the autumn. This also encourages the

production of sprouts. Leave the top growth intact until all the sprouts are cleared, when the top may be cut and used as greens. Remove any of the lower leaves which turn yellow in autumn. Do not cut the tops or heads till late winter or the stems will stop growing and the production of sprouts will cease.
Varieties Early sowing, 'Bedford Fillbasket', 'Peer Gynt' and 'Roodnerf-Early Button'; main crop, 'Citadel', and 'Perfect Line'.

Cabbages
Soil The ground should be deeply dug and moderately manured a few months previous to planting. Water cabbages liberally at all stages of their growth.
Sowing For an early spring supply, sow seed about the end of July and again about the middle of August. Sow a little seed at frequent intervals, so that the crop may mature in succession. Sow thinly in rows 15cm (6in) apart and about 1cm (½in) deep. Keep the bed moist.
Planting out About six weeks from the time of sowing transplant the young cabbages to their final quarters in firm ground which has not been newly dug but has been prepared some two or three months earlier. Allow 37.5cm (15in) from plant to plant in the rows, and 50cm (20in) between the rows. Soak the ground thoroughly after planting and give liberal supplies of water, especially for the first few days.
Varieties 'April', 'First Early Market', 'Harbinger'.

For a summer supply sow such types as 'Golden Acre', 'May Star' and 'June Star' at intervals during the second half of April and the whole of May. Sow and treat as for spring cabbages, but transplant into richer soil, as their growth is much more rapid.

For early summer cabbages, sow varieties like 'Greyhound', 'Hispi' and 'Primo' under glass in January or February, and harden off in a cold frame before transplanting in April or May.

For autumn crops, sow coleworts in May and the first two weeks of June, and treat as recommended for spring cabbages.

For late autumn, winter and early spring use, sow savoys and hardy winter cabbages at the end of May and first half of June. The small-headed kinds have the best flavour though the drumheads are large and hardy. Good winter cabbages are 'Autumn Supreme', 'Christmas Drumhead', 'Greyhound', 'January King' and 'Winnigstadt'. Savoys: 'Best of All', 'Ormskirk-Rearguard' and 'Winter King'.

Red cabbages are grown almost entirely for pickling, although they can be used as a vegetable. The cultivation resembles that of other cabbages. Seed is best sown in March to provide good compact heads ready for pickling in the autumn. Do not gather red cabbage until the head is thoroughly formed; a touch of frost improves the flavour. Useful sorts are 'Niggerhead' and 'Ruby Ball'.

Cardoons

The prickly French cardoons have better flavour than the Spanish variety, but the latter is easier to handle.

Sowing Sow seed in a cold frame or under glass without heat early in April. Seed may also be sown early in June in the open.

Planting out Early in May take out trenches, some 45cm ($1\frac{1}{2}$ft) apart, to a depth of not less than 45cm ($1\frac{1}{2}$ft), about 15cm (6in) of thoroughly decayed manure being placed at the bottom of the trench, dug in and thoroughly incorporated with the soil. Plant out the seedlings about the end of May.

Blanching When the plants are 45cm ($1\frac{1}{2}$ft) high, support them with stakes and tie the leaves lightly, earthing up the stems at the same time like celery. Throughout the summer water copiously and frequently with soft water. In September earth up the stems again so as to blanch them or cover them with paper collars. Three weeks later the first stems should be ready for use.

Carrots

Soil A rather light, sandy soil which has been liberally manured for previous crops suits carrots best.

Where the soil is cold and heavy it may be greatly improved by trenching and by the liberal addition of weathered ashes, leaf-mould or decayed garden compost. If these ingredients are not available, break the soil up and draw it with the rake into ridges 30cm (1ft) high on which to sow the seeds.

Sowing Make the first sowing in a warm border in early March choosing 'Amsterdam Forcing' or 'Early Nantes'. Sow about 2.5cm (1in) deep in drills 37.5cm (15in) apart, thinning to about 20cm (8in) from plant to plant. Earlier sowings may be made in frames or under cloches. Outdoors, sow the seeds in succession until the middle of April, which is also the time for sowing maincrop varieties to mature for winter use. Good types are 'Chantenay Red Cored', 'New Red Intermediate', 'Scarla' and 'Autumn King'. It is a good idea to make a small sowing at the end of June of a quick-maturing variety, such as 'Early Nantes' or 'Parisian Rondo'. For late spring and summer sown carrots, dust between the drills with BHC to discourage the carrot fly.

Storing Pull carrots as soon as large enough; lift the main crop for storing by the end of October, or even later, unless severe frosts set in. Remove the carrots carefully so as not to damage the roots, twist off the leaves, and store the roots in a frost-proof and fairly dry place in boxes of sand or in a clamp outdoors.

Cauliflowers and Broccoli

There are four groups of cauliflower, which now includes the broccoli

Two of the most rewarding vegetables to grow. Cauliflower 'Unwin's Snowcap' (courtesy W. J. Unwin Ltd), and carrots: these need a well-dug stone-free bed

Two of the most popular hardy fruits: apple 'Worcester Pearmain' and pear 'Conference'

types: summer and autumn cauliflowers, winter and spring cauliflowers, summer and autumn sprouting broccoli, and winter sprouting broccoli. With careful selection, cauliflowers can be harvested throughout the year. Most cauliflowers and broccoli do best on loamy rich soils, although light soils are also suitable if they are liberally enriched with manure dug in during winter. Before sowing or planting, fork in a general fertilizer, and lime if the soil is acid.

Sowing To maintain a succession, make three or four sowings, the first at the end of September, or in January in the greenhouse; harden off the seedlings and plant out in April. Good kinds for this crop, which is ready about June, are 'All the Year Round', 'Rocket' and 'Snowball'. Early in April, make a second and larger sowing in open ground. For this crop such varieties as 'Autumn Giant', 'Dominant', 'South Pacific' and 'White Heart' may be sown, young plants being planted out in May and June. For winter and spring cauliflowers make a third sowing about the middle of August to stand through the winter. For this third sowing use such varieties as 'Late Queen' (May), 'Royal Oak' (May), 'St George' (March), 'Superb Early White' (January), and 'Walcheren Winter' (April). Autumn-sown plants are generally pricked out under frames for protection during winter, giving plenty of air in fine weather.

Planting out When the plants are large enough to transplant set them 10cm (4in) apart in rich and well-manured soil. In June move the April sowings to where they are to grow; in September they will be heading, and will continue to improve until the frosts of early winter. When the heads begin to appear, shade them from sun and rain by breaking down some of the larger leaves so as to cover them. Water well in dry weather.

Wintering On the approach of winter plants that are ready for cutting may be pulled up and hung upside down in a cool, but frost-free place. They will stay fresh for two or three weeks.

Broccoli are treated as cauliflowers and need the same kind of soil.

Sowing Sow seeds of summer and autumn sprouting broccoli under glass in March and plant out in early summer. Winter and spring sprouting broccoli should be sown in a prepared seed bed in April or May, and transplanted to their permanent quarters in late June or July. They will be ready for harvesting from the following February or March.

Varieties Summer (calabrese) kinds, 'Express Corona', 'Italian Sprouting', 'Autumn Spear'. Winter and spring varieties, 'Early Purple Sprouting', 'Improved White Sprouting', 'Late April Purple Sprouting'.

Celeriac

Celeriac is hardy and of easy cultivation, growing well in almost any rich, well-prepared garden soil.

Sowing Sow seeds in late February in the greenhouse at 18°C (65°F).

Prick out the seedlings when large enough to handle, singly into 7.5cm (3in) pots.
Planting out About the end of May transfer the plants to the open. The soil should have been deeply dug and well manured before being made firm. Plant shallowly as the stems swell above ground level. Set them 45cm (1½ft) apart, allowing 30cm (1ft) between the rows. Water freely throughout the summer and when hoeing between the rows to keep down weeds, draw the soil away from the plants rather than over them.
Storing At the approach of winter lift the roots and store them like beetroots.
Varieties 'Globus' and 'Marble Ball'.

Celery
Soil Celery prefers a deep, water-retentive soil. Deep or trench cultivation is necessary, and manure and water throughout the growing season.
Sowing Sow seed under glass at a temperature of 18°C (65°F). March is the month for the principal sowing, but early seed may be sown in February. As soon as the seedlings are able to be handled, about 5cm (2in) high, prick the young plants out singly into 7.5cm (3in) pots containing a good potting mixture and place the pots in a cold frame. Later the plants may be transplanted into bigger pots before the final planting in beds or trenches.
Planting out Plant out when 15cm (6in) high, the main crop about the end of June, the earliest plants from the February sowing about the end of May and a late crop about the end of July.

Except for self-blanching varieties, celery must be grown in trenches. Prepare the trenches in winter, making them 45cm (1½ft) wide and 40cm (16in) deep; break up the subsoil, cover with a layer of manure, and incorporate this well with the soil. When ready for planting the bottom of the trenches should be 15cm (6in) below ground level; if more than one trench is needed, space them 75cm (2½ft) apart. Place the young plants at intervals of about 30cm (1ft), firm well and water liberally. In addition to manure, celery will do better if a liquid fertilizer is given once a month. Keep the soil between the plants mulched with old manure to give additional nourishment and to check evaporation. As growth proceeds, gradually hoe earth up round the plants, about 10cm (4in) at a time, and pat down firmly to keep out the rain. Begin earthing-up in August and finish by about October when the celery should be ready two months later. Hold the leaves together while the earthing-up is in process, so that no soil can enter between the stalks. Keep the hearts well above the earthing-up, and remove any side growths.
Varieties Pink and red, 'Giant Pink', 'Giant Red'; white, 'Giant White'; self-blanching, 'American Green', 'Golden Self-blanching'.

Chicory

Apart from its uses as a salad, the forced and blanched chicories are used as a vegetable, and the tender pale green leaves that develop after forcing can be used as spring greens.

Sowing Sow seeds from the middle of April to the middle of June in rich, loamy soil which has been well manured for a previous crop, in rows 45cm (1½ft) apart; thin the seedlings to about 25cm (10in) apart in the rows.

Forcing About the end of October lift the roots, a few at a time, for forcing. Cut the tops back to 2.5cm (1in) of the crown and place these in pots or boxes of soil. Set the pots under the greenhouse staging or a dark cupboard, at a temperature of 10°C (50°F) and cover them with sacking or other material to exclude all light. After three to four weeks, the chicories will be 15cm (6in) long and ready for cutting. The roots may be left to produce another crop of leaves and thereafter thrown out.

Varieties 'Red Verona', 'Sugar Loaf', 'Witloof'.

Corn Salad

Sow in drills, 2.5cm (1in) deep and 25cm (10in) apart, in light, rich soil in a warm situation. Successional sowings from August until the end of September will give a steady winter supply. Water liberally. Thin the seedlings to 22.5cm (9in) apart and pull the leaves when they are young and tender with about four leaves. Protect from severe frost with a covering of hay or straw.

Courgettes – *See* Marrows.

Cucumbers

Tender cucumbers are grown in the greenhouse or a frame, the hardier ridge cucumbers in a sheltered position in the open.

Cucumbers under glass Prepare a 30cm (1ft) deep bed of sterilized soil over a base layer of straw for good drainage; cover the soil with 12.5cm (5in) of moist peat and another 5cm (2in) of soil. Build mounds of good compost – three parts loam to one part peat – on top of the bed, spacing the mounds 60cm (2ft) apart.

Sow seeds in 7.5cm (3in) pots in February or March and transfer the small plants about two weeks later, one to each mound. It is essential to maintain a day temperature of 32°C (90°F) and a night temperature of 18°C (65°F); do this by ventilating in hot weather, but keep the windows closed at night. Water freely with tepid water and spray them daily, more often in hot weather, with a syringe. In the greenhouse, support the plants with stakes and train them along wires; stop the main stems when they reach the top wires, and the laterals beyond the second leaf joints. In a frame, pinch the stems back to two leaves, on both main stems and laterals. Remove male flowers on all cucumber plants and feed with liquid fertilizer once a week. As the plants grow, mulch with peat and soil to keep the roots covered.

Pick the fruits regularly to encourage more crops and do not let them go to seed on the plants.

Varieties 'Butcher's Disease-Resisting', 'Fertila', 'Green Spot', 'Telegraph Improved'.

Ridge cucumbers Sow the seeds as for greenhouse cucumbers, but prick the seedlings into 12.5cm (5in) pots and harden off before planting outdoors in May or June when all frost is past. Prepare growing ridges as in the greenhouse and plant the seedlings shallowly, 60cm (2ft) apart. Seeds may also be sown directly into the ridges in late May. Stop the plants when seven leaves have formed so that laterals will grow; it is not necessary to remove male flowers. Water well with fine sprays of water and do not let it collect round the stems. When the first fruits have set, give a liquid fertilizer once a week.

Varieties 'Baton Vert', 'Burpless Tasty Green', 'Marion', 'Perfection'.

Dandelions

Sow from March till June in drills 30cm (1ft) apart and thin the seedlings to 15cm (6in) apart in the rows. In late autumn lift the roots and store in sand until they are wanted for blanching, as for Chicory, p. 137. The plants may also be left out of doors and the young leaves gathered from March till June. The roots can be roasted dry, ground and used as a coffee substitute. 'Thick-leaved Improved' is a good variety.

Endives

Soil Endive thrives in light moderately rich soil, preferably manured for a previous crop. Rake in a general fertilizer and add lime if necessary.

Sowing The first sowing can be made about the middle of May. For the main crop sow in the middle of June, and again about the middle of July. Plants to stand the winter should be sown early in August. Sow thinly, 1cm (½in) deep, in drills 30cm (1ft) apart and thin the plants, when ready, to 25cm (10in). Water freely in dry weather and give liquid manure occasionally.

Blanching When nearly full-grown, the plants must be blanched. In the case of earlier crops and broad-leaved kinds tie them up loosely when dry and draw the soil up about each plant. Late crops intended for winter use are liable to be injured by frost and these and the curly-leaved kinds should be blanched by covering the plants with inverted pots, blocking out the drainage holes. Blanching should be done at intervals, so as to have a continuous supply. Late-sown seedlings are best planted out in sheltered situations.

Varieties 'Batavian Green', 'Exquisite Curled', 'Winter Lettuce-leaved'.

Kale

Kale or borecole is one of the most neglected vegetables, although its season extends from October to April. It is extremely hardy.

Soil Kale will grow in any, even the poorest, soil, provided it is well drained.

Sowing Sow the seed from March to May in drills about 2.5cm (1in) deep. Thin the seedlings to 10cm (4in) apart where necessary as soon as they appear.

Planting out Set out the seedlings when about six to eight weeks old, allowing about 75cm (2½ft) between the plants in all directions. Water liberally until the roots are firmly established.

Varieties Early, 'Fribor', 'Verdura'; main crop, 'Dwarf Green Curled', 'Frosty', 'Pentland Brigg' and 'Thousand-Headed'.

Kohl-rabi

Soil The kohl-rabi is especially useful as an alternative to the turnip where the soil is light, as it will stand severe drought – frost has no effect upon it. The roots are most palatable if harvested when at the size of tennis balls.

Sowing For a summer supply, sow the seed in March in drills about 1cm (½in) deep, and 40cm (16in) apart. Thin the young plants as soon as possible to about 25cm (10in) apart. For autumn and winter supplies sow seed towards the end of July. (Store as for Turnips.)

Varieties 'Earliest White', 'Purple Vienna'.

Leeks

Soil Leeks do best on deep, rich soil.

Sowing For an early crop sow the seed in boxes early in February and keep at a temperature of 13°C (55°F). When some 5cm (2in) high prick the seedlings off 5cm (2in) apart. Keep in a moderate heat till the middle of April, then transfer to a cold frame, harden off and plant out in May. Seed may be sown thinly in the open in a warm border from the end of February till the end of March, 1cm (½in) deep in drills about 15 or 20cm (6 or 8in) apart. Soaking the seeds in lukewarm water for about 12 hours previously speeds up germination.

Planting out As soon as they are large enough to handle, thin out the young plants and transfer them to their permanent sites at the end of June. If the ground is rich and moderately heavy, plant leeks on the flat in rows, 30cm (1ft) apart, about 15cm (6in) being allowed from plant to plant. When the soil is not so rich and heavy it is better to grow leeks in trenches. These should be about a spade's width wide, about 60cm (2ft) apart, and about 30cm (1ft) deep; rake a good amount of well-rotted manure into the soil. Firm and return about 7.5cm (3in) of soil to the trench. Before transplanting the seedlings, trim their tops by at least a quarter and the roots by half. Drop the leeks into 15cm (6in) holes made at 15cm (6in) intervals in the trench bottom; do not firm, but water them in. Give liberal dressings of liquid manure in late summer, and at all times keep the roots moist.

Blanching As they grow gradually earth the leeks up from the sides of the trenches to keep an increasing portion of the stem buried and blanched. When grown on the flat draw up with the hoe.

Storing Leeks can remain in the ground through the winter and be dug up as needed, or they may be stored in sand in a dry shed.

Varieties 'Early Market', 'Lyon', 'Musselburgh', 'Marble Pillar', 'Winter Crop'.

Lettuces

There are two kinds of lettuces – cabbage types which are round and soft-leaved (butterheads) or curly and crisp-hearted; the second type, cos lettuces, have long, crisp leaves and firm hearts. Most modern cos types are self-folding and so do not as previously need blanching. Some seed mixtures contain cabbage and cos types to give an extended cropping season.

Soil Both kinds like a light, rich and deep soil. For the main crop of summer lettuces, prepare a piece of ground that has already been well cultivated by incorporating plenty of well-rotted manure. Success with lettuce depends on ample moisture at the roots and ample room for leaf growth.

Sowing Under glass, sow lettuces any time from January to March and in the open make successive sowings once a fortnight from mid-March until August in the bed in which they are to remain. Transplanting is necessary with seedlings raised under glass, but generally the best plants are obtained by sowing in the permanent position. Special varieties for growing to maturity in winter are available for greenhouse and frame cultivation.

Sowing in the open, thinning and planting out Early in March sow thinly in drills 30cm (1ft) apart and 1cm ($\frac{1}{2}$in) deep in the prepared bed. When the plants are big enough to handle thin them to 15cm (6in) apart and later to 30cm (1ft) apart. It is better to leave too few plants than too many. Put slug baits among the young seedlings, and keep them well watered.

Winter lettuces Winter lettuces are sown in succession from August to the latter part of October, the earlier sowings being made both in the open and in frames, but the later ones – those sown in October – under glass only. In the open, sow directly into a bed from which a previous crop has been cleared, or in a seed bed with fine soil and transplant before the winter sets in, either outdoors for spring and early summer harvesting or to a heated frame for winter use. All crops in frames need careful attention with plenty of moisture or warm, bright weather may cause the plants to bolt. Slight protection given to the outdoor crop will keep them safe through the hard weather; they can be left in the seed bed and transplanted carefully in March to a warm sunny border. Give a surface fertilizer of dried blood to start growth; they should be ready for cutting in late spring.

Cos lettuces are sown and treated as cabbage lettuce; varieties that are not self-folding can be helped to heart by slipping a broad rubber band round the plants when nearly fully grown.

Varieties Summer cabbage lettuce, 'All the Year Round' (butterhead), 'Avondefiance' (butterhead), 'Salad Bowl' (non-hearting), 'Tom Thumb' (butterhead), 'Webb's Wonderful' (crisp heart), 'Windermere' (crisp heart); autumn and winter cabbage lettuce, 'Arctic King', 'Imperial Winter', 'May Queen' (under glass), 'Premier' (under glass); cos lettuces, 'Buttercrunch', 'Little Gem', 'Lobjoit's Green Cos', 'Winter Density' (all year).

Marrows and Courgettes

These vegetables, whether of the bush or trailing variety, require a deep, light, rich soil, and a fairly sheltered position, with plenty of water in dry weather. The courgette is a type of marrow, differing only from marrows in the smaller fruits which are cut when they are at the most 10cm (4in) long.

Early marrows can be grown in heated frames in the same way as cucumbers, but usually the plants are raised under glass and planted out when all danger of frost is over.

Sowing Sow seed early in April in 7.5cm (3in) pots filled with a good seed compost, covering the seeds about 2.5cm (1in). Place the seeds flat, on their sides, not vertically in the compost. Peat pots are ideal as the roots will not be disturbed during transplanting. Place near the glass in gentle heat and keep fairly moist. When well established, remove to a cold frame and gradually harden off. Towards the end of May, or as soon as the weather is warm and settled, plant them out and protect them for a time with cloches or upturned glass jars; water well until the roots get hold of the soil. Train and regulate the shoots, so as to prevent them growing too closely together, and stop them at the fifth leaf to encourage laterals and fruit production. In hot seasons, mulch the plants to conserve moisture and scatter slug baits on the ground. After a few of the marrows have set, but not before, give a fortnightly liquid fertilizer. Seeds may also be sown in May on the bed itself. Sow the seeds, 2.5cm (1in) deep in groups of two or three, allowing 60cm (2ft) between each group of bush marrows and courgettes, and at least 90cm (3ft) for trailing marrows. Cover with cloches or inverted jam jars until the seedlings are established, then remove the protection and thin the seedlings to the strongest in each group.

Making the bed Make up the bed for marrows about the second week in May. Take out a trench, about 25cm (10in) deep and wide and fill it with well-rotted manure or garden compost. Throw the soil on top of the filled trench so that it forms a ridge. Set the seedlings of glass-raised plants on the ridge, at the distances recommended for station sowings.
Cutting Marrows and courgettes should be cut while the skin is still tender; regular picking also increases the yield. In the summer, cut marrows before they reach a length of 20cm (8in); at the end of the season the fruits can be left to reach full size, and if frost threatens, cut them and hang in nets to ripen in a cool, but frost-free place.
Varieties Trailing, 'Golden Delicious', 'Long Green', 'Long White', 'Vegetable Spaghetti'; bush, 'Custard White', 'Prober', 'Tender and True', 'White Bush'; courgettes, 'Green Bush', 'Zucchini'.

Mushrooms

Soil and site Mushrooms merely require a supply of compost and a certain degree of warmth, moisture and darkness. They are good crops for growing where space is limited, in sheds and garages, under the greenhouse staging or even in a bucket housed in a dark, well-ventilated cupboard. During summer and autumn, mushrooms can be grown in a patch of grass outdoors as long as this has not been treated with weedkillers.
Making the bed Allow about six to nine weeks from sowing the spawn to the gathering of a crop. Mushrooms grow on a compost of rotted organic matter; this can be made up from fresh stable manure and left to rot down under cover, but it is more practicable to buy ready-made, sterilized mushroom compost from garden centres. Pack this into boxes or suitable containers to a depth of 25cm (10in) or make a similar heap on a shed floor.
Sowing the spawn As soon as the temperature of the compost reaches about 24°C (75°F), the spawn, which must be fresh and which is bought in bricks composed of a mixture of manure and soil, containing dry mycelium of the mushroom, can be broken into 5cm (2in) pieces. Plant these pieces firmly with a trowel about 10cm (4in) deep in the compost and about 25cm (10in) apart. Cover the compost with a 2.5 to 5cm (1 to 2in) thick layer of sterilized soil, moistened just enough to hold together.
Care of the bed Little or no water should be given to the bed until the mushrooms begin to come up. As soon as the mushrooms appear, a moderate amount of tepid water may be given once a week if necessary.

Mushrooms should not be cut but twisted off, separating the stalk as near the base as possible. Add fresh soil to fill the holes after picking, and when the compost is exhausted it can be used for a mulch outdoors.

Mustard and Cress

These salad plants can be had throughout the year as they only take about two weeks to mature. In summer they can be sown outdoors in fine soil, and in autumn, winter and spring in trays of moist peat in the greenhouse or on a window-sill. To avoid soil particles on the seed leaves, seeds germinate equally quickly on damp sacking. In spite of their name, mustard and cress are usually rape and cress seeds. Sow the cress seeds four days earlier than the rape or mustard seeds so that they will mature at the same time.

Onions

For a steady supply of onions, seeds are sown at different times of the year; in early spring for lifting in autumn and in autumn for use the following summer. Salad or spring onions can be sown in either autumn or spring, and the thinnings from maincrop onions can also be used as salad onions. Onion sets which do away with the need for sowing, thinning or transplanting can be planted in April.

Soil and site Onions need a sunny, open position, and prefer a deep and rich, friable loam, though they grow quite well in any good light soil. Clay is not very suitable, and a newly-broken soil should be avoided as the foliage grows at the expense of the bulbs which are also open to attack by insect pests, always present in freshly-broken soil. In autumn, dig over the ground and incorporate plenty of well-rotted manure; leave the ground rough for the winter weather to break it down. In the spring, before sowing, rake in a top-dressing of 125g (4oz) of bone meal and 50g (2oz) of sulphate of potash per sq m (yd). On soils low in lime, also rake in carbonate of lime at 150g (5oz) to the sq m (yd).

Sowing in the open Sow the autumn main crop as soon as the ground is in working condition, between January and mid-March. Make the seed bed and place cloches in position to warm up the soil for a couple of weeks; sow thinly in drills 1cm (½in) deep and 30cm (12in) apart. Seed may also be sown under glass in a temperature of 16°C (59°F) early in January. Harden off in April, and plant out early in May.

Outdoors, thin the seedlings as soon as they are large enough to handle, to 2.5cm (1in) apart and later to 15cm (6in) apart. Transplant seedlings and onion sets to the same distances. Water well during dry weather.

About the middle of August make a second sowing of maincrop onions for use next summer before the main crop is ready. Leave the spring-sown seedlings where sown until the end of February, then transplant, fairly deeply, to their permanent bed in soil not recently manured.

Sow salad onions in drills 1cm (½in) deep and 20cm (8in) apart; do not thin. Sowings can be made in early March for a summer supply, and at intervals until September. Hardy varieties can be sown in late September for pulling in spring.

Storing Towards the end of August the bulbs should be well formed and the tops show indications of ripening. Bend or break the tops down with the back of a rake. As soon as the bulbs are properly ripened, take them up and spread in a sunny situation in the open air until thoroughly dried. Store in an airy shed or tie them up in ropes.
Varieties Spring-sowing, 'Bedfordshire Champion', 'Dura', 'Polina', 'Superba', 'Giant Zittau'; autumn-sowing, 'Autumn Queen', 'Express Yellow', 'Kaizuka Extra Early', 'Reliance', 'Solidity'; winter-sowing, 'Ailsa Craig'; salad onions, 'White Lisbon' and 'White Lisbon Winter Hardy'.

Parsnips
Soil To grow parsnips properly, deeply dug, rich, sandy soil, which has been manured for a previous crop, is recommended. If fresh manure is added it will encourage the production of side roots. Before sowing rake in a general fertilizer as recommended on the packet.
Sowing Sow seeds at intervals from February to April (the best-flavoured, though not the largest roots, are obtained by sowing at the later date). Make drills 1cm (½in) deep and 37.5cm (15in) apart, sow thinly, lightly cover the seeds and firm with the rake. When the young plants appear begin thinning until ultimately 15cm (6in) remain between the plants. As soon as they are large enough, they may be pulled.
Storing During the winter the roots are best left in the ground, but if the ground is needed, the remainder can be lifted, their tops trimmed off and stored in a clamp outdoors or in boxes of sand in a shed.
Varieties 'Avonresister', 'Hollow Crown Improved', 'Tender and True'.

Peas
Soil and site Peas require deep loam, which has been well enriched and deeply dug or trenched in the autumn. Where space permits it is a good plan to dig a shallow trench on each side of the rows, so that during the summer months manure and water can be easily supplied. Shortly before sowing, rake in a mixture of 50g (2oz) of superphosphate of lime and 25g (1oz) of sulphate of potash to every sq m (yd).
Sowing under glass The earliest peas are obtained by sowing wrinkle-seed types in February. Sow singly in 6cm (2½in) peat pots of a good seed compost and keep in gentle heat. Harden off in a cold frame and plant out in a warm, south border in early April, 22.5cm (9in) apart.
Sowing in the open The first sowing in the open may be made towards the end of February, provided the soil is not wet or frozen. To secure a succession sow once a fortnight from this time up till the middle of June. Sow the seeds 5 to 7.5cm (2 to 3in) apart in flat-bottomed drills 7.5cm (3in) deep and 10cm (4in) wide. Before sowing, dust the drills with a

proprietary seed dressing. Dwarf peas should be planted in rows about 60cm (2ft) apart, tall varieties 1.2m (4ft) apart.
Supporting When the plants are 7.5cm (3in) high, insert small sticks to give the peas a start and later push in taller pea sticks along the rows and among the plants. Mulching is important to conserve soil moisture, and in hot, dry weather, peas need plenty of water, and syringing overhead.

Pods should be picked as soon as ready; any pods left to grow ripe will result in lower yields.
Varieties First early, 'Feltham First', 'Kelvedon Wonder', 'Little Marvel', 'Meteor', 'Progress No. 9'; second early, 'Achievement', 'Hurst Green Shaft', 'Miracle', 'Onward', 'Chancellor', 'Senator'.

Potatoes

Soil Potatoes do best in a deep, sandy, well-drained loam. In the autumn dig the ground deeply and mix into the soil well-rotted manure at the rate of one bucket for every metre (yd); leave the ground rough over winter, but at planting time rake into the topsoil a general fertilizer at the rate of 50g (2oz) per sq m (yd); never add lime, which potatoes dislike
Sprouting Tubers which are intended to be used for seed should be selected at the time of lifting or bought in fresh every year. They should be evenly shaped and weigh from 50 to 75g (2 to 3oz) each. Spread them on the floor in an open shed until the skin is set and hard, and then pack them in single layers in trays and store in a frost-free, dark and airy place. It is, however, advisable to buy fresh seed potatoes each year as they will have a certificate of disease resistance. Start the tubers sprouting by setting them in trays, rose end upwards, in a slightly heated room with plenty of light and air. Allow about four weeks for the tubers to produce sprouts, which should be short and sturdy, not long and spindly. Allow only three sprouts on each tuber and rub out any others that appear.

For the earliest potatoes choose a sunny sheltered plot; potatoes are particularly susceptible to frost, and it is generally useless to plant before the middle of February even in an ideal situation. In heavy soils it is better to plant after the middle of March. For the main crop March is the best month in the south, in the north wait until April.
Planting After preparing and levelling the soil, take out drills about 12.5cm (5in) deep; for early potatoes leave 60cm (2ft) between the rows, 75cm (2½ft) for maincrop varieties. Lay the tubers at the bottom of the drills, about 37.5cm (15in) apart; draw soil over them with the hoe. When the plants are about 15cm (6in) high, begin the first earthing-up and continue every three or four weeks until nearly full grown.
Lifting and storing Early potatoes for immediate use are dug up as required; maincrop tubers should not be dug up until the tops are quite dead. Lift one plant as a trial; if the potatoes are ripe the skin of the tubers will be set and the potatoes ready for eating. If they are to be stored leave

them in the ground for another three weeks. They are best lifted with a fork inserted deeply under the tubers. Dry by exposure to the sun for a day or two, then store in a dry cellar or other dark frost-proof place or a frost-protected clamp outdoors.
Varieties First early, 'Arran Pilot', 'Duke of York', 'Home Guard', 'Pentland Javelin', 'Ulster Chieftain'; second early, 'Catriona', 'Craig's Royal', 'Maris Peer'; maincrop, 'Desirée', 'King Edward', 'Majestic', 'Maris Piper', 'Pentland Crown'.

Radishes
Radishes can be grown successfully almost all the year round by sowing seed in frames and under cloches in early spring and late autumn and in the open ground at fortnightly intervals from March till September.
Soil Radishes thrive in a light and slightly limed loam, manured for a previous crop.
Sowing Sow thinly in drills, 1cm (½in) apart for long radishes, and from 10 to 15cm (4 to 6in) apart for the globe-shaped types. Thinning should not be necessary if the seed is sown thinly. Remove frame lights or cloches from early sowings in April. Sheltered positions facing south are best for the early crops. When the weather is hot and the ground dry water before sowing and keep the soil moist until the crop is finished.
Varieties 'Cherry Belle', 'French Breakfast', 'Icicle', 'Scarlet Globe', 'Sparkler'.

Rhubarb
Soil and site To produce succulent stems a deeply dug soil, heavily manured a few weeks before planting, is necessary. The situation should be sheltered from east winds, and as the crop is a permanent one the site cannot be included in a rotation plan.
Planting Plant healthy crowns 90cm (3ft) apart in spring with the top bud just above the surface. Cut no stems during the first season and do not weaken the plants by pulling too many stems even when well-established, but leave four or five to maintain health and vigour. Any flower heads should be cut off as soon as they appear.
Forcing For early tender stems in late winter, one or two crowns can be forced, either outdoors or in the greenhouse. Choose two-year-old plants and in the open cover the crowns with deep upturned boxes. Straw or fresh manure may be heaped round the boxes to generate heat. Alternatively, lift the crowns in winter and put them into boxes of soil, kept slightly moist. Place in a dark shed or greenhouse or cover with boxes or black polythene; at a temperature of 7°C (45°F), stems should be ready for pulling after eight weeks.
Varieties 'Hawke's Champagne', 'The Sutton', 'Timperley Early' (good for forcing).

Salsify

Soil Salsify does best in a deep, sandy soil which has been manured for a previous crop such as celery or peas. Before sowing, rake in a general fertilizer at the rate of 125g (4oz) to the sq m (yd).

Sowing Sow thinly about the end of April in drills 2.5cm (1in) deep and 30cm (1ft) apart. As soon as the seedlings are about 5cm (2in) high, thin them to 15 or 20cm (6 or 8in) apart. They will be ready for use in the early part of November.

Lifting and storing The roots are best left in the ground throughout the winter and pulled as required for use. If the frosts are severe the roots can be protected with ashes, straw or bracken. Any roots that remain in late winter can be lifted and stored like carrots, or they may be left in the ground and recommence growth which will result in leafy above-ground shoots. These chards may be cooked as a vegetable or blanched like endive.

Varieties 'Mammoth' and 'Sandwich Island'.

Savoy – *See* Cabbage.

Scorzonera

Scorzonera requires similar treatment to salsify.

Variety 'Russian Giant'.

Seakale

Soil This is a permanent crop and needs deeply cultivated soil with a liberal dressing of manure incorporated. Being a native maritime vegetable, seaweed is the best form for manure. Prepare the ground in autumn and leave it rough during the winter. Seakale can be raised from seeds, which is a long process, or from root cuttings known as thongs. Whichever process is used, fork over the bed in early spring, rake it level and firm it with the feet.

Sowing Sow thinly in March or April in drills about 5cm (2in) deep and 45cm ($1\frac{1}{2}$ft) between the drills. As soon as the seedlings have made six leaves, transplant them to rows 45cm ($1\frac{1}{2}$ft) apart, with 22.5cm (9in) from plant to plant. Water liberally and apply liquid fertilizer frequently in hot weather. The following spring move the plants to leave 75cm ($2\frac{1}{2}$ft) either way.

Propagation by root cuttings The quickest way to produce cropping plants is by root cuttings. Plant small roots, or rather pieces of root, about the size of the little finger, about 15cm (6in) long and 1cm ($\frac{1}{2}$in) thick, vertically about the end of March. The thongs are usually supplied with a straight cut at the top and a slanting cut on the bottom; set the thongs, straight side up, with the tops just below the soil surface. Allow 45cm ($1\frac{1}{2}$ft) between the rows and about 37.5cm (15in) between the thongs.

Suppress weeds by frequent hoeing or with a 5 or 7.5cm (2 or 3in) mulch as a top-dressing. Early in May remove all weak growths and cut away any flower stems so that strong crowns form for forcing in the winter. Water should be given liberally throughout the summer.

Forcing and blanching If intended for early use, lift the roots about the end of November, as soon as the leaves part readily from the crowns. Pack them closely together in boxes of light soil, the crowns being level with, or just below, the surface. Place in a dark cellar or darkened part of the greenhouse with a continuous temperature of about 10°C (50°F). Keep the soil gently watered and covered with a layer of dry leaves or straw. Cut the shoots when about 18.5cm (7in) long, and for a continuous supply force roots in succession. The roots which have been lifted for forcing and which are not wanted immediately may be stored in soil, crown uppermost, so that they can be forced as required. Forcing takes about five weeks.

Seakale can also be forced in the open by covering them with large inverted pots or drain pipes and slates being placed over the plants about the second week in November and the space between the pots piled up with leaves, or fresh manure. Every fortnight cover a fresh supply of plants so as to yield a continuous supply. As soon as the crop has been cut remove the bulk of the heating material, but leave a little as protection against frost.

Variety 'Lily White' is the only one generally available.

Shallots

Soil Shallots do best in an open situation, and in a medium, well-drained soil that has been deeply dug and well manured for previous crops. Before planting fork in 75g (3oz) of superphosphate of lime to every sq m (yd).

Planting Plant the bulbs, which should be of medium size, in February or early in March just deep enough to make them firm, but without covering them with soil. Allow 15 to 20cm (6 to 8in) from bulb to bulb and 30cm (1ft) between the rows. At the beginning of July draw the soil away from the bulbs so that they can ripen and about the end of July or early in August, when the stems begin to die down, lift and dry the bulbs before storing them in a dry, moderately light room.

Varieties 'Giant Yellow', 'Russian Shallot'.

Spinach

Soil A deeply dug, rather moist soil is preferable for summer spinach, a rather lighter soil for winter spinach. Sandy, quick-draining soils are not suitable. On poor soils, dig in well-rotted compost or manure in autumn, otherwise fork in a general fertilizer when preparing the seed bed in spring, at the rate recommended by the manufacturer.

Sowing Soak the seed in water for twenty-four hours before sowing. Sow thinly in the permanent quarters, in drills 2.5cm (1in) deep and 30cm (1ft) apart. When about 7.5cm (3in) high, thin the seedlings to 15cm (6in) apart. Sow summer spinach at three-weekly intervals from the end of February to early in May. When gathering spinach, pick only the largest leaves; do not pick all the leaves from any one plant.

For winter supplies of spinach sow early in August and at fortnightly intervals until mid-September. In cold areas, it may be necessary to protect the plants with straw or bracken through the winter.

Varieties Summer, 'Greenmarket', 'Long Standing Round', 'New Zealand' (perpetual); autumn-winter, 'Long Standing Prickly', 'Sigmaleaf'.

Spinach Beet

This is also known as perpetual spinach and is hardy enough to stand through the average winter. Regular pulling of the leaves encourages further cropping.

Soil and site Spinach beet grows on most kinds of soil, but does best on ground that was manured for a previous crop. A sunny sheltered site, especially for an autumn sowing, is recommended, and it is essential that it is well-drained.

Sowing For a summer supply, sow seeds in April, in 2.5cm (1in) deep drills 40cm (16in) apart. As soon as the seedlings are large enough to handle, thin them to leave 20cm (8in) from plant to plant. Pick the leaves as they are ready as this will help the plants to produce more leaves. For a winter supply, make another sowing about mid-August.

Varieties are usually listed in catalogues as perpetual spinach or leaf beet.

Swedes

This root vegetable is grown like main crop turnips, but the roots, which are larger and sweeter, are in the ground over a long period.

Soil and site The best soil is one that has been well manured for a previous crop; fresh manure will make the roots fork. Acid soils should be limed to prevent club root disease.

Sowing Sow seeds thinly, early in May in the north and late May in the south, in drills 2.5cm (1in) deep and 45cm ($1\frac{1}{2}$ft) apart. When the seedlings are 2.5cm (1in) high, thin them to 25cm (10in) apart.

Storing Swedes can be left in the ground through winter and dug up as required for use. When there is danger of prolonged frost, dig up some roots and store them in boxes of sand in a cool, but frost-free shed.

Varieties 'Bronze Top', 'Chignecto', 'Purple Top'.

Sweet Corn

Maize or sugar corn need a hot summer for the cobs to ripen properly, and are best raised in the greenhouse to give them a good start.

Soil and site Sweet corn requires a deep, rich, well-drained soil that has been well manured either for a previous crop or several weeks before planting out. The position should be open and sunny, sheltered from prevailing winds.

Sowing Sow seeds in individual pots in the greenhouse in late March or early April and keep them at a temperature of 13°C (55°F). Harden the seedlings off in a cold frame in May and put them out in their permanent quarters in late May, setting them 37.5cm (15in) apart in rows 60cm (2ft) apart. It helps pollination if sweet corn is planted in square blocks rather than in long rows.

Seeds can also be sown in the open in May, two seeds being sown at each station and later thinned to the strongest seedling.

Water freely in dry periods; it is a good idea to mulch round the plants so as to conserve moisture. When the silky tassels at the top of the cobs turn brown, sweet corn should be ready for picking. Test for readiness by pulling the green sheath back and pressing a few of the pale yellow grains: they should ooze a thick liquid. Cut the cobs just before they are required.

Varieties 'Earliking', 'First of All', 'Kelvedon Glory', 'North Star', 'Sugar King'.

Tomatoes

In most part of Britain, tomatoes of good quality can be grown in the open if the right varieties are chosen and the season is warm and sunny. But in cold exposed areas and cool summers, better success is ensured by growing tomatoes under glass.

Soil The best soil for the successful growing of greenhouse tomatoes is fibrous loam, mixed with a little sharp sand, with leaf-mould and some well-decayed manure. Do not give too much soil at first; start the plants in small mounds of soil, well up near the light, and add further top dressings of peat as the roots grow and demand fresh compost. Many greenhouse tomatoes are also grown by ring culture in which the plants are set in bottomless pots of roofing felt and grown on a bed of aggregate. The new growbags – large plastic bags filled with peat-based compost and fertilizers – are also suitable for growing tomatoes, both in the greenhouse and in the open.

Sowing Sow seeds at weekly intervals through February and March, sowing 6mm ($\frac{1}{4}$in) deep and 5cm (2in) apart in pans covered with glass and paper and placed close to the glass in a warm greenhouse or moderately warm frame. (Night temperature 16°C (59°F); day temperature 21°C (70°F).) Shade from the strong sun till the seeds germinate. Seed sown in February should produce fruit in July. As soon as two true leaves appear on the seedlings prick them off singly into 7.5cm (3in) pots, a good half of the stem being buried in the soil. In a small greenhouse keep the young seedlings near the glass, to keep them short-jointed. As they grow move them on into larger pots, and in about 10 or 12 weeks they should be ready for planting out into borders, 45cm (1½ft) apart in the row, or into the final pots, some 25cm (10in) across. The first truss of bloom should be formed before the plants are finally planted out. Potting must be firm.

Cultivation under glass Generous watering is essential at every stage of growth, but avoid water-logging. Support each plant with a strong stake and tie the stem in as growth progresses. When the first flower truss has set, begin a weekly liquid feed with a proprietary tomato fertilizer. Pinch out all side shoots, only the flower trusses being allowed to break from the main stem. The plants should have the growing point of the main

Removing side shoots from tomato plants; these arise in the leaf axils and should be pinched off with the tips of the finger and thumb as soon as they are large enough

stem pinched out when nine flower trusses have set. Pollination can be aided by tapping the stakes gently to release the pollen. Although warmth is necessary, over-heating should be avoided. A night temperature of 13 to 16°C (55 to 59°F) and a day temperature of 18 to 21°C (65 to 70°F) are the extremes. Give ample ventilation. Seeds may also be sown in June and July to produce tomatoes through the winter.

Cultivation in the open For outdoor tomatoes sow seeds in March as for a greenhouse crop. When the young plants are about 20cm (8in) high harden them off in a cold frame and plant out in June. A medium loam is the most suitable soil, and good drainage is essential. The best situation for tomato plants is against a south wall fully exposed to the sun. For the first week or so protect the plants with cloches or inverted pots. Feed the plants weekly as for greenhouse tomatoes. Stop the side shoots by nipping them off in the leaf axils, and stop top growth by the first week in August. Keep the plants tied to stakes and restrict watering except during droughts.

If all the fruits have not ripened by the end of the season, cut them off and ripen them on a window-sill indoors or wrapped in newspaper in a drawer.

Varieties Greenhouse, 'Ailsa Craig', 'Alicante', 'Eurocross', 'Big Boy', 'Harbinger', 'Moneymaker'; outdoor, 'Ailsa Craig', 'Moneymaker', 'Outdoor Girl', 'Primatel', 'Sugarplum' (small, sweet fruits), 'The Amateur' (dwarf variety).

Turnips

Soil The most suitable soil for this vegetable is a sandy loam which has been deeply dug and well manured for a previous crop.

Sowing For early turnips, make successional sowings in the open in March, April and May, choosing varieties such as 'Golden Perfection', 'Purple Top Milan' and 'Snowball'. 'Jersey Navet' can be sown extra early under cloches or in frames, or later in the open for a main crop. Thin the plants to about 15cm (6in) apart as soon as possible. Turnips for autumn and winter use can be sown in an open situation in July, the varieties 'Golden Ball', 'Red Globe', 'Green Top White' and 'Manchester Market' being recommended.

Storing When frost sets in cover winter turnips with straw or leaves and leave in the ground. In the spring any roots left will send up a crop of young green shoots – turnip tops – which make a good green vegetable.

Watercress

This salad plant is best grown in a stream of pure running water with a good gritty bed, but will also crop well in a shallow trench or trough that can be kept permanently moist. Sow seeds thinly in boxes of compost in a cold greenhouse in April, prick them out into pots when large enough to handle, harden off in a cold frame and plant them out 15cm (6in) apart on the surface of the bed in May. Gradually admit water until the plants have become established. The watercress will be ready for cutting about July. Cut as soon as ready to encourage more shoots to grow, and snip off any flowering stems as they appear. Bronze and green-leaved varieties are available, the former with larger leaves, but the green type is the easiest to cultivate.

Sowing Guide to Vegetables

The following table shows which seeds should be sown during the various months of the year. Full cultural details will be found in the paragraphs on the particular plants.

Seed or Tubers	Jan.	Feb.	Mar.	Apr.	May	Jun.	Jul.	Aug.	Sept.	Oct.	Nov.	Dec.
Artichokes												
Chinese	–	–	*	–	–	–	–	–	–	–	–	–
Globe	–	–	–	*	–	–	–	–	–	–	–	–
Jerusalem	–	–	*	–	–	–	–	–	–	–	–	–
Asparagus	–	–	–	*	–	–	–	–	–	–	–	–
Aubergines	–	*	–	–	–	–	–	–	–	–	–	–
Beans												
Broad	–	*	*	*	*	–	–	–	–	*	*	–
French or Kidney	–	–	–	*	*	*	–	–	–	–	–	–
Haricot	–	–	–	*	–	–	–	–	–	–	–	–
Runner	–	–	–	–	*	*	–	–	–	–	–	–
Beetroot	–	–	–	*	*	–	–	–	–	–	–	–
Broccoli	–	–	*	*	*	–	–	–	–	–	–	–
Brussels Sprouts	–	*	*	–	–	–	–	–	–	–	–	–
Cabbages	*	*	*	*	*	*	–	*	–	–	–	–
Cardoons	–	–	–	*	–	*	–	–	–	–	–	–
Carrots	–	–	*	*	*	–	–	*	–	–	–	–
Cauliflower	*	*	–	*	–	–	–	*	–	–	–	–
Celeriac	–	*	–	–	–	–	–	–	–	–	–	–
Celery	–	*	*	–	–	–	–	–	–	–	–	–
Chicory	–	–	–	*	*	–	–	–	–	–	–	–
Corn salad	–	–	–	–	–	–	–	*	*	–	–	–
Cucumbers	–	*	*	–	–	–	–	–	–	–	–	–
Dandelions	–	–	*	*	*	*	–	–	–	–	–	–
Endives	–	–	–	–	*	*	*	–	–	–	–	–
Kale	–	–	*	*	*	–	–	–	*	–	–	–
Kohl-rabi	–	–	*	–	–	–	*	–	–	–	–	–
Leeks	–	*	*	–	–	–	–	–	–	–	–	–
Lettuces	*	*	*	*	*	–	–	*	*	*	–	–
Marrows and Courgettes	–	–	–	*	*	–	–	–	–	–	–	–
Mushrooms	*	*	*	*	*	*	*	*	*	*	*	*
Mustard and Cress	*	*	*	*	*	*	*	*	*	*	*	*
Onions	*	*	*	–	–	–	*	*	*	–	–	–
Parsnips	–	*	*	*	–	–	–	–	–	–	–	–
Peas	–	*	*	*	*	*	–	–	–	–	–	–
Potatoes	–	*	*	*	–	–	–	–	–	–	–	–
Radishes	*	*	*	*	*	*	*	*	*	*	*	*
Rhubarb	–	*	*	*	–	–	–	–	–	–	–	–
Salsify	–	–	–	*	–	–	–	–	–	–	–	–
Seakale	–	–	*	*	–	–	–	–	–	–	–	–
Shallots	–	*	*	–	–	–	–	–	–	–	–	–
Spinach	–	–	*	*	*	*	*	*	*	–	–	–
Spinach Beet	–	–	–	*	–	–	–	*	–	–	–	–
Swedes	–	–	–	–	*	–	–	–	–	–	–	–
Sweet corn	–	–	*	*	*	–	–	–	–	–	–	–
Tomatoes	–	*	*	–	–	–	–	–	–	–	–	–
Turnips	–	–	*	*	*	*	*	*	–	–	–	–
Watercress	–	–	–	*	–	–	–	–	–	–	–	–

* Shows when to sow or plant.

Crop Rotation at a Glance

The table overleaf shows which crops a certain vegetable may follow and which it may *not* follow. It also shows which crops a vegetable may be followed by and the crops that should not come after it.

Principal crop	Crops it may follow	Crops it may not follow	Crops it may be followed by	Crops it may not be followed by	Catch-crops which may be planted between rows
Beans	Asparagus, broccoli, cabbages, kale, turnips, parsnips, carrots, potatoes	Leguminous plants of its own family, ie, peas, etc	Beet, carrots, celery, leeks, lettuces, parsnips, salsify, turnips, and any of the cabbage group	Leguminous plants of its own family, ie, peas, etc	Brussels sprouts, kale
Beet	Cabbage family, and any crops but those specified in next column	Spinach, turnips, parsnips, carrots, salsify, and scorzonera	Peas, beans, cabbages, cauliflowers, lettuces, onions, and any spring-sown crop except those in next column	Spinach, turnips, parsnips, and carrots	—
Brussels Sprouts and Kale	Peas, beans, lettuces, potatoes	Cruciferous plants of own order, ie, any of cabbage family, turnips, etc	Peas, beans, beet, carrots, parsnips, onions, potatoes, French beans, celery, salsify, leeks, lettuces, endive, spinach	Cruciferous plants of own order, ie, any of cabbage family, turnips, etc	Beans
Broccoli	Peas, beans, French beans	Cruciferous plants of own family	Any crop to be sown or planted when cleared off	Cruciferous plants of own family	—
Cabbages	Peas, beans, French beans, potatoes, lettuces, onions, leeks, celery, etc	Cruciferous plants of own family	Peas, beans, French beans, potatoes, lettuces, carrots, parsnips, beet, salsify, celery, seakale, onions, leeks, radishes, endive, shallots, etc	Cruciferous plants of own family	—
Carrots and Parsnips	Cabbage family, and any crops except those in next column	Any crops except root crops and umbelliferous plants	Any crops except those in next column	Any crops except root crops and umbelliferous plants	
Cauliflower	Peas, beans, potatoes, celery, French beans, onions, carrots, lettuces, beet	Cruciferous plants of own family	Peas, beans, potatoes, celery, onions, carrots, leeks, salsify, endive, lettuces, beet, parsnips	Cruciferous plants of own family	Spinach, lettuces, endive
Celery	Any crop except those in next column	Parsnips, carrots, parsley	Peas, beans, French beans, onions, potatoes, turnips, and any of the cabbage family	Parsnips, carrots, parsley	Lettuces, endive, dwarf early peas, French beans
Endive and Lettuce	Asparagus, potatoes, peas, beans, and any of the cabbage family	Chicory, salsify, scorzonera, artichokes, cardoons, and any plants of the family *Compositae*	Peas, beans, potatoes	Chicory, salsify, scorzonera, artichokes, cardoons, and any plants of the family *Compositae*	—
French Beans and Peas	Potatoes, carrots, parsnips, turnips, broccoli, and any of the cabbage family	Beans, and leguminous plants of own family	Broccoli, cabbages of any kind, spinach, turnips, potatoes, celery, parsnips, beet, salsify, onions, leeks, lettuces, endive, shallots	Beans and leguminous plants of own family	Summer spinach, radishes, lettuces, broccoli, turnips, early carrots, kale, and Brussels sprouts between dwarf sorts
Leeks, Onions, Shallots, etc	Cabbage family, celery, potatoes, peas, beans, lettuces, endive, spinach	Garlic, chives, and any crop of the onion family	Cabbages, carrots, celery, cauliflower, parsnips, potatoes, peas, beans, beet	Garlic, chives, and any crop of the onion family	—

Principal crop	Crops it may follow	Crops it may not follow	Crops it may be followed by	Crops it may not be followed by	Catch-crops which may be planted between rows
Potatoes	Any crop except those specified in the next column	Carrots, parsnips, beet, salsify, scorzonera	Any crop requiring a loose, clean, well-worked soil, and all cruciferous plants, peas, beans, etc	Root crops generally, such as carrots, parsnips, beet, etc	Brussels sprouts, cabbages, broccoli, and late celery if there is space enough for trench
Seakale	Potatoes, peas, beans, carrots, parsnips, beet, celery, etc	Cruciferous plants of own family	Potatoes, peas, beans, carrots, parsnips, beet, celery, etc	Cruciferous plants of own family	—
Spinach	Peas, beans, cabbages, cauliflower, lettuces, etc	Beet	Peas, beans, cabbages, cauliflower, lettuces, etc	Beet	—
Turnips and Swedes	Potatoes, spinach, peas, beans, lettuces, etc	Cruciferous plants of own family	Potatoes, spinach, peas, beans, lettuces, beet, carrots, parsnips	Cruciferous plants of own family	—

Note – *Cruciferae* – cabbage, cauliflower, broccoli, turnip, radish, cress, seakale, mustard, horseradish; *Leguminosae* – Peas, beans; *Umbelliferae* – Carrot, parsnip, parsley, celery, fennel;*Compositae* – Globe artichoke, Jerusalem artichoke, scorzonera, salsify, endive, lettuce, chicory.

Herbs

Angelica

A short-lived perennial, angelica may grow to 3m (10ft) high. It needs a rich, deep, well-manured soil, in full sun or light shade.It is raised from seeds sown in shallow drills in the open in August or March. Thin the seedlings as soon as they can be handled and transfer them to their permanent quarters, about 37.5cm (15in) apart. The young stems are candied and used for cake and dessert decoration.

Balm

Also known as lemon balm from the aroma of the leaves, balm is a perennial herb that will thrive in any ordinary soil and in sun or light shade. The leaves are used in salads, sauces and omelettes and in wine cups and cool summer drinks. Plant in autumn or spring, 45cm (1½ft) apart, and propagate by division of the roots in autumn.

Basil

This half-hardy annual herb is much used to flavour tomato and egg dishes and delicate white sauces. Sow seeds under glass in March and transplant the seedlings in late May, setting them 30cm (1ft) apart in good, rich soil and a sunny sheltered situation.

Bay

Bay is an invaluable herb in *bouquets garnis* and as a flavouring of any kind of savoury dishes as well as milk puddings. It is an evergreen shrub that can be trained and clipped into mop-headed standard trees, often grown in deep tubs. In open ground, bay needs ordinary, but well-drained soil and shelter from north and east winds. Plant in the autumn or spring and propagate by cuttings in late summer.

Borage

This is a good plant for bee-keepers; the young leaves are used to flavour claret cups and salads and the candied flowers for cake decorations. An annual, it grows in any good, ordinary soil, and should be sown in March or April, in shallow drills; thin the seedlings to 30cm (12in) apart.

Caraway

Grown mainly for its seeds, caraway is an annual that requires rich, deep soil and sun. Sow seeds in March or April, thinning the seedlings to 30cm (1ft) apart. The young leaves may be used in salads; the pungent seeds, borne in umbels, are harvested in late summer, dried and used in breads and cakes, cheese and vegetable dishes.

Chervil

Chervil repays careful cultivation, deep digging, and moderately enriched soil. In the warmer parts of the country seeds may be sown early in September in a warm, dry situation; thin the seedlings to about 20cm (8in) apart. This crop will need protection when the nights are frosty. In other parts of the country, sow seeds in shallow drills in succession from March to August. An annual, chervil leaves are used to flavour soups, sauces and egg dishes.

Chives

Chives are of the onion family, and its shoots are used in soups and salads, sauces, omelettes and for garnish. It likes a good garden soil, and is propagated by division in March or October every three years. The plants should be in rows 30cm (1ft) apart, with 15cm (6in) between the plants. Seed may be sown in the open in April. Remove all flower heads as they appear. The stems die down in the autumn and appear again early in the spring.

Coriander

An annual herb that is raised from seeds sown in the open in April and thinned to 15cm (6in) apart. Coriander needs a light, but rich and well-drained soil in an open and sunny situation. The seeds are gathered in late summer, dried and stored for use in curries, milk puddings and mixed into cream cheese.

Dill

This resembles fennel with its fine ferny leaves and graceful habit. It is an annual herb, and both the leaves and the dried seeds are used to impart an aniseed flavour to salads, fish and egg dishes and vinegars. Sow seeds in March in shallow drills in rich, moisture-retentive soil in a sunny situation. Thin the seedlings to 30cm (12in) apart.

Fennel
Fennel is a perennial herb, it likes a rich soil, and is best propagated by seed. Sow in April in drills 2.5cm (1in) deep; when the plants are about 7.5cm (3in) high, thin them to a distance of 60cm (2ft). Root division may be done in March, but they are slow to become established. Use the leaves to flavour fish dishes and sauces, salads and salad dressings. The dried seeds are used to flavour vinegars and pickling liquids.

Garlic
Belonging to the onion family, garlic is used to flavour a wide variety of savoury dishes. Plant the small bulblets or cloves just beneath the soil surface, about 15 to 20cm (6 to 8in) apart in late February or March. Garlic needs a light, fertile soil in full sun. Remove the flower buds as soon as they appear.

Horseradish
Horseradish is grown for its long edible and pungent roots; once established the roots are difficult to eradicate from the soil, and for this reason horseradish is best grown as an annual. It thrives in well-drained but moist soil that has been deeply dug and manured for a previous crop; fresh manure will make the tap roots fork. In early spring plant out young roots or thongs; they are usually about 30cm (1ft) long and should be inserted in deep holes with the tops 5cm (2in) below the soil surface. Allow 30cm (1ft) between the roots and 45cm (1½ft) if more than one row is planted. Dig up the roots as required for use, and in November lift the remainder and store in boxes of sand in a frost-free place. The smaller roots can be used for planting out the following March.

Marjoram
Marjoram likes a sunny spot and good soil. There are two kinds, sweet marjoram, which is the most common kind, an annual, which is raised from seed sown in gentle heat in March and planted out in May 22.5 to 30cm (9 to 12in) from plant to plant. Pot marjoram, which is a hardy, more bitter perennial, is raised from seed in the same way or increased by root division. Both kinds can also be sown out of doors in April and later thinned as above. The pot marjoram needs a dry soil and a warm position, or a cold winter may injure it. The leaves of both, fresh or dried, are used to flavour stuffings for meat and poultry, soups, stews and tomato dishes.

Mint

Mint will do well in a not too sunny corner of the garden, though not in full shade. It is a perennial herb and spreads rapidly through underground runners. For this reason it is advisable to confine the roots by sinking slates round them or growing them in a bottomless zinc bucket sunk in the ground. It needs a moist soil. The young leaves are used fresh to flavour young vegetables, in sauces, jellies and chutneys and in long cool summer drinks.

Parsley

Parsley requires light, rich, deeply dug loam that is well-drained, in sun or light shade. Make two sowings, one for the summer crop, sown in April, the other for winter and spring, sown in July. Sow thinly in drills 2.5cm (1in) deep. Not until about seven or eight weeks after sowing will the seed begin to show above ground, when it must be carefully weeded and well watered. Thin out the seedlings when large enough to handle to 22.5cm (9in) apart. Any flower-buds should be nipped off. The crop for winter use can be picked closely in September when a fresh crop of leaves will shoot up. If a frame is available, plants can be transferred to it in August or September, about 12.5cm (5in) apart; cover the frame with matting in frosty weather. Parsley runs to seed in the second year, and it is therefore necessary to make annual sowings.

Rosemary

This highly aromatic, evergreen shrub has narrow green and white leaves; small sprigs are used to flavour roast lamb and pork, game and fish dishes. It bears pale blue flowers in early spring. Rosemary thrives in most ordinary soils, but needs a sunny and sheltered position. It is propagated by cuttings in April and planted out, 60 to 90cm (2 to 3ft) apart, in September or the following spring.

Sage

The grey-green woolly leaves of this evergreen shrub are used mainly in stuffings for meat and poultry and to flavour sausage meat. Sage needs a well-drained soil in an open sunny situation. It can be raised from seed, sown under glass, the seedlings being planted out when well-grown, 37.5cm (15in) apart. It can also be propagated by cuttings in late summer.

Savory

There are two kinds, summer savory which is an annual, and winter savory which is a perennial. The leaves of both are slightly bitter, winter savory more so, and should be used young, to flavour salads and soups, egg dishes and vegetables. Savory likes a rich but not too heavy soil. Sow summer savory in April and thin the seedlings 22.5cm (9in) apart. Winter savory may be raised in the same way, or old plants may be divided and replanted in March.

Sorrel

A perennial herb grown for its bitter young leaves which are used fresh in salads or to flavour soups and stews; they can also be cooked like spinach. Sorrel needs a deep, rich and moist soil in a sunny situation. It can be raised from seeds sown in the open in drills in March and thinned to a distance of 15cm (6in) apart. Propagation can also be by division of the roots in the spring.

Tarragon

This perennial herb is not always fully hardy in cold districts; it is often cut by strong frosts but usually springs again from the base. The aromatic leaves are used to flavour egg, fish and chicken dishes, in sauces, butters and vinegars. Tarragon requires a deep, rich soil well enriched with manure, and sun and shelter. Set small plants 7.5cm (3in) deep with a distance of 45cm (1½ft) between the plants. Cut the stems down in autumn and cover the crowns with a winter mulch of weathered ashes, leaves or bracken. The plants are propagated by division of the roots in spring.

Thyme

A spreading low shrub with highly aromatic foliage, thyme thrives in any well-drained, rich soil and in full sun. The leaves are used in *bouquets garnis*, to flavour roasts of meat, stuffings, egg dishes, soups and fish. Thyme can be raised from seeds or planted out from rooted cuttings in the spring or autumn. Thin the seedlings or set the young plants out 30cm (1ft) apart. Though shrubby, thyme is short-lived and should be replaced every three years; propagation can also be by division of the roots in March.

14
The Fruit Garden

Somehow a garden does not seem complete without some fruit trees – even if they are only grown for shade. Unfortunately pests and diseases attack a number of fruits, but the newer spray materials are effective enough to give reasonable control of the few serious troubles while the others cause only superficial damage. The satisfaction of having really fresh fruit straight from the garden makes it easy to overlook a small pimple, or a patch of russet, which, while it may mar the beauty of the fruit, in no way impairs its flavour or dietetic value.

Situation

It is generally unwise to attempt to grow apricots, figs, grapes, peaches or nuts in a cold climate, but all the fruits dealt with here can be grown in the open anywhere in a temperate situation with a reasonable chance of success. For apples and pears the ideal conditions are found where there is enough sun to give good colour to the fruit and to ripen the young wood at the end of the year, which is necessary to ensure a crop the following season. In colder situations only in good season will these conditions prevail and crops will consequently be rather uncertain, though this can be overcome to some extent by choosing particular varieties. In areas with a high humidity and consequent favourable conditions for the fungus causing scab, it is more difficult to produce clear-skinned fruit, but intrinsically the fruit is just as good, and the milder conditions prevailing have compensating advantages.

Local conditions As far as local conditions are concerned, the best position is one fully open to the sun and air, and preferably part-way up a slight slope facing south or west. The position must not be too exposed however. It is difficult to get well-shaped trees or bushes in such a position, but what is much worse is that bees are very loth to fly in districts in which strong winds persist during flowering time, and without bees there may be no pollination and hence no crop. If shelter is not already provided it is best to get it established before the trees are planted. Gooseberries and red currants are particularly liable to have branches blown out by strong winds. Even worse than high exposed positions are those which are known as frost-holes, or frost-pockets.

These are low-lying places into which cold air drains from adjoining higher land, and which are consequently liable to early and late frosts. The greater the area of higher land which is feeding the frost-pocket with cold air, the more severe will the effect be, the worst position of all being where the garden forms the centre of a bowl, with the cold air coming in from all directions. In such a position it is best not to attempt fruit growing. In other positions it is sometimes possible to drain the cold air still lower, away from the fruit, by removing a hedge or other obstruction that is holding it up. In a 'frost-bowl' nothing can be done. In some seasons trees in a frost-pocket will bear no crop at all up to a sharply defined level, above which there may be a full crop, the dividing line being the height to which the frost rises at flowering time. Thus the lower-growing the plant, the more liable it is to be damaged, with strawberries the most susceptible.

Soils for fruit

Most fruits grow best on a slightly acid soil, one with a pH of 5.5 to 6.5, but the topsoil is not the most important factor where fruit growing is concerned. A good deep but well-drained subsoil is more important. For tree fruits, particularly apples, good drainage is essential and if water lies for any time within 5 or 7.5cm (2 or 3in) of the surface, the trees will suffer. If the subsoil is shallow, as often happens on chalk or gravel, it is difficult to grow fruit satisfactorily, because the roots quickly dry out. Chalk has the added disadvantage of making the iron in the soil unavailable to plants, which results in pale sickly foliage and poor crops, and it is best not to attempt bush fruits or strawberries on really chalky soils. Given a good subsoil, the topsoil can be heavy clay or light sand, as long as the trees or bushes receive the appropriate treatment to enable them to cope with any topsoil shortcomings until their roots get down to the subsoil. Nevertheless, a good medium loam as a topsoil is an added advantage in getting the trees away to a good start, especially the shallow-rooting ones.

Forms of trees

Different varieties vary in vigour, and the degree of vigour can be even more markedly controlled by the rootstock on which the fruit tree is grafted. Particular attention should be given to selection of suitable rootstocks when choosing trees for individual sites. For details *see* individual fruits.

Trees or bushes can be trained into almost any shape, but the most common and practical are the cordon, which is the most restricted form, the espalier, the fan, the pyramid and the bush, which are all of medium size, and the standard and half-standard which form the largest trees.

Cordons A cordon consists of a single stem with fruiting spurs along its

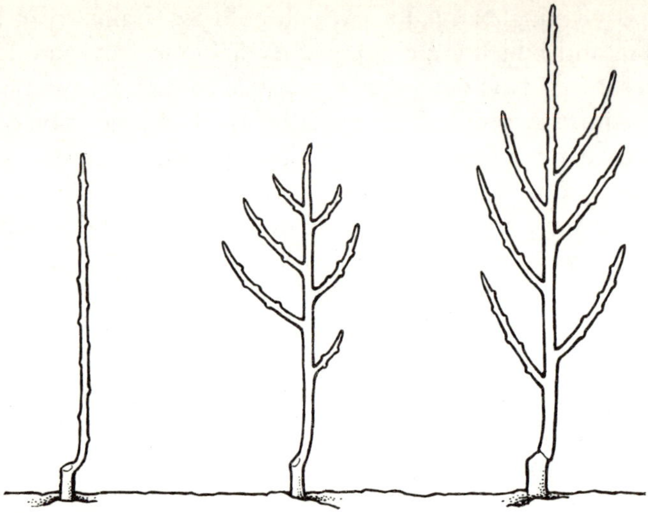

Types of young fruit trees. *Left:* a maiden
Centre: a feathered maiden *Right:* a two-year whip growth

whole length. It may be grown vertically, horizontally, or at any angle, but is generally most successful at an angle of 45°, as that ensures regular growth along its whole length. Cordons by their very nature need a permanent support of wire trellis, fence or wall.

Espaliers An espalier is in effect a tree bearing a number of cordons. It can consist of a central vertical stem with the side branches trained horizontally, or the main stem can be stopped about 30cm (1ft) from the ground and two or more branches taken up vertically. This latter form was previously known as a multiple cordon. The espalier needs similar support to a cordon, though usually of a more substantial nature as it makes a bigger tree. It is not a form suitable for stone fruits.

Fans In this form the branches, of roughly equal vigour, radiate fanwise from a main stem stopped about 30cm (1ft) above ground level. It is most suitable for stone fruits, red currants and gooseberries.

Pyramids These can be grown on a stock which gives small trees of about 1.5m (5ft) high, known as dwarf pyramids, or on a stronger stock giving trees up to 2.7m (9ft) high. In both cases the main stem continues to its full height, the branches radiating from it getting shorter towards the top. It is a good type of tree for producing high-quality fruit, since all parts get adequate sunlight and air.

Open-centred trees The open-centred bush tree is formed of a single main stem to a height of 60 to 90cm (2 to 3ft), above which point three or four main branches spread out to form the framework of a cup-shaped tree with no central stem. The standard tree is like a bush, except that the main unbranched stem is continued to a height of from 1.5 to 2.1m (5 to 7ft), while a half-standard has a stem height of about 1.2m (4ft).

Planning the fruit garden

The first thing to decide is which fruits are to be grown, and this will largely be a matter of personal preference within the limitations of the site. In most cases it is best to decide first which berry fruits are to be included, as their vigour is not complicated by the use of rootstocks, and the space that they will need can be easily reckoned. Then the tree-fruit requirements can be adjusted to the remaining available space by choosing the appropriate form of tree on the most suitable rootstock. Most gardeners like to include strawberries, gooseberries and loganberries and black currants, but raspberries are often excluded. There is only a limited use for red and white currants, so that generally one or two bushes are enough.

The distances between fruit trees and bushes vary and it is best to get this information from your nurseryman. Make sure you buy the right number of plants to fill the space allocated. When the bushes and trees are first put in at the correct distances they look very isolated, but they will quickly fill the space and will benefit from having sufficient room in which to develop freely. Even if there is adequate room for the larger type of tree, it may be felt that a greater number of smaller trees such as cordons or dwarf pyramids will be preferable, in view of the fact that they come into fruit slightly earlier in their life and that they are more likely to produce top-quality fruit. Remember though, that the initial expense of a large number of trees may be considerable, and that they must have regular attention.

The more vigorous bush or standard trees, once they have been formed to a reasonable shape, will survive a good deal of later neglect and come to little harm, but if cordons or dwarf pyramids are neglected they quickly get out of hand. So the amount of time which is likely to be available to look after them will have to be taken into consideration. Nevertheless, with the advantages that these smaller trees have, it is well worth while utilizing existing fences, walls, or other supports for cordons, and for having a few dwarf pyramids as a special interest.

Pollination With tree fruits it is advisable to have at least two varieties of each sort, flowering at the same time, so that cross-pollination can take place. This is because many varieties, especially of pears and plums, are self-sterile; that is, they will not set fruit with their own pollen. In some cases the neighbour's trees will serve as pollinators, but it is best to be sure and to plant one's own.

Birds It is unwise to plant cherries in the open in a built-up area, because it is unlikely that the birds will leave any to be picked. The only way to ensure a crop is to have them on a wall and net them when they start to colour. Even with soft fruits birds will take their share and in some districts a fruit cage is the only solution, in which case all the fruits to be netted must be arranged in as compact an area as possible to keep the cost of netting to a minimum. The cage is best formed of a permanent side framework of metal or wood, covered with 1cm (½in) wire mesh or nylon netting, the top being covered at fruiting time with fish netting. Wire netting over the top often causes injury to the plants through a fine deposit of zinc being washed down by rain, or if left in position in the winter may collapse under heavy snow and even bring the whole structure down. For the strawberry bed 38mm (1½in) square posts, driven in at intervals with 60cm (2ft) out of the ground, and with strong wire stretched in each direction from their tops, gives a framework on which to rest fish netting for the fruiting season.

Layout Do not combine fruit with vegetables, except possibly in the case of strawberries. Fruit needs quite different cultural and manurial treatment as well as specific spraying for disease control so that it is impracticable to combine the two successfully. If possible, fruits requiring the same manures should be put together. Dessert apples, gooseberries and strawberries want only limited amounts of nitrogen, whereas cooking apples, plums and bush and cane fruits want more, and black currants will take large amounts. Raspberries, blackberries and gooseberries will tolerate moderate shade.

Selection of trees

There are three main points to bear in mind in choosing fruit trees. They should be as young as is practicable, have good root systems and, except in the case of maidens, a good skeleton framework of branches. In general terms, the younger a plant is, the better it will stand transplanting. For trees, the ideal would be to buy them as maidens, that is one year old from budding and consisting of a single stem. Some amateurs, however, may prefer to let the nurseryman get the first main branches established, as he will be able to get them well-positioned, and this will mean that the tree will be two or three years old when bought. The shape of the mature tree will depend on the positioning of its main branches, and while the branches must be sturdy, they need not be imposingly large; a good root system will soon put extra vigour into them. Old thick-stemmed trees that are really the nurseryman's discards should be avoided. Bush fruit should be bought as two-year-old bushes, except that raspberries will be one-year-old canes and strawberries will be newly-rooted runners. As with all plants, the root system should be adequate with a good supply of fine fibrous roots. A tree with a fat stem-base, with thick fangs in place of roots, should go straight back to the seller or on to the bonfire.

Tree planting and staking

For general information on care and planting of new trees, *see* Ch. 6. In planting grafted trees, take out the hole to such a depth that the

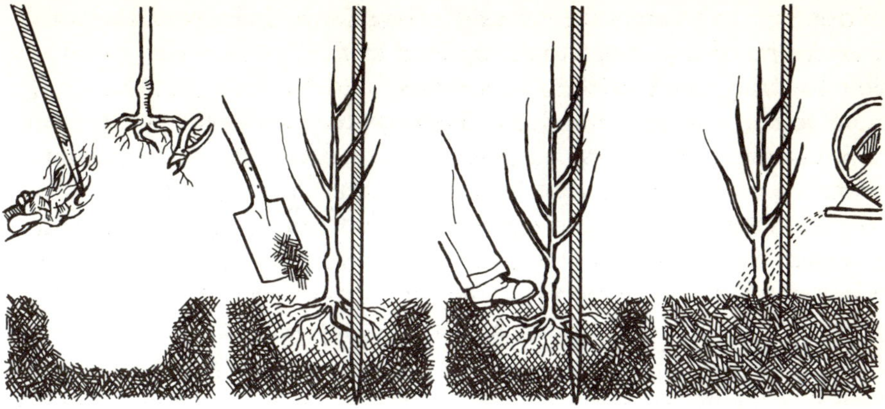

Planting a fruit tree. Note that the stake is singed to prevent the wood rotting. Ensure that the point of union with the rootstock is above ground and that the tree is planted firmly.

union between stock and scion will be 15cm (6in) above ground level when filled in completely. *Oblique cordons* should be planted at the angle at which they are to be trained, and with the scion on the upper side to avoid breaking at the union. *Pyramid trees* worked on very dwarfed stocks will need support all their lives. The best thing is to plant such trees in rows, so that support can be given them by two wires, at about 45 and 90cm ($1\frac{1}{2}$ and 3ft) from the ground, stretched between stout posts.

For *cordons* a strong wire fence is needed, with posts at 3 to 3.6m (10 to 12ft) intervals, and with stronger posts with straining bolts at the end to keep the wires taut. It is well worth making a good job of this right at the start. The trees are usually taken to 1.8m (6ft) high, and the posts should be the same height. It is best to have three wires, with the bottom one 90cm (3ft) from the ground, using gauge 10 for the top wire, but slightly thinner gauge for the lower wires. In the early stages at any rate it is best to fix strong bamboo canes to the wires by wiring, or tying with strong string, in the positions the trees are to occupy. The trees can then be tied to the canes with soft twine, which will not cut into the bark.

Where trees are to be grown against walls, fit the wires at least 10cm (4in) from the walls.

Management of tree fruits

Manuring With trees planted in a reasonably fertile soil, no additional manure should be needed for at least a season, though a mulch over the root area will keep the soil cool and moist, and will help root action. An annual dressing of sulphate of potash at 25g (1oz) per sq m (yd) and half that amount of superphosphate, is generally beneficial. If the leaves turn bluish-green towards autumn, with scorched edges, then more potash is needed, while if they take on bright autumn tints of reddish purple, extra phosphate should be given. The amount of nitrogen to be applied will be decided by the vigour of the trees. Sufficient is needed to maintain active growth, but not so much that the wood formed is excessive or remains soft and unripened by the autumn. It should not be applied later than June. It will only be on poor soils that nitrogen will be needed at all in the first two or three years, but when the tree has settled down and is cropping, a dressing of sulphate of ammonia at 25g (1oz) per sq m (yd) or its equivalent, in spring and repeated two months later, will be about the amount required.

Spraying Control of specific pests and diseases is dealt with in Ch. 9. It is, however, possible to anticipate some of these troubles or to take them in one's stride, if a regular spraying programme is carried out. The following table sets out such a programme.

Stage of growth	**Month**	**Treatment**	**Troubles dealt with**
Dormant	Dec.–Jan.	Tar-oil wash or DNOC/petroleum	Aphid, apple-sucker, and generally cleans up trees
Pink bud	Late Apr.	BHC, malathion or dimethoate	Blossom weevil and winter moth caterpillar
Petal fall	Late May	Lime-sulphur+ malathion, fenitrothion or malathion	Mildew, aphid, red spider, and apple sawfly

In addition, monthly sprays with either malathion or fenitrothion are likely to be needed to keep down aphids coming in from surrounding gardens, and in humid areas these should have lime-sulphur or other fungicide added to control scab.

Fruit-thinning In a good fruit year, much more fruit is set than the trees can hope to develop to a good size, and under those conditions some thinning should be done in addition to the natural fruit drop. It should be deferred until mid-July, as in the first half of that month trees often shed some fruits naturally, and if thinned before that a short crop can easily result. Young developing trees often set fruit which takes nourishment needed to build up the tree framework, and most of these fruits should be removed early.

Frost prevention While fruit trees generally are quite hardy, the flowers can be killed by slight air frost of even short duration. Snap frosts occurring at flowering time can often be countered by temporary protection. Such frosts almost always occur under still windless conditions, and newspaper, muslin, old curtains, or similar material laid over the plants will generally stay in position till the frost is past. It may look untidy for a few hours, but the benefit is reaped later in the season. Where blossoms are only slightly frozen they can sometimes be saved by

This patio has been made into a complete outdoor room

If an outdoor paved area is constructed with partial walls and roof, a wide variety of quite tender plants can be grown, especially climbers covering them from the early morning sun, as it is the quick thawing which does most damage.

Training and pruning trees

Pruning is not an exact operation and it is impossible to lay down hard and fast rules for it. Varieties differ in their habit of growth; rootstocks affect the type of growth as well as the vigour; soil and weather have their effects, and pruning has to be adjusted to meet these variations. It is therefore only possible to state the general principles leaving the rest to the discretion of the gardener. The expert pruner does not blindly concern himself with making a tree conform to a given shape. If a tree tends to grow away from the shape he had in mind for it, he will adjust his ideas to what he thinks is best for that individual tree.

The usual forms of young, trained fruit trees as supplied by nurseries. From left to right these are standard, half standard, dwarf standard, bush and dwarf pyramid

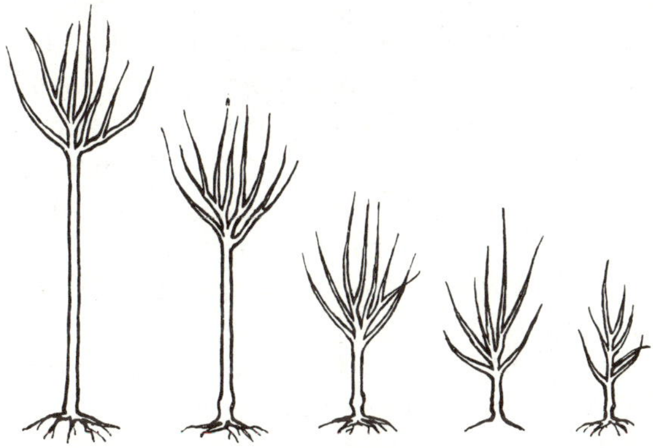

There are two stages in pruning. The first is the formation of a sound basic framework for the tree, generally with a definite shape in mind. The second is the maintenance of balanced growth which will result in ample fruit buds and adequate wood growth, with the branches spaced wide enough to let the sun and air get in so as to keep the tree healthy and to ripen the fruit.

Cordons For cordons choose maiden trees, though they may or may not have small lateral branches. If they do not reach their full length in one season, continue the main stem for a second year. If the main stem bears a fruit bud at the end, cut this back to a wood bud in the winter; if the main stem is weak cut back one third of its length to induce greater vigour in a continuation shoot. Later on, to hasten the formation of fruit buds, carry out summer pruning. This involves cutting back all the firm, mature, lateral shoots to three or four leaves, not counting any in the rosette of leaves at the base, in early July in the south, and about fourteen days later in the north. Smaller shoots coming out from the lateral shoots should be cut back to one bud, and any soft immature shoots should be left until

September when they should be treated similarly. This concentrates the nourishment into the buds at the base of the shoot, and hastens their formation into fruit buds; this may take two or more years, during which time any laterals should be pruned to one or two buds. Spurs may carry two or more fruit buds in young trees, and many more in older trees; these may need to be thinned, or even taken out altogether to prevent the over-crowding of the trees.

Espaliers For a horizontal espalier, cut a maiden back about 45cm (1½ft) from the ground in the winter. The top bud continues the main stem vertically and the lower two opposite buds form the first two horizontal branches. Train these branches at an angle of 45° during the growing season to induce stronger growth; the following winter train these down horizontally. Excessive growth of either shoot can be reduced by putting it at a lower angle, and lack of growth can be stimulated by raising the angle. Other laterals on the main stem which are not needed for branches should be stopped at three or four leaves, and secondary shoots at one leaf, later removing them altogether. Each tier is formed in the same way in successive years, and each branch is pruned as if it were a cordon. The 'U' espalier starts off in the same way as the horizontal except that no central stem is taken upright. The first two branches are, however, brought down to the horizontal when about 45cm (1½ft) long, and from that point trained vertically to form the two main arms, and are pruned as for cordons. Should they not send out sufficient laterals to form spurs, cut them back to induce the buds to break.

Fans These can be formed by planting out a maiden tree, and cutting it back to a good bud about 60cm (2ft) from the ground. Rub out all buds except the top three. The resulting top shoot is then pinched back to a few buds once or twice during the growing season to concentrate vigour into the two lower shoots, and then removed altogether the following winter. The two lower shoots should be trained at an angle of about 30° from the horizontal, using canes secured to the wires, and these form the two main arms of the fan from which the other shoots radiate. If one shoot is more vigorous than the other it can be checked by temporarily lowering it a little. The next winter cut back these two shoots one third to one half their length according to vigour, and then allow three strong and evenly spaced shoots to develop on the top side of each, and one on the underside, rubbing out all other buds. The following winter cut these branches back and select shoots from them, as was done with the two main branches the previous year. This is repeated each year until the allotted area is covered with the branches spaced about 30cm (1ft) apart.

Pyramids In the winter after planting cut a maiden tree back to a bud 60cm (2ft) from the ground, and cut back the resulting shoot the following winter to about half its length, but to a bud on the opposite side. Repeat each successive winter, to keep the central stem upright. Cut back lateral shoots which form the branches a third of their length if strong growing and to half their length if weaker. Laterals from these branches should be shortened to three or four buds and sub-laterals to one bud, or removed altogether if too crowded. On dwarf pyramids summer pruning can be done as with cordons. Once the tree has begun fruiting, less extension growth will be made and pruning will merely consist of keeping the branches well spaced.

Open-centred bush and standard trees The pruning of these trees is very simple. Cut the maiden stem to a bud at the required height, and select three or four of the resulting shoots to form the main branches. Those coming out at a wide angle are best, and for this reason the top one or two are often cut out, as they tend to be too upright. From then on pruning is aimed at building up a cup-shaped tree with well-spaced branches. Nothing in the way of detailed spur pruning need be attempted. Remember that hard pruning makes for more vigorous growth, so where weak shoots need to be urged to grow stronger, they should be cut back to a few buds, but where vigour needs to be reduced, only light cutting back should be done.

Root-pruning and bark-ringing Where trees are making excessive growth with few fruit buds, they can be checked by root-pruning. A young tree can be lifted and its main roots cut back, but with an older tree the work involves marking out a half circle at least 90cm (3ft) away from the trunk and digging a trench 60cm (2ft) deep and wide. Chop off the roots thus exposed and fill in the trench again. It is best to root-prune one side of the tree one winter and the other side the following year. The considerable amount of work involved can be avoided in the case of apples and pears by bark-ringing. This consists of taking out a ring of bark about 6mm ($\frac{1}{4}$in) wide half way round the trunk, about 15cm (6in) below the first branches. Make a similar cut about 7.5cm (3in) lower on the opposite side of the trunk, being careful to cut into the surface bark only. Ringing is best done at flowering time, when the bark will come away easily. Cover the cuts with adhesive tape to encourage healing.

Harvesting

Soft fruit should be gathered when it is cool and dry. The best time is as early as possible in the morning after the dew is off, but before the sun has sufficient power to warm the fruit. Plums, too, should be picked dry. With apples and pears it is not so important as long as they can be spread out to dry after picking, but even so, varieties for long storage are best picked dry. Pick all fruit carefully and handle it gently. Even hard fruit like apples bruise easily, and though no damage may be visible at the time, its keeping quality will be affected. In picking do not grip the fruit with the finger-tips, but let the palm of the hand take the weight, then lift the fruit until it comes away easily.

Cultivation of Fruits

Apples

Rootstocks All nurserymen specializing in fruit trees give a choice of rootstocks on which their trees are worked. Most of the apple stocks now in use were raised at the East Malling Research Station, and their numbers are prefixed with 'M', or where raised in conjunction with the John Innes Horticultural Institute, by 'MM'. The rootstock most suitable for the very restricted type of tree, the small cordon or the dwarf pyramid, is the M9. It brings them into bearing quicker than any other stock, but it has a restricted root system and the trees therefore have to be supported all their life. While M9 is useful for its specialist purpose, a slightly more vigorous rootstock, but one which gives a small enough tree to be grown as a cordon, small pyramid or bush in the average garden, is the one that most practical gardeners will be looking for. The best for this purpose is MM106, and it is particularly good on sandy soil. M26 is also very good, as it grows vigorously in its early years, but soon settles down to give good crops. For the larger bush tree with a 3.6 to 4.5m (12 to 15ft) spread, or for espaliers, the best stocks are MM106 and M2, in that order of vigour, though there is not a lot of difference between them. MM109 is a little more vigorous, and stands up to drought conditions better on a sandy soil.

For very vigorous trees, which will generally be trained as standards or half-standards, and planted 5.4 to 7.2m (18 to 24ft) apart, the best stocks are MM111 and M25.

Pollination Most varieties will pollinate any other variety, but 'Worcester Pearmain' is probably the most effective for the purpose. There are a few varieties which are of limited value as pollinators. These include: 'Bramley's Seedling', 'Belle de Boskoop', 'Ribston Pippin', 'Blenheim Orange', 'Warner's King'.

Other varieties, including 'Beauty of Bath', 'Crawley Beauty' and 'Edward VII', are of little use as pollinators because they flower later than most other varieties.

Varieties There are over 2,000 varieties of apple in the National Fruit Trials alone, so that there is no dearth of varieties from which to choose. The difficulty is making a short list of those varieties likely to give the best results in a particular situation. The following lists are an attempt to do this, though many varieties of merit have by necessity had to be left out. In choosing varieties account should be taken of any which do particularly well in the locality, even though they may not be included in the lists, for generally a moderately good variety will, if local conditions suit it, be equal to others more generally preferred. Thin apples in June, dessert varieties to 10cm (4in) apart, and cooking varieties to 20cm (8in) apart, after the natural fruit drop.

* = Varieties of special merit
S/T = Suitable for dwarf and trained trees
S/S = Self-sterile, needs a pollinator
N/S = Does well in colder, northern regions
B = Tends to biennial bearing, fruiting only in alternate years
F/R = Resistant to frost
C/G = Compact grower, particularly suitable for small gardens
B/A = Tree in blossom is particularly attractive

Cooking varieties

'Arthur Turner'* July–October. Good flavour and regular cropper. B/A.

'Bramley's Seedling'* November–March. Is the best keeping cooker and a heavy cropper if it misses frost damage, to which it is particularly subject. Is vigorous and spreading so requires little pruning. S/S, B.

'Early Victoria' July–August. A regular heavy cropper needing heavy thinning. Upright habit. Reasonably tolerant of heavy soils. N/S.

'Edward VII' December–April. Very good quality. Flowers late, so misses frost. Upright habit, C/G, S/S.

'George Neal'* September–October. An improvement on 'Grenadier'. Fruit large and crisp, and an excellent cooker. Regular cropper.

'Howgate Wonder' December–February. Large flat apple, striped, and regular cropper.

'Lane's Prince Albert'* November–April. Reliable cropper. Fruit soft so needs careful handling. Prune fairly hard. Rather liable to mildew, but sulphur must not be used on it after flowering. N/S, C/G.

'Monarch' December–April. Fruit soft, needs careful handling, but stores well. Regular cropper, needs thinning. N/S.

'Newton Wonder' December–March. Heavy cropper of excellent quality. Can be used for dessert late in season. Vigorous grower. B (strongly).

'Rev. W. Wilks' September–December. Bears very heavy crops. Cooks frothily. C/G.

Dessert varieties

'Advance'* August. Of better quality than the more usually grown 'Beauty of Bath', and only about a week later. Juicy, with a Cox's flavour. It has a good habit, but is not a heavy cropper. S/T, S/S.

'Blenheim Orange' November–January. Excellent flavour and appearance. Growth is vigorous, but crops are light in the early years. S/S.

'Charles Ross'* October. Large and attractive fruit of good quality. Thrives on chalkly loam. N/S.

'Cox's Orange Pippin' November–December. Unsurpassed quality.

Is a difficult variety to grow even in mild situations, and is only a moderate cropper. S/T, S/S. 'Crimson Cox' is inferior.

'Egremont Russet'* October–December. The best variety of russet apple. Fine flavour and a regular cropper. S/T, C/G.

'Ellison's Orange' Late September–October. Looks like a Cox but has an aniseed flavour. Has only a short season. An easy variety to grow and a regular cropper. N/S, S/T, F/R, B.

'Epicure' Late August–September. Good cropper of excellent flavour. Short season only. Spreading habit. S/S.

'Fortune'* September–October. Good quality and flavour, and moderately good cropper. Upright habit. N/S, S/T, S/S, B.

'James Grieve'* September–October. Very good flavour, but flesh tender so needs careful handling. Vigorous and upright, and easy to grow. N/S, S/T.

'Orleans Reinette'* November–February. A moderate cropper with fruit of excellent flavour, does not store well.

'Ribston Pippin' November–December. Regular cropper and of excellent flavour. B/A, S/S.

'Sturmer Pippin' December–May. The best very late keeper. Leave on the tree as long as possible. Does well on most soils.

'Sunset'* November–December. Good quality of Cox's flavour, but fruit sometimes rather dull in appearance. Strong upright grower. B/A, S/T, S/S.

'Superb' November–January. Good quality but rather dull appearance. Keeps well. Is rather an erratic cropper. Resistant to canker so suitable for heavier soils. Prune lightly. N/S, B.

'Winston' December–April. A heavy cropper of fair quality.

'Worcester Pearmain' September–October. Good colour and a regular cropper, but of moderate quality. Upright grower, tip bearing. N/S, F/R.

Apricots

The apricot will ripen only in favoured spots, and even there will need a south or west facing wall as it comes into flower early. The soil must be of open texture and preferably of a chalky nature. The general treatment is the same as for the peach, to which it is related. It differs in bearing fruit on spurs as well as on one- and two-year-old wood, and unwanted laterals should be cut back to two buds instead of being removed altogether. Fruit-thinning need be less drastic than with the peach, the fruits being left at about 10cm (4in) apart.

All varieties are self-fertile. While trees in good situations will crop heavily, they are usually short-lived, often succumbing to die-back disease for which there is no cure. The best variety is 'Moorpark'.

Blackberries and hybrid berries

The cultivated blackberries crop heavily and have much finer and larger fruits than the wild type, though not all varieties are of superior flavour. They will grow in any reasonable soil, preferring one with ample organic material, but tolerating even a very chalky one. They will grow in almost any position, so are suitable for the odd corners in light shade. If too shaded or too sunny, the fruit flavour will be poor. They are easily propagated by layering the tips of the new shoots in July, which can be severed from the parent plant and planted out the following spring. When planting mature plants cut the existing canes back to 15 to 22.5cm (6 to 9in) from the ground. The fruit is borne mainly on one-year-old wood, so pruning and training consists of cutting out old fruited canes and replacing them, fanwise, with the new shoots and removing any weak or surplus ones. Ample feeding is needed to maintain vigour, though 'Himalaya Giant' may be tamed a little by less generous treatment. Where trained to a wire trellis, erect three wires at 60cm, 1 and 1.5m (2, 3½ and 5ft) from the ground, though for 'Himalaya Giant' they will be better at 90cm, 1.3 and 1.8m (3, 4½ and 6ft). Plants of most varieties should be 1.8 to 2.4m (6 to 8ft) apart. To avoid cane spot, train the fruiting canes to one side in a fan and the new canes to the other side, so that the spores do not fall from the old canes on to the new. Alternatively, train the fruiting canes on the lower wires and the new canes straight up. The best varieties are: 'Himalaya Giant', very strong-growing, needing up to 4.5m (15ft) apart, with large fruit of only moderate flavour, and with vicious thorns, ripens July; 'Bedford Giant', ripens July; 'Oregon Thornless', late August, thornless canes.

A well-trained screen of blackberries; they should not be left to form a wild tangle

Loganberries

This is a hybrid, and is similar in growth habit to the blackberry, but has dark red, raspberry-like fruit of a more acid flavour. It is not so robust a grower, so sites exposed to severe frost or cold winds should be avoided. While it can be grown on a wide range of soils it does not like very chalky ones, or any of an extreme nature. Plant 2.4 to 3m (8 to 10ft) apart. To maintain good growth give an annual application of 25g (1oz) per sq m (yd) of a nitrogenous and potassic fertilizer and the same amount of superphosphate every third year. Pruning and training is the same as for blackberries. In addition to the ordinary type of loganberry, there is the 'Merton Thornless', which crops equally heavily.

Other hybrid berries include: 'Boysenberry', 'Youngberry' and 'Wineberry'. They need the same treatment as the above, but are generally inferior to them.

Black currants

Black currants are the most accommodating of the bush fruits and will thrive on most soils, though the best results are obtained on a deep loam that keeps moist during the summer. While they will not tolerate waterlogged conditions, they are less fastidious as to drainage than most fruits. They will also tolerate heavy dressings of farmyard manure which may be needed to enrich a poorer soil, and which would upset the balanced growth of other fruits. Indeed, they are such gross feeders that a good dressing of farmyard manure, worked into the soil before planting, is desirable on all but the most fertile land. They dislike acid conditions, so where these exist, give a good dressing of lime, though not at the same time as the manure. As black currants flower early in the year, they are particularly liable to injury from frost and cold winds, and suitable precautions must be taken against these.

Raising new bushes Propagation is by cuttings of mature shoots taken in October or November, all the buds being left on, as the more shoots coming from below ground the better. The following winter cut the resulting shoots back to one or two buds, or to ground level. A further year's growth will result in bushes with up to twelve shoots, and the next autumn they can be put in their fruiting positions, as bushes older than two years do not establish themselves well. Strong bushes can be planted out at one year, and will give equally good results. Plant deeply in order to get shoots from below ground, and cut down all shoots to ground level immediately after planting. There should be no suggestion of a 'leg' to the bush.

General care Black currants send out a lot of surface roots, so once the root system is formed, deep hoeing or cultivating should be avoided. If a good thick mulch of farmyard manure or peat can be given late each winter, it will keep down most of the weeds, and will go a long way to meet the plants' nutritional needs. Additional food should be given each year in the form of 50g (2oz) of nitrogenous fertilizer, 50g (2oz) of sulphate of potash, and 25g (1oz) of superphosphate per bush when growth has started in March or April, doubling the amount of nitrogen if no farmyard manure has been given.

Pruning After the initial cutting-down, all young shoots should be left intact, as it is on these that the fruit is borne. The only exception is with weak shoots, which should be cut hard back to induce stronger growth. If the bushes are growing well, little pruning will be needed for the first two or three years after planting, and after that, the aim should be to induce vigorous young shoots from as low down as possible by cutting out older dead branches. Some varieties tend to become straggly as they get older; remove straggling branches to obtain a more upright bush.

Varieties The following is a selection of good varieties.

'Boskoop Giant' The earliest, with large berries, but only a moderate cropper.

'Laxton's Giant' Almost as early as 'Boskoop', and has large exhibition berries. Not a heavy cropper.

'Wellington XXX' A good general-purpose variety, though of rather spreading habit. Second-early.

'Blacksmith' A good general-purpose variety, though it makes rather a large bush. Mid-season.

'Baldwin' Probably the best all-round variety, though it is the only 'temperamental' one, and will not thrive everywhere. A compact grower and regular cropper, though the berries are not impressively large. Rich in vitamin C. Mid-season.

'Raven' A regular heavy cropper, but makes a very big bush not suitable for small gardens. Mid-season.

'Westwick Choice' Very similar to 'Baldwin', and likely to succeed where that variety fails to do so.

'Amos Black' The latest fruiting. Upright grower. Moderate cropper.

Blueberries

While the blueberry is not a popular fruit it can be successfully grown in acid moist soil. The 'high bush' is the only suitable type, and good varieties are 'Berkley', 'Burlington' and 'Kengrape'. It needs an acid soil of pH 5.8 or below, and one that keeps moist even in the driest summers, but must also be well drained. A layer of peat at least 15cm (6in) thick, overlaying ordinary soil, is most likely to supply these requirements. It will not thrive on high exposed places but needs a position at a lower altitude. Cross-pollination is desirable, so at least two varieties should be grown. Precautions will have to be taken against birds, which are very fond of the fruit.

Cherries

Cherries, and especially sweet cherries, are not really suitable for growing in the open garden. In the form of tree needed for the open garden they take a long time to come into bearing, and even when they do start fruiting it is difficult to prevent the birds taking most of the crop. By purchasing wall-trained trees, they can be brought into fruit more quickly, and can also be netted against the birds, and the flowers covered to protect them from frost. Even so, it is generally unwise to attempt cherries on a wall lower than about 2.4m (8ft), as this would involve servere pruning to keep them in bounds, and would almost certainly lead to serious gumming. Unfortunately there are no really dwarfing rootstocks which can be used to restrict the vigour. Sweet cherries will have a spread of 6 to 7m (20 to 24ft), and sour cherries 4.5 to 5.4m (15 to 18ft). Sweet cherries prefer walls facing south or west, but sour cherries will do well on any wall. The best form for trained trees is the fan.

Varieties All the sweet cherries need cross-pollinating, but unfortunately all varieties do not cross-pollinate each other. The Morello is self-fertile, and will pollinate any other variety flowering at the same time. The following are good varieties and are listed with suitable combinations for pollinating.

Variety	**Season**	**Pollinator**
Dessert		
Bigarreau Napoleon	Late July	Roundel Heart, Bradbourne Black
Bradbourne Black	July	Bigarreau Napoleon, Merton Heart
Early Rivers	Late June	Merton Heart, Waterloo
Merton Heart	Late June	Early Rivers, Bradbourne Black
Roundel Heart	Early July	Bigarreau Napoleon, Bradbourne Black
Waterloo	Late June	Early Rivers
Sour		
Morello	August–September	Self-fertile

Soil and manuring Cherries are rather fastidious as far as soil is concerned. It must have a fair amount of body in it, but must be deep and well-drained, and preferably overlay a chalk subsoil. They do not like heavy clays. With wall trees the vigour must be kept within bounds, so they should not be overfed. An annual mulch of well-decayed manure, and 25g (1oz) of sulphate of potash and 15g ($\frac{1}{2}$oz) of superphosphate per sq m (yd) should be ample.

Pruning of established trees of sweet cherry should be done during the growing season. All laterals, except any needed as replacement branches, should be pinched back to four or five buds in July, and back to two or three buds in September. This helps the formation of spurs on which the sweet cherry fruits, as well as on younger wood. Remove surplus shoots and shoots growing towards the wall in September. Sour cherries bear most of their fruit on the previous year's growth, so the shoots are not pinched back, but older branches should be cut back and replaced by younger growths. Young shoots can be left at from 10 to 15cm (4 to 6in) apart.

Harvesting For really rich flavour the fruit should be left on the tree until it is fully ripe. If the stalks do not part easily from the tree, cut them with scissors, as tearing them off may make wounds in the bark through which fungus disease may enter.

Cobnuts and filberts

In a filbert the outer husk extends beyond the end of the nut and enfolds it while in the cobnut it is much shorter. The soil should only be of moderate fertility, though not too hungry, and manuring must be done in moderation to avoid excessive growth. At least two varieties should be planted to ensure adequate pollination. Delay pruning until early March when the male catkins and female flowers can be seen, and sufficient left to give a good crop. The nuts are borne mainly on rather weak lateral growths, and other shoots should be removed or cut back to two buds. Bushes can be allowed to grow naturally, merely thinning the branches occasionally, but they will then form big trees and the nuts will be smaller. Good varieties are: 'Pearson's Dwarf Prolific' (Cob), 'Kentish Cob' (Cob), 'Cosford' (Cob), 'Red Filbert' (Filbert).

Figs

Fig trees are quite hardy but a sheltered position, such as a warm sunny wall, is needed to ripen the fruit. The soil must not be too rich, and in most cases it is necessary to restrict the root-run to induce fruiting. For each tree, take out a hole about 1m (yd) square and 90cm (3ft) deep and line the sides with bricks, concrete or asbestos sheeting. Pack rubble or bricks into the bottom to allow for drainage but prevent root penetration. The soil can be given extra nutrients by adding 250g (8oz) of coarse bone meal, and 2 to 2.5kg (4 to 5lb) of mortar rubble or limestone. Training the tree consists in spreading the shoots fanwise as they grow; keeping them as evenly spaced as possible, but precise training is impracticable. The fruit is borne at the tips of well-ripened shoots made the previous summer, and is visible in embryo form in the autumn. The main pruning is done in March, when sufficient of these fruiting shoots should be retained, and all surplus, weak or frost-damaged ones removed. In June it helps to swell the young fruits if the tips are pinched out of the fruiting shoots. This does, however, result in a lot more side-shoots developing lower down the tree, and these may have to be thinned out later. Frost damage can be reduced by protecting with straw mats or sacking secured over the tender shoots against wind, but it must be removed in good time in the spring. With a restricted root-run, watering may be needed in a dry summer, or the fruit may drop off, and a mulch will often help under these conditions. Manuring will not generally be needed as excess vigour must be avoided, but on occasion a dressing of a general fertilizer may be given to maintain adequate growth. The best varieties are 'Black Ischia', 'Brown Turkey' and 'Brunswick'.

Gooseberries

Gooseberries need a fertile soil of open texture, and a good dressing of farmyard manure applied during digging operations will help them. They are susceptible to potash deficiency, especially on light land, so a dressing of 50g (2oz) per sq m (yd) of sulphate of potash worked into the top 10cm (4in) of soil prior to planting is advisable. They can be grown in almost any form, except as standards. For 'rough' growing on poor soil the stool form where there is no leg but shoots come up from the ground is best. The best general purpose form for the garden is the ordinary bush on a 15 to20cm (6 to 8in) leg, and this will give good size and quality fruit adequate for most needs. Where special dessert quality is desired, these bushes can be spur-pruned, and where suitable varieties are chosen, this will give smaller bushes which can be planted at 1m (4ft) square instead of the usual 1.5m (5ft) apart either way. They can also be trained as cordons or espaliers, and in these forms can be planted against a north facing wall to prolong the season. On a south wall they are too liable to severe attacks of red spider.

Manuring In planting, take care that no fresh manure is in contact with the roots. The best subsequent manuring programme is a good 2.5cm (1in) thick mulch of farmyard manure or similar material in the early spring, plus about 25g (1oz) per sq m (yd) of sulphate of potash. An alternative to this is a dressing of about 75g (3oz) per sq m (yd) of a general fertilizer with a high potash and phosphate content. Care must be taken to keep vigour under control or they will almost certainly be attacked by mildew, especially the variety 'Whinham's Industry', while too lush shoots are liable to be blown out by strong winds.

Training and pruning Propagation is by straight shoots of one-year-old wood, about 30cm (1ft) long, taken just before the leaves fall in the autumn. They should not be allowed to dry out between cutting off and planting. Pinch out the soft tip, and, except for the stool bush, remove all but the top three or four buds and spines to give a clean leg of 15 to 20cm (6 to 8in). The cuttings do not take root readily, so they should be given good conditions. The resulting growths can be pruned according to the form of bush wanted. After planting in their permanent positions, cut the leaders back by about half, according to vigour, and side shoots to a bud at about 2.5cm (1in) from the base. Subsequently trained forms should be spur-pruned by cutting laterals back to two or three buds, and this can also be done on bushes, but for heavy crops of good-sized berries it is best to leave the laterals at six to eight buds, as fruit will be borne along these laterals as well as on spurs. This type of pruning is done in March for the first few years, thereafter branches should be thinned out as necessary to keep the bush open, and old branches and spurs removed and replaced by new shoots. Unripened shoot-tips, and any attacked by mildew, should be cut off and burned, also any shoots arising on the leg or from below ground, except in the case of stool bushes. A sprawling habit can be counteracted by cutting the straggling branches to upward-pointing buds. In cultivating care should be taken not to damage surface roots.

Varieties These are not sharply divided between cooking and dessert, the general practice being to pick some berries from each bush when green for cooking, and use the rest later for dessert. The following are good varieties:

'Bedford Red' Red, can also be picked green for cooking. Vigorous grower.

'Careless' Green-white. Heavy cropper.

'Golden Drop' Yellow. Small fruit of good flavour. A regular upright cropper.

'Green Gem' Yellow-green. A heavy cropper of good quality fruit.

'Leveller' Green-yellow. The best dessert variety, but it needs good, well-drained soil conditions, spur-pruning and careful attention. Must not be sprayed with sulphur.

'Whinham's Industry' Red. A vigorous grower and a heavy cropper. Tolerates heavy soil.

'Whitesmith' Green-yellow. A good general-purpose variety.

Grapes

Grapes will ripen outdoors only in favoured positions, preferably on south- or west-facing walls, or on a warm southern slope. Excessive vigour delays ripening so much that the crop does not mature, so soil of only moderate fertility, but of open texture, is essential. For the same reason manuring must be kept to a minimum, except that well-timed applications of fertilizer given while the berries are swelling will increase the crop. Training is generally as cordons, planted 1.2m (4ft) apart. Laterals are produced and these are stopped at two leaves beyond the flower-cluster, and secondary laterals at one leaf. Only one or two bunches should be taken off a vine in the first fruiting season, gradually increasing the number in subsequent years. These fruit-bearing laterals are cut back to one bud in the winter so that a spur system develops. If trained as horizontal espaliers, laterals should only be taken from the top side of the horizontal branches, and spaced at about 45cm ($1\frac{1}{2}$ft). More informal training can also be quite successful with outdoor grapes; all that is needed are supports to keep the fruiting canes off the ground, these canes being replaced by new canes as they are formed. Indoor varieties are not suitable for outdoor cultivation. The following are suitable: 'Brant', black; 'Müller-Thurgau', white; 'Muscat Hamburgh', black; 'Précoce de Malingre', amber; 'Siegerrebe', golden.

Thinning will need to be done for dessert berries. Birds are likely to be troublesome, and mildew will have to be combated.

Medlar

The medlar is easy to grow, as it thrives in almost any soil, and makes an attractive tree with its crooked picturesque habit. The training and treatment are the same as for the apple, except that medlars are not suitable for the trained forms of tree. The fruit is very much an acquired taste. It should be left on the tree until late October or early November, and then stored in a cool place until it is 'bletted', that is, until the flesh has become soft with slight rotting, when it is ready to eat.

Mulberry

The mulberry can be grown as a bush or standard, but in colder conditions it will need to be grown on a south or west facing wall. It likes a well-drained soil, and under good conditions will have a spread of 7.5 to 9m (25 to 30ft). Once the tree shape is obtained the only pruning needed will be occasional thinning out of the branches. It propagates readily by cuttings or layers from late summer onwards. The tree takes many years to begin fruiting.

Peaches

Outdoor peaches and nectarines can be grown as bush trees, at about 4.5m (15ft) apart, but are better against a warm wall. They prefer a light loam, slightly alkaline, but not a strongly chalky soil. The best rootstock is 'St Julien A'. Once the tree head is formed, pruning should be kept to a minimum, only thinning out crowded branches. The only way to be reasonably assured of crops outdoors, however, is by growing the trees on a south- or west-facing wall, and even then it will probably be necessary to protect the blossom from frost. Treatment for these walled trees is the same as for those growing under glass, enough young shoots being trained in to replace the fruiting shoots, and the surplus shoots disbudded. For outdoors, early varieties are recommended and among the best are 'Duke of York', 'Hale's Early' and 'Peregrine', and the nectarines 'Early Rivers' and 'Elruge'.

Pears

The cultivation of pears is very similar to that of apples, but it requires rather more detailed attention. Pears need ample warm sunshine to ripen the fruits. As far as soil is concerned they are rather more tolerant of poor drainage than are apples, yet they are likely to suffer more from drought.

Forms of tree There is an old adage that 'Pears are planted for heirs', and that was true of trees on their own roots or worked on seedling pear rootstocks. On dwarfing stocks they will come into bearing as quickly as apples if they are grown as restricted trained trees to which they lend themselves very readily. They will succeed in any of the trained forms described earlier in the chapter, and as dwarf pyramids. There are only two rootstocks for pears, the quince for restricted or dwarf trees, and the seedling pear for the large standard trees. There are two varieties of quince, the 'Angers' (Malling A) and the 'Common Quince' (Malling B) which give trees of about equal vigour. For large standard trees, or even for very large espaliers, the seedling pear stock must be used, but they take many years to come into bearing. Certain varieties of pear do not make a good union with quince, and for these 'double working' is practised; that is, a 'compatible' variety must first be worked on to the quince rootstock and the required 'incompatible' variety worked on to it the following season. Consequently such trees are more expensive.

Planting and after-care As pears start into growth before apples they should be given priority for planting and be given a warmer situation but the method is the same. Special care must be taken to keep the union well above ground, because if the scion sends out roots this is likely to cause excessive vigour and delay fruiting much more than with apples. Pear trees on quince tend to make a lot of fruiting spurs at the expense of extension growth, especially when young, and more severe pruning is needed to counteract this. Older pear trees need to have some of the spurs cut out altogether and others shortened. For the same reason pears on quince stock need more nitrogen and less potash than do apples, in order to maintain adequate growth. A good general manuring programme would be to give the trees an annual mulch with farmyard manure or compost, plus a dressing of 25g (1oz) of a nitrogenous fertilizer, 15g (½oz) of sulphate of potash and 15g (½oz) of superphosphate per sq m (yd) in the spring. On trained trees and when good specimen fruits are wanted, thin the fruits to about 10cm (4in) apart so that they are not touching when fully grown. This will usually mean removing one to three fruits per spur according to the fruit size of the variety. It should be done in June. Thinning is not generally necessary on bushes in the open.

Harvesting and storing Practical experience is needed to harvest pears just at the right time, as it is unwise to go too much by the colour. With the September and early October varieties, it is best to pick them two or three weeks before their season, at which time some of them may still be quite green. Others should be picked when they part easily from the tree if raised in the hand. Pears do not store well, and they need careful watching to see that they do not become mushy. Never store them with apples. A good storage temperature is around 7°C (45°F). Bring them into a warm room for a day or two at about 16°C (59°F) to ripen.

Varieties Since most pear varieties are unable to set fruit with their own pollen, at least two varieties must be planted to ensure cross-pollination. Most varieties will pollinate any other variety, except 'Beurré d'Amanlis' and 'Bristol Cross', which are useless for pollination, while 'Conference' will not pollinate 'Beurré d'Amanlis'. There are special cooking varieties such as 'Catillac' and 'Bellissime d'Hiver', but the following dessert varieties can also be cooked while slightly under-ripe.

'Beurré d'Amanlis' August–September. Juicy. Does well in the Midlands and the North.

'Beurré Hardy' October. Does especially well in the south-east.

'Bristol Cross'* September–October. Good flavour and appearance.

'Conference' October–November. Self-fertile. A regular cropper and the best variety for bush trees in the open. Bottle-shaped fruits.

'Doyenné du Comice' Late October–November. Needs a wall for best results. The finest flavoured pear, but not an easy one to grow.

'Emile d'Heyst' October–November. A compact grower and regular cropper.

'Louise Bonne of Jersey' October. A regular heavy cropper.

'Packham's Triumph'* November. A heavy cropper; makes a small compact tree.

'William's Bon Chrétien'* September. The best early pear and a good cropper.

'Winter Nelis' October–November. Heavy cropper.

* Needs double-working.

Plums

While plums will not thrive in waterlogged soils, they are more tolerant of bad drainage than are apples. On poor soils they will make only little growth, damsons doing better than ordinary plums on such soils. As they flower early they are susceptible to frost damage, so the site for them must be chosen with care.

Forms of tree The plum does not lend itself to undue restriction, and it is impracticable to train it in the form of cordons or dwarf pyramids. The espalier form also involves considerable cutting back, which in turn produces more vigour, and the only successfully trained form is the fan. A high wall with ample spread is required for it, otherwise even in this form it will have to be severely pruned. For trees in the open the bush and half-standard are the best forms. Varieties with drooping habit, like 'Victoria' and 'Early Laxton', are best as half-standards.

Rootstocks There are no really dwarfing rootstocks for plums, but the Common Plum gives the smallest trees and is best for walls and for garden trees generally. Unfortunately damsons and a few varieties of plums will not take on Common Plum, and the alternative for these is Common Mussel, though it is not quite such a good stock, being prone to suckering. For bigger trees for the large garden or orchard, the 'St Julien A' stock is best, and 'Pershore' grown on its own roots is also used as a rootstock.

Manuring Plums are gross feeders and need ample nitrogen. It must, however, be given with discretion in the case of wall trees, otherwise they will become too vigorous. The best basis for the feeding programme is a good mulch annually, and it can be of fresher manure than would be safe for most crops. This will probably suffice for wall trees, but trees in the open should also have a dressing of 25g (1oz) of a nitrogenous fertilizer, 15g (½oz) of sulphate of potash and 15g (½oz) of superphosphate per sq m (yd) each spring. Should potash deficiency symptoms show, the main one being the drying-up of the leaf edges, the potash application should be increased. This is most likely on light soils.

Pruning Bush or standard plums require comparatively little detailed pruning, and are better without it. Vigour can be controlled by suitable feeding. It is important not to make large cuts in plum trees during the winter, as that allows the entry of the silver leaf fungus, which is often fatal to susceptible varieties. Even the smaller cuts, such as those which have to be made in training the tree, are best made just before growth starts in the spring, rather than in the winter. On wall trees some pruning is unavoidable, and this should consist of pinching out the tips of young shoots at five or six buds, to be cut back later to two or three buds, except that as older branches become less fruitful they have to be replaced by young shoots from lower down the tree; the pruning of these replacement shoots is left until the winter, when they are shortened back according to vigour. The plum fruits on one-year-old and also on older wood.

Varieties The self-fertile varieties can be planted alone and will give good crops. Some self-sterile varieties will pollinate other self-sterile varieties but some will not, and the best thing is to make sure by using a self-fertile variety as pollinator, as they are all efficient for that purpose. Early-flowering varieties cannot, however, be relied on to pollinate late-flowering ones and vice versa, as they may not be in flower at the same time. The following is a selection of the best varieties, most of the cooking varieties being of good eating quality when fully ripe.

S/F = Self-fertile
P/S/F = Partly self-fertile
S/S = Self-sterile
E/F = Early-flowering
M/F = Mid-season flowering
L/F = Late-flowering
T/T = Suitable for trained trees

Cooking varieties

'Belle de Louvain' Late August. Red-purple. An upright grower, but rather slow coming into bearing. S/F, L/F.

'Czar' Mid-August. Dark Blue. Not a top-quality plum, but the most regular and heavy cropper. A compact grower. S/F, M/F.

'Early Laxton' Late July. Yellow. A good cropper and excellent cooker and dessert. A rather straggly grower, but resistant to frost damage. E/F, P/S/F.

'Kirke's Blue' September. Purple-blue. Best on a wall. Fine dessert and cooker. Not a heavy cropper. S/S, M/F.

'Marjorie's Seedling' September–October. Dark blue. Upright grower. S/F, L/F.

'Merryweather' (damson). Being only of moderate vigour is the best garden damson. A heavy cropper of large fruit. S/F, M/F.

'Pershore' ('Yellow Egg'). Late August. Probably the best cooker. Is resistant to silver leaf disease. S/F, L/F, T/T.

'Victoria' For cooking or dessert. Late August. Red. The most popular general-purpose plum. Susceptible to silver leaf disease. S/F, M/F.

Dessert Varieties

'Cambridge Gage' Green. Late August. A heavy cropper, with greengage-flavoured fruit. Rather spreading habit. P/S/F, L/F.

'Coe's Golden Drop' Late September. Yellow, will keep two or three weeks after picking. S/S, E/F.

'Comte d'Althann's Gage' Deep red. Mid-September. S/S, E/F, T/T.

'Denniston's Superb' Yellow-green. Mid-August. Vigorous and regular cropper. S/F, E/F.

'Early Transparent Gage' Golden-yellow. Mid-August. A regular cropper. S/F, E/F, T/T.

'Oullin's Golden Gage' Early August. An upright grower. A little slow at coming into bearing. S/F, L/F.

Harvesting For full flavour, all plums should be left until they are fully ripe. This is not generally practicable because they have to be handled and possibly transported, and in the case of the gages, because of their tendency to split if left on the trees. Most varieties, however, will keep and continue to ripen for at least a few days, especially if carefully wrapped in tissue paper.

Quince

This fruit is not grown as often as it deserves to be. It makes excellent jams and jellies and is a very attractive tree, especially when in flower or fruit. Unfortunately it is only in the warmer parts of the country that it can be relied on to ripen its fruits. It is best grown as a bush or half-standard, and needs the same treatment as the pear to which it is closely related. The fruit should not be gathered until the end of October unless severe frost threatens earlier. Store in a cool frost-proof place, in a layer of straw and away from other fruits, or it may affect their flavour. The fruits will keep for two or three months under those conditions, and are ready for use when they turn yellow. The two best varieties are 'Portugal' and 'Vranja', both of which have pear-shaped fruits, larger in 'Vranja'.

Raspberries
These will grow in any situation that is not excessively wet or dry. They like a deep moist soil, but will not tolerate bad drainage such as occurs on heavy soil. On the other hand, very light soils tend to dry out in the summer and this makes it very difficult to mature a good crop. Chalky soils are not suitable.

Planting A good dressing of farmyard manure, around two buckets to the sq m (yd) should be worked into the soil during the preparation of the land. Raspberries need adequate potash, and if there is a shortage in the soil work about 50g (2oz) per sq m (yd) into the top 15cm (6in). Planting can be done at any time from November to March when the soil is workable. Comparatively small canes of about 60 to 90cm (2 to 3ft) long, with plenty of fibrous roots on them form the best plants, and should be set fairly deeply, from 30 to 60cm (1 to 2ft) apart according to the variety. The rows should run from north to south, and be at least 1.8m (6ft) apart. After planting cut down the canes to 25cm (10in) from the ground.

After-care The less root disturbance there is in the way of hoeing or other cultivation the better. Weeds are best kept down by a good annual mulch of farmyard manure or compost, applied in February or March. This should be supplemented by 25g (1oz) of sulphate of potash per m (yd) run, with about 25g (1oz) of superphosphate every third year. It is possible to grow raspberries without any artificial support by bending over the canes of one stool and tying the tops to the canes of the ones alongside, and so on along the row, but this is not satisfactory. The best method is to stretch two wires, the lowest at 60cm (2ft) from the ground and another at 1.2m (4ft), or three wires at 45cm, 1m and 1.5m (18in, 40in, and 5ft) for the taller varieties. Stretch the wires between posts at about 6m (20ft) apart, but if posts and wire are stout enough they can be as far as 18m (60ft) apart.

Pruning The canes which have fruited should be cut out as soon as fruiting is finished to allow the sun to get to the new canes to ripen them. The new canes should be tied in about 15cm (6in) apart, cutting out the surplus or weaker ones. In the spring, cut any dead tips on the canes back to a good bud. Certain varieties, of which 'Lloyd George' is one, will fruit in the autumn if the young canes are cut right down to ground level in the early spring.

Varieties Most of the older varieties of raspberry have gone out of cultivation because of deterioration of stocks due to virus infection, and care has to be taken to prevent the same thing happening with modern varieties. Some varieties, notably 'Norfolk Giant', show the presence of virus disease in the leaves by numerous small yellow spots or small areas of uneven shape, but many varieties exhibit no visible symptoms until general degeneration sets in. Care should therefore be taken to obtain virus-free stocks from a reliable source. The following are among the best varieties:

'Glen Clova' A new Scottish variety with heavy crops of good quality fruit, ripening over a long period. Early.

'Lloyd George' An excellent all-round variety having most of the virtues of a good raspberry. Unfortunately it is susceptible to virus disease, and is liable to degenerate quickly if grown close to other varieties. As they may be carriers of the disease it is best grown by itself. Early. May also be grown as an autumn-fruiting variety.

'Malling Exploit' Vigorous and tends to make too many canes. Early and of good appearance and flavour.

'Malling Jewel' A very good garden variety and makes an attractive picture when in fruit. Mid-season, and of good flavour. Resists wind damage so is good for moderately exposed positions. Makes few canes, which are practically thornless, so can be planted closely.

'Malling Promise' One of the easiest varieties to grow, and of good general merit. It is very similar to 'Malling Exploit', though the fruit is less excellent; heavy cropper. Early.

'Norfolk Giant' An old variety, and of only moderate dessert quality but it is a heavy cropper and its fruit is attractive in appearance. It is a strong grower, making very tall canes. As it flowers late it is the variety most likely to miss damage by late frosts.

'September' A new American variety with good crops of bright red fruits from early September. Canes should be cut to the ground in spring and new canes tied in as they grow. Autumn.

Red and white currants

These require identical treatment, which is different from that needed by black currants. They are not fastidious as to soil, but do best on a light open one. Propagation is by 30cm (1ft) cuttings of well-ripened one-year-old wood, of pencil thickness, taken in October; remove all buds other than the top three or four to give a 15cm (6in) leg. From this stage they can be trained as bush or as cordons. The fruit is borne mainly at the base of the previous year's shoots, so that modified spur-pruning should be practised. This can include summer-pruning in July, followed by cutting back the laterals to two or three buds in the autumn.

Red currants are very sensitive to potash deficiency so an annual dressing of about 50g (2oz) per bush of sulphate of potash should be given, with other fertilizers to maintain growth. Muriate, or other chloride-containing potash salts should never be used.

Varieties

'Laxton's No. 1' The best all-round variety. A vigorous grower and heavy cropper. Wind-resistant. Early.

'Red Lake' Compact upright grower. Long trusses of large berries. Mid-season.

'White Versailles' White sweet berries. Upright growth. Early.

'Wilson's Long-bunch' Strong-growing and heavy cropper. Late.

Strawberries

Strawberries are particularly liable to blossom damage by spring frosts, so avoid planting them in frost pockets. Since early fruit is especially prized, a warm sheltered position, preferably on a south-facing slope, should be chosen for at least a few early plants. Some virus disease can be carried over from the debris of an old crop, and it is best not to plant on the site of a recently discarded strawberry bed.

Soil Strawberries will do reasonably well on most soils, except very chalky ones, but best results are obtained on deep well-drained soils with plenty of organic matter in them. This will ensure that they do not dry out, which is one of the dangers with this crop. Some varieties show a preference for a certain kind of soil, so it is worth while enquiring which varieties do particularly well in the district. In preparing the soil for planting, work a good heavy dressing of farmyard manure into the soil. This is particularly valuable because strawberries require only small amounts of nitrogen; an initial application in a slowly released form enables the plants to build themselves up during the first summer, with a small but steady supply available later. The soil should be reasonably

When propagating strawberries from runners use only the strongest which are closest to the parent plant

firmed before planting, as strawberries do not like a loose, open soil.

Propagation Use only healthy strawberry plants for runners to prevent any disease from spreading. If in doubt buy new runners that have been grown in isolation. Where propagation is considered safe, do it by layering, and the first plant on each runner gives the best results. Use the pot method as the roots are not disturbed when the plants are planted out, but make sure they do not dry out while in the pot. A stone placed on a runner will keep it in position until it is rooted. Peg down the runners as soon as the soil is in a suitable condition from mid-September to mid-November. If not done by then it should be delayed to mid-February. Planting distances range from 30 to 45cm (1 to 1½ft) between plants, and from 60 to 90cm (2 to 3ft) between the rows, according to the variety and the fertility of the soil. Planting at the correct depth is important to ensure successful growth.

General attention Spring-planted runners, or any autumn-planted ones which are not doing well should have all the flower trusses removed before the flowers open, so that they will not produce a crop in their first season. The sacrifice will be more than repaid in subsequent crops. Summer care consists of keeping down weeds, but since a large proportion of the strawberry's roots are near the surface, hoeing should be done with care, and the weeds removed when small. A severe attack of greenfly in April is common, and since it can cripple the plants, keep a sharp lookout for it and take prompt action. If an initial dressing of farmyard manure was given, little additional feeding should be needed during the three or four years of the bed's life. If the plants lack vigour they can be mulched annually, or a nitrogenous fertilizer at up to 25g (1oz) per m (yd) of row can be given annually, plus the same amount of sulphate of potash. Too luxurious foliage often means virtually no crop. To keep the fruit clean, spread a layer of straw, peat or polythene strips over the beds as soon as the fruits begin to swell, working it under the berries. The bed is also best netted against birds. Towards the autumn the plants will begin to send out runners which should be cut off in order to concentrate the vigour into the crowns for the following year, unless they are needed for propagating.

Varieties Among the many varieties available, the following are generally the best:

'Cambridge Favourite' A very good second-early, though not happy on heavy soils. Small foliage, so needs to be planted closely, and is useful for growing under cloches.

'Cambridge Late Pine' A late variety with distinctive 'pine' flavour. Very resistant to frost and mildew and a heavy cropper.

'Cambridge Prizewinner' Second-early. Very attractive fruit, but not quite such a heavy cropper as some.

'Cambridge Vigour' This variety ripens very early, and crops very heavily in its first year, but in subsequent years it is later and gives a smaller crop. If planted early in the autumn it is worth treating as an annual, discarding it after the first crop.

'Grandee' Enormous individual berries of good quality on vigorous plants.

'Red Gauntlet' Mid-season to late. Probably the best maincrop variety. A vigorous grower, and good quality fruit.

'Royal Sovereign' Of very high quality, and given good conditions it will crop heavily; under average conditions only a moderate cropper. Succeeds on heavy soil.

'Talisman' Mid-season to late. Fairly vigorous and a heavy cropper. Often gives a second crop in the autumn.

Alpine Strawberries, such as 'Baron Solemacher', fruit from July to October. They are propagated by division or by seed, and like a soil rich in humus. Plant 30cm (1ft) apart each way.

Perpetual Strawberries will tolerate a chalky soil better than will the ordinary type, and will crop from June to October, giving their heaviest crop the first season. To maintain cropping they need replanting each season, in a fertile soil. They do better in the warmer parts of the country. Varieties include 'Red Rich', 'Sans Rivale' and 'St Claude'. 'Gento' is a new German variety, producing heavy crops of large berries with its main season from August to October.

15 Gardening under Glass

A greenhouse or frame adds considerably to the scope of a gardener's activities. It makes possible the raising of half-hardy plants, the early starting of vegetable crops and the propagation of a wide range of plants. While a frame will provide enough protection for the raising of early seedlings a greenhouse can be put to additional use either as a garden feature, filled with flowers and attractive foliage plants, or used to supplement the family diet with tomatoes, cucumbers, early salad crops or fruit such as early strawberries, grapes, figs and peaches.

Siting the greenhouse

For most purposes as much light as possible and shelter from the north and east are most important. If the only position available is in shade this will severely limit the range of plants which can be grown. It is better to treat the greenhouse as a garden feature in its own right than to hide it in some shaded corner. Where a south-facing wall is available, this could support a lean-to house. The heat stored in the wall during the day will be released to warm the air at night, and the wall itself might support trained fruit trees. Often the functions of a greenhouse are incorporated into a conservatory adjacent to the house but this is only suitable for raising vegetables and fruit if it has a glass roof. There are also difficulties in fumigating conservatories that lead directly into living rooms.

Choice of greenhouse

The main choices lie between a free-standing or a lean-to greenhouse, a solid base or glass to the ground, a wood or metal framework, and whether glazed with glass or clear plastic.

Free-standing structures give better illumination and ventilation than lean-to houses and are preferable in most instances. However, if a greenhouse has to be sited near the wall and light will be reduced anyway, it is often better to use a lean-to house and to take advantage of the wall which acts as a free night-store radiator. Free-standing houses are usually rectangular but round, octagonal or dome-shaped structures are available for situations in which appearance is more important than growing space.

A lean-to greenhouse made of cedarwood. Such greenhouses are particularly useful where spaced is confined, and are ideal on south facing walls.

When plants are to be raised on staging at a pleasant working height there is much to be said for having solid walls of wood, asbestos or brick below the staging. Heat loss is reduced, the risk of breaking glass at ground level is removed and the walls hide pots and other sundries which may be conveniently stored below the staging. However, if plants are to be grown in borders at ground level, glass to the ground is essential. Even if staging is installed, there is still scope for growing begonias, ferns and other shade-tolerant plants beneath the staging if the glass comes down to ground level.

A traditional half-wall cedarwood greenhouse. The understaging can be used for storing greenhouse gardening equipment

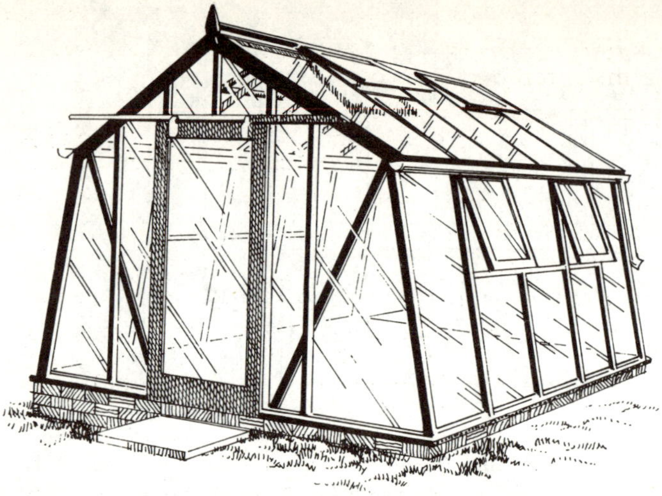

A greenhouse with sliding door. Note the sloping side-walls to the ground; these give greater penetration of winter light than vertical side walls

Modern pressure-treated wood-framed houses last indefinitely without the need for painting, as do good red-cedar structures. Other wood-framed houses need regular maintenance and are less good investments. Metal-framed houses need only thin glazing bars and afford maximum light with minimum maintenance. They should have a solid base on the ground, however, as being light-weight they are easily blown over in strong gales.

Plastic – usually polythene – houses have the advantage of being extremely light weight, and very low in initial cost, but the covering needs replacing at least every second year. It is also difficult to ventilate plastic houses for many crops. Too many ventilation flaps with the resulting extra framework and the need to replace the plastic remove the main advantages of this type of structure. For most gardens, especially where the greenhouse is not in a concealed part of the garden, a glass fitted house is more permanent, more attractive and more manageable.

In choosing a design, pay particular attention to adequate ventilation if the greenhouse is to be used for summer crops or alpines. Extra ventilators can usually be installed.

Greenhouse temperatures

The minimum temperature at which the house is to be maintained depends on its purpose. Most plants will survive at 5°C (41°F) for short periods without harm. For seed-sowing a temperature of 10°C (50°F) is better and some plants and seeds may require temperatures of 15°C (59°F) or higher. The cost of heating increases rapidly as higher temperatures are required. A minimum of 10°C (50°F) will cost more than twice as much to maintain as a minimum of 5°C (41°F).

Greenhouses are roughly divided into cold, cool, warm or intermediate, and hot houses, and as a rough guide the following may be taken as the mean temperatures of the last three.

	SUMMER		WINTER	
	Day	Night	Day	Night
Cool house	15°–18°C (59°–65°F)	13°–15°C (55°–59°F)	13°–18°C (55°–65°F)	7°–10°C (45°–50°F)
Warm house (Intermediate)	18°–24°C (65°–75°F)	15°–21°C (59°–70°F)	15°–21°C (59°–70°F)	13°–18°C (55°–65°F)
Hot house	21°–29°C (70°–85°F)	18°–24°C (65°–75°F)	18°–24°C (65°–75°F)	15°–21°C (59°–70°F)

Unheated greenhouse This type of house depends solely on the heat of the sun for its warmth and so its temperature varies enormously at different times of the year. It requires no artifical heat even in winter. Remember, however, that glass will not keep out frost and the plants selected for the cold house must necessarily be hardy and able to stand a few degrees of frost. A lot can be done by placing sacking and canvas over the glass to keep frost from the more tender plants and such hardy plants as bloom too early in the season to withstand the frost in the open.

The cold house must have plenty of ventilation, but take care to exclude all draughts. On warm summer nights the ventilators may be kept open all night, in cooler and damper weather it is best to ventilate thoroughly in the morning and to close the ventilators soon after midday. For shading, the roller type of blind is most suitable as these may be pulled down as protection against frosts on winter nights.

Watering requires a good deal of care and is best done in the morning; the foliage and atmosphere will then have time to dry off before the cold night air can cause damping-off. This applies especially to watering in autumn, winter and spring; in summer watering may be done in the evening. In hot weather plants may be sprayed from overhead and the paths and staging damped down as advised for the warm house, but this should be done with caution and only in the hottest periods, as the majority of cold house plants do not like a damp and humid atmosphere.

Cool house The cool house will need artificial heat during the colder periods of the year only. Between October and March a day temperature of 13°C (55°F), with a minimum night temperature of 7°C (45°F), is necessary. During April and May, in a normal year, a temperature a few degrees above that of the outside air, both night and day, will be enough.

The cool house provides a home for a very large number of tender and half-hardy plants, and will generally be found the best all-round house for the amateur.

Warm (intermediate) house The warm or intermediate greenhouse requires a minimum night temperature of 13°C (55°F) and a day temperature of 15°C (59°F) during the winter and from 18°C (65°F) to 24°C (75°F) during the day in spring and summer.

The warm greenhouse will give the amateur a very wide range of choice, for many of the plants which will just survive in the cold and cool houses, thrive in the slightly warmer house.

The warm house also allows much greater scope for forced and out-of-season flowers. *See* Selection of Greenhouse Plants.

Hot house The hot house requires considerably more heat, at an almost prohibitive cost. In winter the night temperature should never fall below 15°C (59°F), while the day temperature in summer should range between 21 and 29°C (70 and 85°F). Avoid giving too much heat in winter at a time when most plants are resting. Forcing them during the dormant period will often weaken them and impair the beauty and quality of their flowers. Exposure to the open air and sun matures the wood and strengthens all plants. Where possible, all except the more tender greenhouse plants should therefore be kept in the open from the end of May until early in September, having first been hardened off for a fortnight in a cold frame and then shaded from the strong sun for the first ten days in the open. On returning the plants to the greenhouse before the first frost, given them free ventilation. The plants are not usually taken out of their pots, but plunged to their rims into beds, preferably of ashes or peat, which will keep them well drained and prevent worms from entering and disturbing the roots.

Heating the greenhouse

For large greenhouses, hot water circulating in pipes round the house provides an even temperature. Water may be heated in solid-fuel, oil or gas-fired boilers. In small houses, direct heating is more common. Electric fan heaters provide flexible heating and good air circulation while electric tubular heaters give more gentle heat and higher humidity. Paraffin heaters are the least expensive, but must be well-adjusted to avoid fumes which could damage plants. Natural gas or bottled gas burners have the added advantage of producing not only heat but carbon dioxide which increases the quality of plant growth.

Relative costs of the different methods of heating vary from time to time and from place to place. Electricity is usually the most expensive, but the most convenient. Installation costs must be considered along with running costs and, as efficiency and economy increase as the size of installation increases, there is much to be said for having the same type of heating installed in the greenhouse as in the dwelling house. To economize on heating, the greenhouse can be lined with clear plastic film in the winter after cleaning the glass, inside and out.

Propagating cases

It is much easier to maintain the humid atmosphere needed for propagation in a small enclosure than in the larger space of an airy greenhouse. Also, when only a small area of bench is required for raising seedlings early in the year a propagating case can be easily heated by low voltage cables or even by one or two 40 watt light bulbs, cutting down on the cost of maintaining the whole greenhouse at a high temperature.

A propagating case may be either a permanent fixture, built in a position where it can include some portion of the heating pipes; or it may be portable, so that it can be cleared out when not wanted. Where the pipes are built in they should be covered with a good depth of coconut fibre, and the pots or boxes containing the plants plunged in that.

The propagating case needs careful watching. Cover the glass with paper to shield newly inserted cuttings and seeds from the sun, and keep it in position until the cuttings have rooted, or the seeds have germinated. Remove all wilting leaves regularly as they encourage damping-off, and wipe the condensation off the glass every morning.

Place the cuttings or seeds of nearly all cool house plants under glass in a temperature of 10 to 15°C (50 to 59°F). Warm house plants need a propagating temperature of from 18 to 24°C (65 to 75°F). (*See also* Ch. 5.)

The cold frame

The cold frame is a useful adjunct to the greenhouse as it enables plants from the greenhouse to be thoroughly hardened off before being planted out in the open. Plants may also be brought on in a cold frame for final display in the greenhouse or home and, in a small garden, a well-managed frame can entirely replace the greenhouse for plant-raising and production of salads, melons, strawberries and other low crops out of season.

Span-roof frames are excellent as the lights can be opened on either side and it is therefore possible to ventilate whatever the direction of the

A frame is useful as a half-way stage between the greenhouse and the outside garden and also provides additional space when the greenhouse is full

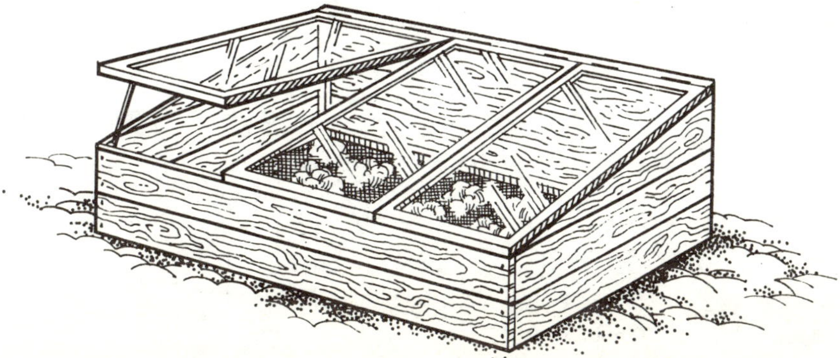

wind. The span-roof frame is best placed to run north and south; either side then gets its share of sun. Lean-to frames should face due south so that they get full sun, unless shade and a low temperature are necessary, when the frame should face north.

The substance used to form the bed of the frame depends on its uses: if pots are to be kept in it, a dry and hard bottom of ashes or shingle, some 7.5cm (3in) deep, is the most suitable. This will keep out worms and other pests and give good drainage. If a seed bed is made, raise the four corners of the frame with bricks, place a layer of leaves at the bottom and cover with 15cm (6in) of well-sieved compost of loam, leaf-mould and sand. Make the bed firm and sprinkle the surface with coarse sand. The surface of the bed should be not more than 15 to 22.5cm (6 to 9in) from the glass, otherwise the plants will become drawn and weak.

The heated frame

The heat is supplied by either low-voltage soil-heating cables buried in the soil or by air-warming cables running along the walls; both types should ideally be installed with a thermostat.

Take great care to provide ventilation and to maintain an even temperature. With a frame heated to 15 to 21°C (59 to 70°F) it is possible to raise plants for early transplanting and also to have crops of almost any vegetable practically all through winter, until the vegetables from the open are ready.

Cloches

Cloches are available in many forms from the simple tent consisting of two or four sheets of glass held in position by galvanized wire to the larger and taller kinds which resemble frames or miniature glasshouses and are made up on a framework of wire or rigid metal. All serve the same purposes: they protect young plants, warm the soil and encourage early growth and final maturity. They are easy to handle and can be placed end to end to cover continuous rows. They are particularly useful for covering crops grown for successional harvesting. In winter or early

Using a polythene cloche is a good way to protect seedlings from frost in early spring and getting plants off to an early start

spring they may be used on lettuce, flower seedlings or salads and from March to May put over seedlings such as sweet corn or tomatoes or over early strawberries. When not in use clean the cloches and stack them neatly out of sight.

Plastic cloches are lighter and more convenient to handle and many fold flat for storage. They do not break as easily as glass panes but they trap less heat, deteriorate in strong sunlight and cannot be expected to last more than three or four years in most circumstances.

Ventilation and heat regulation

Much of the greenhouse's success depends on proper ventilation and regulation of heat and moisture. It is easy to kill, or at least severely injure a house full of plants by injudicious opening or closing of all ventilators. Both top and side ventilators should only be opened simultaneously in summer when the temperature is too high, and then only in moderation, as a chilly draught between the two openings may cripple the less hardy plants. At other times of the year open only the ventilators on the side opposite to that from which the wind is blowing.

The amount of air admitted will depend on the nature of the plants; young growing plants and seedlings require a warm and moist atmosphere, while plants in bloom require the air to be drier. Where there is ample top ventilation there is often less need for side ventilation as well. When a dry atmosphere is necessary, as it may be in houses built for particular plants, small sliding shutters placed in the side of the house and below the hot-water pipes may provide side ventilation. The air is warmed slightly as it passes over the pipes and before it circulates in the house. It is important that the temperature of the house should be carefully watched, especially in the morning – the sun will often come out suddenly with surprising power, and unless the ventilation is regulated in time the heat will become intense. To avoid the risk of scorching, slightly open the ventilators early in mild weather, and gradually admit more air as the sun becomes more powerful, reversing the process towards evening as the temperature falls. Violent changes of temperature are harmful to plants, and the sudden check given to foliage, which is in a state of great heat and transpiration when the temperature of the surrounding atmosphere drops abruptly, will almost certainly give rise to mildew. If this occurs, spinkle flowers of sulphur over the plants affected.

Watering

Plants will need most water in the spring and summer, both because the air is then drier, and because the plants are in full activity and are using up water at a great rate. Water at least once a day, sometimes twice, at this season, and in very hot weather stand moisture-loving plants in saucers of water. Dormant plants and freshly-potted plants are best kept fairly dry until growth begins. A watering once a week will be enough for most plants in winter although the soil should never become dust-dry. In the greenhouse, watering is often as useful for keeping the air in a proper state of moisture as for anything else, and in hot weather the walls, staging, and floor should be frequently damped down by syringing. When the air is very hot and dry, the floor may be thoroughly watered, this will evaporate into the air and keep it moist. This is better than too much overhead watering, which tends to produce weak, insipid foliage.

In the summer, the watering of the plants themselves should be done when the sun's heat is at its lowest, early in the morning or in the early evening, but in spring, late autumn, and in winter it is essential to water in the morning so that excessive moisture may drain off before the evening. Plants should never be allowed to become so dry as to droop as this may cause irreparable damage, but if it does occur stand the whole plant, pot and all, in water deep enough to cover the pot. When thoroughly soaked, do not replace it on the staging at once but put in the shade for an hour or two to recover. Nearly all plants, and especially those that have not recently been re-potted, will be the better for a watering with liquid fertilizer every ten days while the buds are forming. Feeding should be stopped as soon as the flowers are out.

Shading the greenhouse

During the summer, from about March to the end of September, the house will need shading from the strongest sunshine, or there is great risk of the plants being scorched and dried up. No definite dates or hours for shading can be given, as this depends on the weather. The cool house, however, usually needs shading from about the end of February and should be shaded each day as soon as the direct rays fall on the house. Remove the blinds as soon as the rays have passed. The plants in the warm house can do with more sun and heat. Let the rays play for half an hour or so on the house before shading it and remove the shading about half an hour before the sun's rays leave the glass, to maintain the heat of the house. Protect only from the direct rays of the sun. Where constant attention can be given, an arrangement of roller blinds is the most suitable, as the amount of light can be better regulated, and the blinds can be left up on dull and sunless days. Where the greenhouse must be left to look after itself for a good part of the day the simplest and most satisfactory method, is to wash the glass over with an electrostatic shading paint. This is waterproof but can be washed off when cloudy weather sets in and more light is necessary.

Greenhouse automation

With the uncertainties of a temperate climate, the regulation of heat,

Try to include some autumn colour in the garden – this is *Crataegus prunifolia*

Camellias will grow well against a north facing wall

ventilation, watering and shading could easily become a full-time occupation. It is, however, possible to automate these operations, saving much effort and making successful greenhouse management possible for the gardener who has to be away all day or even all week.

Many heaters can be regulated by a thermostat which, set accurately, will easily save its initial cost by reducing fuel consumption. Solenoid-operated ventilators can also be purchased and regulated automatically to open as the temperature increases and to close as the temperature falls. By adjusting ventilation automatically, extremes of temperature are avoided and the need for shading may be reduced.

Automatic watering is achieved by plunging the plant pots into a sand bed in which a constant water level is maintained by means of a cistern and float. Some adjustment is needed initially to obtain the right degree of moisture but plants may then be left for as long as the water supply will last. Such a sand bed with a controlled water level is known as a capillary bench.

Automatic shading is not always readily available and is comparatively expensive. The keen electrician could devise a roller blind which raised and lowered itself at pre-determined temperatures, and a method has been developed which uses coloured water circulated over the roof glass by a thermostatically controlled pump. However, with well controlled heaters and ventilators plus a ready supply of water the dangers of too much or too little shading are almost eliminated and a simple screen of laths, net curtains or proprietary shading material in the hottest summer months will be enough for most plants.

Soil sterilization

Soils in the greenhouse that have been under cultivation for some time frequently become pest-ridden. The presence of pests is indicated by the poorness of crops and by the weak and sickly state of individual plants. This is particularly so with tomato and cucumber which are very susceptible to many serious disorders if grown repeatedly in the same soil.

The problem can be overcome either by sterilizing the soil or by changing it entirely. In the latter case it is important to prevent infection of new soil from the deeper layers of a border; plants may be grown in pots, in proprietary polythene bags of peat compost or in raised beds of compost separated from permanent border soil by polythene sheets.

Sterilization consists in burning, or heating the soil to such a degree that all pests and seeds of weeds are destroyed and plant growth is stimulated.

Plants in sterilized soil will at first be slow in growth, as numbers of the bacteria which promote this are destroyed with the pests. Those remaining, however, are free from the influence of pests and quickly multiply, so that after a time the growth of the plants becomes surprisingly vigorous. There are several methods of effecting sterilization.

Steaming This is undoubtedly the best and most effective method of sterilizing soil. It consists of passing quantities of steam into the soil until the temperature rises to 100°C (212°F) and retaining this temperature in every part of the soil. For the amateur who requires a small but effective outfit, electric steam sterilizing plants can be purchased and operated according to the maker's instructions. For those who prefer to make their own plant, construct a wooden box with several parallel pipes running at intervals across the bottom; provide the pipes with holes. Fill the box with soil and cover the top. Force steam at the pressure of 35kg (70lb) to the sq cm (1in) along the pipes and up through the soil until it is heated to a temperature of 99°C (210°F) or as near that as possible. Maintain this temperature for about twenty to thirty minutes.

Chemical sterilization The two chemicals most commonly used are formaldehyde and cresylic acid. Both are applied in liquid form and both control diseases as well as pests. Cresylic acid is less effective against diseases but more effective against pests. The soil in the glasshouse border should be deeply dug, brought to a fine condition and if dry, watered two or three days before being treated. The chemicals should be applied at the correct dilution and quantity and all parts of the house should be washed down with the solution at the same time. The house must be empty of plants and remain empty for six to eight weeks after treatment.

Where small quantities of sterilized soil for potting or seed sowing are required, loam can be sterilized in an ordinary kitchen steamer, but it is usually easier to purchase sterilized composts.

General hygiene

Cleanliness inside the greenhouse is most essential. Aphids, thrips, red spiders, mealy bugs, scale insects and woodlice are the chief pests met with here. Keeping every corner of the house and the stem of every plant as clean and free from rubbish as possible will do a great deal to keep down insect pests, but annual fumigation of the greenhouse is also desirable unless biological controls are being used against red spider mites and white flies. (*See* Ch. 9 Pests and Diseases.)

Principles of potting

Before use scrub old pots thoroughly in disinfectant. Leave new clay pots to soak in water for several hours. There is little to choose between clay and plastic pots. Clay pots absorb water more quickly than plastic pots, but the latter because of their light weight are easier to knock over. For sowing and potting on prior to planting out, peat pots are ideal as there is no root disturbance.

Pots are usually measured by size, ranging from 5cm (2in) to 50cm (20in) or more.

Potting composts

It is possible to make up composts to suit different types of plants, but most will grow satisfactorily in John Innes composts which may be purchased ready-made or mixed at home.

John Innes Seed Compost (JIS)

2 parts sterilized loam

1 part moss peat

1 part coarse sand

To every 0.35hl (1 bushel) of this mixture add 40g (1½oz) superphosphate of lime (18 per cent P_2O_5) and 20g (¾oz) ground limestone or chalk.

John Innes Potting Compost (JIP)

7 parts sterilized loam

3 parts moss peat

2 parts coarse sand

To every 0.35hl (1 bushel) of this mixture add 125g (4oz) John Innes base fertilizer and 20g (¾oz) ground limestone or chalk for JI No. 1, and twice and three times these amounts for JI No. 2 and No. 3. The JI base fertilizer consists of:

2 parts by weight superphosphate of lime (18 per cent P_2O_5)

2 parts by weight hoof and horn finely ground

1 part by weight sulphate of potash (50 per cent K_2O)

The basic potting composts may be modified by adding up to 50 per cent by volume of coarse sand for alpines and cacti or up to 50 per cent by volume of peat or leaf-mould for azaleas, saintpaulias, begonias etc. For azaleas and heathers omit lime.

Proprietary loamless potting composts based on peat are used increasingly. They are excellent for raising plants, light in weight but difficult to keep in a nearly dry state through the dormant period. They need less firming than the John Innes composts.

When to re-pot

During the growing season a plant or two of each batch of similar flowers, whether they are biennials being grown on for greenhouse use, soft-wooded perennials or hard-wooded plants, should be turned out of their pots to determine whether re-potting is necessary. As soon as the roots begin to wind round the sides of the pot the plants should be moved into larger pots unless the resting season is approaching, when potting can be delayed until growth begins again. Plants make most growth in April and May and again in August and September; the best time to re-pot is therefore just before growth starts about March and again in

August and early September. March is the better time at which to re-pot established plants as the spring growth is more vigorous than the autumn growth, and fresh compost will be of more use to them.

Some plants, such as clivias, flower only when pot-bound and these can be left in the same pot for years, replacing only a little surface soil each year, until the roots finally break the pot.

Size of pot

It is advisable to put a plant into a pot slightly too small rather than too large. Unless the plant is very pot-bound, or is required to grow very quickly (as in the case of many young and growing plants), put the plant back in the same sized pot if possible, leaving about 2.5cm (1in) of compost between the root ball and the sides of the pot.

It is useless to try to save work or to force a plant on by putting a small subject into a pot too large for it. The small roots will be unable to make use of all the moisture and plant food in the soil; this lies dormant in the compost and it is a long time before any fresh air is able to enter, so that the soil becomes clammy and finally sour. For this reason pot up into small pots, re-potting as necessary as the plants grow and the roots become pot-bound. It is rarely necessary to move a plant into a pot more than two, at the most three, sizes larger than the old one. As soft-wooded plants are as a rule vigorous growers, they may usually be put into proportionately larger pots than would be advisable for slower-growing hard-wooded plants.

Re-potting

Plants should be watered the day before re-potting so that the root ball is moist but not wet for the move.

The potting soil should be moderately moist: if a handful is taken up and pressed firmly together, it should mould to the shape of the hand, but at the same time be dry enough to crumble as soon as it is released. Mix the ingredients well together, but do not sieve the compost; this would rob it of much of its plant food and most of its porosity; large lumps should be broken up. Only for seeds and cutting should the compost be sieved, through a 6mm (¼in) mesh. Young plants with fine fibrous roots need a finer textured compost than mature and vigorous plants being potted on into their final pots.

Drainage and crocks

Place small pieces of broken pots, called crocks, over the hole at the bottom of the pot to aid drainage. This is only necessary for clay pots; plastic pots have many more drainage holes. For cuttings, which are not intended to remain in the pot for any length of time after they have rooted, a single piece of crock, convex side uppermost, is sufficient, but when a pot is to be occupied for months, and perhaps years, it is necessary to fill one-sixth of the depth with broken crocks.

After crocking, add a layer of coarse leaf-mould and settle this by tapping the pot gently against the work bench. Now add compost below, around and over the roots so that the top of the root ball, when firmed in the new pot, is within 38mm (1½in) of the rim.

Turn the plant to be re-potted upside down, placing the first and second finger of the left hand so that the stem lies between them while the palm and fingers lie across the top edges of the pot, and hold the bottom of the pot with the right hand. Tap the rim of the pot gently on the edge of the potting bench, and the roots and soil should come out complete.

If the plant does not come out of the pot, insert a finger or a small blunt stick through the drainage hole at the bottom and apply gentle pressure. The ball will soon drop out.

Potting-up

Remove the old crocks, any sour soil and dead roots carefully so that the roots are not bruised, and draw out some of the thickest roots from the ball with a pointed stick; these will establish themselves in the new soil round the sides of the larger pot. Place the plant in the centre of the new pot, on top of the compost and pack soil with the hand or trowel between the ball and the sides of the pot, knocking it against the bench occasionally and pressing the compost down round the sides with a potting stick or the thumb. Press the new soil firmly about the collar of the plant with the thumbs. When firmly planted and covered with 1 to 2.5cm (½ to 1in) of new soil the crown of the plant should be 2.5cm (1in) below the rim in a large pot and 1cm (½in) in a small pot.

All plants, however hardy, should be kept warm and moist for a few weeks after re-potting. This promotes the growth of the roots – a point of great importance at this stage.

Only remove from the ball any soil that is really sour; it is a mistake to disturb the roots if the soil is still fresh. If, however, the compost has become very sour remove all the soil and wash the roots through with lukewarm water, cutting any dead or diseased parts away.

How firm to pot

With most plants it is best to pot firmly, not to ram the earth down too hard, but sufficiently firm for the plant to offer resistance if it is pulled gently upwards. The degree of firmness varies with the age of the plant, the nature of the roots, and the character of the compost. Young plants of all kinds, whose roots will expand, need planting only moderate firmly, the soil being packed just tight enough to hold the plants in position; each subsequent potting should, however, be firmer. Mature, fibrous-rooted plants should be potted firmly, and the more sandy the compost the firmer the potting. Plants with large fleshy roots require a much looser compost. Between these two extremes there are roots of varying sizes and characteristics, but potting is generally a matter of common sense. Although it may be necessary to tamp the soil firmly round the roots, do not pack the surface down hard or air will be excluded. Lastly, never fill a pot with soil right up to the rim, but leave enough room for watering.

Potting-on seedlings and cuttings

Cuttings and seedlings are best potted-up in the same conditions as those in which they have been grown; they are delicate and if transferred to a cold, draughty place may receive a set-back. Once established in their new pots, they can be gradually hardened off to stand the temperature of their new environment.

The size of the pot depends on the type and size of the plant, but as a general rule 7.5 to 10cm (3 to 4 in) pots are suitable for the first potting-up of seedlings that have previously been pricked-off into boxes, round the sides of pots, or into thumb pots; the new pots should be just large enough to take the roots without their touching the sides; larger pots will be needed as the plants grow. The size of the final pot is decided by ultimate growth at maturity and the longevity of the plant.

The potting-up of seedlings is similar, but the stems should be buried nearly up to the two small seed leaves, or cotyledons. The young roots are very brittle and tender, so do not press down the soil with thumbs and fingers as when potting maturer plants; tapping the pot on the bench and watering afterwards should make the compost quite firm enough. Seedlings grown in boxes or close together in pots should be potted-on fairly early, before their roots begin to intertwine.

Forcing bulbs

Bulbs for flowering indoors by Christmas and late winter should be planted as soon as possible in the early autumn. Set the bulbs of daffodil, hyacinth, tulip and similar flowers so that their tips are just above the surface of the soil; a few other bulbs should only be half buried, while others again should be completely buried – crocuses and scilla, for instance, should be just covered with soil. After planting, soak the pots well in water before standing them in a cool place in the open on boards or slates so that worms cannot get up into the soil. Cover them with a 12.5m (5in) layer of fibre or ashes and a polythene sheet to keep out the rain.

The darkness encourages growth of the roots, which is so essential to good blooms. Bulbs should never be forced on before their roots have sufficiently developed. After seven to nine weeks the roots should have formed and the tops have made about 2.5cm (1in) of growth. They can then be moved to a frame or a cold greenhouse, and kept watered but not saturated.

The less forward plants can be put back in the bed of ashes to provide a succession of later blooms if brought into the greenhouse at intervals.

Do not subject the pots to full light until two or three days after the covering has been removed, and until the pale yellow shoots have turned green. When this has happened move the pots close to the glass and bring them on gradually till the flower buds are well advanced. They can then be moved into the home and given an occasional liquid feed. A good compost consists of a mixture of equal parts of loam, leaf-mould and well-rotted cow manure, together with a little sand.

The number of bulbs that can be planted in a pot depends on the type of bulb and the size of pot used. Snowdrops, crocuses and scilla may be planted so that they practically touch one another, about nine bulbs in a 12.5cm (5in) pot; larger bulbs, such as those of the daffodil and tulip, may be planted six in a 12.5cm (5in) pot, while only three hyacinths can be accommodated in a 15cm (6in) pot.

After forcing, dry off the bulbs and plant them out in borders or use them for naturalizing. The year after forcing, the bloom may not be very spectacular, but in subsequent years they should flower profusely.

Bulbs in fibre

Bulb suppliers usually offer specially prepared bulbs to grow in fibre or compost for early flowering. It is false economy to buy any but the best bulbs for forcing. Any type of bowl or other container, about 12.5cm (5in) deep is suitable, but avoid porous containers. A few lumps of charcoal placed over the base will keep the fibre compost sweet. If the fibre is lumpy pick it over and rub out the lumps between your fingers, then soak it for a day or so and drain it thoroughly until only a drop or two of water comes out when the fibre is squeezed in the hand. Fill the bowls to a depth of about one half for large bulbs, such as narcissus and hyacinth; three-quarters for the smaller, such as crocuses and scillas. On this layer, which should not be pressed down too tightly, place the bulbs; if the bowl is very large, group them in small clumps rather than spacing them regularly over it; if it is small the bulbs may nearly, but not quite, touch. Then fill the bowl almost to the top with the fibre, so that the extreme tips of the bulbs just show above it. Keep the bowls in a dark, cool and airy place, for the first six weeks. A cool, airy cupboard or cellar will do. Once a week or so examine the bowls to see whether the fibre is dry, and if it shows signs of dryness plunge them in a basin of lukewarm water, which should cover them completely. When the fibre is well soaked, take out the bowls and turn them carefully sideways, so that any superfluous water drains off. The fibre should be just damp, never saturated. When the bulbs have made shoots about 2.5cm (1in) long bring the bowls out into the light, but do not expose to full heat and light until the shoots have turned a healthy green. Until this happens the bowls should be kept in a shaded, cool room. When the shoots are green allow more heat, light and air; at night move them away from windowsills if frosts threatens. Remember that the plants will naturally grow towards the light, so to ensure good straight plants and flower stalks, give the bowls a quarter turn each day. Do not feed them.

Crocuses, daffodils, tulips, hyacinths, chionodoxas, fritillarias and grape hyacinths may all be successfully grown in fibre, each kind being raised in a separate bowl. Only specially pre-treated daffodils, tulips and hyacinths will tolerate high temperatures when forcing.

Forcing flowering shrubs

Shrubs for forcing should be vigorous and the shoots firm, well ripened and with plenty of flower buds. Apply heat gradually, giving too little rather than too much. The shrubs are usually potted-up in September or early in October and placed in a cold frame until November. Early potting is essential. About the middle of November transfer them to the greenhouse and place them in a temperature of about 7°C (45°F) for the first fortnight; during this period syringe overhead twice a day in fine weather. After the first couple of weeks the temperature may be raised to 15°C (59°F) and as soon as the plants break into active growth the temperature can be raised slightly. When the colour of the buds begins to show, lower the temperature to 15°C (59°F) and maintain this level while the plants are flowering. After forcing, some of the old wood that has borne flowers should be cut away and weak shoots cut right back, the aim being to let air and light into the centre of the plant so that the shoots become thoroughly ripened and able to produce buds for the season. Keep the plants in the warm for three weeks or so, syringe overhead in fine weather with tepid water and feed once a week with weak liquid fertilizer. After this treatment they can be stood in a cold house or cold frame for a fortnight or three weeks to be gradually hardened off and set out in the open for the summer early in June.

Nearly all shrubs are better if forced every alternate year only, and with lilacs this is essential. Roses, however, can be forced quite successfully for several years in succession.

The following is a selection of hardy shrubs for forcing:

Acer japonicum and vars.
A. negundo 'Variegatum'
Amelanchier canadensis
Azalea mollis
Ceanothus species
Chimonanthus praecox
Choisya ternata
Clematis x *jackmanii* hybrids
Cytisus x *praecox* hybrids
Daphne mezereum
Deutzia gracilis and *D.* x *limoinei*
Forsythia x *intermedia* 'Spectabilis'
Hydrangea macrophylla vars.
Jasminum nudiflorum

Kalmia latifolia
Kerria japonica 'Flore Pleno'
Lonicera standishii
Magnolia stellata
Malus x *atrosanguinea* and *M.* x *purpurea*
Philadelphus coronarius and hybrids
Prunus subhirtella and *P. triloba* 'Flore Pleno'
Pyrus, see *Malus*
Rhododendron vars.
Ribes sanguineum
Rosa (various)
Spiraea x *arguta, S. media* and *S. thunbergii*
Syringa vulgaris 'Charles X' or 'Marie Legraye'
Viburnum carlesii, V. plicatum var. *tomentosum* and *V. opulus*

The forcing of hybrid tea and floribunda roses is similar to that of other shrubs, except that they are potted-up in October, kept outdoors until December and kept dry, then pruned hard back to two buds at the base of the main stems. Thereafter begin to force them gradually into bloom.

Other plants for forcing are *Astilbe japonica, Convallaria majalis, Dicentra spectabilis* and *Polygonatum multiflorum.*

These plants should be potted-up at the end of October or early in November and kept in a cold but frost-proof frame to be transferred to the greenhouse, in batches as required, at any time from December to March or April. This will ensure a good show of bloom all through the winter from December until the end of May. Keep them near the glass for some time after being taken into the house and give ample water. Gradually remove the pots farther from the glass as the days become longer, and shade the plants while in bloom.

Selection of Greenhouse Plants

For cultural details, for colour of flowers, time of blooming, height and the best species and varieties, *see* alphabetical list of Ornamental Plants and Trees, Ch. 23.

The cold house

Aquilegia caerulea
Astilbe japonica
Begonia (tuberous vars.)
Calceolaria (shrubby types)
Campanula pyramidalis
Chrysanthemum (large decorative types)
Clarkia elegans
Convallaria majalis
Dianthus (perpetual vars.)
Dicentra spectabilis
Fuchsia species and vars.
Godetia grandiflora and vars.
Lobelia cardinalis
Matthiola incana (and vars.) (stock)
Myosotis sylvatica
Pelargonium vars.
Phlox divaricata

Polygonatum multiflorum
Primula vulgaris (primrose)
P. auricula hybrids
P. vulgaris elatior (polyanthus)
P. malacoides
Schizanthus retusus and types
Trollius asiaticus
T. europeaus
Viola odorata (violet)

Bulbs

Anemone blanda
A. x *fulgens*
**Chionodoxa luciliae, C. sardensis*
Crinum moorei and *C.* x *powellii*
Crocosmia x *crocosmiiflora*
**Crocus neapolitanus* var.
**Cyclamen coum*
**C. neapolitanum*
C. persicum
Erythronium dens-canis
Fritillaria latifolia, F. meleagris
Galanthus nivalis (snowdrop)
Hyacinthus orientalis and vars.
Iris alata, I. reticulata and vars.
**I. unguicularis*
Ixia
Kniphofia macowanii
Lilium auratum, L. candidum
L. regale
**Muscari botryoides*
**Narcissus bulbocodium*
**N. cyclamineus*
**N. asturiensis*
**N.* 'Paper White'
Ornithogalum arabicum
**Scilla sibirica*
Tulip vars.
Watsonia meriana

* Indicates bulbs suitable for culture in the alpine house. All small bulbs are best grown in shallow pans 12.5 to 15cm (5 to 6in) in diameter.

Flowering shrubs

Azalea mollis
Berberis darwinii
Bougainvillea x *buttiana*
Bouvarida hybrids
Camellia japonica and vars.
Ceanothus rigidus
Chaenomeles japonica
Choisya ternata
Clematis x *jackmanii*
Cytisus x *kewensis* (broom)
Daphne cneorum
Deutzia gracilis
D. x *limoinei*
Erica carnea
E. mediterranea
Forsythia x *intermedia* 'Spectabilis', *F. suspensa*
Hebe speciosa
Hydrangea macrophylla vars.
Jasminum nudiflorum
Magnolia stellata
Pernettya mucronata
Prunus japonica 'Flore Pleno'
P. tenella 'Alba'
Ribes sanguineum
Spiraea x *arguta*
Syringa vulgaris (lilac)
Viburnum tinus (laurustinus)
Wisteria sinensis

The warm house

Summer temperature 18 to 24°C (65 to 75°F); winter temperature 13 to 15°C (55 to 59°).

Flowering in early spring

Acacia armata (mimosa)
Azalea mollis
Camellia japonica and vars.
Convallaria majalis
Cytisus canariensis
Erica hiemalis
Freesia hybrids
Kerria japonica 'Flore Pleno'
Lachenalia aloides 'Nelsonii'
Olearia gunniana
Philadelphus lemoinei
Prunus serrulata, etc
Ribes aureum
R. sanguineum
Senecio (cineraria) all types
Syringa vulgaris (lilac)
Viburnum plicatum var. *tomentosum* (snowball tree)
Weigela florida
Wisteria sinensis

Flowering in late spring

Calceolaria x *herbeohybrida*
Deutzia gracilis
Dicentra spectabilis
Hippeastrum equestre hybrids
Kalmia polifolia
Lilium longiflorum
Pelargonium (zonal and regal)

Flowering in summer

Abutilon striatum 'Thompsonii'
Achimenes vars.
Agapanthus orientalis
Begonia species and vars.
Campanula isophylla
Canna indica and hybrids
Celsia arcturus
Cobaea scandens
Crinum moorei and *C.* x *powellii*
Fuchsia species and vars.
Gardenia jasminoides vars.
Gloxinia hybrids
Hebe hybrids
Heliotropium hybrids
Hibiscus rosa-sinensis
Hydrangea macrophylla
Impatiens balsamina
Lilium auratum
L. speciosum
Mimulus moschatus
Nerium oleander
Oxalis species
Pelargonium (zonal and regal)
Petunia violacea
Plumbago capensis
Salvia patens

Flowering in autumn

Begonia species and tuberous-rooted
Chrysanthemum (florists')
Nerine bowdenii
Polianthus tuberosa
Reseda odorata (mignonette)
Salvia coccinea, *S. involucrata*, etc
S. splendens vars., etc
Streptocarpus hybrids
Vallota speciosa (Scarborough Lily)

Flowering in winter

Begonia (fibrous-rooted)
Chrysanthemum (florists')
Cyclamen persicum and hybrids
Daphne odora

Erica hiemalis, etc
Euphorbia fulgens
Freesia hybrids
Narcissus tazetta vars.
Pelargonium, all zonal types
Primula floribunda
P. malacoides, etc
Senecio (cineraria)
Solanum capsicastrum
Sparmannia africana
Tropaeolum peltophorum
Zantedeschia aethiopica

Houseplants

Choosing the positions

Select positions for the plants carefully. Good light is essential for encouraging flowering plants and most variegated foliage plants, though few will tolerate full exposure to strong sun in summer. Plants that do not receive enough light should be changed regularly with those in better positions, or if good light falls on one side only, should be given a quarter turn every day. Windows that give the best light may also be draughty in winter or if they face south may be too hot at midday and should be shaded. Above or near a fireplace or radiator the air may be too dry or too hot, and near a door or on the stairs there may be constant or sudden draughts, and lack of light.

Group several plants in a tray containing 2.5 to 5cm (1 to 2in) of small pebbles, kept moist, for this not only displays the plants to best advantage but also makes it easier to create a humid atmosphere in which they will thrive. Alternatively, plunge the base of the pots into peat and keep this moist.

Some tough plants will survive indefinitely in the house but the appearance of many flowering plants is vastly improved if they are merely displayed for a week or two before being returned to a greenhouse to recuperate.

Management

Watering is usually the most difficult problem; some plants need water every day, some not more than once a week, but the majority need attention every two or three days during the growing season. You can get a good idea by tapping clay pots with a piece of wood; a dull sound will show that the soil is moist enough, a ring that it needs water. Plastic pots are more difficult to gauge, but they conserve moisture better than clay pots. Too much water is far more damaging than too little, because the soil may become water-logged, and lead to rotting and death of the roots. It is important that the compost is free-draining and that the pots are not placed in water-tight holders or stood in deep saucers filled with water. If a plant becomes too dry and the soil does not absorb water, put the pot into a bucket with water coming up to the rim of the pot; remove it when thoroughly soaked and bubbles stop rising and allow it to drain. Pick off dead or wilting leaves and flowers regularly and sponge plants with large leaves that collect dust easily; brush hairy leaves gently. Regular application of weak liquid fertilizer during the growing season keeps houseplants healthy.

A Selection of Flowering Plants

Astilbe
Aphelandra
Azalea indica
Begonia (winter-flowering)
Beloperone
Calceolaria
Celosia
Chrysanthemum
Cineraria
Clivia
Cuphea
Cyclamen
Erica
Euphorbia pulcherrima
Exacum
Fuchsia
Hibiscus
Hippeastrum
Hydrangea
Impatiens
Kalanchoe
Pelargonium
Primula
Saintpaulia
Sinningia (gloxinia)
Solanum

A Selection of Foliage Plants

Araucaria
Aspidistra
Begonia
Bromeliads
Cacti
Caladium
Chlorophytum
Cissus
Codiaeum (Croton)
Coleus
Cordyline
Dieffenbachia
Fatshedera
Fatsia
Ferns
Ficus
Gynura
Hedera
Maranta
Monstera
Palms
Peperomia
Philodendron
Pilea
Rhoicissus
Sansevieria
Scindapsus
Syngonium
Tradescantia
Zebrina

16
The Flower Garden

Situation and design

The flower garden would ideally be situated so that it is sheltered from the cold north and east winds whenever possible; the shelter, whether natural or artificial, should protect quite tall-growing plants without excluding light and air.

A shelter belt can take the form of a hedge, an attractive border of shrubs, or staggered rows of trees, all pleasing backgrounds for flowering plants.

Although full sunshine and fertile, well-drained soil are desirable for the cultivation of the majority of plants, there is a large choice of beautiful plants for shaded situations and poorer soils. While the choice of fruits and vegetables is limited and all must have good growing conditions if worthwhile crops are to be obtained, it is quite possible to create beautiful flower gardens in shady, poorly-drained or very dry situations by suitable choice of plants from the enormous range available. This is not to say that preparation of the ground is not important. The more attention that is given to drainage, cultivation and enrichment of the soil before planting, the more rapid and successful will be the results.

Backgrounds and settings

Form is an aesthetic consideration in the arrangement of the garden – the selection of plants beautiful in themselves, and their arrangement singly or in groups, as specimen plants, backgrounds for dwarfer flowers, as screens, boundaries and hedges. When we think of form in the matter of plants, we think in the extreme examples of landscaped gardens, of the cypress, whose silhouette is such a beautiful feature of the Italian landscape, of the tropical palms, the poplar groves of France, and the many beautiful varieties of English and American trees. But on the smaller garden scale, form is just as pronounced and important and can be expressed in the windswept appearance of a dwarf mountain pine, the silvery plumes of a pampas grass and the elegant beauty of smaller garden trees, such as the silver birch and the mountain rowans.

Among the many trees with beautiful foliage, which are of value as background settings are the willow, acacia, asparagus, various specimens of bamboo, reeds, prunus, cypress, cedar, yew and fir, and numerous hardy evergreen and flowering shrubs. Such plants can be used for a variety of purposes: the larger as screens, and to shelter more delicate specimens, others as specimen plants to break up the expanse of a lawn and maintain the beauty of the garden even through the winter. The sheer beauty of some is sufficient justification for their inclusion. The azalea, magnolia, rhododendron, broom, *Chaenomeles speciosa*, to mention but a few, need no recommendation. In the use of evergreens use your discretion to obtain a balanced harmony. In moderation their usefulness as hardy and enduring plants cannot be too highly praised, but some are gross feeders. Their roots are voracious and spread widely, and when they are used as backgrounds in flower beds and planted too widely or allowed to multiply unchecked, they impoverish the soil and weaken other plants.

Siting of trees and shrubs

Trees and shrubs give permanence and frame to the garden and provide a sheltering background as well as a foil for brighter flowers. So it is wise to consider the choice and arrangement of these plants carefully before designing flower borders round an open lawn, and to ensure that this backbone of the garden is planted in its allotted space before turning to the design and layout of secondary features such as beds and borders or rock gardens and pools.

The many varieties of beautiful flowering shrubs which grow well in Britain should ideally be chosen for more than their purely outdoor qualities. Most people who have gardens like to decorate their houses with flowers, but where space limits the choice of shrubs, these should be equally attractive in foliage, autumn colour and berries.

As an immediate setting for the house, no form of planting is more satisfactory than groups of flowering evergreens. Here, above all other places in the garden, permanence is a quality to aim at, for this is the view which is most constantly in evidence. In winter it may be regretted but not deplored that the remoter parts of the garden are not bright with colours, but if the immediate view from the windows is equally desolate then the whole garden will seem drear. For this reason, evergreens with beauty of form or flower near the house are recommended.

Beds and borders

The first and essential purpose of a flower bed is to display flowers and shrubs to their best advantage. The more simple the shape the better it will fulfil its purpose, and at the same time it will be all the more easy to construct, plant and keep in order. Elaborate geometrical designs have, except in the large more formal Dutch and French gardens, gone right out of fashion. Many of these older designs have sharp-pointed extremities, which are very awkward to plant and care for; the most useful shapes are circles, ovals, gently scalloped borders, squares and rectangles.

Rectilinear beds are generally situated in the more formal parts of the garden, near the house, if they harmonize with the straight lines of the architecture or along flowing lines for a modern, more fluid design. Beds laid out on the lawn should be designed so that their edges repeat or complement the edges of the lawn. Except when they are permanently to accommodate shade-loving plants, place the beds so that they are open to the sun, but at the same time have shelter from cold or strong prevailing winds. When beds are made on a lawn leave enough space for the lawn-mower to operate easily; grass verges or walks between beds should be not less than 60cm (2ft) wide, otherwise even a small machine will have difficulty in cutting them well.

Try to incorporate flower beds as part of an overall plan or pattern. Isolated beds of varied and complicated shapes serve only to break up the garden and create a cluttered appearance. In small gardens, it is often more satisfactory to abandon seasonal flower beds altogether and to group flowers of various kinds among shrubs and herbaceous perennials in wide mixed borders and to leave the lawn clear.

Making new beds

Having pegged out the design to the required size and shape, remove the turf on a dry day, with a turfing-iron in grass sods 5cm (2in) deep. Then dig the soil thoroughly, if necessary to a depth of two spits, keeping the top layer on top and breaking up the subsoil below this with a fork. If the soil is very heavy, the top 60 to 90cm (2 to 3ft) may be removed, the subsoil broken up as before and up to 15cm (6in) of broken bricks or large stones placed on it to improve drainage. Where the topsoil is moderately good you can add loam to it and then return it to the bed, or if the soil is quite impoverished, clayey or stony, remove it all and replace with fresh loam. In either case dig a liberal dressing of well-rotted manure into the topsoil. Lime may also be required. (*See* Ch. 4.)

Each autumn top-dress the beds with manure, as bedding plants are voracious feeders; they like a rich soil and soon exhaust it especially when spring and summer bedders follow each other in the same bed. If manuring cannot be carried out in the autumn it should be done in April or May when summer bedding plants are put out. Every three or four years thoroughly dig over the soil to a depth of two spits, and if it appears at all sour and sticky, give it a dressing of lime.

17
Trees, Shrubs and Climbers

Shrubs and trees not only have an intrinsic beauty which adds to the attractiveness of a garden, but they also provide shade, backgrounds for herbaceous borders and focal points and can be used as screens to divide the garden into several parts. These are only a few of the many uses to which shrubs and trees can be put, but they are sufficient to show the importance that must be given to them when a garden is being planned. The variety of deciduous and evergreen trees and shrubs available is enormous.

Climbers also add much beauty to the garden by clothing walls, fences, sheds and other structures, extending the area of a garden to the vertical plane. Simple screens supporting climbers may also be used to divide various parts of the garden; they occupy less space and obscure less light than a thick hedge.

Before planting, dig the ground deeply, preferably to a depth of 60cm (2ft) and enrich it with well-rotted manure and leaf-mould. Allow sufficient space to each individual plant for the free and full development of its particular habit of growth. Remove the turf within a radius of 90cm (3ft) round bushes planted in lawns for the first four years to simplify mowing and reduce the competition from grass roots.

For climbers, the ground preparations should be particularly thorough as their roots are often confined between a path and the footings of a wall, in positions screened from much rainfall and in soil that is generally poor and starved. Prepare a generous planting hole for each climber to a depth of 90cm (3ft), with the lower soil enriched with rotted manure, leaf-mould or garden compost and the topsoil similarly improved with a heavy dressing of manure. Soak the ground well and leave it to settle before planting.

Methods of planting

Small plants move more satisfactorily than fully-grown specimens and adjust more readily to new soil conditions. They are also less expensive to buy. Each shrub or tree should be allotted the full space it will eventually occupy, but annuals, herbaceous plants or quick-growing temporary shrubs may be used to fill the gaps until they mature. Usually the best time to plant deciduous shrubs is from the middle of October, when the leaves begin to fall, to the middle of November, or in February and March. Evergreens are best planted in September and early October, or better still in April and the beginning of May. Never plant evergreens – or any other plant – in the depth of winter when their vitality is at the lowest, nor when cold, drying winds are prevalent. Container-grown plants may be planted out at any time during the year, weather and soil permitting. In the case of both deciduous and evergreen shrubs it is usually wise, at the time of planting, to thin out and reduce the length of the branches by about one third; This will relieve the strain on the roots while they are establishing themselves. Climbers should not be planted with the roots right up against a wall but 30 to 45cm (12 to 18in) away from the wall, so that they may receive adequate air and moisture. Do not use creosote on fences or wooden supports of a pergola as it is harmful to plant growth.

During the spring and summer keep the soil free of weeds; a mulch of peat or well-decayed manure or compost will do much to maintain healthy growth. In dry weather give a good watering to all wall plants.

Purpose and design

The arrangement of shrubs varies according to the purpose they are to fulfil. In small gardens single plants of different species can be used so that a wide variety of plants can be included, but great care must be taken to ensure that the plants blend to form a harmonious scheme. It is usually better to place groups of about three plants of the same kind together, but full space should be allowed for each individual to develop.

The fact that by careful selection we can have a continued sequence of bloom from flowering shrubs almost throughout the year is often overlooked. Select shrubs not only for the beauty of their flowers and suitability for their situation, but also for the time of year at which they flower. Take care that specimens whose colours clash are separated and that those whose blooms harmonize in colour and time of flowering are allowed to be set off and enhanced by the foliage of shrubs whose flowers are over or still to come. The stronger growers must be kept in check by periodical pruning or they may overpower less vigorous plants.

A straight or boldly curved edge to the mixed border is more satisfactory than unnecessary wiggles, and if the border is edged with stone, brick or concrete slabs the dwarfer plants will be able to droop forward gracefully without encroaching on the lawn.

Although boldness combined with simplicity greatly improves the appearance of a mixed or shrub border do not regiment the height and placing too strictly. Let groups of plants make projections and bays, sometimes pressing out into the border, sometimes forming a recess in which herbaceous plants and bulbs may find shade and shelter.

Conifers
These include many species that may well be planted singly as specimen trees on the lawn. Among the best for large gardens are: *Abies alba*, *A. homolepis*, *A. procera*; *Cedrus atlantica*; *Cryptomeria japonica*; *Chamaecyparis lawsoniana* and *C. obtusa*; *Cupressus macrocarpa*; *Picea abies*, *P. smithiana*, *P. pungens* 'Glauca'; *Pinus wallichiana* (*P. excelsa*, *P. griffithii*), *P. nigra* and *P. sylvestris*; *Pseudolarix amabilis*; *Pseudotsuga menziesii*; *Taxodium distichum*; *Thuja plicata*, *T. orientalis*; and *Tsuga heterophylla*. In small gardens *Juniperus chinensis* 'Pfitzereana', *J. communis* 'Hibernica', *J. horizontalis*; *Picea glauca* 'Conica'; *Pinus mugo* var. *mughus* and *Thuja orientalis* 'Elegantissima' provide a similar range of forms.

Coloured autumn foliage
In planting trees and shrubs it is well worth considering their appearance not only in spring and summer, but also in autumn. When the garden is losing its colour, trees and shrubs may provide much cheerful and striking colour. A useful selection of these foliage trees and shrubs will be found in the following lists.

Hardy Ornamental Trees and Shrubs

Evergreen

Abies (fir)
Araucaria (monkey puzzle)
Cedrus (cedar)
Chamaecyparis
Cryptomeria
x *Cupressocyparis*
Cupressus (cypress)
Elaeagnus glabra, *E. macrophylla*, *E. pungens*
Eucalyptus
**Ilex aquifolium* and vars. (*s*)
Juniperus (juniper)
Laurus nobilis
Ligustrum (privet) (*s*)
Picea abies, etc
Pinus (pine)
Pseudotsuga menziesii
Quercus ilex
Sequoiadendron giganteum
Taxus baccata and vars. (*s*)
Thuja (various) (*s*)
Tsuga heterophylla
Ulex europaeus

Deciduous

†*Acer* (maple)
Alnus glutinosa, etc
Betula
Catalpa
Elaeagnus angustifolia
**E. commutata*
**Euonymus latifolius*
†*Fagus sylvatica* (beech)
Fraxinus americana
†*Ginkgo biloba*
**Hippophae rhamnoides*
Larix decidua (larch)
†*Nyssa sylvatica* (tupelo)
Platanus x *hybrida*
P. orientalis
Populus alba 'Bolleana'

†*Pseudolarix amabilis*
Quercus cerris
Q. coccinea 'Splendens'
†*Rhus typhina*
†*Sorbus*
Taxodium distichum
Tilia
Ulmus

Pendulous or weeping trees

Betula pendula (birch) and vars.
Crataegus monogyna 'Pendula'
Fagus sylvatica 'Pendula' (beech)
Fraxinus excelsior 'Pendula' (ash)
**Ilex aquifolium* 'Pendula' (holly)
Populus tremula 'Pendula' (aspen)
Prunus mahaleb 'Pendula' *(St Lucie cherry)*
P. subhirtella 'Pendula' (Japanese cherry)
Quercus robur 'Pendula' (oak)
Salix babylonica (willow)
Pyrus salicifolia 'Pendula'
Ulmus glabra 'Pendula'
U.g. 'Camperdownie' (Wych elm)

Note – * denotes berry-bearing shrubs; † coloured foliage in autumn; *s* suitable for shade; *r* suitable for the rock garden; E = Evergreen; D = Deciduous; *w* = winter-flowering shrub.

Hardy flowering trees and shrubs

Note – For colour of flowers, time of blooming, heights, cultural details, and the best species and varieties, *see* the alphabetical list of Ornamental Plants and Trees, Ch. 23.

Abelia triflora (D) and *A.* x *grandiflora* (E)
**Ailanthus altissima* (D)
*†*Amelanchier canadensis*
Andromeda polifolia (E)
**Arbutus unedo* (E)
**Aucuba japonica* (E) (*s*)
Azalea vars. (E or D)
**Azara* (E)
**Berberis darwinii* (E)
Buddleia vars. (D)
Buxus sempervirens (E) (*s*)
Calluna vulgaris (E) (*r*)
Calycanthus floridus (D) (*s*)
Camellia species (E)
Castanea sativa (D)
Catalpa bignonioides (D)
Ceanothus species (E)
Cercis siliquastrum (D)
Chaenomeles japonica, *C. speciosa* (D)
Chimonanthus praecox (D) (*w*)
Chionanthus retusus (D) (*s*)
Choisya ternata (E) (*s*)
Cistus (rock rose) (E) (*r*)
†**Clerodendrum trichotomum* (D)
**Colutea arborescens* (D)
**Cornus* (D) (*w, r, s*)
†**Cotoneaster* (E and D) (*r, s*)
†**Crataegus* (thorn) (D)
Cytisus (D and E) (*r*)
Daboecia cantabrica (E) (*r*)
**Daphne* species (E and D) (*r*)
Deutzia species (D)
†*Enkianthus* species (D)
Erica species (heath) (E) (*r*)
Escallonia species (E and D)
Eucryphia species (E)
Euonymus japonicus (E)
Exochorda racemosa (D)
Forsythia species (D) (*s*)
Fuchsia magellanica and vars.
Garrya elliptica (E) (*w*)
*†*Gaultheria procumbens* and

G. shallon (E) (*r, s*)
Genista species (D) (*r*)
Halesia carolina (D)
†*Hamamelis mollis* (D) (*w*)
Hebe (E) (*r*)
Hibiscus syriacus (D) (*s*)
Hydrangea species (D) (*s*)
Hypericum (E or D) (*s*)
Jasminum species
Kalmia latifolia
Kerria japonica 'Flore Pleno' (D)
Laburnum (various) (D)
Lavandula spica (E)
†*Liriodendron tulipifera*
Lonicera (honeysuckle) (D)
Lupinus arboreus (D)
Magnolia species (E and D)
**Mahonia* species (E) (*s, w*)
†**Malus* species (D)
Morus nigra (D)
Myrtus communis (E)
Olearia × *haastii* (E) (*r, s*)
Osmanthus heterophyllum (E)
Paeonia suffruticosa (D)
†*Parrotia persica* (D)
**Pernettya mucronata* (E)
Philadelphus species (mock orange) (D) (*s*)
**Phillyrea latifolia* (E) (*s*)
Phlomis fruticosa (E)
Pieris floribunda, P. forrestii, and *P. japonica* (E)
Potentilla species (D)
Prunus amygdalus (D)
P. avium 'Flore Pleno' (D)
P. cerasifera (cherry plum) (D)
P. persica (peach) (D)
P. serrulata vars. (Japanese cherry)
**Pyracantha* species (E)
Rhododendron (E)
†*Ribes aureum, R. sanguineum* (D) (*s*)
Robinia hispida (D)
Romneya coulteri (D)
**Rosa* species (D)
Rosmarinus officinalis (E)
Salix babylonica (D)
**Sambucus canadensis* 'Maxima' (E) (*r*)
Senecio greyii, S. laxifolius (E)
**Skimmia japonica* (E) (*s*)
Spartium junceum (E)
Spiraea species (D) (*s, r*)
**Symphoricarpos albus laevigatus* (D) (*s*)
Syringa vars. (lilac) (D) (*s*)
Tamarix pentandra (D)
†**Viburnum opulus* 'Sterile' etc
†**V. tinus* (E) (*w, s*)
Vinca major 'Elegantissima' (periwinkle) (E) (*s, r*)
Weigela (D)
Wisteria sinensis (D)
Yucca gloriosa (E)
Y. recurvifolia (E)

Climbing and wall plants

Some climbing plants cling to walls by aerial roots, but the walls themselves should be in good condition to avoid crumbling mortar. Others twine their stems, tendrils or leaf stalks round supports and will not cling to a wall. These require a frame of trellis work, wires or netting attached to the wall. Also included in this group are many plants that are not true climbers but thrive in the sheltered conditions of a wall. They are known as wall shrubs and may be left to grow freely or trained back against the wall as fan-shaped plants. In this case branches are tied back to nails or vine eyes in the wall or to wires or other framework. Methods of climbing for each plant are shown in the list below.

Some half-hardy plants need the shelter of a warm wall in all but the most sheltered gardens; others are particularly sensitive to frost or drought and thrive in moist borders along west-facing walls or fences while many good hardy plants will tolerate a north or east aspect. Again preferences are given in the list below.

Many of the more slender climbers can be used as they would grow in nature, rambling through other shrubs or trees either to decorate them when they are not in flower, to enhance them by harmonious combinations of flowers or to hide dead tree stumps. The possible combinations are endless, and climbers appropriate for this purpose are indicated in the list below.

The most valuable of garden climbing plants are perennials, but annuals also provide a number of beautiful climbers which, by their quick growth and easy culture, are often of the greatest value, particularly where a quick result is needed, perhaps in a new garden, before more permanent plants are established. Annual climbers are also very useful in window boxes and tubs.

Selection of Climbing Plants

For cultural details and for colour of flowers, time of flowering, height and the best species and varieties, *see* the alphabetical list of Ornamental Plants and Trees, Ch. 23.

T. *Aristolochia macrophylla* (syn. *A. sipho*), S.W.
L. *Azara microphylla* (warm sheltered), S.
*T. *Berberidopsis corallina* (Southern counties only), S.W.
L. *Calycanthus occidentalis*, S.W.
*C. *Campsis grandiflora* (trumpet vine), S.
*L. *Carpenteria californica* (Southern counties), S.
L. *Ceanothus* species, S.
T. *Celastrus scandens*, N.E.
L. *Chaenomeles japonica, C. speciosa* vars., E.W.
L. *Chimonanthus praecox* (winter sweet), S.W.
*L. *Choisya ternata*, S.
T/R *Clematis flammula*, E.W.
C. florida vars., E.W.
C. x *jackmanii* vars., E.W.
C. lanuginosa vars., E.W.
C. montana vars., N.E.W.
C. patens vars., E.W.
C. vitalba (traveller's joy), N.E.W.
C. viticella vars., E.W.
L. *Cotoneaster henryanus*, N.E.W.
L. *C. horizontalis*, N.E.
*T. *Eccremocarpus scaber*, S. Treat as an annual
L. *Escallonia species*, S.
L. *Forsythia suspensa*, S.W.
L. *Garrya elliptica*, N.E.W.
C. *Hedera colchica*, N.
C. *H. helix* (common ivy)

C. *Hydrangea petiolaris*, N.W.
T. *Jasminum nudiflorum*, N.E.W.
T/L. *J. officinale*, N.E.
J. mesnyi, S.W.
J. humile 'Revolutum', S.W.E.
L. *Kerria japonica*, S.W.
T. *Lathyrus grandiflorus*, S.W.
L. latifolius (everlasting pea), S
T. *Lonicera caprifolium*, E.
L. japonica vars. N.E.
L. sempervirens (trumpet honeysuckle), N.S.E.W.
L. *Magnolia denudata*, W.
L. *M.* x *soulangiana*
L. *Myrtus communis*, S.
C. *Parthenocissus henryana*, S.N.E.W.
C. *P. quinquefolia* (Virginia creeper), N.S.E.W.
C. *P. tricuspidata* 'Veitchii' (syn. *Vitis veitchii*), N.S.E.W.
T. *Passiflora caerulea* and *P.c.* 'Constance Elliott' (passion flower), S.W.
T. *Polygonum baldschuanicum*, N.S.E.W.
L. *Pyracantha* species, N.S.E.W.
L. *Rosa*
T. *Rubus henryi*, E.W.
*L/R. *Solanum crispum*, S.W.
*T. *S. jasminoides* (sheltered), S.W.
*T. *Trachelospermum jasminoides*, S.
T/R. *Tropaeolum speciosum* (flame nasturtium), N.
C. *Vitis coignetiae* (crimson glory vine), S.
T. *V. vinifera* 'Purpurea' (sheltered), S.W.
T. *Wisteria* species, S. or S.W.

Annuals

*T. *Cobaea scandens* (grown as annual)
*T. *Cucurbita* (gourd)
T. *Humulus* (grown as annual)
T. *Ipomoea purpurea* (syn. *Pharbitis purpurea*) (morning glory)
T. *Lathyrus odoratus* (sweet pea)
*T. *Tropaeolum peregrinum* (Canary creeper)
T. *T. majus* (climbing nasturtium

Note – N.S.E. or W. indicates the most suitable position, eg wall facing north, south, east or west. * denotes half-hardy. C = self-clinging. T. = twining on wires etc. L = loose growing wall shrub. R = rambling.

Pruning

The time and method for pruning depends on the season of flowering, and on whether the blooms are borne on new or old wood. (For details *see* Ch. 7.) Many plants require only occasional thinning out to remove dead wood, improve their shape or restrict their size. The natural form of the plant should whenever possible be allowed to predominate.

April is the best time to trim evergreens, except conifers, which are best pruned in September or October. Conifers, except when grown as hedge plants, are not usually cut hard back. When such conifers as the cupressus or yew are used as hedges, they may be pruned hard back to the height desired.

18
Roses and their Culture

Roses occupy a special place of affection in British gardens for their extended flowering season, their fragrance and the beauty of their blooms. They range from 12m (40ft) high climbers to dainty miniatures of less than 30cm (1ft) and in between these extremes is such a vast range of other types. The modern hybrid tea and floribunda roses flower for months on end and are easily forgiven their rather stiff and dull appearance during the winter months. Old species and shrub roses, though often with a short, but delightful flowering season, are always attractive in leaf and many have outstanding hips in autumn.

Types of roses

The main groups of roses are hybrid tea, floribunda, old-fashioned, shrub and climber, although the divisions between these groups are somewhat fluid. Hybrid tea roses have one or sometimes a few, well-shaped flowers on each stem and flower repeatedly throughout the summer. Floribunda roses are similar in growth, but with large trusses of flowers, less double and less perfectly formed than hybrid tea, on each stem. These two groups have largely replaced the older weaker polyantha roses which are particularly liable to mildew.

Old-fashioned roses are the ancestors of the modern rose. Many have rather weak growth, most flower briefly in June, but some with a second flush in early autumn, and brilliantly coloured hips. They have, however, their own particular charm, in beautifully shaped large flowers of exquisite fragrance, and are deservedly returning to popularity. Shrub roses are mainly vigorous species or forms of the old species roses, with one brief flowering season but often with additional qualities of foliage and form or decorative hips to recommend them for garden use. Modern shrub roses are crosses of hybrid teas, old-fashioned roses and shrub species which have produced a range of roses combining the vigorous constitution of shrubs, the shape and fragrance of old-fashioned rose flowers and the continuous flowering habit of hybrid teas to a greater or lesser extent. Climbing roses include the tall sorts of hybrid teas, the true climbing roses flowering mainly on the laterals of established stems, and the vigorous rambler roses which flower on strong new shoots.

The list of roses within each category is legion and is constantly increasing as new varieties are introduced. Before buying it is advisable to consult an up-to-date specialist catalogue or to visit large gardens and parks to see roses in bloom.

Roses as garden plants

Hybrid tea and floribunda roses are midway in character between bedding plants and permanent shrubs. In large gardens a separate formal rose garden forms a delightful feature and hybrid teas in particular do best in a bed of their own. In small gardens, the more vigorous floribundas, such as 'Masquerade', 'Iceberg' and 'Irish Mist' are suitable as groups in a mixed border. Formal rose beds can also be underplanted with violas, low geraniums and short bulbs to extend the season of interest.

Old-fashioned roses need generous treatment and room to display them well. They are superb massed in large gardens where they combine

Training a climbing rose on a fence: by spreading out shoots as near horizontally as possible side shoots will be encouraged. The stems need to be tied to supports

well with pinks, lavender, iris for a brief but brilliant display, and in small gardens they can make dazzling specimen plants. Species and modern hybrid shrub roses are very useful in mixed borders especially if those with good foliage (*R. rubrifolia*, *R.* x *alba*) and attractive hips (*R. rugosa*, *R. moyesii*) are chosen. Climbers and ramblers are ideal for clothing walls and fences, climbing up trees and hiding ungainly features. In large gardens they make attractive walks supported by pergolas or rustic screens, they mix happily with clematis and the lower stems can be concealed with groups of lilies.

Soil and situation

The very best soil for roses is a deep heavy loam. Peaty soils, if rich in character, are quite good for roses, a general rule being that the more gravelly or sandy a soil the less favourable for the rose. The soil must be well drained, and this means a substratum of porous material, chalk or gravel, not too deep below the surface. Gravel has had a bad reputation for roses, but it is not altogether deserved. Often considered too dry and hot for roses to thrive in, it will grow very good roses if a little care is taken to improve it. Many of the briars and the hybrid teas enjoy such a light dryish soil. Chalk, provided that it is deep enough below the surface, and that there is a good depth of soil on top, is not a bad subsoil. It is well drained, and not too dry in hot weather. Where it is very close to the surface it needs a lot of work and preparation if it is going to grow good roses. A layer, 45cm (18in) deep of good loam is the minimum for roses on chalk, and where the loam is shallower than this, special planting holes must be prepared for the plants and extra soil supplied.

Roses like shelter from strong winds, an open sunny situation away from frost hollows and not too close to high hedges or trees. Shelter from north and east winds is desirable, and if there is room for choice, the rose garden should be on the highest part of the available land, other conditions of soil and shelter being equal.

Planting

Early November is the best time for this operation, though it may be done right through the winter – should conditions be favourable – until the end of March, spring planting being preferable on light soils. Plants bought in containers may be planted at any time.

Break up the soil to a depth of at least 60 or 90cm (2 or 3ft) and improve drainage if necessary. Before the roses arrive turn over the soil to a depth of about 45cm (1½ft) and incorporate plenty of well-rotted manure in it. The lowest layer of soil in the bed should consist of rich, fairly retentive soil, which will hold a certain amount of water, while the upper layers should be lighter and more friable, to encourage the plants to produce plenty of good fibrous roots. Dig the holes to receive the roots from 30 to

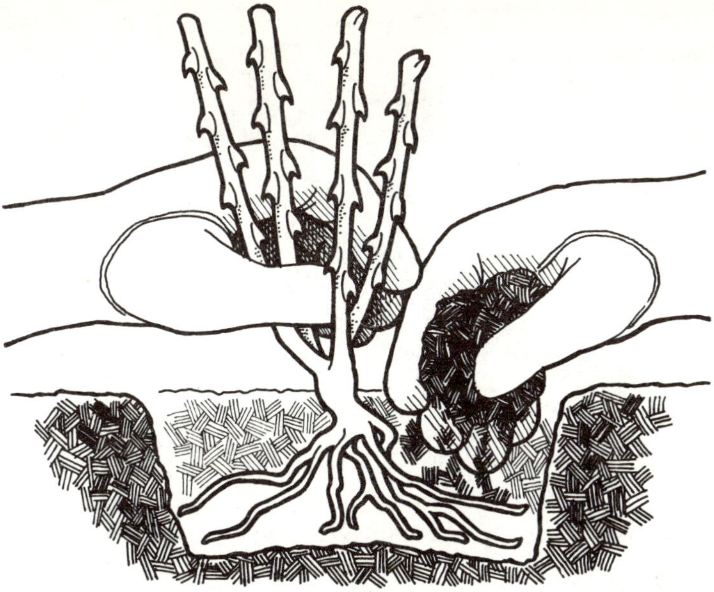

When planting roses make a hole wide enough for the roots to be spread out and deep enough for the union to be just below ground level

45cm (1 to 1½ft) square and deep enough for the point of junction of the scion and the stock to be covered to a depth of about 2.5cm (1in).

Soil may become 'rose sick'. If roses are to be planted in ground previously occupied by other roses the soil needs to be liberally enriched with manure and ideally put to other use for a year or two. When this is not possible, for example when you are replacing worn-out roses in a rose garden, take out a hole, discard the soil, work a generous supply of rotted manure into the bottom of the hole, and plant the roses in rich new loam or growing compost.

Pruning roses after planting

When roses are planted during the autumn and winter months their first pruning should be left until the spring, but when spring-planted it should be done when they are put in. Go over the bushes carefully and cut all dead wood clean out, together with weak and sappy, unripened wood and any shoots which have been injured. Standards should then be cut back to within about 10cm (4in) of their union with the stock and bush trees dealt with a little less severely, leaving about 15cm (6in) of every shoot above the ground. This pruning is only carried out at the time of planting. Subsequent treatment varies with the variety.

Pruning established roses

Hybrid tea and floribunda roses can be lightly pruned in autumn to reduce the risk of blowing about in winter gales. In early spring, remove

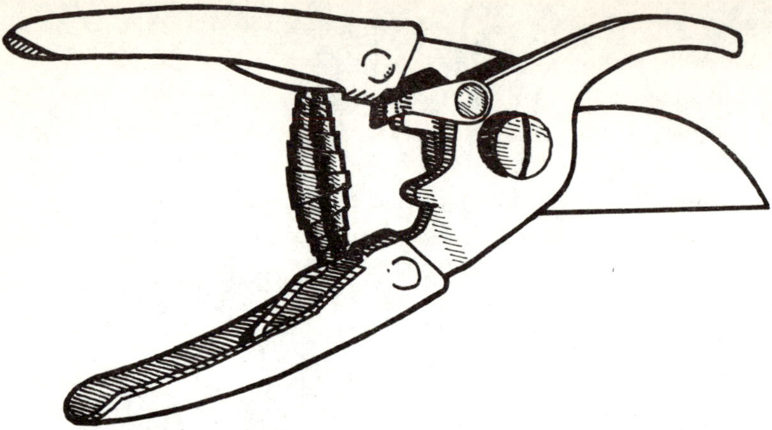

A good sharp pair of secateurs is the most useful tool for successful pruning operations

all dead, weak and misplaced shoots to open out the centre of the plant and cut back all remaining shoots of hybrid teas to four or six buds of the base. Although the result looks severe, the remaining buds will rapidly produce strong shoots to begin flowering in June. Floribunda roses are pruned less severely than hybrid teas, cutting the shoots back to five or seven buds. Dead-heading is a modified form of summer pruning. Instead of cutting off the remains of the dead flower, shorten the shoot back by about a third of its length to encourage further shoots.

Old-fashioned roses require a similar but much less drastic pruning. The centre should be kept open, vigorous new shoots being retained.

Prune established hybrid tea roses back to four or six strong, outward growing buds

Occasional old shoots may be cut out almost to the base and the remainder lightly tipped; shorten the laterals to three or five buds.

Shrub roses do not require regular pruning except for *R. omeiensis* which is grown for the bright prickles on its young stems. This is pruned hard back to encourage new growth.

Climbing roses, which have one main flush of flowers, are pruned as soon as they have finished flowering. Climbing hybrid teas and true climbing roses are thinned only lightly, any strong new shoots being retained for replacement shoots, and the flowered laterals are pruned almost to their base to encourage new lateral growth. Rambler roses are much more vigorous, and flowered shoots should be removed at base and new shoots tied in to take their place.

Care of roses

All roses benefit from careful cultivation. Many are subject to black spot, mildew, aphids (greenfly) and occasionally red-spider mites. These should be watched for and treated at the first sign of attack. (*See* Ch. 9, Pests and Diseases.)

A thick mulch in May will encourage vigorous healthy growth and if this is followed by a fertilizer rich in potash in June, flowering will be improved. Fertilizers especially blended for roses are available. Careful dead-heading (*see* Pruning above) prolongs the flowering season, and although roses are deep-rooting and should not require watering on good soils, a thorough watering during prolonged drought is beneficial.

At the end of the season tip the plants lightly and burn all debris to reduce the risk of diseases being carried over into the following year.

Propagating roses

The most usual method of propagating the rose is by budding, which is a form of grafting in which a rootstock is joined with a scion. But instead of joining a branch or shoot, in roses only a bud is selected. The selection of the bud is most important and should be chosen from a shoot which is mature enough to have borne or to be able to bear a flower – what is called a 'ripe' shoot. Try the shoot with your finger; gently rub it over the prickles. If these fall off easily, the shoot is ripe for budding. Propagation is done in summer, between June and September; the earlier season being suitable if really ripe shoots can be found. Choose the stock in relation to the soil or situation in which it is to be grown and raise these from seeds, cuttings or bought in from nurseries. Certain kinds, such as 'Polyantha Simplex', do best in light soils, others like *R. canina* in heavy, some in dry, and some in moist ground. Some varieties of rose do better on one stock than another, and it is worthwhile checking with the nursery for a suitable stock. (*See also* the chapter on plant propagation.)

Roses are sometimes propagated from cuttings, and where the roses are grown on their own roots this type of propagation is easier to deal with than budding. There is always a risk in budding that the stock may prove too vigorous for the more delicate scion. As a rule climbers and ramblers do well grown in this way, as do the species and old roses and shrubs. Take cuttings from well-ripened wood, which carries a good number of strong healthy leaves, in late summer after the roses have finished flowering. These hardwood cuttings can be rooted in the open. Select a non-flowering shoot about 25 to 30cm (10 to 12in) long and remove all leaves except the top two or three as well as any buds in the leaf axils. Prepare a trench 20cm (8in) deep in a sheltered situation and mix the soil with a little decayed manure, sand and leaf-mould. A frame is better than open ground, but is not essential. Set the cuttings 10cm (4in) apart, water them in well, and spray with a sprinkler morning and evening if the weather is dry. The cuttings may also be planted in pots where they often seem to root more quickly. A cloche or a cold frame placed over them will help rooting. Cuttings will usually be rooted enough for planting out the following autumn.

Species roses can also be grown from seed, a method employed commercially where new varieties are being raised. The seed must be allowed to ripen well and hand pollination is usually necessary. Leave the hips on the plant until almost dropping, then stratify them in damp sand until the next October or November, when the seed can be sown. The seeds often take a whole year to germinate, so do not give up hope if the seedlings show no signs of life for many months. Where seedlings are being raised for new varieties, the tiny plants are budded on to briars during their first year, otherwise grow them on in a nursery bed for two years before planting them out in their growing positions. It is advisable to remove flower buds in the initial stages to prevent the small plants from exhausting themselves.

19
The Herbaceous Border

The herbaceous border can be one of the most attractive features of a garden. Provided that it is of manageable size and the plants are carefully selected it need not require any more labour than the upkeep of the beds filled with annuals, and less than the laying out of more severe bedding designs. Once planted it lasts for many years, merely requiring weeding, staking, occasional mulching, and forking over and feeding annually. The width of the border should harmonize with the size of the garden and other considerations. Where possible it should be not less than 1.2m (4ft) wide, and where there is plenty of space it could be double that.

Site and background

The herbaceous border may occupy almost any position in the garden, but the best results will be obtained if it faces due south and has some protection in the form of a wall or a hedge from the cold north and east winds. But take care that the hedge is far enough away for its roots not to take nourishment from the flowers in the border. A good distance is 60 to 90cm (2 to 3ft).

The background can make or mar the border. A wall or trellis covered with roses or other flowering climber is good, so also is a wall planted with fruit trees, but the dark green background provided by a yew hedge is very hard to beat.

Most perennials will grow in almost any soil, but a deep, rich, well-drained loam is preferred by most.

Preparing the border

The ground should be thoroughly prepared several weeks in advance. This is even more important than in the case of beds for annuals or for tender plants, which will occupy the ground for a single season only. The properly prepared and properly planted border should not require remaking or replanting for several years to come; one of its chief charms consists in the 'settled down' appearance, which is only possible with plants which have occupied the same ground for some time.

The border may be prepared either in September for planting in October or November or in early January for planting in March or April.

The ground needs to be well drained and should ideally be dug to a depth of 60 to 90cm (2 to 3ft), taking care not to bring any sour or heavy subsoil to the top. Mix good farmyard manure with the bottom spit if the soil is heavy, or cow or pig dung if the land is light, while weathered ashes, bone meal, or basic slag will help to break up and lighten the top spit. If the soil is too light it can be improved by adding leaf-mould or thoroughly moistened peat.

Leave the border for a month or so after digging so that it can settle down before the plants are put in.

Time for planting

As a general rule the best time to plant the border is in October or November, but in the north and in very exposed positions it is often advisable to defer planting until March or April. The plants that bloom early should be planted in the autumn if possible so that the roots can get well established before they have to bear the strain of flowering. This applies to such plants as lupins and paeonies. Autumn planting is also advisable in light soils, as very dry weather in late spring may prove disastrous to plants newly set in a light soil that will soon dry out and parch the unestablished roots. In wet, cold soils spring planting is best; if plants must be put in during autumn, do it in September. Thick succulent-rooted plants are more apt to decay if planted in autumn; these should be spring-planted whenever possible.

In planting dig holes sufficiently deep for the roots to be placed without being doubled up, and wide enough to allow them to spread out; cover with fine soil which should be pressed firmly round the crowns. Firm planting is essential and care must be taken that the crowns are not placed lower than ground level, as water may collect and lead to rotting of the crowns. Insert the plants so that the crowns are just level with the surface of the soil. Some herbaceous plants are tap-rooted, such as the anchusa and sunflower, and these demand an extra deep hole for planting, otherwise their long roots will be bent up and prevented from penetrating deeply into the soil to obtain the nourishment and moisture they need. When planting, study the habits of the roots, and allow them to follow what seems to be their natural course, rather than directing them in one special way. Some roots want to run perpendicularly downwards. others grow horizontally; each should be assisted and humoured.

Gradation of flowering plants

As a general rule the taller-growing plants, such as the rudbeckia, sunflower, hollyhock and delphinium, should be placed at the back of the border and there should be a gentle gradation down through plants of medium height, like the phloxes, campanulas and carnations, to the

A dry stone wall breaks the line of a large open space and makes an ideal home for many rock plants

Wisteria cascading over a sheltered wall

violas, daisies, silenes and other dwarfs at the front. But do not follow this pattern too rigidly or you will end up with a stiff effect and lose the freedom and apparent irregularity. Group clumps of the taller plants in prominent positions well to the front while some small-growing and creeping plants can go at the back, at the base of the taller ones, to break up the general outline; a border loses a good deal of its charm if it can all be seen at once from one end. Set the plants in groups of from three or five to seven or nine of each kind in one clump, but not too closely together; the dwarfer the plants the more in a group. It is one of the greatest mistakes to plant perennials singly in various parts of the border, as this gives a patchwork effect; the ideal is masses of striking but well-harmonized colours.

The distance at which plants should be set apart depends on the height and spread to which they will grow at maturity. A good guide is that the dwarfer kinds should be planted about 20cm (8in) apart, the medium sorts 38cm (15in) apart; and the tallest kinds 60cm (2ft) from one another. The aim is to show practically no bare earth in the fully established border, and yet to avoid any overcrowding which interferes with individual development. So to know the habits of the plants helps as much as taste in arrangement. It is also a good idea to introduce low ground cover plants which provide an attractive carpet while also suppressing weeds.

Each plant should be clearly labelled when it is planted to avoid confusion in the colour scheme and the gradation of height. When all plants are in, neatly fork over the soil around them to give the border a tidy and finished look.

Colour groupings

This is perhaps the most difficult problem, as so much depends on the correct solution and individual taste. Aim at large splashes of colour without strong contrasts, and let the tints merge gently from one into the other and lead up from the paler shades to the most vivid. In a red group, start with the pale pinks, next to them put the deeper shades, and so on, finishing with the most vivid and powerful reds; from this work gradually back to the palest of pink again.

The purples, blues and yellows can be arranged in the same way. But do not place these groups against one another indiscriminately or there will be hard lines and clashing colours. However, pink colours harmonize delightfully with lilac so link these up with the purple group, and the blue group with the yellows, for pale yellow blends very well with pale blue.

Also remember that tints may be made to lead from one to another to blend harmoniously. The yellows can run into orange, the orange through orange-scarlet to scarlet and on to the deepest crimson. In the same way link dark blue with pale blues, then purple and down again through lilac to pale blue, lavender-grey or white. Plants with ample green foliage should not be neglected, as nature uses green very liberally in her colour schemes. White, if not used to excess, is invaluable. It can be placed next to the strongest colours as well as against the palest to bring about a cool effect. On a more ambitious scale, an all white and silver border can be a most relaxing and soothing feature in an otherwise colourful garden.

Many of the strong colours may be associated without going through a gradation of their paler tints. Deep blue or purple, for instance, blends well with gold, orange or yellow, but take care not to use any clashing colours in close proximity. The ultra vivid colours are better sited at the far end of the border as they strike the eye so quickly and are apt, if used too freely, to overpower the more delicate tints.

Do not fall into the common mistake of placing all the bright colours at the back and middle of the border; there should be some groups of vivid colouring well to the front. Innumerable edging plants such as aubrietas, dianthus (pinks) and saxifrages provide brilliant tints for this purpose. The groups of colour should not be bounded by hard straight lines; make each group irregular in shape and merging gradually and imperceptibly into the next.

Do not feel disheartened if the colour scheme is not perfect the first year; very few gardeners are infallible in their colour grouping, and errors can be corrected in subsequent years.

Flowers from April to October

The sequence of flowering presents a problem nearly as difficult as the colour scheme itself. The aim is to secure a continuity of bloom from early spring until late in the autumn. So the plants chosen for the border must be not only brilliant in their colours, but have as long as possible a period of bloom. If the border is wisely planned, there is no reason why there should not be plenty of colour from the beginning of April right up to the end of October.

Bulbs such as snowdrops, crocuses, tulips, scillas, chionodoxas, anemones and fritillarias and such early-flowering plants as alyssum, anchusa, aubrieta and the earlier delphiniums will give a good show in spring. During May, June and July, paeonies, lupins, delphiniums, irises, inulas, erigerons, antirrhinums, and many others will provide all the colour needed; there is no trouble at this period. In August and September there are sweet peas, thalictrums, phloxes, sunflowers, penstemons, antirrhinums and late delphiniums; while gladioli, red-hot pokers, aconitums, rudbeckias, dahlias, sunflowers, chrysanthemums and Michaelmas daisies and sedums will carry on the bloom well to the end of October.

Replacements

By midsummer, or even before, the early-flowering plants will have finished blooming and will begin to look untidy however carefully dead flowers have been picked off. So try to plant later-flowering and taller-growing flowers which will screen these as they grow up. This is more difficult than at first appears, for a plant that will grow tall enough totally to obscure the plant behind it, but not until after that plant has flowered, must be chosen. Nor will *any* later-flowering plant do, even though it grows to the correct height and flowers at the right time, for the substitute plant must also fit into the colour scheme: replace a yellow flower with a yellow one or with one whose flowers will harmonize with yellow.

Annuals may be used to fill vacant spaces, and for this purpose alyssum, asters, centaureas, clarkias, stocks, mignonettes and nemophilas are hard to rival.

Care of the border

If the border is constructed and planted in the autumn it will require little attention through the winter although it is wise to cover the crowns of the less hardy perennials, such as penstemons and aquilegias, with straw or small mounds of ashes to protect them from hard frosts. The winter, too, when there is little foliage and most pests are dormant, is the time to wage war on slugs and other pests. (*See* Ch. 9, Pests and Diseases.)

At the beginning of spring, weeds will begin to grow and a great deal of labour later on will be saved if these are kept down from the start. Hoe throughout the spring and summer to aerate the soil and conserve the moisture in hot, dry weather. When the buds are forming help the plants by giving an application of general fertilizer applied just before rain if possible; if no rain comes the chemical should be well hoed in. A suitable mixture is one part of sulphate of potash to two parts of nitrate of soda, applied at the rate of 50g (2oz) to the sq m (yd). If preferred a top-dressing of two-thirds well-decayed farmyard manure and one-third leaf-mould may be given in spring instead of a fertilizer.

Watering and manuring

During very dry weather, the plants will benefit if watered about every other day. Dead flowers should be cut off at once as this will promote further flowering; once a plant is allowed to go to seed, it soon stops flowering. As the plants die and turn yellow, cut them down to within 7.5cm (3in) of the ground; this keeps the border tidy and gives room to other plants; in November, when all flowers are over, cut down all the plants and label them clearly. Evergreen plants, such as red-hot pokers, should not be cut down. At this time, or late in February, dig some well-decayed manure and leaf-mould in between the plants, but do not let the manure cover the crowns or they may rot off, and take care that the digging fork does not injure the roots.

Renewing the border

About every three to four years the border will be all the better for a thorough digging over and manuring; many of the plants will be getting over-bulky and will need dividing, partly because they will crowd less vigorous neighbours and partly because their flowers will have deteriorated both in size and colour. The border is best renewed in November, when all the plants, with the exception of those like paeonies, delphiniums, lilies, daffodils and irises, should be removed, carefully labelled as to colour, height, species, etc, and laid aside in a warm and sheltered position. If they are to be left out of the border for more than a couple of days or so, heel them into the reserve garden. Then dig the border thoroughly, digging as close as possible up to the plants left in position, and manuring the subsoil well. If the soil is at all sour dress it with lime at the rate of 275g (10oz) to the sq m (yd). Divide the plants,

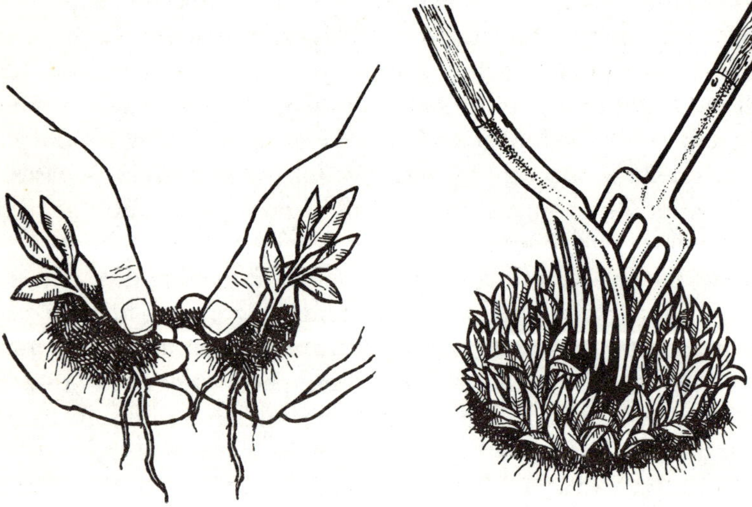

Root division. This is the simplest method of increasing most herbaceous and alpine plants. Lever large fibrous clumps apart by means of two forks

discarding the inner and older stems and replanting the outer and younger crowns in the same way as when the border was first made.

This work may also be done in February or March; this is wiser in colder localities where the plants might not stand a severe winter directly after replanting.

Propagation of herbaceous perennials

Herbaceous perennials may be propagated from seeds, cuttings, offsets, layers, and root divisions, the method most generally used. Seeds are, however, perfectly feasible, especially in the case of new species, although it is a somewhat lengthy process, as the plants do not reach their best for three years. Seed is best sown in the open in May or June, or in shallow boxes in a cold frame. First-year plants should not be allowed to flower at all; second-year plants may be permitted to bloom in moderation but they must not be allowed to go to seed. Full instructions for the various methods of propagation will be found in Ch. 5.

Hardy Herbaceous Perennials

For details as to colour, height, season of flowering, culture and the best species and varieties, *see* the alphabetical list of Ornamental Plants and Trees, Ch. 23.

Acanthus longifolius
A. mollis and *spinosus*
Achillea clypeolata
A. filipendulina
A. ptarmica 'The Pearl'
Aconitum carmichaelii
A. japonicum
A. napellus
Adonis amurensis
A. vernalis
Alcea rosea (hollyhock)
Alstroemeria aurantiaca
A. ligtu
Anchusa italica
Anemone apennina
A. blanda
A. x *fulgens, A.* x *hybrida* and vars.
Anthemis tinctoria vars.
Antherium liliago (St Bernard's Lily)
Aquilegia caerulea
A. longissima
A. vulgaris
Armeria maritima
A. plantaginea and vars.
Artemisia lactiflora
Asphodelus cerasiferus
Aster amellus and vars.
Aster novae-angliae vars.
Aster novi-belgii and vars.
Astilbe x *arendsii*
A. davidii
Aubrieta deltoidea vars.
Bellis perennis (daisy)
Bergenia cordifolia
Buphthalmum salicifolium
Campanula lactiflora
C. latifolia
C. persicifolia
Catananche caerulea
Centaurea macrocephala
C. montana
Centranthus ruber and vars. (valerian)
Cephalaria gigantea
Chelone lyonii
C. obliqua
Chrysanthemum maximum
C. uliginosum
Cimicifuga americana
Coreopsis grandiflora
Corydalis nobilis
Delphinium hybrids
Dianthus caryophyllus (carnation)
D. plumarius (pink)
Dicentra spectabilis
Dictamnus albus

Dodecatheon hendersonii
D. meadia, etc
Doronicum plantagineum and vars.
Echinacea purpurea
Echinops ritro and others
Eremurus (various)
Erigeron speciosus
Eryngium (various)
Erysimum petrovskianum
Filipendula palmata
Gaillardia aristata
Galega officinalis, etc
Gaura lindheimeri
Geranium (various)
Geum (various)
Gypsophila paniculata
Hedysarum (various)
Helenium (various)
Helianthus (sunflower)
Helleborus niger
Hemerocallis hybrids
Heuchera sanguinea
Horminum pyrenaicum
Hosta fortunei
Hypericum calycinum
H. olympicum
Iberis sempervirens
Incarvillea delavayi
Iris germanica and vars.
Kniphofia (various)
Linaria dalmatica
Linum flavum
L. narbonense
L. perenne
Lobelia (various)
Lupinus (various) (lupin)
Lychnis chalcedonica
Lysimachia clethroides
Lythrum (various)
Macleaya cordata
M. microcarpa
Malva moschata
Meconopsis cambrica
Mimulus luteus
Monarda didyma
Myosotis sylvatica (forget-me-not)
Nepeta x *faassenii*
N. sibirica
Oenothera fruiticosa
O. perennis (evening primrose)
Paeonia lactiflora
Papaver orientalis vars.
Penstemon (various)
Phlox paniculata vars. and hybrids
Physostegia virginiana
Primula elatior
P. vulgaris and many garden vars.
Salvia haematodes
S. virgata nemorosa
Saponaria officinalis and vars.
Saxifraga (various)
Scabiosa caucasica vars.
Sedum spectabile and vars.
Senecio clivorum
Sidalcea candida
Smilacina racemosa
Solidago canadensis and hybrids
Stokesia laevis
Thalictrum aquilegiifolium
T. dipterocarpum
Tradescantia virginiana and vars.
Trillium grandiflorum
Trollius asiaticus
T. x *hybridus* and vars.
Veronica incana
V. longifolia (speedwell)
Viola (various) garden vars.

20
Annuals, Biennials and Bedding Plants

Annuals are plants which grow from seed, flower and die within one growing season. Hardy annuals may be sown outside, usually where they are to flower; half-hardy annuals are sensitive to frost and need to be started under glass and planted out later.

Biennials grow from seed in their first year, flower usually rather early in the second year and then die. Some, such as wall flower, pansy and large-flowered polyanthus, are in fact short-lived perennials but their flowers deteriorate in subsequent years so are best treated as biennials.

Bedding plants may be annuals, biennials, bulbs or even herbaceous perennials or shrubs. They are plants used temporarily in geometrically arranged masses for colourful display, being replaced entirely by a fresh arrangement of plants when their flowering season is finished.

Hardy annuals

Any ordinary garden soil is suitable for hardy annuals and for annuals generally. It does not need to be too rich, since this encourages luxuriant leaf growth rather than the production of flowers. Annuals do best, however, in light, sandy soil, and they should have this where possible. Good drainage is essential.

It is always wise to incorporate a generous allowance of leaves or other decomposing vegetable matter with the soil to help create humus.

Very hardy annuals may be sown in autumn, not earlier than the last week in August and not later, even in sheltered spots, than the last week in September. Autumn-sown plants, if they survive the winter's frosts, will bloom earlier in the following spring and flower over a longer period. The best situation for autumn sowing is one sheltered from strong and cutting winds, but free from shade and exposed to the sun. Spring sowings for blooming in summer may be made at any time from the middle of March to the middle of April. Make later sowings for flowering in autumn from the middle of May to the middle of June. The different conditions and climates in various areas make it impossible to give exact times and details.

Sow annuals for transplanting in V-shaped drills about 1cm (½in) deep and 25cm (10in) apart in a nursery bed and remove when about half grown to the position in which they are to flower. On average about 22.5cm (9in) should be left between each plant. Plant them firmly then water well to settle the soil round the roots. There is always some danger in transplanting annuals, unless it is very carefully done or unless they are raised in pots, from which they can be turned out without disturbing the roots. It is usually a better idea to sow the seed where they are to flower and thin the seedlings later to the proper distance.

Half-hardy annuals

Sow the seeds in March or April in well-drained pots or pans, in a seed compost or in a mixture of loam, leaf-mould, well-decayed manure and silver sand, and either shelter in a frame or plunge the pots in moderate bottom heat in a heated greenhouse or frame. The temperature should not rise above 24°C (75°F) by day or fall below 13°C (55°F) at night. Harden off gradually and remove to flowering quarters about the middle of May, but delay transplanting to the end of the month if the weather is cold and unfavourable.

Biennials

Hardy biennials may be sown at a later period of the year than annuals – in May, June or July, sometimes in August. It is wise to sow as early as possible, as this enables the plants to become well established before the colder weather sets in, and to ensure well-developed plants for flowering the next year. If a frame is available early sowing is not so important, as the plants can continue development in the frame at a time when cold and bad weather would impede any growth in the open. Raise biennials in drills 20 to 45cm (8 to 18in) apart in partially shaded nursery beds. As soon as they are tall enough to be handled thin them out to 15cm (6in) apart or transplant with the same distance between plants. Plant out in moderately good, deeply worked soil in their blooming quarters in the spring, or in October if they were started in early summer.

Sow half-hardy biennials in boxes from March to June. They should be protected during the winter in a frame or greenhouse and be planted out in their flowering positions the following spring, from April to June.

Selection of Annuals and Biennials

For notes on colour, height, season of flowering, culture, and the best species and varieties, *see* alphabetical list of Ornamental Plants and Trees, Ch. 23.

Half-hardy annuals

Ageratum houstonianum
Alonsoa warscewiczii (mask flower)
Brachycome iberidifolia
Callistephus chinensis (china aster)

Celosia argentea (Prince of Wales' feathers or cockscomb)
Dianthus chinensis vars.
Dimorphotheca aurantiaca
Helichrysum bracteatum, etc
Helipterum manglesii
H. roseum
Impatiens balsamina
Kochia scoparia trichophylla
Limonium bonduellii
L. sinuatum
L. suworowii
Lobelia erinus vars.
Mesembryanthemum crystallinum
Nemesia strumosa vars.
Nicotiana affinis (tobacco plant)
Petunia vars.
Phlox drummondii vars.
Salpiglossiss inuata
Salvia horminum
Schizanthus pinnatus
Senecio elegans
Statice (see *Limonium*)
Tagetes erecta
T. patula
T. tenuifolia (African and French marigolds)
Verbena vars.
Zinnia elegans

Hardy annuals

Alyssum maritimum (lobularia)
Calendula officinalis (pot marigold)
Centaurea cyanus (cornflower or bluebottle)
Centaurea moschata (sweet sultan)
Clarkia elegans and vars.
C. pulchella
Collinsia bicolor
Convolvulus tricolor and vars.
Coreopsis tinctoria
Delphinium ajacis
Eschscholzia californica (Californian poppy)
Gaillardia pulchella
Gilia lutea
G. capitata
G. tricolor
Godetia, single and double
Gypsophila elegans
Helianthus annuus
H. debilis
Iberis umbellata (candytuft)
Lathyrus odoratus (sweet pea)
Lavatera trimestris
Limnanthes douglasii
Linaria maroccana, etc
Linum grandiflorum 'Rubrum'
Lupinus hartwegii and hybrids (lupin)
Malcolmia maritima (Virginian stock)
Malope trifida
Matthiola bicornis (night-scented stock)
M. incana (ten-week stock)
Nemophila menziesii
Nigella damascena
N. hispanica (love-in-a-mist)
Papaver rhoeas vars. (Shirley poppy)
P. somniferum (opium poppy)
Pharbitis purpurea
Reseda odorata (mignonette)
Silene pendula, var. *compacta*
Tropaeolum majus (nasturtium)
T. peregrinum (canary creeper)

Biennials

Alcea (Althaea) rosea (hollyhock)
Anchusa capensis
Campanula medium
C. pyramidalis

Cheiranthus cheiri (wallflower)
Dianthus barbatus (sweet william)
Digitalis purpurea (foxglove)
Lavatera arborea
Lunaria annua (honesty)
Matthiola (Brompton stock)
Matthiola (East Lothian stock)
Matthiola (intermediate stock)
Myosotis sylvatica (forget-me-not)
Oenothera biennis (everlasting primrose)
Papaver nudicaule (Iceland poppy)
Silene compacta
Trachelium caeruleum
Verbascum species

Although some two or three of the species included in this list are not actually biennials in a true sense, they are most satisfactory when grown as such.

Bedding plants

The term 'bedding plant' commonly refers to certain half-hardy or tender flowering plants which are grown under glass during the winter and spring, and are planted out during summer only to be lifted again as soon as the warm months are over. Pelargoniums or geraniums, as they are commonly called, begonias, verbenas, petunias, calceolarias and lobelias are the plants most frequently grown in this way. But there is no reason why other plants should not be used to create formal beds of flowers or foliage. Almost all flowers can be treated in this way, and it is common practice to use for this purpose such beautiful annuals as saponaria and myosotis (forget-me-nots) or hardy plants like pansies and violas with tulips or other bulbs for spring and chrysanthemums in the autumn.

Planting the bed

With both spring and summer bedding it is best to mark the positions of each plant with stakes and string before starting the actual planting.

To plant a round bed, insert a stake at the exact centre and attach a piece of string to it. It you fix a peg at different distances along this string, you can trace out circles on which the plants, still in their pots, should be spaced out evenly. You will then be able to see more or less how your scheme will look when planted and the number of each kind of plant you need to fill the bed.

In bedding-out small beds most gardeners find it easiest to work from the edges inwards towards the centre; in large beds, however, mark the centre accurately and work outwards from this, using a board to stand on so that you do not tread down the soil.

Do not bed-out while the soil is very dry. Give the bed a good soaking with water the evening before and again after the bedding-out has been completed. Insert each plant to about the same depth as it stood in its pot or in the box. Keep the ball intact and plant so that the top of it is just

1cm ($\frac{1}{2}$in) below the ground level. If the plant is set in too low there is the possibility of it 'damping-off'. Always remove the crocks at the bottom of the pot before the plants are bedded-out, otherwise the bed, in the course of time, will become littered with these bits of broken pots.

Pot plants make better bedding subjects than those grown in boxes, as the roots are not so liable to damage when removed for bedding-out. In planting, use a trowel to scoop out just sufficient earth to make a hole to take the roots without crushing. Do not use a dibble as this is apt to make a hole so deep that an air pocket is left under the roots, which will be parched and will also not have a hole wide enough to accommodate them. Press the soil *very firmly* round the roots with the hands after planting or the plants will be slow in becoming established and will be greatly handicapped. If the weather is warm, bedding-out should be done in the late afternoon or evening.

Spring bedding

At one time bulbs were practically the only plants used by the gardener for spring bedding. But this use of bulbs alone had many drawbacks; the beds were plain and bare all through the winter, then as soon as the bulbs had flowered the beds would become untidy and uninteresting. Today we use a ground cover of alyssum, arabis, aubrieta, daisies, myosotis, polyanthus, silenes, violas, wallflowers, and other dwarf hardy plants, through which the bulbs rise to form a mass of colour over a carpet that is chosen either to harmonize or contrast with them. This ground cover clothes the ground and looks neat all the winter and also keeps the bed tidier and interesting for some time after the bulbs have flowered. Spring bedding has become less formal and stiff, and the period of bloom has been extended.

Do not delay the bedding-out until the early spring when bloom is coming and the roots are not in a favourable condition to establish themselves. As soon as the summer bedding is cleared away in the autumn fork some well-rotted manure, leaf-mould and thoroughly decayed vegetable refuse into the beds to a depth of about 30cm (12in), this will draw the roots well down.

Put in the plants that are to form the ground cover just far enough apart so that, when grown they will cover the surface of the bed. Insert the bulbs in the gaps between these at the correct depth of each kind.

Clearing spring bedding

As soon as the spring bedding is over, all bulbs used in bedding schemes should be lifted, planted in the reserve garden and watered occasionally until the leaves have turned yellow. They should then be dried off and stored. With care they may be used for three or four years in succession without any appreciable deterioration in the blooms. The amateur is often worried as to what he should do with the spring bedding he takes out; should he save any of it or should he destroy it all? As space is usually a consideration, all plants that are easily raised from seed should be destroyed, but such perennials as arabis, daisies, erysimum, polyanthus or violas may be divided into small plants and placed in the reserve garden where they are shaded from the hottest rays of the sun to be grown on for the next year's spring bedding.

Summer bedding

It is best to have bedding plants as well advanced as possible; late and consequently undeveloped plants bear poor flowers. Sow the annuals in heat, if possible, in February or in the open, if hardy, in March or April.

Cuttings of most half-hardy plants, such as pelargoniums and verbenas, are taken in July and August, and of ageratums, calceolarias and salvias in September. They may be kept in the open till the end of September, when they should be wintered in a cold frame or near the glass in a greenhouse in slight heat. For cuttings in early spring place old stock in gentle heat and induce to grow, and the young shoots can be taken as cuttings when sufficiently large. Root them also in gentle heat. (*See* Ch. 5 Plant Propagation.) Begonias and similar tuberous-rooted plants need to be started in heat early in spring and will then be ready for planting out with other bedding plants at the end of May or early in June.

Never bring plants straight out of a heated frame or warm house into the beds, harden off by gradually admitting more and more air for three weeks to a month before the time for bedding-out, which is usually about the middle of May. Planting out without adequate hardening off is a common reason for failure. It usually results in checked growth, late and poor flowering, or complete loss of the more tender plants.

Although it is unwise to bed-out too early, this does not mean that the preparation of the beds should be left until just before it is time to put the plants in. After the beds have been dug over, make them thoroughly firm by treading, if the soil is light, and then rake them over.

Antirrhinums, calceolarias, chrysanthemums (marguerites), and violas are among the most hardy summer bedding plants and a start can be made with these as soon as the beds have been cleared. This will not only help to get the work forward at this time, but will also give these plants time to become established before the warmer weather comes.

Taller subjects may need stakes. Split canes are often strong enough for slender plants and are less obtrusive than entire bamboo canes. Thorough watering in dry weather, occasional application of a high potash fertilizer throughout the summer, and regular removal of weeds and dead flowers will maintain most summer bedding subjects in good condition until the first frosts.

Clearing of summer bedding

As summer bedding plants are nearly all either half-hardy or tender they will require the protection of glass through the winter. From August until mid-September, and certainly before there is any risk of frost, make a start on striking cuttings of tender perennials, calceolarias, fuchsia, helichrysum, heliotrope, pelargonium and penstemon, for example. Later, large standard plants and foliage plants that take several years to grow to the most effective size should be taken up with as complete a ball of roots as possible and planted in suitably-sized pots, trimming the branches back if necessary; at the same time trim back the roots. Store the plants in a frost-proof frame or on shelves in the greenhouse and water occasionally. Bulbous- and tuberous-rooted plants such as begonias, dahlias and gladioli should also be lifted, cleaned and kept dry for the winter. Annual plants raised from seed should be discarded. The beds can then be prepared to receive spring bedding once more.

Bedding colour schemes

Take care with colour schemes; to avoid clashing colours, the colours should either harmonize or gently contrast. Do not use too many colours, two or at the most three are best massed together; only two or three kinds of flowers should be used in each bed. It is necessary, too, to remember the height and habit of plants put together; some make ideal carpet plants, others are excellent for use as the principal plants or for dot plants while, a point sometimes forgotten, all subjects in a bedding scheme should flower at the same time. Never overcrowd, as this leads to weak, straggly plants with poor and scarce blooms. No plant, unless very small, should be planted nearer than 15cm (6in) to its neighbour, while the average-sized plants need to be 25 to 38cm (10 to 15in) apart. Dot plants are placed about 90cm (3ft) apart, while edging plants are best set about 25cm (10in) from the edge of the bed, otherwise they may be damaged when the grass is cut.

Cannas or standard fuchsias make very striking dot plants in a large bed of begonias, as do standard heliotropes or kochias in a bed of salmon-pink geraniums. Abutilons and plumbagoes also make excellent dot plants. Bear in mind the beauty of pale pink flowers thrown up by a ground cover of mauve, dark blue or purple; a group of dark blue or purple flowers if edged with yellow violas makes a most striking display.

Bedding designs should be as simple as possible, especially in small beds, and should aim at providing masses of one colour rather than small patches of highly contrasting shades in a small area. Where the plants themselves are very small, more complicated designs are possible.

Carpet bedding

This consists of masses of low, compact-growing plants with various coloured leaves arranged in a pattern. It is usual to have a background of plants of one colour, and to run plants of other colours in masses, stripes or ribbons to produce the effect desired. Among the more common plants used for this purpose are sempervivum of various colours (grey and green), encheverias, *Senecio maritima* (silvery grey), *Cerastium tomentosum* (silver) and *Chrysamthemum parthenium* (yellow).

Carpet beds are very artificial, very expensive to produce and very laborious to maintain. Although a well-maintained bed can be an impressive sight it is not really suited to the private garden.

Summer bedding

Principal plant	*Ground, edging or dot plant*
Ageratum houstonianum (pale blue)	*Pelargonium* 'Madame Crousse' (rose pink)
Ageratum houstonianum 'Blue Chip'	*Alyssum maritimum* 'Minimum' (white)
Antirrhinum majus 'Rocket', 'Sentinel', 'Nanum' and F_1 hybrids	*Browallia viscosa* (blue) *Lobelia erinus* 'Cambridge Blue'
Begonia semperflorens 'Flamingo' (white), 'Carmen' (rose pink)	
	Alyssum maritimum (white)
Begonia tuberous-rooted vars. (various)	
	Phlox drummondii 'Nana Compacta' (white)
Calceolaria x *herbeohybrida* Monarch strain	
Calendula officinalis 'Kelmscott Giant Orange'	*Anchusa capensis* (blue)
Cineraria cruenta 'Multiflora Nana'	*Gladiolus* 'Rosy Maid' (salmon and apricot)
Dahlia 'Coltness Gem' (scarlet)	*Viola* 'White Swan' (white)
Fuchsia (various)	*Phlox drummondii* 'Nana Compacta' (mixed vars.)
Pelargonium 'Paul Crampel' (scarlet)	*Abutilon striatum* 'Thompsonii' (yellow)
Gladiolus 'Jo Wagenaar' (scarlet)	*Antirrhinum majus* 'White Spire'
Godetia 'Kelvedon Glory' (coral pink)	*Dianthus chinensis* 'Snowball' (white)
Heliotropium x *hybridum* vars.	*Eucalyptus globulus* (silver blue leaves)
Kochia scoparia var. *trichophylla* (burning bush)	*Tagetes erecta* 'Double Eagle' (orange)
Lobelia fulgens 'Queen Victoria' (scarlet)	*Antirrhinum* 'White Spire' (white)
Nicotiana affinis 'Lime Green'	*Polygonum affine* 'Darjeeling Red' (crimson)
Nigella damascena 'Miss Jekyll' (blue)	*Verbena* x *hybrida* 'Ellen Willmott' (salmon pink)
Penstemon hartwegii 'Myddleton Gem', (carmine)	*Phlox drummondii* 'Nana Compacta' (white)
Petunia 'Dream Girl' (rose)	*Callistephus chinensis* (white)
Phlox drummondii (rose and pink shades)	*Gaura lindheimeri* (white, tinted red)
Salvia horminum 'Oxford Blue'	*Calocephalus brownii* (silver leaves)
Tagetes erecta (orange)	*Lobelia erinus* 'Sapphire' (sapphire blue)
Tropaeolum majus 'King of Tom Thumbs' (yellow)	*Penstemon hartwegii* 'Pennington Gem' (cerise)
Verbena 'Mammoth Firefly' (scarlet)	*Antirrhinum majus* 'Yellow Monarch'
Verbena venosa (rosy purple)	*Artemisia lanata* (grey leaves)
Zinnia elegans (scarlet and yellow vars.)	*Ganzania* x *hybrida* 'Hazel' (golden brown)

Spring bedding

Principal plant	*Ground, edging or dot plant*
Alyssum saxatile 'Compactum' (yellow)	*Cheiranthus* 'Blood Red'
Anemone 'St Brigid' (mixed)	*Iris*, Spanish (mixed)
Cheiranthus 'Vulcan' (crimson)	*Tulipa* 'Orange Parrot' (parrot)
Cheiranthus 'Ruby Gem' (ruby violet)	*Tulipa* 'Absalon' (Rembrandt, brown yellow)
Hyacinthus 'City of Haarlem' (yellow)	*Myosotis alpestris* 'Blue Ball' (blue)
Hyacinthus 'Jan Bos' (cerise pink)	*Aubrieta deltoidea* (lavender)
Hyacinthus 'L'Innocence' (white)	*Primula* (polyanthus) var. (red)
Hyacinthus 'Eclipse' (red)	*Viola* 'William Robb' (lavender)
Iris, Dutch (mixed)	*Viola* (blue, yellow and white)
Iris, Spanish (mixed)	*Viola* (blue, yellow and white)
Muscari armeniacum 'Heavenly Blue' (blue)	*Tulipa* 'Bellona' (early)
Narcissus 'Polindra' (yellow and white)	*Muscari armeniacum* 'Heavenly Blue' (blue)
Narcissus 'Polar Ice' (white)	*Myosotis sylvatica* 'Blue Bird' (blue)
Primula (polyanthus) var. (white)	*Bellis perennis* 'Rob Roy' (red)
Primula (polyanthus) var. (orange)	*Crocus* 'Queen of the Blues' (lavender)
Tulipa 'Keizerskroon' (early, scarlet yellow)	*Arabis albida* (white)
Tulipa 'Brilliant Star' (early, scarlet)	*Viola* (winter flowering) 'Helios' (yellow)
Tulipa 'Mr van der Hoef' (early double, yellow)	*Myosotis alpestris* 'Blue Ball' (blue)
Tulipa 'Clara Butt' (Darwin, pink and rose)	*Myosotis sylvatica* 'Blue Bird' (blue)
Tulipa 'William Pitt' (Darwin, blood red)	*Iberis sempervirens* (white)
Tulipa 'Pink Supreme' (Darwin)	*Silene pendula* 'Compacta Mixed' (salmon rose)
Tulipa 'Scarlett O'Hara' (Darwin, pink, yellow)	*Narcissus* 'Rippling Waters' (white)
Tulipa 'Elizabeth Arden' (Darwin hybrid, rose purple)	*Cheiranthus* 'Golden Bedder'
Tulipa 'Apeldoorn' (Darwin hybrid, deep red)	*Cheiranthus cheiri* (white)
Tulipa 'Smiling Queen' (cottage, pink)	*Tulipa* 'Inglescombe Yellow' (cottage)
Tulipa 'Chappaqua' (cottage, scarlet)	*Cheiranthus* 'Fire King' (orange scarlet)
Tulipa 'Groenland' (cottage, green and pink)	*Viola* 'Marie Louise' (lavender)
Viola odorata 'Princess of Wales' (purple)	*Tulipa* 'Princess Margaret Rose' (cottage, yellow orange)

21
The Rock Garden

Rocks and stones are used in a rock garden to simulate the alpine conditions of their natural environment, to provide coolness for the roots and to store moisture in crevices for the plants. But the idea that rock plants grow best in practically nothing but rock is mistaken. A generous allowance of good soil between, amongst and beneath the stones is essential for their healthy growth. As the rocks are meant to provide shelter for roots, it is useless to dump slabs of rock or stone perpendicularly in the soil. This gives no protection; the roots cannot get beneath them, and they do not preserve any moisture. Stones, appropriate in size to the finished rock garden, should be sunk firmly in the earth on a slight slant – tilted backwards, not forwards, so that the rain trickles down to the roots of the plants. If the rocks lean forward, over the plants, the roots will be sheltered from the rain and probably parched. Although the visible portions of the rocks should be as pleasing as possible, and all slant in the same direction to represent a natural outcrop or stratum of stone, they should not only represent a miniature rocky landscape, but should also protect the roots of the plants growing among them. The slopes of the mounds in which the boulders are set should not be too steep and should be as natural in appearance as possible; there should be miniature ranges and mountain peaks dividing them, with valleys into which spurs from the hills project.

In flat gardens it is possible to create the necessary undulations by making a water garden near by. The earth removed from the pond site can be used to raise the rock garden (taking care not to bring subsoil to the surface) and the irregular lines of an informal water garden will set off the rock garden beautifully, especially if water can be led in streams through the rock garden to cascade into the pool (*see* Ch. 22, The Water Garden).

In large rock gardens, it is a good idea to provide winding paths, 45 to 60cm (1½ to 2ft) in width, with stepping stones to cut through the gorges so that every part of the rock garden is easily reached. Make the pockets in which the alpines are to be planted irregular in shape and ranging from a few centimetres (in) in diameter to nearly 1m (yd) across; they should be up to 45cm (1½ft) in depth, and built so that the soil will not wash out of them. If there is any chance of the soil in the pockets becoming sodden, provide clinker and rubble drainage.

It is essential that there are no spaces and hollows under and around the stones, and that the earth is well bedded round them, or the air within the hollow spaces will dry up the soil and drain the moisture from the roots of the plants, while the stones may subside and upset the general effect.

Soil for alpines and rock plants

The great majority of alpines and rock plants like a rich soil, containing a large portion of coarse sand or grit, leaf-mould and other decayed vegetable matter. As a whole these plants are not fussy as to soil and most thrive well in the compost mentioned above. However, there are some which only grow best in certain soils. For these it is easy enough to scoop out a hollow and substitute a little special compost in which the rock plant may be inserted.

Alpine plants in their native habitat receive a yearly top-dressing of vegetable matter from the material carried down by the melting snows, and alpines in a rock garden are all the better for a top-dressing applied in imitation of this natural process.

In their natural conditions the soil around the roots of rock plants is almost always completely covered by stalks and leaves. Each plant touches its neighbours, and practically no soil is left exposed. This arrangement is of the greatest use to the plants: it protects the soil from the action of sun and wind, preserving natural moisture and this protection should be provided as far as possible. This is rather difficult to do at first; while the plants are still small and need protection most they are unable to cover the surface of the ground, and to plant them closer together would mean starving and overcrowding them. In such a case the best thing to do is to cover the intermediate surface of the soil with chips of stone, small enough to be easily pushed aside by a shoot, but sufficient to prevent over-drying of the soil.

Site and and selection of stones

Where possible the rock garden should have an open sunny position, preferably facing all aspects for the benefit of various plants, and away from walls and overhanging trees. Rock gardens always look best where they are not in contrast to any formal arrangement of garden or shrubbery; a natural-looking simulated wild site, where the rock of the district crops up here and there, is best if there is any choice. Local stone should be used if possible, to cut down on transportation costs, but most natural stone is suitable except the very crumbling slates or magnesian limestone. Two of the best are weathered limestone and sandstone. Artificial stones in various shapes and colours are readily available.

In small suburban and town gardens where the natural aspect of a rock garden is out of place, it is often a better idea to create a raised bed between dry walls and to use only one or two fissured stones for picturesque effect. The range of alpines and other low plants which can be grown in a paved garden, raised beds, sinks, troughs, steps and dry walls is no less than those used in a rock garden, and because the former fit more sensibly into a small garden, more room can often be allocated to an individual plant than in a rock garden. (*See* Ch. 10 for construction of dry walls and Ch. 11 for paved gardens, and ideas for planting.)

Plants for the rock garden

When selecting plants it is important to provide interest over the longest possible period of the year. Some of the smaller-growing bulbs which bloom in the winter and early spring are ideal, while late flowering alpines, such as *Astilbe simplicifolia*, *Saxifraga fortunei* and *Zauschneria californica* provide colour long after most rock plants have finished blooming. Bulbs are often overlooked when planting the rock garden and yet some of the smaller-growing bulbs make a lovely sight blooming above a carpeting of *Acaena microphylla*, *Arenaria balearica* or other dwarf trailers. Specimen plants of dwarf conifers like *Juniperus communis* 'Compressa' and *Thuja occidentalis* 'Caespitosa' are attractive throughout the year.

Times and methods of planting

Rock plants should be planted out either in the spring or better still in early autumn, but not later than September since the roots make little growth after that, and the plants are liable to be washed out of the earth by heavy rain, or lifted from the soil by frost. However, with care all alpines can be planted out any time between early April and the end of September. Container plants may be planted at any time providing the weather is neither too dry nor too wet or cold.

When planting in a crevice, it is essential that no air-pocket is left at the bottom. This would drain all moisture from the roots and might cause them to shrivel. To avoid this, ram plenty of good gritty soil well into the crevice and make sure that the hole is well filled, then scrape out some of the soil at the top and set the plant in firmly, pressing the soil well round the roots, and fix it in tightly by means of a small stone. Be careful to give shade-lovers, like the ourisias and shortias, congenial situations such as a sheltered position at the base of a rock facing north or east. Sun-loving plants such as alyssum, arabis, onosma, aubrieta, etc, should be planted in crevices where they can hang over the face of the rocks. On the flat parts and in moist low-lying situations, gentians, primulas of the japonica types and all the more luscious plants will thrive. When planting do not overcrowd. An occasional dwarf evergreen shrub or conifer will accentuate or detract from the heights and enhance the natural look.

The Moraine Garden

Many of the more fastidious alpines will not prosper in an ordinary rock garden. They grow naturally on mountain slopes covered with loose stones, where melting snow in summer provides them with plenty of ice-cold water and where a blanket of snow protects them during the winter.

So we have to try to provide adequate moisture for the roots in summer while the plants are growing, but at the same time good drainage, and protection from damp and excessive cold in winter.

Siting and constructing a moraine bed

An ideal and natural position for the moraine would be at the lower end of a valley between two rocky spurs, the gorge gradually expanding into a flat bed of scree with occasional boulders strewn over it. To make a moraine bed, dig out about 75cm (2½ft) of soil and make the bottom of the basin or trench slope slightly towards the front; the slope should not be too steep or the moraine will become over-dry in summer. Make the lower 25cm (10in) of this basin watertight by puddling with clay or cement. Make an outlet in front, which when closed keeps about 25cm (10in) of water, but not more, in the lowest part of the basin, while, when the outlet is open, none at all remains. Now cover the bottom of the trench with about 25cm (10in) of rubble, stones or any material that will provide good drainage. Above this place another 7.5cm (3in) or so of small stones; these will fill the gaps between the larger stones and prevent the small grit above from sinking through and blocking the drain. Fill up the hollow with a mixture of stone chips and gravel, good loam, and leaf-mould. Cover this with a 5cm (2in) layer of stone chips. Granite or limestone chips are excellent and easily obtained; flint chips should not be used as they do not conserve moisture. Place a few boulders in the moraine bed in order to break up the surface and to give the plants protection. A natural trickle of water may be led into the top of the moraine, or sufficient moisture given from a watering-can each day to cause an overflow from the outlet at the bottom. From November to May, when no additional moisture is needed in the moraine bed, leave the outlet open. Many plants that have proved failures in the rock garden proper will flourish in a moraine bed.

Protection in winter

Silver foliage plants and others whose leaves are covered with hairs or down are, in their natural habitats, usually protected from frost and damp during the winter by a coat of snow. When they are grown out of doors in this country, they must be given protection nestling in a crevice between the rocks; it is often possible to cover it with a sheet of glass resting on the surrounding stone, but when this cannot be done, insert four pieces of stiff galvanized wire firmly in the ground and bend over at the top to hold the glass in position over the plant. If the weather is especially severe or the plant very delicate, pieces of glass may be set in the soil and supported by the wires to form four walls protecting the plant. Sufficient space between the glass roof and the tops of the four walls should be left for adequate ventilation (but not enough to admit rain or snow) or the plant will be liable to damping-off. Frost will often raise plants from the soil, especially those planted the previous autumn. In spring go over each plant carefully and, if necessary, firm it gently down into the soil.

Care of the rock garden

All through the summer months weed the rock garden by hand and pick off all dead flower heads. Water the choice species during dry spells and in May top-dress with a thin layer of sandy loam and leaf-mould. By July most of the plants will have borne the best of their bloom, and many of the most vigorous will be pushing out new growth and beginning to overcrowd the less spreading types. Trim these plants back, including the shrubby subjects, and at the same time remove the older portions of the plants and all dead stems and foliage. Do not, however, cut them back so symmetrically that they look like shrubs in a topiary garden; try to encourage a wild and natural appearance, and where a plant is not throttling its neighbours and has ample space let it ramble over the rocks.

Propagation of rock plants

Rock plants may be increased by seed sown as soon as it is ripe or, failing this, in early spring. Sow in pots or pans under glass. Some germinate better if the pots are plunged out of doors where they are exposed to all weathers and in spring removed to a warm house or frame. Propagate also by cuttings or by division of the roots in April or September. It is easier to raise alpines from cuttings or by division of the roots rather than from seed, which is a lengthy and, in some cases, a difficult process.

If seedlings are raised from a plant which is a cultivar or of hybrid origin, the chances are that they will not come true to the original plants. In such cases increase by means of cuttings, division or root cuttings. (*See also* Ch. 5, Plant Propagation.)

The Alpine House

There are some choice alpines that cannot be cultivated in the open to the best advantage in our uncertain climate. To say that they are choice does not necessarily mean that they are delicate, but that the blooms of many are apt to be spoilt by inclement weather. The alpine house protects these while they are in bloom and also prolongs their season of flowering.

Most of the species can be brought on in pans sunk to their rims in ashes in the open or in frames until they are about to flower, when they should be transferred to the alpine house and removed again to the open after flowering.

After the beginning of October all choice alpines should be housed in a frost-proof frame and moved to the house as the blooms become visible.

The alpine house does not require artifical heating; a low span-roofed type, so situated that it runs north and south is ideal as both sides then receive their fair share of the sun. (For management, *see* The Unheated Greenhouse, Ch. 15.)

Compost and potting

Two-thirds fibrous loam and leaf-mould with one-third coarse, gritty sand makes an excellent compost for most of these plants. Many of the finer saxifrages like a peaty compost with a little ground limestone in it.

Study individual tastes as far as possible. Pot-up in pans from 15 to 22.5cm (6 to 9in) in diameter and about 12.5cm (5in) deep, and as ample drainage is required place 2.5 to 5cm (1 to 2in) of broken crocks in the bottom of the pots for plants like androsaces and saxifrages. For plants of a more vigorous nature and for bulbs, 2.5cm (1in) of crocks will be enough. Re-potting is only needed every second or third year. The staging should be covered with a 5cm (2in) layer of shingle or ashes so that the atmosphere can be kept moist.

Selection of Rock Plants

For details as to colour, height, season of flowering, culture and the best species and varieties, *see* the alphabetical list of Ornamental Plants and Trees, Ch. 23.

**Acaena* species
†*Achillea clavenae*
A. rupestris
A. tomentosa
Adonis vernalis
†*Aethionema pulchellum*
Alyssum montanum
†*Androsace lanuginosa*
**Aquilegia glandulosa*
Arabis albida 'Flore Pleno'
**Arenaria* species
†*Armeria caespitosa*
*†*Campanula* species
Cerastium tomentosum
Corydalis cheilanthifolia
**Cyclamen* (hardy vars.)
Cytisus x *kewensis*
C. x *beanii*
**Dianthus* (various) (pink)
†*Draba* species
Dryas octopetala
Erica carnea (heath)
†*Erodium* species
Erysimum rupestre
Gaultheria procumbens
Genista dalmatica

Genista delphinensis
†**Gentiana* species
Geum species
Gypsophila repens
**Haberlea rhodopensis*
Helianthemum (sun rose)
Heuchera sanguinea vars.
†*Hypericum* species
**Iberis* species
Iris (dwarf bearded, hybrids and bulbous)
†*Lewisia tweedyi*
†*Linaria alpina*
Linum (flax) species
Lithospermum diffusum
Lychnis alpina (campion)
†**Mertensia echioides*
†*Morisia monanthos*
Nierembergia repens
Oenothera missouriensis
†**Omphalodes verna*
Onosma echioides
**Ourisia coccinea*
Oxalis enneaphylla
†*Papaver alpinum*
Penstemon scouleri
Phlox (dwarf) species
†*Potentilla* species
†**Primula* species
†**Pulsatilla vulgaris*
**Ramonda myconi*
†**Ranunculus alpestris*
Saponaria ocymoides
†**Saxifraga* species and vars.
Sedum species
Sempervivum species and hybrids
Silene species
Soldanella alpina
Thymus species
**Viola* species
Zauschneria californica

Note. Plants that will grow in light shade are marked *; those suitable for the moraine garden are marked †.
In addition to the plants named in this list there are many dwarf annuals which, though not rock plants in the true sense, deserve a position in the rock garden. Hardy bulbs afford masses of colour in the early spring and many ferns are also suitable. For dwarf shrubs for the rock garden, *see* alphabetical list of Ornamental Plants and Trees, Ch. 23.

22
The Water Garden

A water garden can be constructed if a source of natural water is available or if it can be artificially introduced. A very small supply, even a trickle artificially laid on, will do if it is continuous, but a water garden is liable to dry up in the summer if it is very shallow. Select a low-lying piece of land, preferably one where a natural depression already exists, so that the plants can be viewed from above. A pool need be no deeper than 45cm (1½ft) with a maximum depth of 75cm (2½ft) at the deepest end for vigorous water lilies.

Siting and design

Try to incorporate a pool in a natural way in the existing garden design. Siting a wild or rock garden often helps the natural look. Size can be made to suit requirements and surrounding conditions, and shape is dependent on space and other features of the garden; aim for naturalness and avoid a series of sharp erratic curves. The design should be simple and can be either formal and rectangular or in long sweeping curves. In a formal setting, and certainly as a central feature in a paved garden, the severely simple square or rectangular pool has great charm. In such cases the pool is often bordered with a paved walk with the crevices set with trailing wall or rock plants. For more informal shapes, let the grass run down gently sloping banks to the water's edge, with marsh plants and other marginals planted in groups from the brink up to the higher parts, where bamboos and other moisture-loving shrubs can be used to form a screen and background.

Left: a small round pool can be made by lining a hole with strong plastic sheeting *Right:* a pool with different levels created by soil and stones

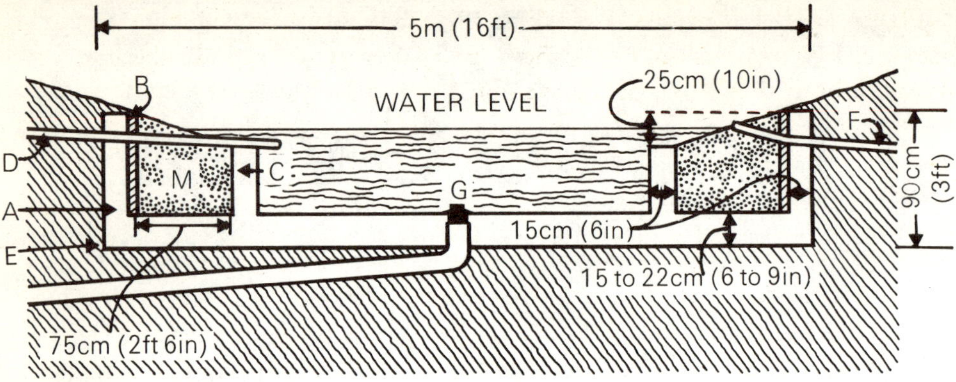

The construction of this formal pool is described opposite *see* Concrete lining of pools

Construction of a pool

Few water plants, except very strong growers, require a greater depth of water than 45cm (1½ft). But to allow for the thickness of the pool lining and for the inclusion of soil to nourish the roots, excavate to a depth of about 75cm (2½ft). The actual walls of the pool are best cut perpendicularly if it is to be lined with concrete; throw the earth well back from the pool so that the banks, on which the marginal plants are to grow, slope gently down to the water.

Various materials can be used for an impervious lining to keep the water in; concrete or plastic sheeting being the most often used. The latter is the easiest; concreting is hard work and needs to be painted with a neutralizing material to protect plants and fish from the lime in concrete.

Plastic lining of pools

Heavy duty plastic sheeting has made the construction of pools much easier. Although concrete still has some advantages for formal pools, irregular pools are usually lined with plastic. Polythene will last for a few years only but it is inexpensive. Butyl sheeting is stronger, longer-lasting and elastic, so that it will mould itself to the bottom of a pool, with no unsightly creases.

To construct a plastic-lined pool take out a hole 15cm (6in) deeper than the proposed depth of the water, sloping the sides at 1 in 3 instead of the nearly vertical sides required for a concrete pool. Spread a thick layer of fine sand over the pool area as the weight of water pressing down on any sharp stones will puncture the lining. Weigh down the lining all around the edge with heavy stones and let it sag into the hole without quite touching the bottom, then introduce the water. The weight of this will stretch the butyl and mould it firmly to the required shape. Cover the bottom of the pool with a further layer of sand, perhaps adding pebbles to provide a pleasing effect. Preformed glass fibre pools are easier to install, needing only an excavation to fit the chosen shape neatly.

Plants are best grown in baskets of heavy loam to facilitate re-arrangement or division, but a 15cm (6in) layer of soil can also be put over the bottom and the plants weighted down on this until they have rooted in.

Concrete lining of pools

Remember that all constructional work will have to be hidden and that there should be a permanently moist margin of soil about 60 to 90cm (2 to 3ft) wide round the pond to accommodate marginal plants. Excavate to a width that will allow for this: for a pool 3m (10ft) wide, a hole 90cm (3ft) deep all over and about 5m (16ft) wide will have to be dug. This allows for a 75cm (2½ft) margin of moist earth, as well as 15cm (6in) for the thickness of the walls on each side. The pool bottom need not be more than 15 to 22cm (6 to 9in) thick.

When the excavation is done, remove all loose soil and firm the bottom thoroughly. If the soil over which the concrete is to be laid is left loose, it may shrink away and cause the concrete to crack.

A useful mixture is one part of cement, two parts of sand and three parts of gravel, broken stone or brick. Turn the material over two or three times while it is still in the dry state. Then wet the heap with water poured over it from a large can fitted with a fine rose, and mix the whole again by turning it over once or twice, so that the materials are throughly amalgamated.

When the concrete is well mixed and in a semi-liquid condition, place a good 15cm (6in) layer over the bottom of the pool and smooth it down firmly. Next build a retaining wall of boards parallel to the earth walls, but 15cm (6in) nearer the centre of the pool. The gap between the wood and the earth sides, when filled up with concrete, will form the walls 'A'. The supporting boards 'B' should not be removed until the concrete is thoroughly set. Now construct the two inner walls 'C', each 75cm (2½ft) from the outer retaining walls, but 25cm (10in) shorter than these.

Insert an inflow pipe 'D' and an outlet pipe 'F' before the concrete work is completed. As soon as the concrete is drying, rough it over, wet and then thoroughly work over with cement wash, 5cm (2in) thick. Take care to see that the corners 'E' are perfectly watertight. It is unwise, apart from the shade cast and the dead leaves and twigs that will fall into the water, to construct a pool under or near trees, as their roots run a fair distance underground, and are in time likely to crack the concrete unless it is very strong.

Water supply and level

A constant flow of water is not necessary for aquatic plants, although it is a good idea to have water circulation of some kind to prevent stagnation. Also for the border of marginal plants round the pond to be successful, the water should never be allowed to fall below the tops of the inner walls 'C' to achieve marshy conditions of the banks within the outer containing walls. In the same way the water level should be kept just below the tops of the walls 'A' or too much of the surrounding ground will become marshy. The outflow pipe 'F' is essential to carry off superfluous rainwater. A plug and outflow 'G' at the bottom of the pond is useful; the water can be periodically drained away and the pool thoroughly cleaned.

When the concrete is quite dry, paint it with Silglaze or fill the pool up with water and drain out several times to wash the lime out of the cement. Fill the spaces 'M' between the retaining walls 'A' and 'C' with a compost of loam and peat, or loam and leaf-mould; bank this up so that the tops of the walls 'A' are covered with soil and hidden from sight. The surrounding ground should slope up gently from this point so that turf may run right down to the water's edge in places, and the water and marsh plants be seen at their best.

At other points rocks may be firmly cemented on the tops of the walls ('A') sometimes just below the water. These shelves will form ledges on which aquatics can be planted and if the rocks are built up as miniature cliffs on one side of the pool they will present a good contrast to the smooth turf running down to the water on the other.

Plants for the water garden

Plant bog or marsh plants in the moist pockets 'M', placing those that require 10 to 15cm (4 to 6in) of water over their crowns under water lower down the bank with those that flourish on cool, moist, swampy banks, a little higher on the moist shelf. Cover the bottom of the pool with a layer of soil 15 to 30cm (6 to 12in) deep, in which plants may root.

The best method of planting water plants in a pool is in pans, small tubs, or special aquatic baskets, in which the plants are placed in fibrous loam and a little well-decayed manure. The pans or baskets are then gently lowered into the water. If a layer of enriched mud covers the bottom of the pool the baskets rest in this and the roots of the plants can work out and ramble at will.

Hide the edges of the pool with plants that spread out on the surface of the water, while rooting in the firm soil at the margin. Among these are the water forget-me-not, *Myosotis scorpioides*, *Potentilla palustris*, *Caltha palustris* and *Veronica beccabunga*. These, prettily grouped, will clothe the actual margin, while beyond them can be set taller-growing plants such as astilbes, irises, marsh marigolds, with sedges, grasses and rushes which all thrive on the slightly swampy bank. Many of the ferns love a situation like this, among them the beautiful *Osmunda regalis*.

Care of water garden

Once planted, many aquatic and marsh plants are better left undisturbed and only lifted and replanted when they appear to be unhealthy or outgrowing their space. Others, however, are much like hardy perennials in their requirements and thrive best if lifted, divided and replaced every third or fourth spring, or when they appear overcrowded. Some of the water lilies make tremendous leaf growth – and consequently little bloom – which covers the water surface, and prevents the sun's rays from warming it, which is essential to most aquatics. Such strong growth should be periodically cut away, and the roots divided.

Many pools are troubled by a slimy green growth called blanket weed. This may cover the surface of the water in hot, dry weather, usually in spring and summer. Unless the outbreak is severe, remove the weeds by hand; otherwise purchase one of the proprietary chemicals designed for use on pools and adhere strictly to the manufacturer's directions.

Note – To find the capacity of a pool, multiply the length, breadth and average depth in centimetres (in) then multiply by 6; this will give the approximate number of litres of water it contains.

Propagation of aquatic plants

Aquatic plants are propagated by seed or by division of the roots, which is best carried out in early spring just before growth commences. The seeds, when sown, should be placed under water. In other respects plants require the same general treatment as other herbaceous plants.

(*See also* Ch. 23, for the culture of individual aquatics.)

The Bog or Marsh Garden

The site of the bog garden should be low-lying and where surface drainage will naturally collect. If the subsoil is of sticky clay, a mere trickle of water will keep the soil in a marshy condition. If the subsoil is light and well drained, a certain amount of excavation will be necessary.

Dig out about 60cm (2ft) of the topsoil and introduce a little clay to form a basis; over this spread a 12.5cm (5in) bed of rubble or large stones and then a layer of coarse soil. Now fill in the hollow, almost to the level of the surrounding land, with a compost of half loam and half leaf-mould or peat. Unless a natural flow of water is available, an artifical trickle, just sufficient to keep the bog marshy, must be introduced. Bog plants should never suffer from drought so the marsh garden should be kept quite moist; it must not become stagnant, however, and slight bottom drainage is necessary. The bog should never be more than 60cm (2ft) in depth. Make paths of rough stones or bricks through the bog, and over these place flat stepping-stones to make every part of the bog accessible.

Selecting the plants

Almost any moisture-loving plant may be used, as may all the plants that thrive at the margins of streams and ponds. Do not overcrowd the plants; group together three to five plants of the same kind, leave a space, and again plant a group of some different colour, type and height. If the area is small, greater variety and beauty can be obtained by the use of small-growing species, while the freer-growing varieties are invaluable as a background where space permits.

Selection of Plants for Water and Bog Gardens

Note – For cultural details, and notes as to colour, height and time of flowering, *see* the alphabetical list of Ornamental Plants and Trees, Ch. 23.

Water Garden

Alisma plantago-aquatica
Aponogeton distachyos
Butomus umbellatus
Calla palustris
Nymphaea alba
N. 'Attraction'
N. 'Ellisiana'
N. 'Gladstoniana'
N. 'James Brydon'
N. 'Laydekeri Fulgens'
N. 'Marliacea' vars.
N. 'Robinsonian'
N. odorata 'Helen Fowler'
N. o. 'Minor'
N. o. 'Sulphurea Grandiflora'
N. tuberosa 'Richardsonii'
Pontederia cordata
Ranunculus lingua
Sagittaria latifolia
S. sagittifolia

Bog or Marsh Garden

Acorus calamus
A. c. 'Variegatus'
Anagallis tennella
**Aruncus sylvester*
Arundinaria (bamboo) species
Arundo donax
**Astilbe* species and hybrids
Caltha palustris 'Flore Pleno'
**Cimicifuga racemosa*
Gentiana pneumonanthe
Geum rivale
Gunnera manicata
G. chilensis
Hemerocallis vars.
**Hosta* species and vars.
Iris aurea
I. fulva
I. kaempferi
I. sibirica
Leucojum aestivum
Lysimachia clethroides
**L. nummularia*
Lythrum salicaria 'The Beacon'
Mimulus cardinalis, etc
Osmunda regalis
Parnassia palustris
Phormium tenax
Pinguicula grandiflora
**Polygonatum* x *hybridum*
**Primula beesiana*
P. bulleyana
P. juliae
**Rodgersia aesculifolia*
Scirpus lacustris
Thalictrum species
Trollius species and vars.
Typha angustifolia

Those plants marked * will grow in semi-sh

23 Ornamental Plants and Trees

Recommended species and varieties together with details of their individual culture

Note – *The words in the brackets following the varieties indicate first the colour of the flowers, then the time of blooming, and lastly the average height to which the plants may be expected to grow*

Abelia – Hardy and half-hardy evergreen and deciduous shrubs which in mild, sunny, sheltered positions can be grown out of doors. *Culture* – Take cuttings in the late summer and strike in frame or layer in August. Plant out in March or October in well-drained peat, loam and leaf-mould, or pot-up for the cool greenhouse. Trim to keep in shape only, cut off dead blooms and thin old wood after flowering. *Species* – *A. floribunda* (purple rose, June to July, 120cm (4ft)); *A. triflora* (pink white, August to September, 1 to 2.4m (3 to 8ft)); and the hybrid *A.* x *grandiflora* (pink white, August to September, 90 to 120cm (3 to 4ft)).

Abies (fir) – Handsome evergreen coniferous trees, which thrive in open positions in good loam. *Culture* – Plant in April or October. No pruning is required. To propagate, sow in the open in March or April. *Species* – *A. alba* (silver fir); *A. balsamea* (balsam fir); *A. homolepis* (Nikko fir); *A. cephalonica* (Grecian silver fir); *A. grandis* (giant fir); *A. nobilis* (noble fir).

Abutilon (Indian mallow) – Handsome half-hardy shrub for the greenhouse or sheltered beds and borders. *Culture* – For bedding-out increase by means of cuttings of young wood struck in moderate heat 15°C (59°F) during the previous autumn, or early in February; grow on and, if for summer bedding, plant out about the end of May. 2 parts fibrous loam to 1 part of peat and sand makes a suitable compost. Trim and cut out old wood in February. *Varieties* of *A.* x ***hybridum*** – 'Ashford Red' (salmon red); 'Boule de Neige' (white); 'Variegatum' (mottled green and yellow foliage). All August to November, 45 to 60cm (1½ to 2ft).

Acacia (mimosa) – Most of these evergreen trees and shrubs are greenhouse shrubs, not sufficiently hardy to plant in the open, except in warm sheltered borders during the summer months. *Culture* – Sow seeds when ripe or take cuttings of half-matured wood with a 'heel' and strike in a close frame in July or August. In the warm greenhouse *A. armata* will flower in early spring. Pot-up in summer after blooming, in 15 to 25cm (6 to 10in) pots, and give liquid fertilizer while growing. Stand in a sheltered position out of doors in summer and take up again in September. Cut back straggling shoots after flowering. For Hardy or Rose Acacias *see* Robinia. *Species* – *A. armata* (yellow, January to March, 90 to 180cm (3 to 6ft)); *A. baileyana* (yellow, January to May, 1 to 6m (3 to 20ft)); *A. dealbata* (mimosa) (yellow, January to May, 1 to 15m (3 to 50ft)).

Acaena (New Zealand burr) – Genus of trailing plants, the dwarf-growing kinds of which are useful rock plants. They do well in sun or shade in ordinary light sandy soil. *Culture* – Sow under glass in March, place cuttings in a cold frame in August or propagate by division in April. Plant out in spring or early autumn. *Species* – *A. buchananii* (yellowish-red, summer, 5 to 7.5cm (2 to 3in); *A. microphylla* (bright red, June to August, 7.5cm (3in)).

Acantholimon (prickly thrift) – Useful little rock plants, which like a warm, dry, sunny position and gritty, well-drained loam. Best propagated by cuttings with a 'heel' in July, in a cold frame, or by layering. *Species* – *A. glumaceum* (pale pink); and *A. oliviere* (pale pink). All July to August, 12.5 to 15cm (5 to 6in).

Acanthus (bear's breeches) – Hardy perennial useful for beds, borders and cold greenhouse. It likes a sunny, sheltered site with light soil. Propagate by root cuttings. *Species* – *A. mollis latifolius* (rose, summer, 60cm (2ft); *A. mollis* (lilac, pink or white, August, 60cm (2ft); *A. spinosus* (purple pink or white, July and August, 90cm (3ft)).

Acer (maple) – Hardy deciduous trees for pleasure grounds and parks in positions with well-drained ordinary soil. *Culture* – Plant in November. No pruning is required. Propagate by means of seed, layering and budding in the open in August. *Species* – *A. griseum* (4.5m (15ft), orange bark and autumn colour; *A. palmatum* (Japanese maple), 1.5 to 9m (5 to 30ft); *A. platanoides* (Norway maple), 9m (30ft), yellow autumn foliage; *A. pseudoplatanus* (sycamore) 'Brilliantissimum', 6 to 9m (20 to 30ft), pink leaves in spring.

Achillea (milfoil, yarrow or double sneezewort) – This genus includes a number of hardy perennials. The dwarf-growing kinds are useful for the rock garden. They like a sunny situation and light, dry, ordinary soil. *Species* – *A. clavenae* (white, May and June, 7.5 to 10cm (3 to 4in)); *A. filipendulina* (yellow, July to September, 90 to 100cm (36 to 40in)); *A. millefolium* 'Cerise Queen' (June to August, 60cm (2ft)); *A. ptarmica* 'The Pearl' (white, July to September, 75cm (2½ft)); *A. tomentosa* (yellow, June to August, 15 to 22.5cm (6 to 9in)).

Achimenes – Genus of tuberous-rooted plants, suitable for the living-room or greenhouse. *Culture* – Use a compost of equal parts of leaf-mould, loam and silver sand. Plant 5 to 6 tubers 2.5cm (1in) deep in a 15cm (6in) pot in February and place in the cool house. Shade from the hot sun and feed with liquid fertilizer. To keep up a succession, start them in heat in January and continue until May. Dry off after flowering, lift rhizomes and store. Propagate by offsets in February or by cuttings in May under glass. *Species and Varieties* – *A.* 'Admiration' (red purple); *A.* 'Celestial' (pale mauve); *A. erecta* (scarlet); *A. grandiflora* (violet); *A. longiflora* (blue); *A. l.* 'Alba' (white). All July to September, 30 to 45cm (12 to 18in).

Aconite – *See* **Eranthis.**

Aconitum (monkshood or wolfbane) – Hardy perennial, poisonous plants. Propagate by root division in winter.
Species – *A. fischeri* (pale lilac blue, September to October, 90cm (3ft)); *A. vulparia* (yellow, July to August, 90cm (3ft)); *A. napellus* (blue and white, June to October, 120cm (4ft)).

Acorus (sweet flag, sweet sedge or myrtle grass) – Genus of hardy perennials 15 to 75cm (6 to 30in) high, flowering in July and August. *Culture* – Propagate by means of division in March and plant out in sunny, marshy situation or in shallow water.

Adenophora (gland bellflower) – Hardy perennials which thrive in sunny borders, in well-drained ordinary soil. *Species* – *A. ornata* 60cm (2ft); *A. liliifolia* (30 to 100cm (12 to 40in)). Both have blue flowers from June to August.

Adonis (pheasant's eye) – Genus of useful rock plants, annuals and perennials, thriving in shade in a mixture of loam, peat and leaf-mould. *Species* – *A. aestivalis* (crimson, May to June, 30cm (1ft)); *A. annua* (blood red, June to August, 30cm (1ft)); *A. amurensis* (yellow, February to April, 30cm (1ft)); *A. vernalis* (yellow, March to April, 25cm (10in)).

Aesculus (horse chestnut and buckeye) – One of the most handsome of flowering trees. *Culture* – Plant in November in a sunny position with ordinary soil. Thin out branches when overcrowded only. To propagate, sow in March, layer in autumn or graft in the spring. *Species* – *A.* x *carnea* (red horse chestnut, 15m (50ft)); *A. hippocastanum* 'Flore Pleno' (double horse chestnut, 15m (50ft)).

Aëthionema (burnt candytuft) – Genus of dwarf-growing shrubby perennials that are excellent subjects for the rock garden. They thrive in the sun in gritty or sandy loam. *Culture* – Sow under glass in March or insert cuttings in a cold frame in July. *Species and varieties* – *A. coridifolium* (rose, June to July, 15cm (6in)); *A. grandiflorum* (rose, May to July, 30cm (1ft)); *A.* x 'Warley Rose', hybrid (carmine rose, May, 22.5cm (9in)).

Agapanthus – Beautiful African lilies blooming in August and September. They thrive in the open in warm sunny borders in rich sandy loam and leaf-mould, but are more suitable for pot culture. *Culture* – Pot-up in March using a 22.5cm (9in) pot and compost of 2 parts loam to 1 part of leaf-mould, rotted manure and sand. A large pot or tub is needed for several plants. During summer give abundance of water and liquid fertilizer twice a week. In winter protect from frost and water sparingly. Large plants may be stood out during the summer. Sow seed under glass or propagate by means of division in March. *Species* – *A. orientalis* (blue); *A. orientalis albus* (white). Both August 45 to 100cm (18 to 40in). The 'Headbourne Hybrids' are hardier and may be grown outside in light soil (light to dark blue, August to October) 45 to 75cm (1½ to 2½ft).

Agave – Best known variety is the *Agave americana*, or American aloe, which, in the cool greenhouse, usually grows from 50 to 100cm (20 to 40in) high, though much larger plants are obtainable. *Culture* – Pot-up firmly every 4 to 5 years in a well-drained compost of 2 parts of rich fibrous loam to 1 part of leaf-mould, sand and brick rubble. The plants may be stood out of doors in summer. Propagate by seed in heat in February or by offsets in summer. *Species* – *A. americana* (yellowish-green, August, 75cm (2½ft)); *A. americana* 'Marginata' (variegated); *A. filifera* (August, up to 90cm (3ft)).

Ageratum (floss flower) – Useful half-hardy annual for the rock garden, and for edgings to beds or borders. *Species* – *A. houstonianum* (blue and white, May to September, 15 to 45cm (6 to 18in)). *Named varieties* – 'Blue Mink' (amethyst blue); 'Imperial Dwarf' (deep blue); 'Blue Powderpuffs' (soft blue); 'North Sea' (violet blue); 'White Cushion' (white).

Alcea Althaea (hollyhock) – Though really perennials, these are best treated as biennials. They like a sunny position in well-drained and deeply worked rich loam. In summer give a liberal supply of water, and a good mulch of well-rotted manure. A dose of weak liquid fertilizer every 10 days should be given as soon as the plants reach a height of 1 to 1.2m (3½ to 4ft). *Propagation* – Sow seed thinly in drills 2.5cm (1in) deep early in May in the open. When about 10cm (4in) high transplant 20cm (8in) apart in a nursery bed, and plant out 90cm (3ft) apart in October. On cold heavy soils it is better to sow in boxes in May or June, pot-up in winter, place in a frame, and plant out in April. Cuttings may be struck in sandy soil under a cloche in spring or the plants can be increased by division just as the new growth is starting. *Species and varieties* – *A. rosea* (pink, single or double); *A.* 'Chater's Double' (single or mixed colours); *A.* 'Summer Carnival' (pink, red, white, yellow, double); *A.* 'Triumph Supreme' (large colour range, double, rust-resistant); *A. ficifolia*, 'Fig-leaved Hollyhock' (red, orange or yellow, single or double). All flower from July to September and grow to 2 to 3m (6 to 10ft) in height.

Alisma (water plantain) – Hardy perennials useful for bog or water margin in ordinary soil. *Culture* – Sow in March in peat, or propagate by division in April, and plant in sunny position with from 2.5 to 30cm (1 to 12in) of slow-moving water above the crowns.

Allium – Attractive hardy bulbous plants which grow from 15 to 45cm (6 to 18in) high and bloom from May to July. They like a sunny position and light loam to which a little sand and leaf-mould have been added. *Culture* – Plant in September or October 7.5cm (3in) deep and 10cm (4in) apart. Lift from the ground when overcrowded and replant immediately. Propagation is by seed in frame in slight heat in March or by offsets in October. *Species* – *A. beesianum* (blue); *A. caeruleum* (blue); *A. moly* (yellow); *A. neapolitanum* (white); *A. roseum* (lilac rose) and many others. All May to July, 15 to 45cm (6 to 18in).

Alnus (alder) – Deciduous tree which grows well in sunny open positions in moist swampy soil. *Culture* – Plant in November. No pruning is necessary. Propagate by seed, layering or grafting.

Aloe – *See* **Agave.**

Alonsoa (mask flower) – Pretty half-hardy dwarf annual suitable for sunny beds, or for pot culture in the cool greenhouse. If 'stopped back' periodically through the summer some can be lifted and potted-up in September for flowering indoors during autumn and winter. *Pot culture* – Pot-up in 12.5 to 15cm (5 to 6in) pots, keep close for 3 weeks, then give ample light and air. Pinch out young shoots occasionally. Water carefully and give weak liquid fertilizer until buds show colour. *Species* – *A. linearis* and *A. warscewiczii*. Both scarlet, July to August, 45cm (1½ft).

Aloysia – *See* **Lippia.**

Alstroemeria (herb lily or Peruvian lily) – Tuberous-rooted perennials, some of which are hardy and suitable for sunny borders, in which the soil is well drained, rich and light, with a little old mortar, leaf-mould and sand mixed with it. They are also useful for pot culture. *Culture* – Plant 10cm (4in) deep and 25cm (10in) apart. Water freely and mulch in summer when growing and protect from severe frost in winter. Do not lift the rhizomes. Propagate by division in spring or autumn. Seed may also be sown in gentle heat in January, and seedlings planted out in May or June. *Species* – *A. aurantiaca* (orange red, May to August, 75 to 90cm (30 to 36in)); *A. chilensis* (red, pink or yellow, July, 75cm (30in)); *A. ligtu* (lilac, streaked purple, July, 45 to 60cm (1½ to 2ft)); **A pelegrina* (pinkish with purple spots, July, 30 to 45cm (12 to 18in)); *Greenhouse species.

Alyssum (madwort) – Useful dwarf annuals and perennials for sunny beds, edgings or rock garden with sandy soil. *Species* – *A. maritimum* (sweet alyssum) (white, May to July, 10 to 15cm (4 to 6in)); **A. montanum* (yellow, May to June, 7.5cm (3in)); **A. saxatile* 'Citrinum' (yellow, May, 15 to 25cm (6 to 10in)). Perennials species marked.*

Amaranthus (love-lies-bleeding and The Prince's feather) – Half-hardy annuals growing from 30 to 90cm (12 to 36in) high and flowering from July to October. They thrive in sunny beds or borders with shallow, light soil, or in the cool greenhouse. *Species* – *A. caudatus* (crimson, July to October, 25 to 100cm (10 to 40in); *A. c.* 'Ruber' (crimson, with carmine foliage, July, 75cm (30in); *A. c.* 'Tricolor Splendens' (crimson, with red, yellow and green foliage, July, 90cm (3ft)).

Amaryllis belladonna (belladonna lily) – This beautiful species is very variable in the size and colour of its flowers, frequently producing flowers variously shaded from white to a reddish or purplish hue. There is

Every garden has room for spring flowers. This picture shows daffodils and an assortment of tulips behind grape hyacinths

For those with no space for a rockery, a complete miniature landscape can be created in a sink garden only one species. Some of the varieties are *A. belladonna ruber major*, *A. belladonna* 'Pallida' and *A. belladonna* 'Parkeri'. This plant succeeds outdoors in well-drained soil at the foot of warm walls. The bulbs should be planted during the summer, when they are dormant, being covered with about 15cm (6in) of rich loamy soil mixed with leaf-mould and silver sand. If planted too deep they do not flower freely. The blooms are produced during August and September, and the leaves, in common with those of many South African bulbs appear during the winter and spring. Leave the bulbs in the ground but protect with straw in winter. *Greenhouse culture* – If grown in the greenhouse, they require very large pots or pans. Even so, they do not flower freely.

Amelanchier (June berry) – Hardy deciduous trees and shrubs that thrive in sunny sheltered positions and in moderately light and moist soil. *Culture* – Plant in October or November. Do not prune, but cut out dead wood and thin when necessary after flowering. Propagate by seed in March, by grafting on the thorn in March, by cuttings struck in the open in October or by layering. *Species* – *A. alnifolia*, *A. canadensis* 6 to 9m (20 to 30ft), *A. ovalis* 1.8 to 4.5m (6 to 15ft). All white, April to May.

Anagallis (pimpernel) – Half-hardy annuals, suitable for a warm, sunny rock garden or greenhouse. *Species* – *A. arvensis*; *A. linifolia*, etc. (various, summer, 15cm (6in); *A. tenella* (bog pimpernel), (pink, July, 7.5cm (3in)).

Anchusa (alkanet) – The annuals are unimportant. The half-hardy biennials and perennials like a sunny position, but do not require very rich soil, *Species* – *A. capensis* (blue, July, 50cm (20in)); **A. italica* 'Dropmore' (rich blue, June to October, 100 to 150cm (40 to 60in)). Perennials species marked*.

Andromeda (marsh or wild rosemary) – Hardy, evergreen, heath-like shrubs, which thrive in the sun in boggy or moist peaty soil, and also make good pot plants for the cold greenhouse. *Culture* – Plant in October. Propagate by means of ripe seed in pans or boxes under glass in October, divide the roots or layer in September. *Species* – *A. polifolia* (rose white, May and June, 50cm (20in)).

Androsace (rock jasmine) – Perennial rock plants which like a moderately sunny position and a mixture of loam, peat and 30 per cent grit. *A. foliosa* and *A. carnea* require some limestone and no peat in the soil. *Species* – *A. carnea* (rose, May, 7.5cm (3in)); *A. foliosa* (rose lilac, May to June, 15cm (6in)) and many others.

Anemone (windflower) – Anemones of both kinds, hardy fibrous-rooted herbaceous perennials and tuberous-rooted, thrive best in semi-shade in a moist, light, rich medium loam, but generally succeed in any which is well drained, well dug and manured. The dwarf-growing kinds are excellent for the rock garden, while St Brigid anemones are favourites for beds and borders. *Culture* (*tuberous*) – Plant from October to the end of March. Set the tubers about 7.5cm (3in) deep and 12.5cm (5in) apart. The roots are best left undisturbed, but may be taken up as soon as the leaves have died down for removal or for drying-off and replanting in the autumn. A change of position is recommended at intervals of 2 or 3 years. These anemones may be propagated by division of dry rhizomes from September to March. (*Fibrous-rooted, herbaceous perennials.*) Sow in a nursery bed in April, thinly in drills 30cm (1ft) apart and 6mm (¼in) deep. Shade from the sun until the seed is up. Thin out the seedlings to 7.5cm (3in) apart and leave them in the nursery bed until the leaves have died down after flowering the following spring, then lift, store and replant in their flowering positions 20cm (8in) apart early in September. *Greenhouse culture* – Plant in the autumn, using 15cm (6in) pans and a compost of deep, rich sandy loam, and place in the cool greenhouse. Dress annually with fertilizer and lift the tubers when the foliage has died down. *Species* – *A.* x *hybrida* (white, rose, August to October, 75cm (2½ft)); **A. apennina* and vars. (blue or white, March to May, 22.5cm (9in)); **A. blanda* (blue, pink, white, March to April, 15cm (6in)); **A. coronaria* (various, May to June, 30cm (1ft)); *A.* x *fulgens* (scarlet, May to June, 30cm (1ft)); **A. nemorosa* and vars. (blue or white, April, 15cm (6in)). Tuberous species marked *.

Anthemis (chamomile) – Hardy perennials that like a sunny border or rock garden with sandy loam. *Species and varieties* – *A. montana* (white, June to August, 30cm (1ft)); *A. sancti-johannis* (orange, June to August, 30 to 45cm (1 to 1½ft)); *A. tinctoria* (yellow, June to October, 45 to 60cm (1½ to 2ft)); *A. tinctoria* 'E.C. Buxton' (pale yellow, June to October, 45cm (1½ft)).

Anthericum liliago (St Bernard's lily) – Hardy tuberous-rooted perennials, which thrive in a warm, sunny border with moist, light, rich soil, or in 15cm (6in) pots in the cold greenhouse. They grow to a height of 75cm (2½ft) and carry white flowers in June and July.

Antholyza – *See* **Curtonus.**

Anthyllis (kidney vetch and ladies' fingers) – Pretty little rock plants which like a sunny position and warm, gritty loam. They flower in June and July, and reach a height of 25cm (10in).

Antirrhinum (snapdragon) – These are grown both as biennials and perennials. They like a dry, well-drained, well-manured loam and a sunny position, and are extremely useful for dry beds, borders, wall, rock and wild gardens. They are also excellent for bedding and cut flowers, with a wide colour range and a height of 15cm (6in) to 120cm (4ft). See catalogues for lists of varieties.

Aponogeton distachyos (Cape water hawthorn or pond weed) – Hardy aquatic plant which produces masses of white flowers from May to October. *Culture* – Propagate by offsets or division in March. Plant in a weighted basket in slowly moving water with from 15 to 75cm (6 to 30in) of water above the crowns.

Aquilegia (columbine) – Hardy herbaceous perennials and biennials, that thrive in rather shady borders in moist, cool, well-drained, deep loam and leaf-mould. They are also useful for greenhouse culture and the dwarf kinds for the rock garden. *Species and varieties* – *A. alpina* (violet blue, May and June, 25cm (10in)); *A. caerulea* (pale blue and white, May to July, 30 to 45cm (12 to 18in)); *A. longissima* (golden yellow, long spurs, May to July (75cm (30in)); *A. skinneri* (dark scarlet and greenish yellow, May to July, 60cm (24in)).

Arabis (rock cress) – Hardy perennial rock plants which like a sunny position in ordinary well-drained soil or sandy loam. *Species* – *A. alpina* (white, May to July, 15cm (6in)); *A. albida* 'Flore Pleno' (white (double), May to June, trailer); *A. androsacea* (rose, May, trailer).

Araucaria (Chile pine or monkey puzzle) – Coniferous trees which like a sunny position and well-drained, deep loam. *Culture* – Plant in April or September. No pruning is necessary. Propagate by seeds under glass. These trees are unsuitable for town gardens. *Species* – *A. araucana*. *Pot culture* – *A. excelsa* (Norfolk Island pine) is only suitable for the cool greenhouse. Pot-up in March, using two parts of sandy loam to one part of leaf-mould. Propagate by cuttings in heat in October.

Arbutus (strawberry tree) – Evergreen shrubs which thrive in a warm, sunny sheltered position in moist, well-drained peat and loam. Trim back the long straggling shoots in April and cut out dead wood. To propagate sow seed in a frame when ripe. Grow in pots till ready to plant out and do not transplant more than necessary. Cuttings of young shoots may also be taken in July and struck in a frame. *Species* –

A. andrachne (white, tinted green, March and April, 3 to 9m (10 to 30ft)); *A. menziesii* (madrona) (white, May, 6 to 30m (20 to 100ft)); *A. unedo* (cream pink, September to October, 3 to 6m (10 to 20ft)).

Arenaria (sandwort) – Dwarf hardy perennial creeping plants, useful for carpeting, for the paved garden and for the rock garden. They like a moist, sandy, gritty loam. *A. balearica* likes a shady spot and ample leaf-mould in the compost, but *A. montana* loves to tumble over the sides of a rock in full sun. *Species* – *A. balearica* (white, May and June, 7.5cm (3in)); *A. montana* (white, May to July, 7.5cm (3in)); *A. purpurascens* (reddish purple, June and July, 7.5cm (3in)); *A. tetraquetra* (white, June, 7.5cm (3in)).

Aristolochia – Some species, such as *A. macrophylla* (*sipho*), the Dutchman's Pipe (brown and yellow, June to July, 6m (20ft)), are hardy herbaceous perennial climbers in sheltered positions, but others are only suitable for the greenhouse. *Culture* – Sow under glass in March, or take cuttings under glass in April. Plant out in the following March (hardy species) or in the greenhouse in a mixture of light, sandy loam and leaf-mould. Thin out during the spring.

Armeria (thrift, sea pink, cushion pink, etc) – Dwarf hardy perennials mainly seen in the rock garden. They like a sunny, open position in dry, deep loam. *Species* – *A. caespitosa* (pinky lilac, June, 10cm (4in)); *A. maritima* (rose, red, lilac, white, June to July, 15 to 30cm (6 to 12in)); *A. pseudarmeria* (rose, May to July, 45cm (18in)).

Arnebia (prophet flower) – Hardy annuals which thrive in the sun in sandy loam and are excellent for border or rock garden. *Species* – *A. cornuta* (yellow, black dots, June to August, 38cm (15in)).

Artemisia (old man, lad's love, etc) – Hardy herbaceous perennials and evergreen and deciduous shrubs thriving in ordinary soil. Most have finely cut silvery grey leaves. Several of the dwarf-growing kinds make excellent rock plants. *Culture* – Propagate by division in October, or by cuttings in July. *Species* – *A. abrotanum* (yellow, August to October, 90cm (3ft)); well known for its fragrance (southernwood); *A. lactiflora* (cream white, August to October, 1.5m (60in)); *A. nitida* (*lanata*) (yellow (silver foliage), July August, 15cm (6in)).

Arum Lily – *See* **Zantedeschia.**

Aruncus dioicus (syn. *sylvester*), (*Spiraea aruncus*) – Hardy herbaceous perennial thriving in moist situations but tolerant of dry shady conditions. Large dissected leaves and plumes of ivory white flowers in June and July persisting into winter. Propagate by division in spring but do not disturb otherwise. Height 1.5m (5ft). *A.s.* 'Kneiffii' is only 60cm (2ft) and very finely dissected.

Arundinaria – Genus of bamboo, the species of which thrive in a moist climate in a deep, rich loam holding ample leaf-mould, and given protection from north and east winds. Of the hardy kinds. *A. japonica* (syn. *Bambusa metake*), 3 to 4.5m (10 to 15ft) is the most generally grown. There are also many half-hardy species for the warm greenhouse. *Culture* – Propagate by division in May and plant in sheltered positions. Cut out all dead wood in April. *See also* Bambusa.

Arundo (great reed) – Perennial which thrives in semi-shade on slightly swampy banks in light, rich loam, and grows to a height of 3m (10ft). *Culture* – Propagate by division in May. *Species* – *A. donax* (glaucous foliage, 3m (10ft)); *A. donax* 'Variegata' (leaves striped white, 3m (10ft)).

Ash – *See* **Fraxinus.**

Asparagus Fern – Hardy and greenhouse evergreen and deciduous climbing and trailing plants which thrive in a compost of 2 parts loam to 1 part leaf-mould, peat and sand. *Culture* – Pot-up in March using 15 to

25cm (6 to 10in) pots. Syringe and water well in summer. Propagate by seed in March in heat, by cuttings in a propagating case at the same period, or by division in March. The hardy species do well in a warm, sunny position in rich, sandy soil. See also Smilax. *Species* – *A. plumosus* and var. 'Compactus'; *A. retrofractus*; *A. densiflorus* 'Sprengeri'.

Asperula (woodruff) – Hardy annuals and dwarf-growing perennials useful for beds, borders, edgings, rock gardens, etc. The annuals like semi-shade; the perennials a sunny site, and soil with ample grit in it. *Species and varieties* – *A. gussonei* (rose, May to August, 10cm (4in)); *A. odorata* (white, May to June, 22cm (9in)); *A. orientalis* (annual, light blue, June to September, 10cm (4in)).

Asphodelus (asphodel) – Mostly hardy perennials that thrive in the sun in any soil, though rich, sandy loam is most suitable. *Species* – *A. acaulis* (pink, May to July, 30 to 60cm (12 to 24in)); *A. albus* (white, May to July, 60 to 90cm (24 to 36in)); *A. cerasiferus* (king's spear) (white, May to July, 60 to 90cm (24 to 36in)).

Aster (Michaelmas daisy) – For the annual 'China Aster', *see* Callistephus. Hardy perennials which thrive in the sun in ordinary well-drained soil and are excellent for borders and wild gardens, while the dwarf kinds make excellent subjects for the rock garden. They flower from July to November, and grow from 15cm (6in) to 1.8m (6ft) in height according to species. Named varieties of *A. amellus* – 'King George' (purple blue); 'Lady Hindlip' (rosy pink); 'Nocturne' (deep lavender); and 'Perry's Favourite' (pale pink). Named varieties of *A. cordifolius* – 'Diana' (lilac) and 'Silver Spray' (pale lilac). Named varieties of *A. ericoides* – 'Blue Star' (pale blue); 'Delight' (white); and 'Simplicity' (blue). Named varieties of *A. novae-angliae* – 'Barr's Pink' (pink); 'September Ruby' (crimson); and 'Purple Prince' (purple). Named varieties of *A. novi-belgii* – 'Blandie' (creamy white, 1m (3½ft)); 'Chequers' (purple, 60cm (2ft)); 'Eventide' (blue, late, 1.5m (5ft)); 'Fellowship' (pink, 1m (4ft)); 'Freda Ballard' (red, late, 90cm (3ft)); 'Marie Ballard' (blue, 90cm (3ft)); 'Orlando' (silver pink, 1m (3½ft)); 'Winston Churchill' (ruby, 75cm (2½ft)). Dwarf varieties of *A. novi-belgii* (all 30 to 45cm (12 to 18in)) – 'Blue Bouquet', 'Little Red Boy', 'Jenny' and 'Snowsprite.

Astilbe – Hardy herbaceous plants for moist, rich soil. Best by water. Feathery plumes of flowers in July. Propagate by division. *Varieties* – 'Bressingham Beauty' (pink); 'Fanal' (red); 'Hyacinth' (pink); 'White Queen' (all 75cm to 1m (2½ to 4ft)); *A. chinensis pumila* (pink, July to September, 30cm (1ft)).

Astragalus (milk vetch) – Hardy dwarf-growing plants of the broom genus, some of which make excellent subjects for the rock garden. They thrive in the sun in deep loam, sand and mortar. *Culture* – Sow in the spring or summer, or propagate by division in autumn. *Species* – *A. alpinus* (purple, June to August, trailing); *A. danicus* 'Albus' (white, May to July, 13cm (5in); *A. tragacantha* (violet purple, May to July, 60cm (2ft)).

Astrantia (masterwort) – Hardy perennials, which like a shady position with cool, moist loam and leaf-mould. The dwarf-growing kinds are excellent for the rock garden. Propagate by means of root division in spring or autumn.
Species – *A. major* (white, tinged pink, May to July, 45cm (18in)); *A. minor* (pale rose, May to July, 15cm (6in)).

Aubrieta (rock cress) – Pretty evergreen perennial trailing plants, which are useful for edgings, or the rock garden. They thrive in the sun in dry, rich, sandy loam and leaf-mould. *Varieties* – 'Barker's Double' (rosy lilac); 'Bridesmaid' (blush pink); 'Crimson King'; 'Godstone' (violet blue); 'Lavender'; 'Lilac Queen' (rose lilac); 'Magician' (purple). All April to June, 10cm (4in).

Aucuba (spotted or variegated laurel) – Hardy evergreen shrub, well suited for shady places and well-drained ordinary soil. It may also be grown in large pots. *Culture* – Plant in March or October. Cut back long weak shoots in May. To propagate, take cuttings and strike in the open in autumn, or sow seed in frame when ripe.

Auricula – *See* **Primula.**

Azalea – This group of plants is classified under the Rhododendrons, but is here treated separately under its old and still used name. A compost of sandy peat and loam or fibrous loam and leaf-mould is suitable for all species, but they will grow quite well in almost any soil which does not contain lime or chalk. *Culture* – For outdoor culture, *see* Rhododendrons. *Pot culture* (*R. simsii* and hybrids) – Pot-up firmly from October to November, using 15 to 25cm (6 to 10in) pots and the compost as described. Keep in a cold frame until late November, then move in succession into the house and gradually acclimatize to moist, warm conditions. After flowering, prune straggling shoots and remove all dead blooms. Re-pot if necessary (usually every second or third year), place the pots in the warmest corner and syringe overhead. Stand in the open in a cool, sheltered position on a bed of ashes or shingle from June to September, and water liberally and syringe overhead morning and evening in dry warm weather. In September return to the house. *A. mollis*, though hardy, is also useful for the warm greenhouse. To propagate, take cuttings of half-matured wood early in summer and strike in a frame (10 to 16°C (50 to 59°F)); sow in moist heat and fine sandy peat in spring: or layer. *Species* (*hardy*) – *R japonicum* (*A. mollis*) (red, yellow, etc.); *R. nudiflorum* (*A. nudiflora*) (pink or white); *R. luteum* (*A. pontica*) (yellow). All May to June, 1 to 2m (3 to 6ft). (*Greenhouse*) – *R. simsii* (Indian azalea, many shades of colour). They flower from December to May, according to the temperature of the house, and grow from 30 to 90cm (1 to 3ft) high. Consult growers' catalogues for named varieties.

Azara – Evergreen shrubs and climbers that are almost hardy, and which like a warm, sheltered position and well-drained sandy loam. *Culture* – Plant in March or October. Thin out the branches when necessary, but otherwise do not prune. Propagate by means of cuttings under glass in summer or by layering in spring. *A. microphylla* is a beautiful shrub with pale yellow flowers in early spring. *A. dentata* is later. Both scented.

Balsam – *See* **Impatiens.**

Bambusa (bamboo) – Most are tropical plants requiring heated greenhouses. For hardy bamboos, *see* **Arundinaria.**

Bartonia – *See* **Mentzelia.**

Begonia – These plants thrive in sunny beds and borders with rich loam, and are also extremely useful in the greenhouse. *Culture* (*tuberous-rooted species*) – For bedding out or for greenhouse decoration June to October. Sow in February under glass (18°C (65°F)) in a finely sifted and just moist compost of ⅔ loam and ⅓ leaf-mould and sand. Water before and after sowing and keep the seed pan moist. Prick off the seedlings into shallow boxes. Pot-off singly into pots and plant out in May or June, or pot-up into 13cm (5in) pots for the greenhouse, keep near the glass, and shade when the sun is hot. Particular varieties may be propagated in spring by leaf-cuttings. Ordinary stem cuttings may also be taken in summer. When starting tubers, they should be planted flat or hollow side uppermost in February or March, and just covered in shallow trays in heat (16°C (59°F)) with moist sandy loam and well-rotted manure for soil. Water in moderation until growth commences. If for summer bedding, harden off in May in a cold frame and plant out in June, or, if for the greenhouse, pot-up in 10cm (4in) pots in a compost of ⅔ loam and ⅓ leaf-mould, well-rotted manure and sand, re-potting when pot-bound into 17 to 20cm (7 to 8in) pots. Water well in summer, shade from hot sun, and once the roots have filled the pots, feed with weak liquid fertilizer twice a week. Stake any shoots that need support and pick off all dead blooms. Greenhouse temperature 13°C (55°F) winter to 21°C (70°F) summer. The tubers should be lifted in October when the frost has turned the foliage black. If they must be removed from the beds before this lift them with a good 'ball' of soil, pack in boxes, and place in a sheltered spot to finish ripening. Then shake the soil and foliage away from the roots, allow them to dry for a day or so and store in dry soil in boxes in a cool but frost-proof place. Tuberous begonias in pots must be gradually dried-off and stored in a frost-proof shed or frame for the winter.

Culture (fibrous-rooted species) – This is a large and varied class, including a large number of species and varieties of a sub-shrubby habit, which require an intermediate greenhouse temperature. Some of them flower more or less all the year round, and a few of them may be used for summer bedding. The most important for this purpose are the many beautiful varieties of *B. semperflorens*, which may be raised from seed sown during January in a temperature of 16°C (59°F) or from basal cuttings from plants lifted and potted up and kept in a warm house over the winter. The sub-shrubby and perennial species generally are propagated by ordinary cuttings, or by leaf-cuttings, in a temperature of from 16 to 21°C (59 to 70°F). The winter-flowering section, which is represented by 'Gloire de Lorraine' and its varieties, may be increased by leaf-cuttings, or by young basal shoots. They are usually taken from plants that have flowered and that have been rested for a few weeks. These are then partly cut back and started in a temperature of from 18 to 21°C (65 to 70°F), cuttings being taken during March. The other winter-flowering section, which is represented by varieties raised from crossing the species *B. socotrana* with the tuberous-rooted varieties are by no means easy to grow successfully, and require very careful management during their resting period. After flowering, they should stand in a house with a temperature of from 13 to 16°C (55 to 59°F). They should have very little water at the roots; on the other hand, they must not suffer from dryness. In May give more water, and when the young shoots are about 7.5cm (3in) in length, they should be taken as cuttings and inserted singly in small pots of sandy compost. They root readily in a close case with a bottom heat of 21°C (70°F). During the summer months they should be grown in an average temperature of from 13 to 18°C (55 to 65°F).

Culture of ornamental and variegated-leaved species – Pot-up in March or April in a compost as recommended above, keep in a moist atmosphere, never letting the temperature fall below 10°C (50°F), and shade from the strong sun. At that time, water liberally and give a little weak liquid fertilizer. Decrease the water supply in winter, but do not dry off entirely. Propagate by seed, leaf-cuttings of unflowered shoots (heat 16 to 18°C (59 to 65°F). For species and varieties *see* growers' catalogues.

Bellis (daisy) – Dwarf-growing hardy perennials, which thrive in the sun in moderately rich soil. They grow from 15 to 30cm (6 to 12in) high and flower in May. Propagate by seed or division.

Benthamia (Bentham's strawberry tree) – *See* **Cornus capitata.**

Berberidopsis corallina (coral barberry) – Half-hardy evergreen climbing shrub which thrives in a cool greenhouse, or in a border in the south in well-drained, light loam against walls facing south or west and partially shaded. It carries coral-red flowers in June, and grows to a height of 6m (20ft). *Culture* – Take cuttings early in summer, or propagate by layering in October. Plant out in April and October and thin out straggly branches when overcrowded.

Berberis (barberry) – Beautiful hardy flowering shrubs, evergreen and deciduous. *Culture* – Plant evergreens from March to April or from October to

November; deciduous, November to March, in ordinary soil or sandy loam. Thin out shoots after flowering when overcrowded and trim to shape. Trimming should be delayed until the spring in the case of shrubs grown for autumn foliage. Most species are propagated by seeds in the open in October, by half-matured cuttings in a frame in July or August, or by layering in August. *B.* x *stenophylla* must be propagated by cuttings or layering. *B. darwinii* is useful for pot culture in the cold or unheated greenhouse. Pot-up in November using 20 to 25cm (8 to 10in) pots and a compost of two parts of sandy loam to one part of leaf-mould and rotted manure. *Species and varieties* (*Evergreens*) – *B. candidula* (yellow, April to May, 60cm (2ft)); *B. darwinii* (orange, April to May, 2.5 to 3m (8 to 10ft)); *B.* x *stenophylla* (yellow, April to June, 2.5 to 3m (8 to 10ft)); (*Deciduous*) – *B. thunbergii* (yellow, April to May, 90cm (3ft)); *B. vulgaris* (yellow, April to May, 1 to 4.5m (4 to 15ft)); *B. wilsonia* (yellow, May, 60 to 100cm (2 to 4ft)); *B. yunnanensis* (yellow, May, 1 to 1.8m (4 to 6ft)).

Bergenia – Hardy plants with rosettes of very large, usually glossy, evergreen leaves. They thrive in sun or semi-shade in ordinary garden loam. Propagate by seed (gentle heat) in the spring; or by division in the autumn. *Species* – *B. cordifolia* (rose, 30 to 45cm (12 to 18in)); *B. ciliata ligulata* (purple rose, 30 to 60cm (12 to 24in)); *B. stracheyi* (pink and white, 25cm (10in)). All April to May flowering.

Betula (birch) – Plant in November in a sunny, open, moist position. All species will thrive in a poor, gravelly soil. No pruning is necessary. Propagate by seeds, layering or grafting. *Species* – *B. pendula* (silver birch); *B.p.* 'Darlecarlica' (Swedish); *B.p.* 'Youngii' (weeping); and *B.p.* 'Purpurea' (purple birch).

Bignonia (trumpet flower) – Some of these are fine half-hardy perennial climbers, related to *Tecoma*. They thrive best planted out in borders of the greenhouse.

Boltonia (false starwort) – Hardy perennial for border or wild garden, thriving in any moist and moderately good loam. *Species* – *B. asteroides* (white, July to September, 1 to 1.5m (4 to 5ft)).

Boronia – Evergreen shrubs which do best in the cool greenhouse in equal parts of sandy loam, peat, and leaf-mould. *Culture* – Pot-up from April to May in 12.5 to 17.5cm (5 to 7in) pots. Stop young plants, give ample air and liquid fertilizer while growing. Prune after flowering, and stand outdoors from June to September. To propagate, take cuttings of young shoots in May and strike in sand and peat under glass (16°C (59°F)). *Species* – *B. elatior* (carmine); *B. heterophylla* (cerise); *B. megastigma* (brownish purple and yellow). All February to April, 60cm (2ft).

Box – *See* **Buxus.**

Brachycome iberidifolia (Swan River daisy) – Beautiful summer-flowering, dwarf-growing, half-hardy annual. Varieties are available in white, pink, red and blue colours.

Brodiaea (Californian or Missouri hyacinth) – Hardy and half-hardy bulbous plants, that thrive in well-drained, deep, sandy soil mixed with leaf-mould, in sunny borders, in the cool greenhouse, or in the rock garden. *Culture* – Plant in October, 7.5cm (3in) deep and 12.5cm (5in) apart. Protect with ashes during winter, and lift the bulbs every fourth year only. Propagate by offsets in October. *Species* – *B. coronaria* (violet blue, June and July, 38cm (15in)); *B. ixioides* (*Triteleia*) (yellow, summer, 15cm (6in)); *B.* (*Ipheion*) *uniflora* (white or blue, April to May, 15cm (6in)); *B. ida-maia* (*Dichelostemma*) (crimson satin flower, dark crimson and green, summer, 50cm (20in)).

Buckthorn – *See* **Rhamnus.**

Buddleia – Beautiful flowering shrubs. Some species are not quite hardy enough to stand severe weather out of doors, but flourish in well-drained, deep, ordinary soil or good loam in warm, sunny, sheltered positions, or in the greenhouse. *Culture* – Plant *B. globosa* in March or October. Others November to March. Do not prune *B. alternifolia* or *B. globosa*, merely cut out old wood after flowering. In the case of *B. davidii* cut last year's shoots back to within 25cm (10in) of old wood in February. Propagation is by cuttings in a frame in late summer or autumn or by seed when ripe. *Hardy species* – *B. alternifolia* (pale, purple, June, 3m (10ft)); *B. colvillei* (rose, July, 6m (20ft)); *B. davidii* and vars. (lilac, August, 3m (10ft); *B. globosa* (orange ball tree) (orange, June, 3m (10ft)).

Buphthalmum (ox-eye) – Tall hardy perennial, which thrives in the sun in well-drained loam. *Species* – *B. salicifolium* (yellow, July to September, 60cm (24in)); *B. speciosissimum* (golden orange, July, 1.5 to 2m (60 to 70in)).

Butomus umbellatus (flowering rush) – Hardy aquatic perennial, which likes a warm, sunny position in a bog or on a muddy bank, on in sheltered still water, with from 2.5 to 30cm (1 to 12in) of water above the crowns. It grows some 75cm (30in) high and carries pink flowers from June to August. Propagate by division in March.

Buxus sempervirens (box) – Hardy, slow-growing, small-leaved, evergreen shrub. Ideal for low hedge or topiary. Plant in April or September, in light, well-drained soil. Clip in May and August. Propagate by cuttings in August or September under cloches; division in September or by layering in October. *Species* – *B. sempervirens* (common box); and vars. 'Aurea Pendula' (golden); 'Argentea' (silver); 'Suffruticosa' (dwarf-growing).

Cacti – Nearly all species may be grown in a moderately heated greenhouse. They like a compost of ½ fibrous loam and ½ a mixture of sand, broken bricks and rubble, and a sunny position, except *Epiphyllum*, *Rhipsalis* and *Zygocactus*, which prefer shade and a compost of ⅔ fibrous loam and ⅓ sand, peat and brick rubble. Pot-up firmly in February or March and re-pot every 3 to 4 years, keeping pots as small as possible. A few pieces of charcoal in the compost are beneficial. Give ample ventilation and syringe with tepid water twice a week from April to September. Decrease water supply from October to April. Propagate by cuttings (partially dried) in summer, by grafting in March, or by offsets. Hardy cacti can be planted in spring in a well-drained, sunny, sheltered site in the rock garden or on a wall or bank in light loam with a mixture of brick rubble, sand and gravel. *Aporocatus*, *Notocactus* and *Mammillaria*, and those with stems likely to hold moisture, should be covered with glass in winter. *Species* (*Hardy*) – *Echinocereus engelmannii* (purple, June, 45cm (18in)); *Mammillaria densispina* (pink, summer, 22cm (9in)). (*Half-hardy*) – *Aporocatus flagelliformis* (whip cactus) (pink, June, 30 to 75cm (12 to 30in)); *Epiphyllum* hybrids (orchid cactus) (many colours, June, 45 to 60cm (18 to 24in)); *Opuntia ficus-indica* (prickly pear) (yellow, June, 75cm (30in)); *Rhipsalis cassutha* (mistletoe cactus) (white, April, 38cm (15in)); *Schlumbergera russelliana* (leaf-flowering cactus (pink, November, 25 to 60cm (10 to 24in)).

Calamintha (*Acinos*) **alpina** (calamint) – Hardy aromatic plant forming a thick carpet of foliage, and carrying sprays of violet flowers all through the summer. Grow in a sunny site in gritty loam. Propagate by seeds in March, or by division in March or September.

Calandrinia (rock purslane or portulaca) – Dwarf-growing, annual and perennial plants that thrive in the sun in sandy loam. *Species* (*Annual*) – *C. discolor* (lilac, 30 to 45cm (12 to 18in)); *C. grandiflora* (rose, 45cm (18in)); *C. ciliata* (purple, 22.5cm (9in)). (*Perennial*) – *C. umbellata* (crimson, 22.5cm (9in)). All July to September.

Calceolaria (slipper flower) – There are three distinct kinds of calceolaria, the *her-*

baceous, raised and reared under glass; the *shrubby*, grown for bedding out; these thrive in fibrous loam mixed with leaf-mould and sand. The third type, being hardy perennials and annuals, make excellent subjects for the rock garden. *Culture* (*Herbaceous Calceolarias*) *C.* x. *herbeohybrida* – Sow thinly in a propagating case in June. Pot-up singly in July and keep in a cold frame; re-pot into 7.5 to 10cm (3 or 4in) pots in September and take into the greenhouse. Keep warm and moist at night and give a steady even temperature. Pot-up finally in February or March (before the flower buds begin to show), using 17.5 to 20cm (7 to 8in) pots and a compost of 2 parts loam to 1 part of leaf-mould and sand, and keep near the glass in a cool greenhouse. Stake securely, shade from the strong sun, and do not over-water. Weak liquid fertilizer should be given at fortnightly intervals, as soon as the buds appear. Seeds should be sown afresh each year to obtain the best results. *Culture* (*Shrubby Calceolarias*) *C. integrifolia* – Take cuttings of vigorous young basal shoots in September and strike under glass, or in a warm north border, and cover with cloches. If the weather turns frosty, cover the cloches. About the middle of February, the cuttings should have their growing points pinched back. A fortnight later they may either be potted or kept as cool as possible 7.5 to 10cm (3 to 4in) apart in a nursery bed, and finally transferred to the flower garden about 22.5cm (9in) apart towards the end of May or early in June. Seed may also be sown under glass in March. (Temp. 10 to 16°C (50 to 59°F). Transplant the seedlings into boxes as soon as they can be handled and next pot-up singly into 7.5 to 10cm (3 or 4in pots). Transfer to a cold frame in May, and before the plants become pot-bound re-pot into 12.5 to 15cm (5 to 6in) pots, if for greenhouse use, or if for summer bedding, harden off and plant out early in June. *Culture* (*third type*) – As for other annuals and rock-garden plants.

Calendula (pot marigold) – Hardy annuals which thrive in beds or borders in almost any soil. All double, flowering from June to October, with flowers of bright orange or yellow, 45cm (18in).

Calla palustris (bog arum) – Hardy aquatic plants which spread over the surface of shallow still water. They like a sunny position in firm soil at the margin of ponds. Propagate by division in March. The white flowers are borne from June to August.

Callistemon (bottle brush plant) – Greenhouse evergreens which thrive in full sun in a cool house, in equal parts of sandy peat and loam. They carry crimson and golden flowers in May and June on stems from 1 to 2m (3 to 6ft) in height. *Culture* – Pot-up in 15 to 25cm (6 to 10in) pots, stand out of doors from June to September, and trim after flowering. To propagate take cuttings of matured wood in the late spring and strike in a frame.

Callistephus chinensis (China aster) – Half-hardy, autumn-flowering annuals particularly adapted for small beds, edgings, the rock garden, or pot culture. All varieties thrive best in a deep rich light soil and in hot dry weather should be mulched with well-rotted manure, and frequently watered with liquid fertilizer. *Pot culture* – Sow in May. Pot-up three plants in a 15cm (6in) pot in a compost of $\frac{2}{3}$ fibrous loam and $\frac{1}{3}$ well-decayed manure. Stand in the open and transfer under glass as soon as the buds begin to colour. *Species and varieties* – *Callistephus chinensis* (single) 45cm (18in); 'Chrysanthemum-flowered' 30cm (12in); 'Comet' (broad florets) 30cm (12in); 'Dwarf Bouquet' 15 to 22.5cm (6 to 9in); 'Giant Ray' (stiff and prominent florets) 45cm (18in); 'Mignon' 25cm (10in); 'Ostrich Plume' (branching with double flowers) 45cm (18in); 'Quilled' (tubular florets); 'Paeony-flowered' (incurving florets) 45cm (18in); 'Queen of the Market' (double) 38cm (15in).

Calluna vulgaris (ling, heather) – Hardy evergreen shrub thriving in full sun in peaty non-calcareous soil. *Culture* – Plant in October or April, trim off dead flower-heads in April. To propagate, take cuttings in summer and strike in peaty soil in a frame or layer. *See also* Erica. *Varieties* – *C.v.* 'Alba Plena' (white Scotch heather); *C.v.* 'H. E. Beale' (pink, July to September, 38cm (15in)); *C.v.* 'Aurea' (golden foliage, July to September, 30cm (12in)); *C.v.* 'Robert Chapman' (orange red foliage, 38cm (15in)).

Calochortus (butterfly tulip, star tulip, and mariposa lily) – Half-hardy bulbous plants that thrive in full sun in sandy leaf-mould. *Culture* – Plant in late October, 7.5cm (3in) deep and 7.5cm (3in) apart. Cover with straw in winter and lift the bulbs when the leaves die down. *Pot culture* – Pot-up 10 bulbs in a 10 to 12.5cm (4 to 5in) pot in November in a compost of $\frac{2}{3}$ sandy loam and $\frac{1}{6}$ part each of peat and leaf-mould. Keep covered with straw in a cold frame until late December, when transfer to the greenhouse; dry off after flowering. Propagate by offsets in November. *Species* – *C. albus* (white, June to July, 20cm (8in)); *C. venustus* and vars. (yellow and red, July and August, 38cm (15in)).

Caltha (marsh marigold) – Useful hardy perennial for the water-side or moist border. *Culture* – Propagate by division of roots in March or July and plant out in moist, rich soil and in full sun or partial shade. *Species* – *C. palustris* 'Flore Pleno' (rich yellow (double), May to July, 30cm (12in)); *C. leptosepala* (deep yellow, flushed maroon, May to July, 38cm (15in)); and *C. polypetala* (golden, May to July, 50cm (20in)).

Calycanthus floridus (Carolina all-spice) – Hardy, scented, deciduous shrub which likes a partially shaded moist position and carries purple-red flowers in May and June, growing 1.5m (5ft) or more. *Culture* – Plant in November, and cut out dead wood after flowering. Propagate by cuttings or layering in summer.

Camassia (quamash) – Hardy bulbous plants which thrive in moist but sunny borders in a mixture of loam, leaf-mould and rotten manure. *Culture* – Plant in October, 10 to 12.5cm (4 to 5in) deep and 25cm (10in) apart; and lift from the soil every fourth year. Propagate by offsets in October, or by seed under glass in March. *Species* – *C. quamash* (purple blue and silver white, May and June, 50 to 75cm (20 to 30in)); *C. leichtlinii* (cream white, May and June, 1 to 1.5m (40 to 60in)).

Camellia – Hardy evergreen shrubs which thrive in sheltered and semi-shaded positions and in practically any soil, provided it is lime-free. They are also useful for greenhouse culture. *Culture* – Pot-up firmly in May, using 20 to 30cm (8 to 12in) pots. They do best when under-potted. Use a compost of one-half part turfy loam and a quarter part each of sand and peat or leaf-mould. As soon as re-established, gradually harden off, stand out of doors in partial shade on a firm base of ashes or bricks, and keep the roots moist, but not too wet. Move the plants into cold frames or the cold house in September. Trim back all straggling shoots after flowering, syringe daily, sponge the leaves occasionally, and disturb the roots as little as possible. Propagate by grafting in a close propagating frame in early spring, using seedling *C. japonica* as a stock, or cuttings of half-matured shoots in a frame in July or August. Seeds may be raised in moist heat. *Species* – *C. japonica* flowers from February to May; *C. sasanqua* from October to April. Varieties of both are numerous and catalogues should be consulted.

Campanula (bellflower) – Genus including annuals, biennials and perennials and providing plants for the greenhouse, border and rock garden. Almost all species thrive in an open position in sun or semi-shade in well-drained light, sandy loam with ample grit and leaf-mould. *Pot culture* (*C. pyramidalis*) – Sow in small pots and place in a well-ventilated frame; move into 13 to 15cm (5 to 6in) pots in October and keep in a frost-proof frame for the winter. Pot-up again in March, using 17 to 20cm (7 to 8in) pots and a compost of $\frac{2}{3}$ sandy loam and $\frac{1}{3}$ leaf-mould, rotted manure, and a little rubble; harden off and stand in the open. Stake as the flower spikes form, move into the house about July, and give liquid fertilizer when the buds form. *C. pyramidalis* and other tall species for the greenhouse may also be increased by cuttings in a frame in March or August. *Greenhouse trailing species* – Propagate by seed in heat in March, by cuttings in a frame in August, or by division in March. *Species* – *C. glomerata* (pale purple, June to September, 45cm (18in)); *C. lactiflora* (blue or white, June to August, 90 to 120cm (36 to 48in)); *C. latifolia* (pale blue, June to September, 60 to 120cm (24 to 48in)); *C. medium* (Canterbury bells) (various, June to August, 25 to 120cm (10 to 50in)); *C. persicifolia* (blue and white, June to August, 60 to 75cm (24 to 30in)); *C. pyramidalis* (chimney bellflower) (blue or white, July to September, 100 to 175cm (40 to 70in)). (*Alpines*) – *C. allionii* (blue, June, 5 to 7.5cm (2 to 3in)); *C. alpina* (violet, June to September, 10cm (4in)); *C. caespitosa* (blue, June to July, 13cm (5in)); *C. carpatica* vars. (purple, blue or white, May to September, 15 to 30cm (6 to 12in)); *C. garganica* (mauve, white or pale blue, June to September, 10cm (4in)); *C. portenschlagiana* (purple blue, June to August, 10cm (4in)); *C. poscharskyana* (powder blue, June, 30cm (12in)).

Canary Creeper – *See* **Tropaeolum peregrinum.**

Canna (Indian shot) – Half-hardy perennials for the cool greenhouse or for summer bedding in warm sunny beds and borders with well-manured rich loam. *Culture* – Sow seed 1cm ($\frac{1}{2}$in) deep in sandy loam and leaf-mould in a propagating case (24°C (75°F)), in February or March (the seed having previously been soaked for a day in warm water). Pot-up singly as soon as possible, or propagate by division of roots in spring, dividing them so that each section of root contains an eye. Pot-up early in March or April in single pots and, if for outdoor culture, plant out in June about 60cm (24in) apart. If for greenhouse culture, pot-up into 15 to 30cm (6 to 12in) pots, using a rich and porous compost of one-half loam and one-quarter part each of farmyard manure and sandy leaf-mould. At the end of September pot-up those grown out of doors and winter under glass. Keep moderately dry and allow the leaves and stems to die off gradually. *Named varieties* – 'Bonfire' (orange scarlet); 'Evening Star'; 'President' (scarlet); and 'J. B. van der Schoot' (yellow, spotted). All August to October, 1 to 2m (3 to 6ft).

Caragana arborescens (pea tree) – Hardy deciduous shrub of the *Cytisus* family, which thrives in sunny positions on dry banks in light sandy or ordinary soil. *Culture* – Plant in October; cut out dead wood after flowering. Propagate by seed in the open in May or by layering in July.

Carnation – *See* **Dianthus.**

Carpenteria californica (Californian mock orange) – Half-hardy climbing shrub which likes a warm sheltered position and well-drained loam. Grows from 1.5 to 3m (5 to 10ft) high, flowers about mid-summer. *Culture* – Propagate by cuttings of young wood in April in a frame, by layering in September, or by suckers in autumn. Plant in autumn and prune out weak wood and dead flowers after flowering.

Carpinus betulus (hornbeam) – Hardy deciduous tree which thrives in sunny, open positions in almost any soil and makes a good hedge plant. *Culture* – Plant from November to February; no pruning is necessary except for hedges which are trimmed in August. Propagate by seed.

Castanea sativa (sweet chestnut) – Hardy deciduous tree which thrives in full sun in light gravelly loam. *Culture* – Plant in November and thin out branches when overcrowded.

Catalpa bignonioides (Indian bean tree) – Hardy deciduous trees which thrive in full sun and in moist, but well-drained rather light loam. They grow 7.5 to 15m (25 to 50ft) high and flower in July and August. *Culture* – Plant from November to February. When seeds are not available, take cuttings of leafy shoots in July and insert them in gentle bottom heat or layer in July.

Catananche – Hardy perennial or annual plants, which like a sunny spot in a warm dry border and ordinary soil. *Species* – *C. caerulea* (blue, July to August, 75cm (30in)); and *C. caerulea* 'Perry's White' (white, July to August, 50 to 75cm (20 to 30in)).

Ceanothus (Californian lilac) – Half-hardy shrubs which like a warmy sunny position and well-drained ordinary soil and leaf-mould. There are two distinct classes, one flowering in spring, the other from July to September. The latter are hardy deciduous shrubs and the others evergreens, suitable for sheltered walls and mild localities. *Culture* – Plant in March or October. Cut spring-flowering species back in May; late-flowering plants must be pruned in early spring. Evergreens grown as bushes will not need severe pruning. To propagate, take cuttings in July or August and strike in a frame, or layer during the same months. *Species and hybrids* (*Evergreen, spring-flowering*) – *C.* x *burkwoodii* (rich blue); *C. dentatus* (blue); *C. rigidus* (purplish blue); and *C.* x. *veitchianus* (bright blue). (*Hybrids* (*deciduous*), *late-flowering*) – 'Ceres' (rose pink); 'Gloire de Versailles' (lavender); 'Henri Desfosse' (dark blue); 'Indigo' (indigo blue); 'Marie Simon' (rose); and 'Perle Rose' (rose carmine).

Cedrus (cedar) – Hardy evergreen trees suitable only for large gardens. *Culture* – Plant in September or October when from 30 to 100cm (1 to 4ft) high, in a sunny position in well-drained, gravelly, chalky or sandy soil. No pruning is necessary. To propagate, sow in March or April. *Species* – *C. atlantica* (Mount Atlas cedar, 24 to 30m (80 to 100ft); *C. deodara* (deodar 46m (150ft)); and *C. libani* (cedar of Lebanon, 30m (100ft)).

Celastrus (bitter sweet, staff tree, etc) - Hardy perennial climbing plants which thrive in most soils and positions. They carry hundreds of brilliant golden yellow fruits exposing scarlet-coated seeds in autumn. *Culture* – Cut out weak wood and tip stray shoots in February and propagate by layering young shoots in October. *Species* – *C. orbiculatus* and *C. scandens*.

Celosia (Prince of Wales' feathers, or cockscomb) – Half-hardy annuals which thrive if planted out in June in a warm, sheltered situation in southern districts. Grown in pots in the greenhouse, they may, with a little trouble, be had in flower the whole winter. *Species and varieties* – *C. argentea* (silvery); *C. a. cristata* (cockscomb) (crimson, July to August, 45cm (18in)); *C.a.c.* 'Coccinea' (scarlet); *C.a.c.* 'Pyramidalis' (scarlet, crimson, or gold, July to September, 75cm (30in)).

Celsia (Cretan mullein) – Half-hardy biennials and perennials which thrive in the cool greenhouse, in a compost of sandy loam and a little leaf-mould. *Species* – *C. arcturus* (deep yellow, spotted purple, June to November, 50cm (20in)); *C. cretica* (golden yellow, spotted brown, June to July, 1.5m (60in)).

Centaurea – Large genus of hardy annuals, biennials and perennials, all of which thrive in a sunny position in any good garden soil. The perennials (knapweed) make good border plants; *C. cyanus* (cornflower) and *C. suaveolens* are annuals. *Pot culture* – *C. gymnocarpa* (dusty miller) and *C. ragusina* are useful in the cold greenhouse. Sow in heat in January and August, or take cuttings in September. *Species and varieties* (*Hardy annuals*) – *C. cyanus* (cornflower) (white, pink, blue, July to October, 15 to 90cm (6 to 36in)); *C. moschata* (sweet sultan) (white to yellow, rose and purple, July to October, 50cm (20in)). (*Hardy perennials*) – *C. babylonica* (yellow, July to September, 2 to 2.5m (6 to 8ft)); *C. dealbata* (rose, silver foliage, July to September, 60cm (24in)); *C. macrocephala* (deep yellow, July and August, 120 to 150cm (50 to

60in)); *C. montana* (blue, white, pink and yellow, July and August, 60 to 90cm (24 to 36in)).

Centranthus (valerian) – Hardy perennial, which likes a sunny position and dry, limy soil, and is useful for borders, rock gardens, or walls. *Species* – *C. angustifolius* (crimson, May to July, 60cm (24in)); *C. ruber* (crimson, June to August, 60 to 90cm (24 to 36in)); *C.r.* 'Albus' (white).

Cerastium (mouse-ear, Jerusalem star) – Genus of dwarf, invasive hardy perennials that are useful for carpeting or for the rock and paved gardens. *Species* – *C. bierbersteinii* (white, silver foliage, May to June, 15cm (6in)); *C. tomentosum* (white, silver foliage, June to August, 15cm (6in)).

Ceratostigma (leadwort) – Low-growing rock plants which thrive in the sun in gritty loam. *C. plumbaginoides* (cobalt blue, September, 22cm (9in)) is well-known.

Cercis (Judas tree) – Tall deciduous shrubs or small trees which thrive in full sun in moist, sandy and well-drained loam. In May they carry rose purple pea-shaped flowers. *Culture* – Plant in October or November. To propagate, sow in a frame or layer in September.

Chaenomeles (cydonia, japonica, flowering quince) – Hardy deciduous flowering trees and shrubs, which thrive in sunny positions in ordinary soil. *Culture* – Plant in October or November. Cut out old wood and shorten side shoots in June. Propagate by seeds, layering, suckers or cuttings in October. *Pot culture* – Pot-up in November, in 20 to 25cm (8 to 10in) pots and take into the cold greenhouse. Sink the pots in ashes outdoors from May to November. *Species and varieties* – *C. speciosa* (orange red), vars. 'Aurora' (rose, shaded yellow); *C. japonica* (orange flame) hybrids. All January to June, 1 to 2.7m (3 to 9ft).

Chamaecyparis (false cypress) – Coniferous trees tolerant of most soils. *Species* – *C. lawsoniana* ('Lawson's cypress', fast growing, suitable for hedges, with many ornamental varieties, 15m (50ft)); *C. obtusa* (rounded, dark green and slow growing. Eventually 9m (30ft)).

Charieis heterophylla (Cape aster) – Pretty little hardy annual, very effective in beds or rock gardens. It grows some 15cm (6in) high and flowers from June to September.

Cheiranthus (wallflower) – Hardy biennials and perennials which may be grown in sunny, open beds or borders, in the rock garden or in the cold greenhouse, in dry, sandy loam with some lime in it. Double wallflowers must be raised from cuttings. The perennial species are usually grown as biennials. *Pot culture* – Pot-up in September, using 12.5 to 15cm (5 to 6in) pots and ordinary soil and keep in a cold frame until the buds appear. *Species and varieties* – *C.* x*allionii* (bright orange, 25cm (10in)); *C. alpinus* (*Erysimum alpinum*) (pale yellow, 15cm (6in)). All April to June. *Named varieties* – (*C. cheiri*) – (pale yellow) 'Primrose Monarch'; (bright yellow) 'Cloth of Gold'; (golden) 'Harpur Crewe' (double); 'Ivory White'; 'Orange Bedder'; (apricot) 'Eastern Queen'; 'Blood Red'; (crimson) 'Vulcan'; (brown) 'Harbinger'; 'Purple Queen'.

Chelone (shellflower) – Hardy perennials, many species of which are now classed with penstemons; they like a sunny or semi-shaded site in moist sandy loam with humus in it. *Species* – *C. lyonii* (rosy purple); *C. obliqua* (pink, June to September, 60 to 90cm (24 to 36in)).

Chimonanthus praecox (winter sweet) - Winter-blooming hardy deciduous shrub, which likes a sunny, sheltered position in deep, moist, sandy loam. It bears pale yellow flowers stained purple, and reaches a height of 2m (7ft) on walls. *Culture* – Plant in October or March, and when grown as a climber cut back side shoots to within 5 to 6 buds of the main stems after flowering. Propagate by layering in August, or by suckers or seed in March.

Chionanthus virginicus (fringe tree) – Hardy deciduous small tree which likes a sheltered position in well-drained, moist loam, and bears white flowers in June and July. *Culture* – Plant from October to November, and trim to shape after flowering if required. Propagate by layering in September, or strike cuttings of half-ripe shoots in a frame during July and August.

Chionodoxa (glory of the snow) – This bulbous plant requires similar treatment to that of bulbs generally and thrives in sun or shade and sandy loam in the border, rock garden or greenhouse. *Culture* – Plant in October 6cm (2½in) deep and from 7.5 to 10cm (3 to 4in) apart. Propagate by offsets in October or raise from seed. *Species* – *C. luciliae* and *C. gigantea* (soft mauve, blue and white, March, 22cm (9in)).

Choisya ternata (Mexican orange blossom) – Half-hardy evergreen shrub which likes a sunny sheltered position in sandy loam. It grows from 1.8 to 3m (6 to 10ft) high and from May to September, bears small white flowers. *Culture* – Plant in April or September, and in April cut out old wood or trim if required. Propagate by layering in August, or by cuttings in a frame in August. *Pot culture* – Pot-up in spring in a 15 to 20cm (6 to 8in) pot and a compost of peaty loam, leaf-mould and sand. Prune straggly shoots after flowering and put out in the open, with pots sunk in ashes, from July to October.

Christmas Rose – *See* **Helleborus.**

Chrysanthemum – The chrysanthemum is one of the hardiest plants, but owing to the fact that it flowers somewhat late its beautiful blooms are subject to injury from the weather when grown out of doors unless some protection is provided. Chrysanthemums may be classified according to the time of their blooming, as early-flowering, blooming from July to October; semi-early, blooming in September and October in the open; and ordinary or late-flowering, blooming in November and December.

Culture of indoor chrysanthemums – If seed is used it should be sown as soon as ripe (February) in a pan of sandy soil at 16°C (59°F); transplant and pot on as necessary. *Propagation by cuttings* – After the plants have finished blooming the stems and all weak shoots from the base should be cut down to within a few centimetres (in) of the ground and the pots stood in the cold greenhouse or a frost-proof frame. A one centimetre (½in) mulch of fine loam and leaf-mould, and a little water, will help the old roots to throw up sturdy young shoots for cuttings. Root these in pots of John Innes potting compost. Once the cuttings are rooted (in from 3 to 5 weeks), stand the pots near the glass in a frost-proof frame and give ample ventilation in fine weather. Cuttings of Korean types should be taken in December or January. Nearly all growers differ as to the best time for striking cuttings of the decorative types. Some recommend November; some succeed admirably by inserting them in May; the latter date only when propagating plants to flower in small pots in December. Perhaps it is better to make a compromise by striking in February or March. *Potting on* – December-struck cuttings should be well rooted by the middle of February and should then be potted-up into 7.5 or 9 cm (3 or 3½in) pots, adding to the compost ⅓ part well-rotted manure. They should receive their next shift into 12.5 or 15cm (5 or 6in) pots about the first week in April. Disturb the roots as little as possible, and add a weak feed and a dusting of bonemeal and powdered charcoal to the compost. The cultivation should be continued in a frame or on a shelf near the glass. Shade from the sun, then in about a fortnight's time harden off, stand out of doors by the middle of May, and give a final shift a month or 6 weeks later. *Summer treatment* – The pots should be stood in the open on slates in a sheltered position, facing south or west. As soon as the pots are full of roots the plants should be placed in 20 to 22.5cm (8 to 9in) pots; about the middle of June is a good time to complete the final potting-up. No soil is better for them than a compost of ⅔ lumpy fibrous loam, ⅙ well-rotted compost and ⅙ leaf-mould and a little rubble and sharp sand liberally coloured with bonemeal. The plants should be properly supported. *Stopping and disbudding* – If bushy plants are to be grown, pinch out the tip of the central shoot when the plants are some 12.5 to 15cm (5 to 6in) high. A second stopping will be necessary in early summer. If you grow blooms for exhibition only, no stopping will be needed until the break bud appears in early summer. Pinch out this bud and all the young shoots just below it, save the three strongest and best placed, and concentrate the whole strength of the plant into these stems and the strength of these stems into a single bud at the top. *Feeding and autumn treatment* – From early in August the plants should be fed 2 to 3 times a week alternately with sulphate of potash and with diluted liquid fertilizer. Feeding must cease as soon as the blooms are 3 parts open, and early in October the plants should be moved under glass. This is a critical change for them, and the leaves should be kept well syringed, except in dull, damp weather.

Outdoor culture of border chrysanthemums – Plant out towards the end of May. They should receive the same general treatment in training and watering as those grown indoors, except that the majority need not be stopped. The soil should be well drained and well dug in winter but it must not be too rich. A mulch in June is beneficial. In planting allow 60 to 90cm (24 to 36in) between each plant and an open, sunny, sheltered position is essential. Most varieties naturally form bushy plants, but with others it is necessary, from time to time, to pinch back the tips of the shoots; this pinching back should not be continued after the end of July. If large blooms are desired the plants should be disbudded. As soon as the flowers are over cut the plants down to the ground, lift them, shake the soil from the roots and place them close together in shallow boxes of light, sandy soil and store in a frost-proof place. In March divide the crowns, retaining the younger and more vigorous portions only and plant out again in the border or take cuttings as advised for the indoor kinds. In light and warm soil it is not always necessary to lift the crowns in autumn. Varieties are numerous and change frequently so specialist catalogues should be consulted.

Chrysanthemum, Annual (corn marigold, crown daisy) – These showy plants thrive in sunny beds or borders. *Named varieties* – 'Cecilia' (white and yellow); (Eastern Star' (yellow, brown eye); 'Evening Star' (golden yellow); 'Morning Star' (primrose); 'The Sultan' (maroon); and 'White Pearl' (double). All flower from June to September, 50cm (20in).

Chrysanthemum frutescens (marguerite) – These popular half-hardy perennial plants like a soil that is not too rich. *Culture* – Sow under glass in April, or strike cuttings of young shoots in a cold frame in September; protect in severe weather. Pot-up into 10cm (4in) pots in March, harden off and plant out towards the end of May, or re-pot into 15cm (6in) pots, harden off and stand in the open until September, then move into 17.5cm (7in) pots and transfer to a cool but frost-proof house for the winter. Young plants grown on for pot culture should be stopped during the spring and summer. *Varieities* – 'Broussonetii' (white single); 'Etoile d'Or' (yellow); 'Queen Alexandra' (white, double).

Chrysanthemum, Perennial (ox-eye daisy, Shasta daisy) – These, like the annual species, make a good show in sunny borders and ordinary soil. *Species* – *C. alpinum* (white, June to September, 12.5cm (5in)); *C. arcticum* (white, tinged pink, October, 45cm (18in)); *C. coccineum* (scarlet, June to September, 90cm (36in)); *C. maximum* (white, July to September, 90cm (36in)); *C. serotinum* (white, September to October, 1 to 1.5m (3 to 5ft)).

Cimicifuga (bugwort, bugbane or snake-root) – Hardy perennial which thrives in a deep, moist loam and fairly sunny position. *Species* – *C. cordifolia* (creamy white, July to August, 90cm (36in)); *C. racemosa* (creamy white, July to August, 60 to 120cm (36 to 48in)).

Cineraria (*Senecio*) – Beautiful greenhouse perennials which, by careful treatment may be had in flower from November to May. They thrive in a compost of 2 parts fibrous loam to 1 part of leaf-mould, well-decayed manure and a little sand, and are best grown from seed. *Culture* – The first sowing should be made in April in pans filled with a good seed compost and placed in slight bottom heat. Cover with glass and paper and keep slightly moist. Stand the seedlings in partial shade, move into 7.5cm (3in) pots as soon as possible, gradually harden off and remove the lights of the frame entirely by day from July to the end of September. Shift the young plants into 11 to 12.5cm (4½ to 5in) pots as required, and give them their final shift in September into 15 to 20cm (6 to 8in) pots. Keep moist and syringe every afternoon in hot weather, then towards the end of September move the plants into a cool greenhouse, and water and feed with liquid fertilizer. Another sowing may be made in a cold frame in May, and a third in June. Pot on as above, but at proportionately later dates. *Cineraria maritima* (*Senecio cineraria*) is a beautiful foliage plant for summer bedding or cold greenhouse. Sow under glass in March. *Species and varieties* – *C. maritima* (*Senecio cineraria*) (silver foliage, summer, 45cm (18in)); and *Senecio cruentus* (*cineraria*), of which there are many varities. (Various colours, winter and spring, 45 to 75cm (18 to 30in).)

Cistus (rock rose) – Evergreen perennial shrubs mostly hardy in warm sheltered sites. They love the sun and do well in dry, well-drained sandy loam or poor soil. *Culture* – Do not prune, merely keep the shrubs in shape by means of stopping in March and by removing dead blooms. Propagate by layering in August, sow seed in April, or take cuttings of half-matured wood in August and strike in a shaded frame. Grow in pots till ready for planting out. *Species* – *C.* x *cyprius* (white, spotted red, June to July, 100 to 150cm (40 to 60in)); *C. ladaniferus* (white, spotted red, June to July, 120 to 150cm (48 to 60in)); *C.* x *purpureus* (purple red, blotched crimson, June to July, 90 to 120cm (36 to 48in)); *C.* x *corbariensis* (white, stained yellow, June, 45 to 60cm (18 to 24in)).

Clarkia – Hardy annuals which thrive in fairly moist rich soil in the border or cold greenhouse. For the greenhouse sow in a frame in August, and pot-up as required, using 15 to 17.5cm (6 to 7in) pots for three plants. *Varieties* – 'Brilliant Rose' (rose); 'Firebrand' (crimson); 'Marginata' (pink, margined white); 'Orange King' (orange); 'Scarlet Beauty' (scarlet); 'Purple Queen' (purple); 'Salmon Queen' (salmon); 'Snowball' (white); and 'Mixed'. All July to October, 60cm (24in).

Claytonia (spring beauty) – Dwarf-growing hardy perennials which thrive in sun or shade and ordinary soil. *Culture* – Sow in March, where the plants are to flower. *Species* – *C. sibirica* (rose) and *C. virginica* (white). Both spring, 15cm (6in).

Clematis – Beautiful hardy climbers which do well against walls and on trellises, facing north, east or west, or in the greenhouse. A sunny position is most suitable, but the lower part of the stems require shade. Although not particular as to soil, they prefer light to heavy soil if it has been well manured; an alkaline soil is most satisfactory. *Culture* – Propagate by layering in summer and plant out in March. Cut away dead and weak wood, giving ample light and air to the growths retained and fasten the shoots up securely. Propagation may also be carried out by grafting, by cuttings or seed. Most varieties require pruning after flowering but *C. vitalba* is best pruned in March, while *C.* x *jackmanii* and *C. viticella* vars. should be cut down to 15cm (6in) in November or to 30cm (1ft) in spring. *Pot culture* – Pot-up in March using 12.5 to 25cm (5 to 10in) pots and a compost of 2 parts peaty loam to 1 part of leaf-mould, well-rotted manure and sand. *Varieties* (*Early-flowering*) – 'Bee's Jubilee' (mauve with deeper stripe); 'Duchess of Edinburgh' (double, white), both May to June. (*Late-flowering*) – 'Ernest Markham' (crimson); 'Jackmanii Superba' (purple);

'Mme le Coultre' (white), all July to September. There is a vast range of named varieties and catalogues should be consulted. *Species* – *C. montana* (white) and *C.m.* 'Tetra Rose' (pink) in April; *C. tangutica* (yellow, followed by silver-haired fruits) and *C. viticella* (slender, purple) in August to September.

Clerodendrum – Beautiful deciduous shrubs or small trees, which thrive in a sunny sheltered position in well-drained, rich loam. *Culture* – Plant in October or November. Propagate by seed, cuttings of half-ripened shoots in a frame or by root cuttings. *C. speciosissimum* is a good plant for the cold greenhouse. *Hardy species* – *C. thomsoniae* (white, red calyx, 3.5m (12ft)); *C. bungei* (rose pink, 1.8 to 2.4m (6 to 8ft)); *C. trichotomum* (white, red calyx, 3 to 3.5m (10 to 12ft)). All July to September.

Clianthus – Evergreen climbing shrubs which succeed best in the sunny border of a cool greenhouse in sandy peat and fibrous loam. *C. puniceus* (crimson) and var. 'Albus' (white), parrot's bill and lobster's claw, blossom freely out of doors against a trellis or south wall. *Culture* – Sow in February singly in pots and when 7.5 to 10cm (3 to 4in) high move into 11cm (4½in) pots and keep in these until ready for planting out in April, or in the case of *C. speciosus* (glory pea) into a border in the house. Syringe house plants daily in hot dry weather and trim back straggling shoots after flowering. They may also be raised by cuttings in a frame. (Temp. 21°C (70°F)) in May or June.

Clivia – Beautiful evergreen plants with lily-like blooms, for the cool greenhouse. *Culture* – Plant in February in 22.5cm (9in) pots in a mixture of rich sandy loam, leaf-mould and old manure, keep in a cool place and let the roots fill the pots, as the plants flourish best when root-bound. Water well in summer, keep cool and on the dry side during winter, and sponge the leaves occasionally with tepid water. Weak liquid fertilizer should be given twice a week while the buds are forming. Propagate by division of suckers in February, or by seed sown when ripe. *Species* – *C. miniata* and vars. (orange scarlet); *C. nobilis* (red and yellow). All March to April, 50cm (20in). Clivias make very useful house plants.

Cobaea (cup and saucer plant) – Beautiful evergreen climbers that thrive in the cool greenhouse. They grow to a height of 6m (20ft) and flower from July to September. *C. scandens* (purple and greenish white) will also thrive in the open in warm sheltered positions in the south and west of England; in more exposed positions it must be treated as an annual and be raised each year. *Culture* – Sow thinly under glass (7°C (45°F)) in light rich soil in February, or propagate by cuttings of young shoots in January or February, and raise in a propagating case. Pot-up into 7.5 to 10cm (3 to 4in) pots, harden off, and if growing in the open, plant out 60cm (24in) apart in June in equal parts of loam, leaf-mould and sand or grow on in pots and keep in the cool greenhouse. In February prune laterals back to two buds and cut out all weak growth.

Colchicum (meadow saffron or autumn crocus) – Hardy bulbous plants usually grown in the rock garden. *Culture* – Plant in July or August in full sun 12.5cm (5in) deep and 15cm (6in) apart, in moist, cool loam. Lift from the ground (triennially) in August to increase. *Species* – *C. autumnale* (lilac rose, September to October, 15cm (6in)); *C. speciosum* (crimson, purple or white eye, September to October, 25cm (10in)).

Coleus blumei – Half-hardy annual and perennial foliage plants, useful for bedding-out or the cool greenhouse. *Culture* – Sow thinly in heat (21°C (70°F)) in March. Named varieties can be propagated by cuttings at any time from spring to autumn, struck singly in pots in a propagating case with good bottom heat (21°C (70°F)) and in a moist atmosphere; the best time is March. These plants like a light, rich soil: 2 parts of loam to 1 part of leaf-mould and sand. Place near the glass, but shade from strong sun. When rooted, re-pot into 7.5cm (3in) pots, pinch back and pot on till they are finally in 12.5 to 15cm (5 to 6in) pots.

Collinsia – Hardy annuals for sunny beds, borders or the greenhouse. *Species* – *C. heterophylla* (reddish purple and white, July to October, 30cm (12in)); *C. grandiflora* (purple blue and white, July to October, 30cm (12in)).

Colutea (bladder senna) – Deciduous broom-like shrub, thriving in almost any position or soil. *Culture* – Plant in October or November, and in March cut the previous year's growth well back. To propagate, take cuttings in September, or sow seed in the open in spring. *Species* – *C. arborescens* (yellow, June to August, 3m (10ft)); *C. orientalis* (red and yellow, June to August, 1.8 to 2.5m (6 to 8ft)); *C.* x *media* (reddish brown, June to August, 3m (10ft)).

Commelina tuberosa (day flower) – Annual and perennial plants, which thrive in a sunny position in warm, well-drained borders and rich light soil. Rich blue, August and September, 45cm (18in).

Convallaria majalis (lily of the valley) – To grow lilies of the valley well the roots should be set in bunches 30cm (1ft) apart in a rich soil of sandy loam. *Culture* – Plant in October, only just covering with soil and mulch with a 5cm (2in) layer of leaf-mould or peat, lift from the soil every fourth year and propagate by division in October. *Pot culture* – Plump crowns should be potted up 2.5cm (1in) apart in November, using 12.5 to 15cm (5 to 6in) pots and a compost of sandy loam and leaf-mould, and so that only the tips obtrude. Water well and keep in a cool frame for a few weeks, then take into the house in batches as bloom is required. The pots should be kept in the dark until the shoots are 12.5 to 15cm (5 to 6in) in height, after this gradually admit light, raise the temperature to between 16 to 21°C (59 to 70°F) and give tepid water in increasing amounts as growth continues. After flowering, plant the crowns in the border.

Convolvulus (bindweed) – Large family of hardy annual and perennial climbing and trailing plants, most of which like a sunny position and rather poor soil. *Species* Annuals – *C. tricolor* (white to purple and blue, June to October, 2 to 2.5m (8 to 9ft)); *C. tricolor* 'Alba' (white, July to October, 30cm (12in)). Perennials – *C. cneorum* (silver foliage shrub with soft pink flowers, June to September, 45cm (18in)); *C. mauritanicus* (blue, June to September, 30cm (12in) herbaceous).

Coreopsis (tickseed) – Hardy annuals, biennials and perennials, most of which are best treated as biennials. The tall varieties are effective in mixed borders and the dwarf kinds make fine bedding plants. A moist sandy loam and a sunny position are most suitable, and ample water is needed in summer. *Species* (*Annuals*) – *C. nuecensis* (orange and brown, 45cm (18in)); *C. drummondii* (golden yellow, 60cm (24in)); *C. tinctoria* (yellow and bronze, 45cm (18in)); *C. douglasii* (yellow, 30cm (12in)); *C. stillmanii* (yellow 45cm (18in)). All July to October. (*Perennials*) – *C. grandiflora* (golden yellow, July to October, 60 to 75cm (24 to 30in)); *C. lanceolata* (yellow, July to October, 60 to 75cm (24 to 30in)); *C. rosea* (reddish pink, July to September, 45cm (18in)); *C. verticillata* (golden yellow, July to September, 60cm (24in)); *C. maritima* (yellow, July to September, 75cm (30in)).

Cornus (cornel, dogwood, cornelian cherry) – Deciduous shrubs and trees and hardy herbaceous perennials. *Culture* – Sow under glass or propagate by layering in October, or by suckers in November. Plant out in spring or early autumn in the shade, in a mixture of moist leaf-mould and peat, or ordinary soil. *C. mas*, the cornelian cherry (3 to 7.5m (10 to 25ft)) thrives quite well in a dry soil. It has tiny yellow flowers in February to March.

Species and varieties – *C. alba* 'Sibirica' (silvery variegation); *C. alba* 'Sphaethii' (golden foliage); *C. capitata* (syn. *Benthamia fragifera*) (cream and pink flowers, spring, scarlet fruits, 3.5m (12ft)). A half-hardy evergreen shrub which may be grown in the open in warm sheltered situations in the south; *C. florida* 'Rubra' (rosy pink floral bracts); *C. kousa* (white floral bracts) (May to June, 2 to 3.5m (7 to 12ft)).

Corokia – Half-hardy evergreen flowering shrubs which thrive in a warm sunny position and in ordinary soil. *Culture* – Plant in April or October, and prune only to keep in shape. To propagate, strike half-matured cuttings in a frame in August. *Species* – *C. buddleioides* (white, April to May, 1m (3 to 4ft)); *C. cotoneaster* (yellow, May, 1.8m (6ft)); *C. macrocarpa* (orange, May to June, 1.8m (6ft)).

Coronilla (crown vetch or scorpion senna) – Half-hardy evergreen or deciduous shrubs, and herbaceous perennials, which succeed well against a south wall with a little winter protection, also in the rock garden or cold greenhouse. *Culture* – Plant in March or October in well-drained ordinary soil or in sandy loam (rock garden species). *Pot culture* – Pot-up in March, using 15 to 20cm (6 to 8in) pots and a compost of 2 parts sandy loam to 1 part of peat. Prune into shape and cut out old and dead wood in February and stand in the open after flowering until September. To propagate, sow in a frame in March or take cuttings of young wood in April or August (greenhouse plants) and strike in a frame (16°C (59°F)). The rock garden species are propagated by seed as above or by division of roots in October. *Species* – *C. cappadocica* (cream yellow, July to August, 10cm (4in)); *C. minima* (yellow, June to July, 7.5cm (3in)); *C. varia* (lilac pink, August to September, 30 to 45cm (12 to 18in)); Shrubs – *C. emerus* (yellow, June to August); and *C. glauca* (yellow, April to May).

Cortaderia selloana (pampas grass) – Perennial grass which thrives in sunny, sheltered positions and well-drained soil. It grows 1.8 to 2.5m (6 to 8ft) high and flowers in autumn.

Cortusa matthioli (bear's ear) – Dwarf-growing rock plants, closely allied to the *Primula*, which thrive in partial shade in rich sandy loam and leaf-mould and flower in July.

Corydalis (fumitory) – Hardy annual and perennial rock garden or border plants, which require shade and comparatively poor soil. *Species* (*Perennials*) – *C. cashmeriana* (blue, May to September, 15cm (6in)); *C. cava* (purple and rose, May, 30cm (12in)); *C. lutea* (yellow, June to September, 15 to 30cm (6 to 12in)).

Corylopsis – Hardy deciduous shrubs which like a sunny, sheltered position, and well-drained, ordinary soil. *Culture* – Plant in October or November. Little pruning is required. Propagate by layering in the summer. *Pot culture* – Pot-up from October to February, using 15 to 20cm (6 to 8in) pots and good loam. Sink the pots in the open from May to December, then take into the cold greenhouse. After flowering prune out weak wood and dead flower shoots. *Species* – *C. glabrescens*; *C. pauciflora*; *C. spicata*. All yellow. March to April, 1.2 to 2.5m (4 to 8ft).

Cosmos (Mexican aster) – Half-hardy annuals and perennials which thrive in warm, dry borders and in ordinary soil. The early-flowering annuals should be chosen. *Species* – Annuals – *C. bipinnatus* (pink, white and crimson, June to October, 75 to 175cm (30 to 70in)); *C. sulphureus* (yellow, June to October, 50cm (20in)); *C. diversifolius* (lilac to rose, June to October, 60cm (24in)); *Named varieties* – 'Gloria' (rosy pink); 'Klondyke' (yellow); 'Psyche' (pink, red or white); 'Bright Lights' (yellow and orange) and 'Diablo' (orange).

Cotoneaster (rockspray) – Hardy shrubs or small trees, most of which grow best in poor or chalky soil. *Culture* – Plant from October to March. No pruning is necessary, though some species require thinning out after flowering. To propagate, take cuttings of hardwood in a frame in July or August, or layer in September or October. Seed may be sown in the open in March or September. *Species* – *C. buxifolius* (E) (white, April 30 to 60cm (1 to 2ft)); *C. dammeri* (E) (white, April to May, prostrate); *C. franchetii* (E) (white, May, 2 to 3m (7 to 10ft)); *C. horizontalis* (pale pink, Apr., 60 to 120cm (2 to 4ft)); *C. microphyllus* (E) (rosy white, May, 90 to 180cm (3 to 6ft)); *C. microphyllus* var. *thymifolius* (E) (pinkish, April, 22 to 30cm (9 to 12in)); *C. salicifolius* (E) (white, May, 180cm (6ft)). (E) = Evergreen.

Crataegus (thorn) – Hardy deciduous trees or shrubs, useful for hedges etc. *Culture* – Plant in October or November in a sunny position and ordinary soil. Thin out the branches when overcrowded. To propagate, sow seed when ripe, bud or graft. *Species and varieties* – *C. crus-galli* (white, with brilliant autumn colour and large haws); *C. oxyacantha* 'Plena' (white, double); *C.o.* 'Rosea Plena' (pink, double); *C.o.* 'Punicea' (scarlet, single). All May, 4.5m (15ft).

Crinum (Cape lily) – Half-hardy bulbous plant for the cool greenhouse. *C.* x *powellii* and var. 'Album' will grow outdoors in a sunny, sheltered, moist border, in well-drained, deep and rich sandy loam and peat. *Culture* – Plant 15cm (6in) deep in March, surrounded with coarse sand and protect with straw in winter. Do not disturb unless overcrowded. *Pot culture* – Pot-up in the spring (triennially) one bulb in each 22.5 to 25cm (9 to 10in) pot in a compost of 2 parts fibrous loam to 1 part sandy peat. Propagate by offsets in March. *Species and varieties* – *C. bulbispermum* (pink or white); *C.* x *powellii* (rose red or white). Both June to August, 60 to 90cm (24 to 36in).

Crocosmia – Almost hardy bulbous-rooted perennials for sunny position in sheltered, well-drained border. Lift and divide every 2 to 3 years when overcrowding reduces flowering and protect with straw or ashes in cold weather at end of winter. *Species* – *C.* x *crocosmiiflora* (montbretia) has grassy foliage and yellow or orange flowers in autumn, 45cm (18in). *C. masonorum* has bold pleated leaves and arching spikes of orange flowers in summer, 1m (3 to 4ft).

Crocus – Besides those which bloom in the early spring there are species and varieties that flower in the autumn and winter. *Culture* – They like a good light soil to which a little bonemeal has been added, and thrive in sun or shade in a warm rock garden, borders or in pots and are also useful for naturalizing in grass or a wild garden. Crocuses are increased by offsets or by seed, the former being the usual method. Offsets are treated the same as old corms and will bloom the second year. Seed should be sown in pans of light sandy loam as soon as ripe and placed in a sheltered situation out of doors until late autumn. During heavy rain and cold weather protect with a cold frame. They may remain in the same pans during summer but lift in autumn and plant in beds of loam in a nursery bed 5cm (2in) apart and 7.5cm (3in) deep; here they will form strong corms and flower the third or fourth spring. Plant mature corms from 5 to 7.5cm (2 to 3in) deep and 10cm (4in) apart, autumn-flowering species from July to August; spring-flowering species in September or October. Divide and replant every third year. *Pot culture* – Plant about 7 corms 1cm (½in) deep in a 12.5 to 15cm (5 to 6in) pot in autumn, using a good compost and keep covered with ashes or soil in a frame until growth commences, then water and transfer to the cool house. Stand out in the open and keep dry in summer and re-pot in September. *Species* (*Early spring*) – *C. biflorus* (white, veined violet); *C. chrysanthus* (orange yellow and red); *C. imperati* (lilac or buff and black); *C. aureus* (golden yellow); *C. sieberi* (lilac blue and gold); *C. tomasinianus* (lavender); *C. versicolor* (white and purple); *C. vernus* and vars. (various). (*Autumn*) – *C. asturicus* (purple); *C. byzantinus* (lavender); *C. ochroleucus* (yellow); *C. pulchellus* (lavender blue and orange throat); *C. sativus* (violet, mauve and orange); *C. speciosus* (violet blue and orange); *C. zonatus* (lilac pink with orange throat). Dutch crocuses are spring-flowering varieties in white, yellow, lavender, purple and purple/white stripes.

Cryptomeria japonica (Japanese cedar) – Handsome evergreen trees which thrive in deep sandy loam in a sheltered, sunny position. *Culture* – Plant from September to November. No pruning is required. To propagate, sow in March or April or strike cuttings under cloches in August. The variety 'Elegans' is an attractive rounded shrub to 2.5m (8ft).

Cucurbita (ornamental gourds) – Half-hardy climbing plants, many of which are very ornamental. Treated in a similar way to ordinary marrows, most will thrive in the open. Any good seedsman's catalogue will give several varieties.

Cuphea (cigar flower) – Hardy and half-hardy annuals, perennials and shrubs, better treated as house or greenhouse plants. (*Shrubby species*) – Propagate by cuttings of young wood in bottom heat (21°C (70°F)) in spring. Trim the following January, and re-pot if necessary in February.

x **Cupressocyparis leylandii** (Leyland's cypress) – A very fast-growing conifer for windbreaks and tall hedges. Plant in November and trim, if necessary, in August.

Cupressus (cypress) – Quick-growing conifers which thrive in sunny, sheltered positions in almost any soil. *Culture* – Plant in April or September. No pruning is required, except in the case of hedge plants. They may be propagated by cuttings in a frame in August or September; some, however, are best raised from seed in March. *C. macrocarpa* (the Monterey cypress), which thrives by the sea, makes a good hedge plant. *See also* Chamaecyparis.

Curtonus paniculatus (*Antholyza paniculata*) – Hardy bulbous-rooted perennial which thrives in a sunny position in well-drained borders with sandy loam and grows to about 75cm (30in) high, carrying scarlet and yellow blooms from June to August. *Culture* – Propagate by offsets in March or October, and plant 12.5cm (5in) deep and 15cm (6in) apart.

Cyclamen – Tuberous-rooted plants, useful for rock garden, border, naturalizing in grass and for greenhouse culture. Of the hardy cyclamen there are two types, the spring-blooming and autumn-blooming. *Culture* (*Hardy species*) – Plant in August 5cm (2in) deep and 6cm (2½in) apart in a shady position in light sandy loam mixed with peat or leaf-mould. Protect with straw in winter and top-dress annually with leaf-mould or peat. Propagate by seed in gentle heat in spring and do not plant the young corms in their permanent positions until of moderate size. *Species* – *C. coum* (purple, red and white, January to March, 7.5cm (3in)); *C. europaeum* (red and white, July to November, 7.5cm (3in)); *C. neapolitanum* (rose, white and purple throat, August to September, 15cm (6in)); *C. persicum* (white to crimson, November to March, 15cm (6in), tender); *C. repandum* (purple/red, April to May, 15cm (6in), slightly tender). *Pot culture* – (*C. persicum*) – Soak the pot and dried off corm in water and stand on a shelf in the greenhouse. Pot-up in August, placing one corm in a 12.5cm (5in) pot in a fresh compost of rich sandy loam and leaf-mould, and keep close for a few days, then give ample air and not too much heat (16°C (59°F)). Moist, steady heat and shade from strong sun are essential. After flowering, decrease water supply, dry off and keep the roots cool and almost dry until next potting-up. Keep the plants indoors from September to May, and in a cold frame with the pots on their sides from June to August. Only use the same corms for pot culture for 2 years in succession. One-year-old plants give the finest flowers; cyclamen are best raised annually from seed. To propagate, sow thinly in pans in a finely sieved compost of ⅔ loam and ⅓ leaf-mould and sand from August to November and place in a cold frame or on a shelf near the light in the cool greenhouse. Prick off into pans, then pot-up singly into small pots and subsequently into larger pots until, in July, they are in 12.5 to 15cm (5 to 6in) pots in which they may be flowered.

Cydonia (quince) – *C. oblonga* is the edible quince. For flowering quince, *see* Chaenomeles.

Cynoglossum (hound's tongue) – Annuals, biennials and perennials which thrive in rather poor, ordinary soil and bear deep blue forget-me-not-like flowers from June to August.

Cytisus (broom) – Genus of shrubs, mostly hardy and deciduous, which thrive in light ordinary soil, in a dry, sunny position. The species and hybrids *C. ardoini* (deep yellow), *C.* x *beanii* (golden yellow), *C.* x *kewensis* (cream), and *C. purpureus* (rose purple), flowering in May and June, are all prostrate or trailing and suitable for the rock garden. *C.* x *praecox* (sulphur yellow, April to May, 2m (6ft)) and the purple-flowered hybrids, *C. scoparius* 'Donard Seedling' and 'Windlesham Ruby' (May, 1.5 to 1.8m (5 to 6ft)) are the best border species, while for pot culture, *C. canariensis* and *C.* x *racemosus* (both yellow, 90cm (3ft)) will flower in the house from January to March. *Culture* – Cut back all branches by at least ⅓ and plant in October. Small plants give little trouble. Except when quite young only trim to keep in shape; pruning must be systematic and regular so that it is not necessary to cut into old wood. Spring-blooming species should be trimmed and pruned directly after flowering; late-flowering kinds should not be pruned until the following February or March. *Pot culture* – Pot-up in May, after flowering, using a compost of 2 parts loam to 1 part lumpy leaf-mould and coarse sand. Prune hard back after flowering, then keep in the warm and syringe in fine weather. Harden off and sink the pots outdoors from May to October, then move into the cool greenhouse. To propagate, sow in the open in September, take cuttings in March or August and strike in a frame and grow in pots near the glass until ready for planting out. Young plants need occasional stopping. The *Genista* genus is closely allied to *Cytisus*.

Daboecia (Irish heath) – Hardy evergreen shrubs which thrive in sandy peat and loam with no lime in it. *Culture* – Plant out in March or October, and cut off dead blooms in October. To propagate, strike cuttings in a frame in July or August, layer in September or sow seed. *Species and varieties* – *D. cantabrica* (rosy purple); *D.c.* 'Alba' (white); *D.c.* 'Bicolor' (purple and white). All June to September, 30cm (1ft).

Daffodil – The word daffodil is popularly applied to those types of narcissi with long, trumpet-like coronas. For culture, *see* Narcissus.

Dahlia – The dahlia is easily grown in rich garden soil and in warm districts may be left in the ground all winter if a heap of ashes or sand is placed over the tubers. It is somewhat tender, however, and it is better to lift it as soon as the plant has died down, and to store the tubers for the winter. The ideal soil is a rich sandy loam containing sufficient humus to make it retentive of moisture. *Culture* – Dahlias may be multiplied by seeds or by dividing the base of the old stem in March taking care that an eye and a tuber or two are attached to each portion. Another way is to cut off the young shoots at their base and strike them in small pots. *Seed* – Sow about 2.5cm (1in) apart in shallow pans or boxes of seed compost in March. Place the pans on a warm shelf and in April pot-up either singly or round the edge of 15cm (6in) pots. Place in a cold frame, gradually harden off and plant out to 60 to 90cm (2 to 3ft) apart, early in June. After flowering, the young tubers are taken up and treated as old tubers. *Cuttings* – In February, March or even the first week in April tubers which have been wintered in a dry place are placed in shallow boxes containing a slightly moist peat compost which does not quite cover them and are set in heat close up to the glass (18°C (65°F)). A number of strong shoots soon appear; when these are 7.5 to 10cm (3 to 4in) long they can be taken off and struck round the edges of 10cm (4in) pots, filled with equal parts of sandy loam and leaf-mould. They should be watered and again placed in heat and shaded from the sun. Pot-up singly as soon as the cuttings have struck (about 3 weeks) and transfer to a cold frame. Pot on as required, harden off and plant out early in June. *Preparing the ground and planting* – In autumn prepare the beds; they should be in an open but sheltered position and should catch the morning sun, but must have a little shade in the afternoon. Damp, low-lying situations should be avoided. Dahlias will be best displayed in beds to themselves. Mark out the beds with stakes; remove 10cm (4in) of the soil and replace with 10cm (4in) of thoroughly rotted manure and bonemeal at the rate of 75g (3oz) to the sq m (yd). The whole should then be dug to a depth of 45 to 60cm (18 to 24in) and the manure thoroughly mixed with the soil. Towards the end of May top-dress the soil with wood ashes or peat which should be thoroughly raked in. Insert 1 to 1.5m (4 to 5ft) stakes at planting time 90cm, 1 and 1.5m (3, 4 and 5ft) apart according to varieties, which are planted 10cm (4in) deep so that the crown is just level with the surface. After planting water thoroughly. Syringe every evening in dry weather and destroy slugs, earwigs and other pests. During June and July water as often as twice a week in hot dry weather. Remove all dead or straggling shoots and keep plants trim and well staked. A surface mulch of peat or rotted manure, 7.5cm (3in) deep, will help to keep the roots cool and moist; if this is not applied, weak liquid fertilizer should be given every third or fourth day throughout August and September. When dahlias are intended either for exhibition or for highly developed flowers, early in July, when the plants are 45cm (18in) high, pinch out the top and thin out the stems that form after this, to 6 at the most and leave only one bud on a shoot. Where a show of colour or flowers for picking is required, 8 to 9 stems may be left; frequent thinning out of stems is necessary. Flowers for exhibition should be protected both from the sun and rain. As the autumn approaches examine the shoots and slacken the raffia or string where necessary. When the frost turns their foliage brown or black, take up the plants, leaving 15cm (6in) or so of stem attached. Stand the tubers to dry with the stem downwards for a few days, then plunge them with a little old soil still left on them into a box of ashes, vermiculite or sand in order to preserve them from damp, frost and heat. Varieties are so numerous that a specialist catalogue should be consulted. All July to October. The colour range is very wide and heights vary from 15cm to 2m (6in to 7ft).

Daphne – Dwarf-growing deciduous and evergreen shrubs, which thrive in a sunny sheltered position in well-drained, deep, sandy loam and peat. *Culture* – Plant in March or October. No pruning is necessary. Propagate by layering in August, grafting in May or seeds. *D. mezereum* (purple, rose and white, 60 to 120cm (2 to 4ft), which is usually propagated by means of seed, is the best known of the hardy deciduous species. It thrives in ordinary garden loam, but needs shade from the hot sun. If trimming is necessary, it should be done in April. For the rock garden none are better than *D. alpina* (white May, 45cm (18in)); *D. blagayana* (ivory, May, 15cm (6in)); and *D. cneorum* (purple pink, May to August, 30cm (12in)). They thrive in partial shade in sandy loam and peat or leaf-mould. *Greenhouse culture* – *D. odora* (pink, 60cm (2ft)) and *D.o.* 'Alba' (white), often but wrongly named *D. indica*, are too tender for the open air, except in the south-west. Pot-up in April using 12.5 to 17.5 (5 to 7in) pots and a compost of peaty loam and sand. Plunge the pots in a cool, shady position out of doors from May to September, syringe daily in fine weather, and keep just moist. Move into the house in September, and gradually give more heat.

Delphinium (larkspur) – Large genus of hardy annuals, biennials and perennials, which like a sunny site in deep, highly enriched and well-drained friable loam and need ample water in hot dry weather. If flower stalks are cut down as soon as they have bloomed a second crop of bloom will be obtained in early autumn. *Pot culture* – Pot-up in October or November in 12.5 to 15cm (5 to 6in) pots, and winter well up near the glass in a cool house. *Species* (*Perennials*) – *D. cardinale* (scarlet); *D. cashmerianum* (purple blue); *D. nudicaule* (orange scarlet); *D. sulphureum* (sulphur yellow). All June to August, 60 to 150cm (24 to 60in). For named varieties of *D. elatum* growers' catalogues should be consulted. (*Annuals*) – *D. consolida* (purple); *D. ajacis* (blue).

Desfontainia spinosa – Evergreen shrub which is almost hardy in England. It thrives in warm, sheltered borders or in pots in the greenhouse, in a well-drained compost of equal parts of loam and peat with a little sand added. It grows to a height of 3m (10ft) and flowers from July to September. *Culture* – Plant in spring or autumn. Propagate by cuttings in slight heat in spring.

Desmodium (tick trefoil and telegraph plant) – Hardy perennials and shrubs, also greenhouse deciduous shrubs. The former thrive in sunny sheltered borders in ordinary soil, the latter in the cool greenhouse. *Greenhouse shrubs* – Pot-up in March in a compost of sandy loam and peat. Propagate by cuttings in frame or from seed. *Species* – *D. gyrans* (greenhouse) (white, July, 60cm (2ft)); and *D. canadense* (lilac, July to October, 1m (3 to 4ft)).

Deutzia – Hardy deciduous flowering shrubs, which thrive in a sheltered, partly shaded position in rich, well-drained ordinary soil in the shrubbery, or in the greenhouse. *Culture* – Plant in October or November, mulch annually after flowering, also thin out well and cut away weak and old wood. To propagate, strike cuttings of soft wood in June in a frame with bottom heat. *Pot culture* – Pot-up from September to November, in rich, sandy loam, using as small a pot as convenient. Keep cool but frost-proof, then in December or January move into the greenhouse and gradually raise the temperature to 18°C (65°F). As soon as the buds form, feed with weak liquid fertilizer once a week until the colour of the flowers is visible. Deutzias are well adapted for forcing but should be exempted from this process every alternate year. *Species and varieties* – *D. discolor* 'Major' (white); *D. gracilis* (white); *D. longifolia* 'Veitchii' (rose purple); *D.* x *magnifica* (double white); *D.* x *rosea* 'Grandiflora' (white and pink); *D. scabra* (syn. *crenata*) 'Plena' (double pink); *D. vilmorinae* (white). All May to June, 1 to 1.8m (3 to 6ft).

Dianthus – Beautiful and extensive genus which embrances the carnation, picotee, pink and sweet william.

Carnations in the border – Three weeks before planting time the bed (well-drained medium loam) should be dug and a little well-rotted manure dug in to at least 15cm (6in) below the surface, but manuring must not be overdone. Plant in September or early in October, but in heavy and cold soils it is often wise to keep the young plants in a frame until May and then plant out. In April the flowering stems should be supported and as soon as it is apparent that the principal bud is a healthy one, the less important ones should be pinched off. A small dose of weak liquid fertilizer twice a week after watering may be given from the time the buds begin to form until the colour shows. Carnations are short-lived perennials and the beds should be replanted every second year.

Carnations under glass – In September or early October pot-up young layers singly into 7.5cm (3in) pots in a compost of ⅔ loam and ⅓ well-rotted leaf-mould and coarse sand, well sifted and sterilized. Then stand the pots in a cold frame for the winter. Keep slightly moist but no water must settle on the leaves. In March, re-pot into 15cm (6in) pots, adding a little well-decayed manure and rubble to the compost. Keep close after potting until established, then give more air and finally remove the lights. In May, re-pot into 20cm (8in) pots and return to the frame for a fortnight. Then stand in the open in a sheltered position, on a firm bed of ashes or on slates. Water liberally, syringe in dry weather and stake, manure and disbud as advised for those in the open border. When the young plants are some 15cm (6in) high, stop the top bud and as soon as the side shoots are from 15 to 20cm (6 to 8in) in length they will in turn require pinching back; not later than mid-June, however, for ordinary July-flowering carnations, or mid-August for perpetual-flowering species. Transfer to a light position in the cool greenhouse as soon as the flowers show colour (about July). *Propagation* – Choice varieties should be raised from cuttings or layers. *Seed* – Sow 2.5cm (1in) apart in April or May in seed pans, in John Innes seed compost and place in a sheltered part of the garden. When the plants show 5 to 6 leaves plant out from 25 to 38cm (10 to 15in) apart in sunny, well-drained beds. Protect during winter with a cold frame. In cold and heavy soil, some gardeners prefer to sow in August, overwinter in a cold frame and plant out in spring. *Layering* – The season for this is in July or August. *Cuttings* – Cuttings may be struck in a frame with a bottom heat of 16°C (59°F) at any time from November to February (the best time is January). Early in March these cuttings, if struck in January, will need potting on into larger pots.

Perpetual carnations are invaluable for winter blooms. The cultivation and soil are much the same as for the ordinary carnation. About the beginning of September the plants may be taken into the house and watered occasionally with weak liquid fertilizer as soon as the roots have filled the pots. Seed may be sown in gentle heat (13°C (55°F)) in February.

Malmaison carnations require treatment as detailed for border carnations, but only require one stopping and a cooler atmosphere; the winter temperature should rarely rise above 7°C (45°F). They should not be placed in the open in summer. Propagate by layers in a frame in July and August, or by cuttings in a propagating frame with bottom heat in May or June.

Clove carnations are hardy border type, best planted out in April.

Marguerite carnations are half-hardy annuals which thrive in open beds in rich, gritty loam. They grow about 45cm (18in) high and flower from August to October. If lifted before damaged by the frost they will provide flowers in the greenhouse through the winter and spring.

Pinks are excellent border and edging plants. March is the best time to plant border pinks out in the open. These resent disturbance and should remain in position for several years; the ground needs to be limed periodically and an annual top-dressing is beneficial. Pinks are easily increased by division if lifted in September, or they may be layered in July and the young plants can be moved to their flowering positions in autumn; seed may also be sown under glass in July. The biennial *Dianthus chinensis*, the Chinese or Indian pink, is best raised from seed in the autumn, wintered in a frame and set out in the following May; a sunny position is essential and a well-limed or chalky soil is a great advantage. Its variety *D.c.* 'Heddewigii' and its named sorts are best treated as annuals. Another delightful class includes the alpine or rock-garden pinks; these are easily grown in a sunny position and in sandy soil. Perpetual-flowering pinks (*D.* x *allwoodii*), if lifted in autumn and potted-up, will continue to bloom in the greenhouse throughout the winter. They are not particular as to soil, will stand the winter in the open border well, and are easily raised from cuttings or by layering in summer.

Sweet William (*Dianthus barbatus*) is a hardy perennial, best treated as a biennial. Sweet Williams can also be propagated by cuttings, by division of roots, or by layering.

The choice of varieties among all the *Dianthus* is legion, so catalogues should be consulted.

Dicentra (dielytra or bleeding heart) – Hardy perennials which thrive in a sheltered, sunny site and a light dry soil with ample leaf-mould in it. Although hardy it is safer to winter them in a frame in cold districts. They are often forced in the greenhouse in late winter. *Pot culture* – Pot-up in September in good sandy loam, stand in the cold frame, plunged in ashes, and keep just moist until November, then move into the greenhouse (13°C (55°F)). After flowering, continue to water until the leaves die down, and stand in the open from May to September. Dicentras require ample water and, when making full growth, the pots may be stood in saucers of water. Propagate by division in April or September, and plant out during those months. In the open the flowers are borne from May to July. *Species* – *D. cucullaria* (white, 12.5cm (5in)); *D. eximia* (pink), 38cm (15in)); *D. formosa* (red, 22.5cm (9in)); *D. spectabilis* (red or white, 60cm (24in)).

Dictamnus (burning bush, dittany or fraxinella) – Hardy perennials, suitable for sunny or semi-shaded borders and dry, light soil. Resent being disturbed. *Species* – *D. albus* (white); and *D.a.* 'Purpurea' (purple red). Both June to August, 75cm (30in).

Diervilla – *see* **Weigela.**

Digitalis (foxglove) – Handsome biennials and hardy perennials, that thrive in the shade in almost any fairly rich soil. *Species* – *D. grandiflora* (yellow, spotted, 60cm (2ft)); *D. ferruginea* (wine-coloured, 90 to 120cm (3 to 4ft)); *D. lutea* (pale yellow, 60cm (2ft)); *D. purpurea* (white and purple). All June to September.

Dimorphotheca (Cape daisy or star of the veldt) – Half-hardy annual which likes a sunny position in light soil and is useful for inclusion in the rock garden. It flowers from July to October and grows 30cm (12in) high.

Dodecatheon – The American cowslip, which thrives well in cool shady borders, or rock or marsh garden in rich, deep loam. *Varieties* – *D. hendersonii* (rose, May, 22.5cm (9in)); *D. jeffreyi* (purple rose, June to July, 45cm (18in)); *D. meadia* (lilac, rose and white, May to June, 30 to 45cm (12 to 18in)).

Dog's Tooth Violet – *See* **Erythronium.**

Doronicum (leopard's bane) – Hardy perennials which thrive in sunny borders and ordinary soil or under almost any conditions. Cut down the shoots that have flowered and dress with well-rotted manure to encourage a second crop of bloom. *Species* – *D. austriacum* (golden yellow, April to May, 45cm (18in)); *D. plantagineum* 'Excelsum' (yellow, March to June, 60 to 90cm (24 to 36in)).

Draba – Dwarf-growing rock plants which thrive in a moderately sunny spot, in well-drained gritty loam. *Species* – *D. aizoides* (bright yellow); *D. dedeana* (white); *D. rigida* (pale golden yellow). All March to May, 7.5cm (3in).

Dracocephalum (dragon's head) – Hardy perennials useful for cool shady borders or rock gardens with light soil. *Species* – *D. grandiflorum* (blue, 38cm (15in)); *D. ruyschiana* (purple, 38cm (15in)). All flower from July to August.

Dronera (sundew or youthwort) – Curious dwarf-growing, insectivorous plants which thrive in a warm, sheltered position in the bog or wild garden. They grow some 7.5cm (3in) high and flower about midsummer. Propagate by seed or root cuttings in March.

Dryas (mountain avens) – Evergreen trailing hardy perennials which like sun or partial shade and a cool gritty loam with lime and leaf-mould in it. They are excellent in the rock garden. *Species* – *D. drummondii* (yellow); *D. octopetala* (white). Both June to July, 7.5cm (3in).

Eccremocarpus – Half-hardy climbers which thrive in any well-drained light loam against south walls, trellises and pillars and are also useful as greenhouse climbers. *Culture* – Propagate by cuttings in a frame in autumn or sow in heat in January; plant out in April. After flowering cut away dead wood and protect the roots in winter. *Species – E. scaber* (orange red), flowering from July to September, 3 to 6m (10ft to 20ft).

Echeveria – Half-hardy dwarf-growing rosette-shaped succulent plants which thrive in warm, sunny sheltered positions but which must be brought indoors in October. The red and yellow flowers are borne on short stems. *Culture* – Pot-up in March in 10 to 12.5cm (4 to 5in) pots in a loam compost. Propagate by means of offsets or leaf-cuttings in summer.

Echinops (globe thistle) – Hardy perennials that thrive in the sun in light loam but do not like being disturbed. *Species – E. banaticus* (blue, July to September, 90 to 150cm (36 to 60in)); *E. commutatus* (white, July to August, 150 to 175cm (60 to 70in)); and *E. ritro* (blue, summer, 90 to 150cm (36 to 60in)).

Edelweiss – *See* **Leontopodium.**

Elaeagnus (oleaster or wild olive) – Hardy evergreen and deciduous shrubs which grow freely in full sun in almost any soil. *Culture* – Plant in March or from September to November, and cut out dead wood when required. To propagate, strike cuttings of matured wood in October in a frame, or layer.

Species and varieties – E. commutata (1.8 to 3.5m (6 to 12ft)); **E. glabra* (4.5 to 6m (15 to 20ft)); *E. multiflora* (1.8 to 3m (6 to 10ft)); **E. pungens* (3 to 4.5m (10 to 15ft)). *Denotes evergreen.

Enkianthus – Beautiful flowering shrubs which like a sunny sheltered position and moist peat or non-calcareous sandy loam and leaf-mould. *Culture* – Plant in October or November; no pruning is necessary. To propagate, sow seeds or strike cuttings of mature shoots in a frame in October. *Species – E. campanulatus* (cream, yellow and red, May, 1 to 2.5m (4 to 8ft)); *E. perulatus* (white, April, 1 to 1.8m (3 to 6ft)).

Epacris (Australian heath) – Heath-like winter-flowering evergreen shrubs that thrive in the cool greenhouse. *Culture* – Pot-up when growth begins (about May), using 12.5cm (5in) pots and a compost of sandy peat. Keep close until established and then stand in a cool greenhouse during the summer months. Water moderately and give liquid fertilizer while growing, but do not syringe. Cut long shoots well back and thin out after flowering. Propagate by cuttings of young wood with a little bottom heat in spring, or sow seed in pots in March.

Epilobium (willow herb) – Hardy perennials, the dwarf-growing species of which are useful for the rock garden, and the marsh or water garden. They do well in sun or shade in moist ordinary soil but prefer a gritty loam with some peat in it. *Species – E. angustifolium* (crimson, July to August, 90 to 100cm (36 to 40in), very invasive); *E. dodonaei* (rose pink, June to August, 60 to 90cm (24 to 36in)).

Epimedium (barrenwort) – Dwarf-growing perennials which thrive in sun or shade in the rock garden in sandy loam with a little peat. *Species – E. alpinum* (yellow and crimson, April to June, 22.5cm (9in)); *E. grandiflorum* 'Rose Queen' (large crimson, April to May, 20 to 30cm (8 to 12in)); *E.* x *rubrum* (rose, April to May, 25cm (10in)).

Eranthis (winter aconite) – These tuberous plants like a shady position in moist sandy loam and leaf-mould. *Culture* – Plant in October 5cm (2in) apart and 5cm (2in) deep. Do not lift from the ground. Propagate by division in October. *Species – E. cilicica* (yellow); *E. hyemalis* (greenish yellow). Both January to March, 10cm (4in).

Eremurus (fox-tail lily, giant asphodel or king's spear) – Tall, hardy perennials which thrive in sunny sheltered borders in rich loam. *Species – E. stenophyllus* (golden yellow, June to July, 90cm (3ft)); *E. elwesii* (soft rose, June, 1m (4ft)); *E. robustus* (pink, June, 2m (7ft)).

Erica – Important genus of hardy and greenhouse evergreen flowering shrubs, often known as heath or heather. *Culture* – (*Hardy species*) – Plant in October in a sunny position in well-drained sand and peat or in any light garden loam without lime in it. *E. carnea* (*E. herbacea*) will tolerate some lime in the soil if peat or leaf-mould is added. Do not prune, but merely keep in shape by removing dead blooms from the spring-flowering species in June, from the summer and autumn bloomers in March; and from winter flowerers in April. To propagate, strike cuttings of half-matured wood in July in a frame, sow seed in March, divide the roots or layer in autumn. *Culture* (*Greenhouse species*) – Propagate by cuttings of tender tips of young shoots in March or April or in September (10°C (50°F)) in well-drained pots or pans of sandy peat. Pot-up into 5cm (2in) pots as soon as rooted. Stop to make bushy plants. Re-pot in September into 12.5cm (5in) pots and transfer to a light, airy position; re-pot into 15cm (6in) pots, if need be, in March and summer on a bed of ashes in a cold frame in full sun. Mature plants should be potted-up in September in 15 to 17.5cm (6 to 7in) pots in a compost of sandy loam and peat in equal proportions and should be stood in the cold greenhouse. Trim after flowering. The winter-flowering kinds should be turned out into the frames after hardening off in April; the summer-flowering species in July, when they have finished blooming. In the cool house *E. gracilis* (red purple) flowers in November and December, and *E. hiemalis* (purple pink) from December to February. (*Hardy species*) – *E. arborea alpina* (white, February to May, 3.5m (12ft)); *E. cinerea* (purple, August to September, 30cm (1ft)); *E.c.* 'Alba' (white); *E. mediterranea* (mauve pink, March to May, 1 to 1.8m (3 to 6ft)); *E.* x *darleyensis* (mauve pink, January to April, 60 to 90cm (2 to 3ft)); *E. carnea* (*E. herbacea*) (purple, red, pink or white, November to April, 15 to 75cm (6 to 18in)). *See also* Calluna.

Erigeron (fleabane) – The species grown are hardy perennials which thrive in sunny borders or in the rock garden in ordinary soil. *Species and varieties* – *E. alpinus* (purple, July, 25cm (10in)); *E. aurantiacus* (orange, July to August, 15 to 30cm (6 to 12in)); 'Darkest of All' (violet mauve); 'Gaiety' (deep pink); 'Quakeress' (pale blue with pink); 'Sulphureus' (yellow). All varieties June, 60 to 75cm (24 to 30in).

Erinus (summer starwort) – Hardy evergreen rock garden or wall plant thriving in sun or shade in sandy loam. *Species* – *E. alpinus* (lilac rose and white); *E.a.* 'Dr Hanele' (carmine). All May to July, 10cm (4in).

Erodium (heron's bill) – Partly hardy and partly half-hardy perennials which do well in sandy loam in dry, warm, sheltered situations in the rock garden. *Species* – *E. petraeum* (white, veined pink, May to September, 7.5cm (3in)); *E. macradenum* (white, tinged rose, blotched violet, June to July, 15cm (6in)).

Eryngium (sea holly) – Tall, hardy perennials, which like a dry, sandy soil and a sunny position in a warm border. *Species* – *E. amethystinum* (metallic blue, June to August, 60cm (24in)); *E. giganteum* (bluish, July to September, 75 to 100cm (30 to 40in)).

Erysimum (fairy wallflower, hedge mustard) – Hardy annuals, biennials and perennials, excellent for sunny borders and rock gardens when grown in gritty and sandy loam. *Species* – *E. perovskianum* (yellow and orange, July to October, 30 to 45cm (12 to 18in)); *E. alpinum* (yellow, May to September, 15cm (6in)); *E. rupestre* (sulphur, June, 22.5cm (9in)).

Erythronium (dog's tooth violet) – Little bulbous plants which do well in light soil; useful as an edging to borders or in the rock garden. *Culture* – Plant 10 to 15cm (4 to 6in) deep and 10cm (4in) apart in partial shade in September in moist, well-drained sandy loam and ample leaf-mould. Surround the tubers with about 2.5cm (1in) of sand and do not lift more than necessary, but mulch annually with well-rotted manure or peat. Propagate by seed in a frame in August. Thin out, but do not plant the seedlings out until the third September after sowing. The plants are also increased by offsets.

Pot culture – Plant in August in 12.5 to 15cm (5 to 6in) pots, using a compost of loam, peat and leaf-mould, and keep in a cold frame during the winter, giving little water only until February. Then increase the supply and take into the cold greenhouse. *Species and varieties – Erythronium citrinum* (yellow); *E. revolutum* (pink); *E. dens-canis* (pink). All April to May, 25cm (10in).

Escallonia (Chilean gum box) – Half-hardy evergreen (except *E. virgata* which is deciduous) and hardy shrubs, which succeed in sheltered, well-drained ground. *Culture* – Plant in October or November, or in March or April. Cut out old wood, shorten laterals after flowering (August) and trim to shape. Autumn-flowering species should not be pruned until the following March. To propagate, strike cuttings of half-matured shoots in July or August in a frame. *Species – E. floribunda* (white, July to September, 1.5 to 3m (5 to 10ft)); *E.* x *langleyensis* (rose carmine, June, 3 to 4.5m (10 to 15ft)); *E. virgata* (white, June to July, 2 to 2.5m (6 to 8ft)); *E. rubra* (deep red, September to October, 1.8 to 3.5m (6 to 12ft)).

Eschscholzia (Californian poppy) – Hardy annuals which thrive in sunny beds or rock garden (dwarfs) in poor, light soil. *Species – E. tenuifolia* (yellow, May to October, 22.5cm (9in)); *E. californica* (orange and yellow, red, etc, May to October, 45cm (18in)).

Eucalyptus (gum tree) – Half-hardy evergreen trees, which thrive outdoors in warm areas. Also suitable for the cool greenhouse in a compost of 2 parts of fibrous loam to 1 part of leaf-mould. *Culture* – Pot-up in March, using 15 to 20cm (6 to 8in) pots; plant outdoors in a sunny position from June to September. To propagate, sow in gentle heat (16°C (59°F)) in early spring or strike cuttings of mature shoots under glass in June.

Euonymus (spindle tree) – Deciduous and evergreen shrubs and small trees, which like a sunny position and good loam. *Culture* – Plant evergreens in April or September and October, deciduous from November to March. No pruning is necessary. Propagate in autumn by cuttings from the previous year's growth, or by seeds. *Species and varieties – E. alatus* (scarlet leaves, autumn, 1.8 to 2.7m (6 to 9ft)); *E. europaeus* (pink fruit, autumn, 3 to 7.5m (10 to 25ft)); *E. fortunei* (evergreen, climber, 3m (10ft)); *E. japonicus* (evergreen, deep glossy foliage, 1.8 to 3m (6 to 10ft).

Euphorbia (spurge) – The hardy perennials are the only ones worth growing; *E. epithymoides* (yellow, 38cm (15in)), and *E. myrsinites* (yellow, 15cm (6in)), both like a gritty loam and full sun.

Everlasting Pea – *See* **Lathyrus.**

Exochorda (pearl bush) – Hardy deciduous shrubs, closely allied to the *Spiraea*. They thrive in sunny, sheltered positions in rich loam. *E. racemosa* (white, May to June, 1.5 to 3m (5 to 10ft)) is the best species. *Culture* – Plant in October or November and cut back straggling shoots after flowering. To propagate, strike cuttings of half-ripe shoots in late summer in a frame.

Fagus (beech) – This well-known tree thrives in chalk soils and is a good tree for woodland planting. *Culture* – Plant in October or November. No pruning is necessary. Propagation of varieties is usually carried out in March by grafting on the common beech. *Species and varieties – F. sylvatica* (common beech); *F.s.* 'Purpurea' (purple beech); *F.s.* 'Cuprea' (copper beech); *F.s.* 'Pendula' (weeping beech); *F.s.* 'Heterophylla' (fern-leaved beech).

Fatsia japonica (Japanese aralia) – Semi-hardy evergreen shrub which thrives well in the cool house; in good loam in warm, sheltered positions it will grow out of doors. It grows some 3.5m (12ft) high and carries cream white flowers in October and November. *Culture* – Plant in March or April, or pot-up in March, using a compost of 2 parts of loam to 1 part of leaf-mould and sand. Water well, syringing in spring and summer, and shade from the sun. To propagate, sow seed when ripe in heat (21°C (70°F)); insert 5cm (2in) pieces of stem in sandy soil in a propagator in spring or September, or increase by suckers.

Ferns – Hardy ferns thrive in sheltered and shady positions in moist but well-drained deep loam with plenty of leaf-mould, peat and coarse sand in it. Dead fronds should be left to act as a protection in winter. Half-hardy kinds require slight artifical heat in winter and tender ferns a temperature of 16°C (59°F). Pot-up in spring when growth commences in a compost of 2 parts fibrous loam and 1 part well-sieved leaf-mould and coarse sand, keep moist and syringe. Propagate, preferably in March or July, by means of spores sown in the same manner as seed, in John Innes seed compost, by division in March or April, or, in some cases, remove and pot-up the minute plants growing on the fronds. *Species (Hardy)* – *Adiantum pedatum* (maidenhair fern); *Asplenium adiantum-nigrum* (spleenwort); *Athyrium filix-femina* (lady fern); *Blechnum spicant* (hard fern); *Dryopteris dilatata* (broad buckler fern); *Osmunda regalis* (royal fern); *Polypodium vulgare* (polypody); *Polystichum aculeatum* (hard shield fern); and *Polystichum setiferum* (soft shield fern).

Forget-Me-Not – *See* **Myosotis.**

Forsythia (golden bell tree) – Hardy deciduous shrubs, thriving in ordinary soil and in sunny positions. *Culture* – Plant from October to November, and cut well back after flowering. To propagate, strike cuttings of soft wood in a frame in June or July and layer. *F.* x *intermedia* 'Spectabilis' is also useful for the cold greenhouse. Pot-up from October to December, using a 20 to 25cm (8 to 10in) pot and a compost of 2 parts of loam to 1 part of leaf-mould and sand; sink the pot outdoors from May to October. *Species and varieties* – *F.* x *intermedia* vars. 'Spectabilis' and 'Lynwood'; *F. suspensa* and *F. viridissima* (golden yellow, March, 1.8 to 3m (6 to 10ft)).

Fothergilla – Hardy deciduous shrubs which like a moist, sandy loam and peat. They grow some 1 to 1.8m (3 to 6ft) high and flower from April to June. *Culture* – Plant from October to March. Propagate by cuttings in late summer, by layering in autumn or sow in heat in spring.

Francoa ramosa (bridal wreath) – Graceful cool greenhouse plant with small white or rosy red flowers in late summer. *Culture* – Sow in March with slight bottom heat (13°C (55°F)) or propagate by cuttings under glass in June. Pot-up from February to March, using 15 to 20cm (6 to 8in) pots and a compost of sandy loam and leaf-mould. Discard the old plants, and raise a fresh batch annually.

Fraxinus (Ash) – These well known trees like a sunny position and ordinary soil. Plant in November. To propagate sow in a frame in autumn. *Species* – *F. excelsior* (European ash, 24m (80ft)); *F. ornus* (flowering ash, scented, 9m (30ft)); *F. pennsylvanica lanceolata* (green ash, for difficult situations, 24m (80ft)).

Freesia – Species of almost hardy bulbous plants for the warm, sunny border or cold greenhouse. *Culture* – Plant in August, 5cm (2in) apart, in light, well-drained soil, protect with straw in winter and lift after flowering. *Indoors* – Pot-up in succession from July to December, 2.5 (1in) deep and 5 cm (2in) apart, in equal parts of sandy loam and leaf-mould. Place the pots under a south wall, or in a frame in the case of coloured varieties, until the bulbs begin to grow (about 6 weeks). Transfer to a cold frame, and in a fortnight place on a shelf near the glass. Thin stakes are necessary for support, and freesias require bi-weekly doses of liquid fertilizer as soon as the buds form. The bulbs will bloom from January to April. Keep dry in a sunny frame from May to July, and shake clear of soil and pot-up each year. They can be increased easily from seed. Sow the seed when ripe, in August or September, in 12.5cm (5in) pots of sandy loam and leaf-mould, and place in a cold frame exposed to the sun; thin out to leave 5 to 6 plants in each pot. Soak the seed for 24 hours before sowing. Freesias do not like transplanting. They may also be propagated by offsets in July or August. *Named varieties* – 'Ballerina' (white); 'Excelsior' (cream); 'Romany' (double, mauve); 'Rose Marie'.

Fritillaria – Hardy bulbous plants, which succeed in any garden soil, although a dry, deep, rich (*F. meleagris* moist), sandy loam gives the most satisfactory results. They are excellent for shady borders, the rock garden, for naturalizing in grass, and (some species) for pots. *Culture* – Plant in October 10cm (4in) deep and 17.5cm (7in) apart (except *F. imperialis*, which should be 25cm (10in) apart) and do not lift from the ground unless overcrowded; when necessary, lift and replant immediately. *Pot culture* – Plant in the autumn in 10 to 12.5cm (4 to 5in) pots in a mixture of loam, peat, leaf-mould and sand, and give occasional doses of liquid fertilizer when the buds form. Propagate by bulbous offsets in October. *Species* – *F. latifolia* (yellow, 20cm (8in)); *F. imperialis* (red or orange and yellow, 75cm (30in)); *F. meleagris* (purple or white), 25cm (10in)); *F. persica* (Persian lily) (violet, 60cm (24in)). All April to May flowering.

Fuchsia – Fuchsias grow in almost any soil and are excellent for the cold greenhouse or the open border in summer. Feeding them with dilute liquid fertilizer is preferable to mixing manure with the soil. A carefully shaded house is the best place for the tender kinds when in blossom. *Culture* – Sow in heat 21°C (70°F) in the spring, but the more satisfactory way is to take cuttings in spring or autumn. Plants that have been at rest during the winter should be started in February or March and large early-flowering specimens will be produced by cutting down the old plants and re-potting them in good rich compost. When re-potted, keep them in a temperature of 13°C (55°F) and syringe overhead daily in fine weather. Insert cuttings taken from these plants in pots filled with a good potting compost and plunge the pots in a bottom heat of 16°C (59°F). In 3 weeks they may be potted into 7.5cm (3in) pots and replunged in the same bed, keeping the temperature from 10 to 16°C (50 to 59°F). As soon as necessary move into fresh pots, until they receive their final shift into 15, 22.5 or 30cm (6, 9 or 12in) pots towards the end of June; or into the open about the end of May. Cuttings can also be taken of semi-matured wood in August. The plants should be kept close up to the glass and will require stopping at least 6 times and careful training. Never stop a plant within 2 months of the time it is required to bloom. A regular, moist temperature should be maintained and the foliage should be sprayed in warm weather. During bright sunshine the glass should be lightly shaded. In July or August the plants can be in a sunny position in the open. *Species (Hardy)* – *F. magellanica* (scarlet); *F.m.* 'Mrs Popple' (violet and purple); *F.m.* 'Riccartonii' (bright red) and numerous named hybrids. (*Half-hardy*) – *F. cordifolia* (red and green); *F. corymbiflora* (scarlet); *F. fulgens* (scarlet). All July to September, 1.5 to 1.8 (5 to 6ft).

Funkia – *See* **Hosta.**

Gaillardia (blanket flower) – Annuals and perennials, both kinds being usually treated as half-hardy. They thrive in any light, rich soil in sunny beds. *Named annual varieties* – 'Lollipops' (yellow, cream and red, double); 'Lorenziana' and 'Picta' (red and yellow). *Named perennial varieties* – 'Burgundy' (deep red); 'Goblin' (22cm (9in) yellow and red); 'Mandarin' (orange). All June to October, 30 to 75cm (12 to 30in).

Galanthus (snowdrop) – Snowdrops thrive in the shade in well-drained moist, gritty loam and are excellent for beds, for the rock garden, for growing in pots or for naturalizing beneath deciduous trees. *Culture* – Plant in August or September, 7.5cm (3in) deep and 7.5cm (3in) apart; lift every fourth year only and propagate by division. *Pot culture* – Plant 2.5cm (1in) deep in September or October, using 10 to 12.5cm (4 to 5in) pots and a compost of 2 parts of ordinary soil to 1 part of leaf-mould and sand, and keep in a cold frame covered with ashes or soil until growth commences. Dry off after flowering. *Species* – *G. elwesii* (white, marked green, January, 20cm (8in)); *G. nivalis* (white, January, 15cm (6in)); *G. plicatus* (white, January, 30cm (12in)).

Galega (goat's rue) – Hardy border perennial, which thrives almost anywhere and in any soil. *Species and varieties* – *G. officinalis* (lilac blue, white and pink, June to October, 1m (48in)); *G. officinalis* 'Her Majesty' (pale lilac blue and white, June to October, 1m (50in)).

Galtonia candicans (Cape hyacinth) – Tall, hardy, bulbous plants, flowering in August and September, and loving a sunny border and well-manured, deeply dug, sandy loam and leaf-mould. *Culture* – Plant in March or October from 10 to 15cm (4 to 6in) deep and 38cm (15in) apart, letting the bulbs rest on sand. If the soil is cold and heavy, the bulbs must be lifted annually. *Pot culture* – Place one bulb 1cm (½in) deep in a 15cm (6in) pot and set in a cold greenhouse. Only grow in a pot for 1 year, after which plant out. Propagate by seed in the open as soon as ripe, or by offsets in autumn.

Gardenia – Evergreen flowering shrubs suitable for hothouse or warm greenhouse and which require much heat and plenty of water when growing. They thrive in equal parts of peat, loam and rotten manure with a little charcoal added. *Culture* – Prune into shape and pot-up in February or March, putting year old plants into 12.5 to 15cm (5 to 6in) pots; 20cm (8in) pots should be large enough for old specimens. Syringe daily, and give liquid fertilizer when the buds form. Propagate in February or March by shoots with a heel in pots in sandy peat, in a propagating frame with a bottom heat of 21 to 27°C (70 to 80°F). *Named varieties of G. jasminoides:* 'Fortunei' (cape jasmine), and 'Florida'.

Garrya – Hardy evergreen shrubs with yellow or greenish-white flowers from November to March. *Culture* – Plant in May in ordinary soil and a sunny, sheltered position. In May trim back long shoots a little and cut out dead wood. To propagate, strike cuttings in August in a frame, or layer. *Species* – *G. elliptica* (1.8 to 3.5m (6 to 12ft) or more).

Gaultheria (winter green, shallon) – Genus of evergreen shrubs, some of which are hardy and suitable for the woodland or rock garden. *Culture* – Plant in April or October in cool, moist, ordinary, lime-free soil and leaf-mould in semi-shaded position. Thin out old shoots when overcrowded. Propagate by seed in heat in March, division or layering in October. *Species* – *G. procumbens* (white and pink, July to August, creeping); *G. shallon* (white and red, May to July, 1 to 1.8m (3 to 6ft)).

Gaura – Hardy perennials which are best treated as annuals and thrive in light, warm, rich soil in sunny borders. They reach a height of 90cm (36in) and flower from June to October.

Gazania (treasure flower) – Showy summer bedding plant with yellow and bronze flowers from June to Oct.; also useful for cool greenhouse. *Culture* – Propagate by basal cuttings in summer in a cold frame. Plant out in June in a sunny position. Protect from frost in winter. For indoors, pot-up in March in sandy loam and peat.

Genista (broom) – Closely related to *Cytisus*, hardy flowering shrubs valuable for the greenhouse, border, shrubbery, or rock garden. *Culture* – Plant in October in dry, light soil in a sunny position. The early-flowering types should have the old wood thinned out and should be trimmed

Sweet peas need a rich soil, and should be planted in a trench. In due course they will need stakes up to 2.5m (8ft) high

Sharp edges to paths and steps can be softened by allowing plants to come beyond the borders into shape directly after flowering; the later bloomers should be cut hard back in February or March. Do not prune but keep in shape by stopping and removing dead blooms. To propagate, sow in a frame when ripe or strike cuttings of half-matured wood in a frame during August and grow on in pots until planted out, as they do not transplant readily. *Species* – *G. aetnensis* (golden yellow, July to August, 3 to 6m (10 to 20ft)); *G. cinerea* (golden, June to July, 2.5 to 3m (8 to 10ft)); *G. hispanica* (the Spanish broom) (golden, May to June, 30 to 90cm (1 to 3ft)); *G. pilosa* (yellow, May to June, trailer); *G. tinctoria* 'Plena' (golden, double, July to August, 30 to 60cm (1 to 2ft)).

Gentiana – Beautiful little rock plants which need as near to alpine conditions as possible. A moist, but well-drained, gritty, peaty loam and leaf-mould, to which has been added a fair amount of rubble, suits them well. Ample moisture is essential through the summer and most species do best in partial shade. The gentians are impatient of root division and indeed of transplanting. *Species and varieties* – *G. acaulis* (deep blue, May to June, 5 to 7.5cm (2 to 3in)); *G. asclepiadea* (violet, September 30 to 35cm (12 to 14in)); *G. lutea* (yellow, May to June, 60 to 90cm (24 to 36in)); *G. farreri* (blue, August to September, 7.5 to 10cm (3 to 4in)); *G. pneumonanthe* (violet, August, 15 to 22.5cm (6 to 9in)); *G. verna* (deep blue, April to May, 5cm (2in)); *G. sino-ornata* (deep blue, September to November, 15cm (6in)).

Geranium (crane's bill) – Ordinary garden soil, provided it is fairly light and well-drained, suits the hardy geraniums; a sunny, open site is essential. The dwarf kinds are suitable for the rock garden, and thrive in poor, sandy and gritty soil. An autumnal dressing of granite chips will help them to survive the winter. *Culture* – Sow in March or August (under glass) or in April in the open, or the plants may be increased by division from October to March. Cuttings of matured side-shoots can also be struck in August in a frame. For half-hardy greenhouse bedding plants and show varieties, *see* Pelargonium. *Species (Hardy)* – *G. psilostemon* (red purple, 45 to 60cm (18 to 24in)); *G. endressii* (rose pink, 38cm (15in)); *G. meeboldii* (blue, 45cm (18in)); *G. pratense* (mauve, blue or white, 50 to 75cm (20 to 30in)). *(Dwarfs)* – *G. farreri* (pink, 15cm (6in)); *G. sanguineum* (crimson purple, 22.5cm (9in)); *G.s.* 'Album' (white, 22.5cm (9in)); *G.s. lancastriense* (rose and crimson, 15cm (6in)). All June to September.

Geum (avens) – Hardy perennials which thrive in sunny borders in almost any well-drained, light, rich soil; the rock garden species love a deep, gritty loam, and *G. reptans* and *G. rivale* require plenty of moisture. *Species and varieties* – *G. coccineum* (orange scarlet); *G.* 'Lady Stratheden' (double, golden yellow); *G. montanum* (yellow); *G.* 'Mrs Bradshaw' (bright red); *G.* 'Fire Opal' (orange); *G. reptans* (golden yellow); *G. rivale* 'Leonard' (crimson pink). All April to October, 15 to 60cm (6 to 24in).

Gilia – Hardy annuals and half-hardy biennials which thrive in ordinary soil in warm, sunny borders. *Species* (*Annuals*) – *G. densiflora* (syn. *Linanthus*) (lilac pink, 30cm (12in)); *G. lutea* (yellow, 12.5cm (5in)); *G. tricolor* (pale purple, white and yellow, 25 to 50cm (10 to 20in)). (*Biennials*) – *G. aggregata* and *G.* (*Ipomopsis*) *rubra* (crimson scarlet 60 to 120cm (24 to 48in)). June to October.

Ginkgo biloba (maidenhair tree) – Hardy deciduous tree thriving in deep loam in a sheltered position. *Culture* – Plant in October. No pruning is required. Propagate in March by seed in a frame. A good town tree growing slowly to 18m (60ft) or more. Leaves butter yellow in autumn.

Gladiolus (sword lily) – Gladioli are divided into large-flowered, primulinus, miniature and butterfly hybrids, blooming from June to September. They like a deep, well dug, firm loam and a warm spot well exposed to the sun and sheltered from winds. *Culture* – Line the pocket in which the corms are to rest with a little coarse sand. Plant in March or April 10cm (4in) deep and 10 to 15cm (4 to 6in) apart, in rows 38 to 50cm (15 to 20in) apart. Large flower spikes will need staking securely. The corms are taken up in October or November and stored. Prepare for planting in succession the following March or April by rubbing off the old roots and soil adhering at the bottom of the corms. *Propagation* – Draw a drill 5 to 7.5cm (2 to 3in) deep on rich soil in the nursery bed and plant the cormlets thinly in March. Keep moist; some of these may flower late in autumn, many the second year and all the third year. These young cormlets require the same treatment as the old ones. Gladioli may also be raised from seed in May in a cold frame. If, however, it is desired that all the young plants shall come true to type, propagation must be effected by offsets. *Pot culture* – Place one corm 7.5cm (3in) deep in a 15cm (6in) pot in a compost of 2 parts sandy loam to 1 part of leaf-mould and sharp sand, in October or November; cover with straw till growth starts and keep in a frame until March. Then put in a light airy position in a cold greenhouse to bloom. Dry off after flowering, store, and keep dry from May to October. *G.* x *colvillii* is good for pot culture, and makes a good room plant. *Species* (*Early*) – *G. byzantinus* (purple red, 50cm (20in)); *G. cardinalis* (scarlet, white spots, 90cm (30in)); *G.* x *colvillii* (purple, white spots. 45cm (18in)); *G.* x *c.* 'Albus' (white, 45cm (18in)). All June to July. Named varieties are innumerable and catalogues should be consulted.

Gloxinia – Tender tuberous-rooted perennials, with large white, pink, red or purple flowers, June to October. Leaves dark velvety green, 30cm (12in). They thrive in a fibrous peaty loam mixed with leaf-mould and sharp sand. *Culture* – Start the tubers in succession from January to April by placing them in a box in a 5cm (2in) layer of compost (16°C (59°F). Keep just moist, and as soon as from 5 to 7.5cm (2 to 3in) growth has been made, plant one tuber in each 10cm (4in) pot. Maintain the same heat and moisture, shade from the sun, and water liberally when well rooted. Pot-up into 12.5cm (5in) pots as soon as pot-bound, and again into 15cm (6in) pots when the buds are forming. After flowering, dry off and store the tubers in peat. Propagate at the end of January by seed in a compost of peat thinly covered with coarse sand only, and exposed to a bottom heat of about 21°C (70°F). Prick off 2.5cm (1in) apart as soon as possible and gradually reduce the temperature to 16°C (59°F); pot-up singly into 10cm (4in) pots and place near the glass. Maintain the temperature and keep moist but do not let moisture touch the leaves. Pot-up by stages, until the flowering pots, 12.5 to 17.5cm (5 to 7in) are reached. Seed may also be sown in a cold house in June. Old tubers, when started in heat in February in boxes of damp peat, supply shoots from which cuttings may be made; these should be placed in a close propagating frame and subjected to moist and gentle heat. Another method of propagation is by leaf-cuttings taken at any time.

Godetia – Hardy annuals, useful for summer bedding. *Named varieties* – 'Crimson Glow' (deep red); 'Kelvedon Glory' (salmon-orange); 'Salmon Princess' (salmon rose); 'Sybil Sherwood' (pink); 'Azalea-flowered' (various). All June to October, 15 to 60cm (6 to 24in).

Golden rod – *See* **Solidago.**

Gunnera – Hardy perennial foliage plants, which thrive in rich soil and sheltered, shady positions. They are valuable for margins of pools and for shrubberies. The crowns require slight winter protection. *G. tinctoria* (crimson fruit, August, 1.5m (5ft)); *G. manicata* (2.5m (8ft)).

Gypsophila (chalk plant or gauze flower) – Hardy annuals and perennials which thrive in dry, well-limed loam, in sunny borders or the rock garden. *Species* (*Annuals*) – *G. elegans* (white, large, 45cm

(18in)); *G. muralis* (pink, 15cm (6in)). (*Perennials*) – *G. cerastioides* (white, veined red, 7.5cm (3in)); *G. paniculata* (white, single and double, 75cm (30in)); *G. repens* (white and pink, 10 to 15cm (4 to 6in)). All May to September.

Haberlea – Hardy perennials suitable for a shady spot in the rock garden in moist soil. *H. rhodopensis* (lilac, May to July, 15cm (6in)) is a favourite.

Habranthus pratensis – *See* **Hippeastrum pratense.**

Halesia (silver bell or snowdrop tree) – Hardy deciduous summer-flowering trees or shrubs 2.5 to 9m (8 to 30ft) which thrive in well-drained, moist sandy loam in a sunny, sheltered position. *Culture* – Plant in October or November; thin out the branches when overcrowded. To propagate sow in a frame in March or take cuttings in October.

Hamamelis (witch hazel) – Small deciduous flowering trees or shrubs which thrive in sunny positions in moist but well-drained loamy soil. *Culture* – Plant in October to November. Just thin out and trim the branches in April when overcrowded. To propagate, sow seed when ripe in a frame, layer in late summer or graft. *Species* – *H. japonica* and *H.j.* 'Arborea' (yellow, January to February, 2.5 to 4.5m (8 to 15ft)); *H. mollis* 'Pallida' (pale yellow, December to February, 1.8 to 2.5m (6 to 8ft)).

Hebe (Veronica) – Shrubs from New Zealand, formerly included with *Veronica*, which can be grown outdoors in mild districts. Hebes are amongst the most valuable of summer and autumn-blooming plants, both for greenhouse culture and for out of doors, where, with a dry subsoil and somewhat sheltered, sunny situation, the plants will generally stand uninjured through the winter. The dwarf species are suitable for the rock garden. *Culture* – Plant in April or September. Trim annually to keep in shape only, but it is usually necessary to prune hard back every few years. To propagate, strike cuttings of matured wood in a frame in August; the young shoots should occasionally be pinched back, but no stopping should be done after June. *Pot culture* – Pot-up in the early summer, using 15 to 20cm (6 to 8in) pots and a compost of 2 parts of loam to 1 part of leaf-mould. Harden off and stand in the open from May to September, then take into the cold house. After flowering, prune severely in March, and place the pots near the glass. *Species and varieties* – *H.* x *andersonii* 'Variegata' (purple, July, 60cm (2ft) with cream and dark green leaves); *H. brachysiphon* (white, July, 1.8m (6ft)); *H. cupressoides* (lavender, July, 1m (4ft) with grey green delicate foliage); *H. armstrongii* (with arching golden foliage); *H.* 'Autumn Glory' (purple, September to November, 60cm (2ft) and purplish foliage).

Hedera (ivy) – There are many kinds of this well-known climber. The common sorts thrive against walls in ordinary rich soil; the variegated kinds prefer walls facing south or west, and like ample lime in the soil. *Culture* – Strike cuttings in autumn in sandy soil in a shady border, or layer; plant out in showery weather between October and April. When established, old leaves and untidy shoots need clipping back in April. *Species and varieties* – *H. canariense* (large, variegated leaves, tender; good house plant); *H. colchica dentata* and *H.c.* 'Variegata' (hardy with very large leaves); *H. helix* (common ivy) with many varieties.

Hedysarum – Genus of hardy biennials, perennials and shrubs, useful for borders and the rock garden. They thrive in the sun and in ordinary soil. *Species* (*Biennials*) – *H. coronarium* (scarlet, June to September, 90cm (36in)). (*Shrub*) – *H. multijugum* (purple red, June to September, 90 to 180cm (36 to 72in)).

Helenium (sneezeweed) – Hardy perennials which thrive in sunny borders in rich, ordinary, well-drained soil. *Species* – *H. autumnale* (yellow, July to October, 1m

(40in)); *H. hoopesii* (orange, July to October, 75cm (30in)). *Named varieties of H. autumnale* – 'Butterpat' (yellow, chocolate centre, August to October, 90 to 120cm (36 to 48in)); 'Moerheim Beauty' (bronze red, August to October, 90 to 120cm (36 to 48in)).

Helianthemum (sun rose) – Low evergreens which love the sun and do best on dry banks, or in the rock garden in sandy soil. For culture, *see* Cistus. *Species – H. lumulatum* (yellow, May to September, 22.5cm (9in)). *H. nummularium* vars. – 'Ben More' (deep orange); 'Ben Nevis' (butter yellow); 'The Bride' (white); 'Wisley Pink' and 'Wisley Primrose' (vigorous).

Helianthus (sunflower) – Hardy annuals and perennials which grow freely in a sunny site in any rich, well-dug soil. *Varieties (Annuals) – Named varieties of H. annuus* 'Flore Pleno' (double); 'Autumn Beauty' (clear yellow); 'Italian White' (pale primrose). All July to October. *Named varieties of H. debilis* – 'Excelsior' (golden red); 'Giant Yellow'; and 'Sunburst' (yellow, red, purple). *(Perennials) – H. decapetalus* (yellow, single or double, August to October, 120 to 180cm (4 to 6ft)); *H. salicifolius* (yellow, black centre, September to October, 2.5m (100in)); *H. rigidus* 'Miss Mellish' (yellow, September to October, 2.5m (100in)).

Helichrysum (everlasting) – These are mostly half-hardy or hardy perennials or annuals, which thrive in sunny positions and gritty loam and are mostly suitable for borders, or as pot plants indoors, while the dwarf species make excellent rock plants. *Species (Half-hardy annuals) – H. bracteatum* and vars. (white, brown, red, pink and yellow, July to October, 90cm (36in)); *H. orientale* (yellow, July to October, 60cm (24in)). *(Hardy perennial) – H. bellidioides* (white, July to October, 12.5cm (5in)).

Heliotropium arborescens (cherry pie) – Soft-wooded shrubs, for summer bedding and pot culture, and succeeding best in light, rich loam and leaf-mould. *Culture* – Seed sown thinly in spring in moderate heat make good plants for summer and autumn decoration. Pot-on in April into 10cm (4in) pots, pinch back when 7.5 to 10cm (3 to 4in) high, harden off and plant out, about 30cm (12in) apart in June. The finest plants are obtained from cuttings taken in the same way as for verbenas and bedding calceolarias. Take the cuttings in spring or autumn (preferably late August) and strike in boxes in a frame in moderate heat; syringe in hot weather and in 5 to 6 weeks pot-up into 7.5 or 10cm (3 or 4in) pots and move into the cool house. *Pot culture* – Pot-up annually in March, using 15 to 20cm (6 to 8in) pots and a compost of 2 parts loam to 1 part of leaf-mould and sand. Stop to make bushy, and prune well back in February.

Helipterum – These half-hardy annuals, which now include the acrocliniums and the rhodanthes, are everlastings, valuable alike for greenhouse and flower garden. They succeed best in a light, rich soil and warm sheltered positions. *Pot culture* – *(Rhodanthes)*. Sow 6mm (¼in) apart in August (10°C (50°F)). Place the seedlings near the glass and keep fairly dry at first. Pot as soon as possible into flowering pots. *Species – H. manglesii* (rose and silver); *H.m.* 'Maculatum' (pink, yellow or white); *H. roseum* (rose). All June to October, 30 to 45cm (12 to 18in).

Helleborus (Christmas rose, Lenten rose) – Hardy perennials which thrive in well-dug, light and moist soil in a border facing preferably east or west. For the greenhouse, pot-up in October in 15 to 20cm (6 to 8in) pots of good potting compost; select fresh plants annually, planting the old ones out in April or May. Otherwise disturb as little as possible. *Species – H. lividus* (light green leaves and flowers, March to April 90cm (3ft)); *H. foetidus* (dark green leaves, pale green and purple flowers, January to June); *H. niger* (Christmas rose) (white flowers, December to March); *H. orientalis* (Lenten rose) (white to purple flowers, February to

April). All 30 to 45cm (12 to 18in) except *H. lividus.*

Hemerocallis (day lily) – Hardy perennials which do well in moist, light, and deep soil in a shady border or marsh garden. Propagate by division in April or November. *Species – H. aurantiaca* (apricot orange); *H. dumortieri* (yellow and red brown); *H. fulva* (bronze yellow), May to August, 30 to 90cm (12 to 36in). Individual flowers only last a day. Many named varieties.

Herniaria glabra and others of the genus are useful little creeping plants for the paved or rock gaden. They like a sunny position and gritty loam, and are propagated by division in the spring.

Hesperis (sweet rocket) – Spring-flowering hardy annuals, biennials and perennials, which grow freely in any light soil in a sunny position, and are excellent for the mixed border. *Species (Perennial) – H. matronalis* (white, red, rose, purple, single and double, June to July, 50cm (20in)); *H. violacea* (violet, May to July, 45cm (18in)).

Heuchera (alum root) – Hardy perennials which do well in warm, rich and light soil, in a sunny border. The dwarf species are useful for the rock garden. *Species and varieties – H.* x *brizoides* (rosy red); *H. sanguinea* (coral scarlet). Both May to September, 50 to 75cm (20 to 30in).

Hibiscus (rose mallow) – Beautiful hardy and half-hardy plants, suitable for borders and indoor decoration. *Culture* – Plant the hardy sorts in sandy loam in March in a sheltered position in sun or shade; do not prune, merely keep in shape by tipping and removing dead blooms after flowering. Propagate by sowing seeds about April, by cuttings in a frame in September, or by grafting. Those intended for indoor culture require a compost of fibrous peat and rich fine loam with a large proportion of sand; a little charcoal added is often beneficial. Propagate these from seeds sown in gentle heat, or by cuttings struck early in spring in a close frame. *Species (Hardy annual) – H. trionum* (purple, July to September, 60 to 120cm (2 to 4ft)). *(Shrubs) – H. coccineus* (bright scarlet, August to October, 1 to 1.5m (4 to 5ft)); *H. syriacus* and vars. (white, blue, pink or crimson, single or double, August to October, 2m (7ft)), *(Greenhouse shrubs) – H. rosa-sinensis* (red, 1.8m (6ft)).

Hieracium (hawkweed) – Hardy perennials, some of the dwarf-growing species of which thrive in ordinary soil in a sunny rock garden or border. *Species – H. alpinum* (yellow, July, 15cm (6in)); *H. aurantiacum* (orange, June to August, 50cm (20in)).

Hippeastrum (equestrian star) – Genus of bulbous plants formerly including *Amaryllis*, *Habranthus*, etc. Jacobean Lily, *Sprekelia formosissima*, is usually grown in pots in the warm greenhouse in rich and heavy loam, but it succeeds at the foot of a south wall. *H. pratense* is suitable for a sunny border, rock garden, or pot culture. Plant in October and protect with straw in winter. *Culture* – Hippeastrums should be planted in February. Water well and give liquid fertilizer when the buds appear. Keep dry after flowering. Re-pot every 3 to 4 years and propagate by offsets treated as old bulbs.

Hippophae rhamnoides (sea buckthorn) – Hardy deciduous shrub or tree 3 to 12m (10 to 40ft) which thrives in moist ordinary soil in open positions (preferably near the sea). *Culture* – Plant in October or February and cut back weak shoots in February. Propagate by seed in the open, by suckers or layers in autumn and by root-cuttings in spring.

Holly – *See* **Ilex.**

Hollyhock – *See* **Alcea.**

Holodiscus discolor (syn. *Spiraea discolor*) – Shrub, 2.5 to 3.5m (8 to 12ft). For culture, *see* **Spiraea** (shrub).

Honesty – *See* **Lunaria.**

Honeysuckle – *See* **Lonicera.**

Hosta (plantain lily) – Hardy herbaceous foliage plants, suitable for the border, rock garden, shrubbery or cold greenhouse. They require rich, well-dug soil and thrive in sun or shade. *Culture* – Propagate by division in spring or autumn or pot-up in March. *Species* – *H. plantaginea* (white, July to September, 45cm (18in)); *H. sieboldiana* (pale lilac, July to August, 30 to 45cm (12 to 18in)); *H. ventricosa* (lilac blue, July to August, 30 to 45cm (12 to 18in)); *H. fortunei* (lilac, July, 60 to 90cm (2 to 3ft)).

Humulus (Hop) – Hardy herbaceous perennial climbers, delighting in rich, deep, sandy loam. *H. lupulus* 'Aureus' (golden hop) and *H. scandens* 'Variegatus' (silver variegated hop), may both be grown as annuals. If grown as perennials the stems should be cut to the ground in autumn.

Hyacinthus (hyacinth) – Can be divided into two classes: the early-flowering Roman hyacinths, useful for pot work and for forcing, and the Dutch hyacinths also good for pot work, and specially suitable for spring bedding. The best soil for hyacinths is a well-manured, deeply dug sandy loam with leaf-mould in it, but they will grow in almost any soil or in compost, fibre or water. *Culture* – Plant in a sunny position from September to November about 10cm (4in) deep and from 12.5 to 25cm (5 to 10in) apart, according to variety. *Pot culture* – To obtain bloom from December to April pot-up in succession from August to November in good bulb compost or fibre. For 3 bulbs a 14cm (5in) pot will be sufficient.

Named varieties – 'L'Innocence' (white); 'City of Haarlem' (yellow); 'Pink Pearl' (pink); 'Lady Derby' (pale pink); 'Jan Bos' (red); 'La Victoire' (red); 'King of the Blues' (dark blue); 'Ostara' (deep blue); 'Myosotis' (light blue).

Hydrangea – The common hydrangea *H. macrophylla* is a summer-flowering deciduous shrub, which thrives in a sheltered position in well-drained and richly manured sandy loam. *H. paniculata* and var. 'Grandiflora' (creamy white) are quite hardy. *Culture* – The same treatment, both indoors and out, will suit these species, bearing in mind that although *H. paniculata* is quite hardy, *H. macrophylla* is less so. The two species also require different treatment as to pruning. *H. macrophylla* need only be trimmed in March; *H. paniculata* should be cut back by half in March. Plant in March. *Pot culture* – Pot-up from February to March, using from 12.5 to 30cm (5 to 12in) pots and a potting compost. When grown in small pots one stem only should be encouraged. After flowering, stand in the open until September. *H. macrophylla* is also suitable for forcing in the warm greenhouse. Blue flowers may be obtained by planting in a lime-free soil and by watering with a solution of sequestrene or with aluminium sulphate. To propagate, strike cuttings of young wood in May, or of strong matured shoots that have not flowered in August; both in a frame. Autumn-struck cuttings should be wintered in a frame with an even temperature of 4°C (40°F).

Hypericum (St John's wort, Aaron's beard or rose of Sharon) – This genus includes a number of hardy shrubs, evergreen and deciduous, as well as hardy annuals and perennials. The annuals are hardly worth growing, but some of the dwarf-growing perennials and evergreen shrubs make excellent rock or edging plants. Sandy loam and a sunny site suit them best. (*Shrubs*) – Plant in November; cut well back in March. Propagate by cuttings in July or sow seed when ripe. *Species* (*Perennial*) – *H. fragile* (20cm (8in)). (*Shrub*) – *H. calycinum* (30 to 45cm (12 to 18in)); *H. elatum* (120 to 150cm (48 to 60in)); *H. hookerianum* (1 to 1.5m (3 to 5ft)); *H.* x *moserianum* (30 to 45cm (12 to 18in)); *H. patulum* 'Hidcote' (45 to 90cm (18 to 36in)). All carry yellow flowers from July to August.

Iberis (candytuft) – Hardy annuals and perennials, both of which succeed in any soil with lime in it, but prefer dry, sandy loam and a sunny position. *Species* (*Annual*) – *I. umbellata* (purple, crimson and pink, July to October, 30cm (12in)). (*Perennials*) – *I. gibraltarica* (lilac pink, May to July, 30cm (12in) this needs a warm, sheltered position); *I. sempervirens* (white, May to June, 15 to 30cm (6 to 12in)).

Ilex (holly) – Hardy trees and shrubs which thrive in sun or shade in almost any well-drained soil. Plant in May or September; prune with secateurs in April (hedges in May or August). To propagate, sow in March in shallow drills in the open. The seeds usually take 2 years to germinate, and many people prefer to strike cuttings of half-mature wood in August in a cold frame or to layer in summer. Consult catalogues for named varieties.

Impatiens (balsam) – Pretty half-hardy annual for sunny beds or borders with rich soil or for the greenhouse. Support with stakes. *Pot culture* – Pot-up as required, using 12.5 to 15cm (5 to 6in) pots and a potting compost of peat and stand near the glass in a cool greenhouse. Syringe overhead, ventilate and water liberally. As soon as the buds begin to form feed twice a week with a weak liquid fertilizer. Do not stop. When large specimens are desired, move into 20 to 25cm (8 to 10in) pots, using a rich compost and feed regularly. *Species and varieties* – *I. balsamina* (many vars.); *I. holstii* (vermilion); *I. oliveri* (mauve); *I. sultani* (syn. *I. walleriana*) (rose).

Incarvillea – Hardy annuals and tuberous-rooted perennials growing from 15 to 90cm (6 to 36in) high and flowering from May to August. They thrive in well-drained rich loam in sunny borders. *Culture* – Sow in pans in a frame in April, thin and plant out in spring and autumn. Seed can be sown in the open early in May; increase also by division in March or October. *I. delavayi* (crimson pink or purple, 38cm (15in)) is the most popular.

Inula (fleabane) – Hardy perennials useful for sunny borders or for the wild garden. *Species* – *I. acaulis* (orange yellow, 5 to 10cm (2 to 4in)); *I. hookeri* (yellow); *I. oculis-christi* (golden yellow, June to August, 60 to 90cm (24 to 36in)).

Ipomoea (morning glory) – Large genus of half-hardy climbing plants, closely allied to the convolvulus, all requiring a rich, light soil. *Culture* (*Annuals*) – Sow seed singly in April in small pots under glass and plant out 60cm (24in) apart in May or June against a trellis or sunny wall. (*Perennials*) – These are best propagated by cuttings of side shoots struck in a frame between March and August. *Species and varieties* – *I. learii* (blue dawn flower, sub-tropical climber). (*Annuals*) – *I. purpurea* (various single and double); *I. violacea* (syn. *I. tricolor*) (sky blue). All June to September, 2.5 to 3m (8 to 10ft).

Iris – Genus of hardy plants usually divided into 2 sections: the bulbous and the non-bulbous or rhizomatous-rooted. To the latter class belong the flags or bearded irises, the kaempferi or Japanese group and the Sibirica irises; to the bulbous class belong the English, Dutch and Spanish irises. The cultivation of irises is simple, the plants succeeding in a sunny position in any light, rich garden soil, though sandy loam with 50 per cent peat or leaf-mould is most suitable for the bulbous species. The English iris needs a heavier and cooler soil than the Dutch and Spanish species, and it is necessary to lift bulbs of the last 2 triennially, rest them for a few months and then re-plant. For the tall bearded iris the soil should be deeply dug, and well-manured. It will, however, grow in almost any well-drained soil. The Japanese irises love marshy land, require a position in full sun, and should occasionally be transplanted and divided in August after blooming. The three following types also belong to the rhizomatous group: the *Evansia* section, the *Oncocyclus* or cushion irises and the *Regelia* irises.

Culture (*Bulbous-rooted*) – Plant 7.5 to 10cm (3 to 4in) deep in September or October with a little sand round the bulbs (Spanish, 10cm (4in), Dutch 12.5cm (5in), and English 15cm (6in) apart). Most spring and autumn-flowering species need to be lifted from the ground in August, summer-flowering kinds should be lifted every third year, in October, after the plants have died down. English irises can be left undisturbed; the Dutch irises need the same treatment as the Spanish. *Pot culture* – Many of the bulbous irises make good pot plants; among these are *I. planifolia*, *I. persica*, *I. reticulata* and the English and Spanish kinds. They need a compost of $\frac{2}{3}$ fibrous loam, $\frac{1}{3}$ leaf-mould and sand; plant 5 bulbs in a 15cm (6in) pot in September or October. They may be propagated by offsets in October.

Non-bulbous or rhizomatous species – Sow seed in April in a cold frame, or propagate by division in August. Plant out in August or September; bearded irises (tall) 50cm (20in) apart; (medium) 38cm (15in) apart; (dwarf) 12.5cm (5in) apart. The upper part of the rhizomes should lie on the surface of the soil, so as to be exposed to the air and sun. The dwarf bearded alpine species may be propagated by seed in September under glass, by offshoots in October or by division in the spring after flowering. Lift and re-plant the rhizomes every 3 years.

Species (Bulbous-rooted) – Spring-flowering – *I. histrio* (lilac blue and yellow, January to February, 15cm (6in)); *I. orchioides* (yellow, lilac spots, March to May, 50cm (20in)); *I. persica* (purple, yellow and green, March, 10cm (4in)); *I. reticulata* (purple, red and orange, January to February, 20cm (8in)). (*Summer-flowering*) – *I. xiphioides* (English iris) (purple, mauve, pink and blue, July, 25 to 63cm (10 to 25in)); *I. xiphium* (Spanish iris) (blue, yellow and white, June, 50cm (20in)). (*Autumn-flowering*) – *I. planifolia* (sky blue and yellow, November to January, 2.5cm (1in)). (*Non-bulbous or rhizomatous*) – *I. fulva* (syn. *cuprea*) (red bronze, June to July, 50cm (20in)); *I. foetidissima* (bluish lilac or yellow, June, 75cm (30in)); *I. kaempferi* (various, July to September, 45 to 75cm (18 to 30in)); *I. monnieri* (yellow and white, June to July, 90 to 120cm (36 to 48in)); *I. ochroleuca* (white and yellow, June to July, 120cm (48in)); *I. sibirica* (blue, white and yellow, May to June, 90cm (36in)); *I. spuria* (deep blue, June, 100cm (40in)); *I. unguicularis* (syn. *stylosa*) (various, November to March 15 to 30cm (6 to 12in)).

Ivy – *See* **Hedera.**

Ixia (African corn lily) – Half-hardy bulbs which thrive in warm, dry, sunny borders or in the rock garden in rich, sandy loam enriched with leaf-mould or peat, or in pots in the cold greenhouse. *Culture* – Plant in September, 10cm (4in) deep and 7.5 (3in) apart. Do not lift, but in winter cover the bulbs with ashes or straw. *Pot culture* – Pot-up from August to September, placing bulbs in a 15cm (6in) pot in John Innes potting compost. Dry off after the foliage dies. Propagate by seed in a frame in September or by offsets in October. Seedlings take 3 years to flower. *Named varieties* – 'Bridesmaid' (white); 'King of the Yellows' (yellow); 'Queen of the Roses' (rose); 'Excelsior' (red); 'Vulcan' (scarlet and orange). All May and June, 38cm (15in).

Ixiolirion (ixia lily) – Half-hardy bulbous plants which grow about 38cm (15in) high, flower in June and do well in well-drained sandy loam in a warm, sunny border or rock garden. *Culture* – Plant in September, 12.5 (5in) deep and 7.5cm (3in) apart; do not lift the bulbs, but protect them with straw during the winter. If grown in pots, treat as Ixia.

Jacobean Lily – *See* **Sprekelia.**

Jamesia americana – Hardy deciduous flowering shrub which likes a damp rich soil and a sunny position. *Culture* – Plant from October to November; thin out branches when overcrowded. To propagate, sow seed when ripe, or in autumn strike cuttings.

Jasminum (jasmine) – *J. officinale*, the common white jasmine which blooms in June and July, is the best known; *J. humile* 'Revolutum', with yellow flowers in May, is better grown in bush form; *J. nudiflorum* has yellow flowers in winter and is useful outdoors or in the cold greenhouse; there are also beautiful hot house species. Hardy kinds like rich loam and most do well against walls and pergolas facing north or west. *Culture* – Strike cuttings of ripe wood in summer in a frame, or layer. Plant out from October to March, and after flowering prune shoots that have bloomed. *Pot culture* (*Cold house*) – Pot-up in February or March, using 15 to 20cm (6to 8in) pots and John Innes potting compost; give weak liquid fertilizer twice a week as soon as the buds form. (*Warm house*) – Pot-up in March; keep moist and syringe frequently until the plants have bloomed, then keep moderately dry.

Juglans (walnut) – Hardy deciduous nut-bearing trees which thrive in well-drained loam in a sunny, open position. *Culture* – Plant in October when 3 to 4 years old. Thin out branches when overcrowded. To propagate, plant nuts 10cm (4in) deep in the open. *J. regia* (common walnut).

Juniperus (juniper) – Handsome coniferous shrubs which thrive in the sun in moist, well-drained and deep loam with mortar rubble. *Culture* – Plant in May or September; no pruning is required. To propagate, strike cuttings in a frame in September, or raise from seed.

Kalmia (American laurel) – Hardy evergreen shrubs which should be treated as rhododendrons; they are also suitable for gentle forcing. To propagate, sow in a frame in spring, strike cuttings in a frame or layer in October. *Species* – the best known are *K. latifolia*, the calico bush, or mountain laurel (rose and white, June, 2.5 to 4.5m (8 to 15ft)); *K. angustifolia*, the sheep laurel (purple red, June, 90cm (3ft)).

Kerria (jew's mallow) – Hardy deciduous shrubs, bearing orange flowers in March and April. *K. japonica* (1m (4ft) single) and vars. 'Pleniflora' (2.5m (8 to 9ft) double) and 'Variegata' are usually grown; as climbers they run up to double the heights mentioned. They do well in sandy soil in sunny positions against walls facing south or west. *Culture* – Strike cuttings of young shoots in a frame in autumn, or propagate by division of roots in late autumn. Plant out from October to March. About June or early July cut out the oldest wood. *Pot culture* – In the cool greenhouse *K.j.* 'Pleniflora' may be had in flower in February. Pot-up annually in October using 20 to 25cm (8 to 10in) pots and John Innes potting compost. Prune after flowering and plant outdoors.

Kniphofia (tritoma, red-hot poker, flame flower, torch lily) – Tall hardy perennials which thrive in well-drained and deep sandy soil in sunny or partially shaded borders; they may also be potted-up in April or November in 20 to 25cm (8 to 10in) pots and grown in the cold greenhouse. *Species* – *K. uvaria* 'Grandiflora' (orange red, July to September, 175cm (70in)); *K. macowanii* (orange, September to October, 45cm (18in)). Named varieties are more readily available.

Kochia (summer cypress) – Half-hardy annuals useful for summer bedding, for borders and the cold greenhouse.

Laburnum (golden rain or golden chain) – Hardy deciduous trees with yellow flowers in May; almost any soil and a sunny position suit them well. *Culture* – Plant in November; trim back weak shoots after flowering and cut out dead wood in winter. To propagate, sow in a frame in spring; budding and grafting are sometimes resorted to. The seeds are poisonous.

Lachenalia (Cape cowslip) – Beautiful bulbous-rooted flowering plants suitable for greenhouse culture. *Culture* – Pot-up in August, 1cm (½in) deep in a compost of peaty loam. Put one bulb in a 10cm (4in) pot or 5 bulbs in a 15 to 17.5cm (6 to 7in) pot. Keep in a cold, frost-proof frame until early December, watering only when dry, then transfer to a shelf near the glass in the greenhouse (10°C (50°F)) and water as growth begins. Keep quite dry in pots from May to August. Propagate by offsets in August. *Named species and varieties* – *L. bulbifera* (red and yellow); *L. aloides* (golden yellow); *L.a.* hybrids (yellow green, tipped red).

Lantana – Bushy evergreen, half-hardy shrubs, 15 to 20cm (6 to 8in) high, flowering from June to September. Useful for the greenhouse and flower garden. *Culture* – Pot-up as soon as the young shoots break after pruning, using 15 to 17.5cm (6 to 7in) pots and John Innes potting compost No. 3. Syringe in spring and summer. If planted out during the summer, they must be wintered indoors. Seeds sown in heat (24°C (75°F) in March make summer and autumn-blooming plants. They are also propagated in spring or autumn by cuttings of half-matured wood in heat.

Lapageria – Beautiful evergreen climbers for the cool greenhouse, which require a well-drained loam mixed with sand and an equal portion of peat. They grow to a height of 3m (10ft) and flower in October and November. *Culture* – Propagate by seed sown as soon as ripe in gentle heat or by layers after flowering, the latter being the best way. Pot firmly, or plant in border in March; shade and water well. Cut out weak shoots only after flowering. *Species and varieties* – *L. rosea* (rose); and *L.r.* 'Albiflora' (white).

Larix (larch) – One of the few deciduous conifers. It grows from 9 to 30m (30 to 100ft) in height and thrives in a sunny position and in ordinary soil. *Culture* – Plant in October. Remove dead wood when necessary. Propagate by seed in the open in November. *Species* – *L. decidua* (*europaea*) (common larch); *L.* x *pendula* (weeping larch); *L. kaempferi* (Japanese larch).

Larkspur – *See* **Delphinium.**

Lathyrus (everlasting pea, sweet pea) – Annual and perennial climbing plants, the most popular of which are the sweet pea and the everlasting pea.

Everlasting pea (*L. latifolius*) – Beautiful hardy climber. Moist, good soil and a sunny position suit it best. *Named varieties* – 'White Pearl' (white); and 'Pink Beauty' (carmine rose). Both June to September, 1.8m (6ft).

Sweet pea (*L. odoratus*) – Sweetly scented annual climber. Sweet peas enjoy a rich soil properly prepared prior to sowing. Dig out a trench 60cm (2ft) wide to a depth of from 60 to 90cm (2 to 3ft) with a good supply of well-rotted manure worked into the lower 25cm (10in). Sweet peas can be sown in the open on a dry day, generally early in March, but rather earlier in a warm sheltered situation. It is often beneficial to soak the seeds in warm water overnight to soften the hard seed coats. The seed should be sown 3.5m (1½in) deep and 7.5cm (3in) apart. When about 10cm (4in) high, thin out to 15cm (6in) apart and support by means of twigs. As the plants grow taller, stakes 2 to 2.5m (7 to 8ft) in height can be placed in position. To secure the finest blooms, however, sow the seeds in late autumn or early in February in 12.5cm (5in) pots, placing 6 seeds in each, or a single seed in a small pot. The seeds may also be sown some 5cm (2in) apart in boxes about 10cm (4in) deep, but the seedlings must be potted off singly as soon as possible. Raise the young plants on a shelf near the glass in a cool greenhouse or in a frost-proof frame. Before being planted out into the open, early in March, when the plants are about 10cm (4in) high, they should be hardened off in a cold frame. Not more than 3 growths should be allowed to develop from each root, and when the plants have grown to 1m (3 to 4ft) high give them a weak liquid feed once a week. Plants raised like this for exhibition should flower from early June to late September; if desired, early in May blooms may be had by growing the peas in the greenhouse. After-care is very simple, but it is of prime importance to remove faded flowers before they set seed. If seeds are required, a portion of the row or one clump may be set apart for the purpose. The tips should be pinched out when they reach 15 to 20cm (6 to 8in) above the top of the stakes, and the soil between the plants should be kept continually stirred. Named varieties are innumerable and catalogues should be consulted.

Laurel – *See* **Prunus laurocerasus;** *P. lusitanica.*

Laurus (bay) – This genus includes two species only, *Laurus azorica* and *L. nobilis* (evergreen), the true bay laurel or sweet bay. The latter thrives in well-drained fibrous loam and peat in a sheltered position in sun or shade. Strike cuttings in a frame in August.

Lavandula (lavender) – The best-known species, *L. spica* (mauve to white), the common lavender, thrives in light and well-drained soil in sunny position, grows about 90cm (3ft) high and flowers in July and August. *Culture* – Plant in March or September and clip after flowering. To propagate, strike cuttings in October.

Lavatera (mallow) – Hardy annuals, biennials and perennials, which thrive in the sun in any soil. *Species* (*Annual*) – *L. trimestris* (rose or white). (*Biennial*) – *L. arborea* (violet). (*Perennial*) – *L. thuringiaca* (blue). All July to September, 75 to 150cm (30 to 60in).

Layia (tidy tips) – Hardy annuals suitable for sunny beds, borders or rock gardens. *Species* – *L. elegans* (yellow, margined white); *L. glandulosa* (white). All July to September, 25cm (10in).

Leontopodium alpinum (edelweiss) – Hardy alpine plant which requires a sunny position, in sandy loam. The cream white, star-shaped flowers are borne from June to September on stems 15cm (6in) high.

Leptospermum – Evergreen shrubs which thrive in the cool greenhouse in a peaty compost. *L. scoparium* (white) may be grown outdoors in a warm, sheltered situation. Propagate by cuttings (with bottom heat) in May or by seed in slight heat in March. *Species and varieties* – *L. scoparium* 'Chapmanii' (rose, 120cm (50in)); *L.s.* 'Nichollsii' (carmine, 2m (80in)). June to August flowering.

Leptosyne – now included in **Coreopsis.**

Leucojum (snowflake) – Hardy bulbs which thrive in any garden soil in semi-shade and are useful for borders or the rock garden. *Culture* – Plant in September 7.5 to 10cm (3 to 4in) deep and 12.5cm (5in) apart; lift every 7 years. Propagate by offsets or by seed. *Species* – *L. aestivum* (white, spotted green, May, 38cm (15in)); *L. autumnale* (white, tinged red, October, 25cm (10in)).

Lewisia (bitter-root) – Useful little rock plants for a dry sunny crevice and in gritty loam. Protect from wet in winter. *Species* – *L. cotyledon* (pink, striped buff or white, May to June, 10cm (4in)); *L. rediviva* (pink and white, May to August); *L. tweedyi* (salmon pink, 20cm (8in)).

Liatris (blazing star or Kansas feather) – Hardy perennials, better grown as biennials. They thrive in almost any soil in a warm, sunny border. *Species* – *L. graminifolia* (pink, 90cm (36in)); *L. spicata* (mauve purple, 45cm (18in)). All August to October.

Libocedrus (incense cedar, syn. *Calocedrus*) – Hardy and half-hardy evergreen coniferous trees, the most popular species of which is *L. decurrens*. It likes a well-drained loam and a warm, sheltered position. *Culture* – Sow seed October to April, or strike cuttings in a frame in September.

Ligustrum (privet) – Hardy evergreen and deciduous shrubs, usually grown as hedge plants but poisonous to cattle. They thrive in ordinary soil and in full sun. *Culture* – Plant from November to March; clip in summer and cut out dead wood. To propagate, strike cuttings in the open in autumn. *Species* – *L. ovalifolium* (common privet) and *L.o.* 'Aureum' (golden privet) are those most used. *L. lucidum* is a tall evergreen privet.

Lilac – *See* **Syringa.**

Lilium (lily) – There are many different species and varieties of lilies, but they are for the most part hardy bulbous perennials requiring practically the same management. Lilies thrive in deep, well-dug garden soil or in a moist, well-drained fibrous loam with well-decayed leaf-mould. A few, such as *L. auratum*, *L. giganteum* (*Cardiocrinum*) and *L. pardalinum*, love a peaty soil.

Culture – Plant in October in groups of 5 to 7, 10 to 12.5cm (4 to 5in) deep (about 3 times their own depth), and from 15 to 30cm (6 to 12in) apart, according to species; the bulbs should, as a rule, when planted, rest on sand, and they should not be disturbed more often than every 3 years. A yearly top-dressing of well-decayed manure each spring will be beneficial. Lilies which form roots from the base of the stem should be planted among low-growing shrubs; these particular lilies may be planted at any time, and somewhat deeper than the non-stem-rooting kinds. When in bloom, all lilies should be carefully staked and all dead flowers should at once be removed, but the stems must not be cut down until they have died off. The madonna lily (*L. candidum*) requires different treatment. Transplant this lily in August, only lift when necessary and top-dress with well-rotted manure each spring. *Pot culture* – Plant in late autumn; a 30cm (12in) pot will take 6 bulbs, a large bulb of *L. auratum* would require a 25cm (10in) pot to itself. The bulbs should be covered by 2.5cm (1in) of soil which should be made firm, and care must be taken that the bulbs do not touch the sides of the pots. They should be treated in their first stage of growth as hyacinths grown in pots, except that the pots must be only partly filled with soil. Bury the pots in ashes or soil, in a frame till the plants begin to grow, when, as the stems grow, the pots are gradually filled up to within about 2.5cm (1in) of the rim. Those intended to flower early should be placed under glass, while late bloomers should remain out of doors in a sheltered situation. Propagation is by offsets in October, by planting scales from bulbs in sandy soil in a cold frame, or seed in pans in cold frames in August. Seedlings of most species do not flower until they are 2 to 5 years old.

Species and varieties – *L. auratum* (Japanese lily) (white, yellow and crimson, August to September, 100cm (40in)); *L. candidum* (madonna lily) (white, June to July, 120cm (50in)); *L. chalcedonicum* (turk's cap) (bright scarlet, July to August, 100cm (40in)); *L. bulbiferum* (orange, July to August, 90 to 150cm (36 to 60in)); *L. formosanum* (trumpet lily) (white, July to August, 75cm (30in)); *L. martagon* (rosy violet, wine red and white, July, 100cm (40in)); *L. paradalinum* (panther lily) (scarlet, orange and yellow, July, 150cm (60in)); *L. regale* (white and yellow, July, 60 to 100cm (24 to 40in)); *L.* x *testaceum* (syn. x *excelsum*) (Nankeen lily) (petals yellow, anthers scarlet, June to July, 150cm (60in)); *L. tigrinum* (tiger lily) (scarlet orange, dark purple spots, August to September, 120cm (50in)). There are numerous hybrids all classified according to origin; consult catalogues for the best varieties.

Lily of the Valley – *See* **Convallaria.**

Limnanthes – Dwarf hardy annuals, which flower in summer and are useful for edging or rock garden.

Limonium (statice, sea lavender) – These beautiful annual and perennial everlasting flowers thrive in sunny borders or in the rock garden in well-drained sandy loam and leaf-mould. Nearly all the annuals are better treated as half-hardy. *Pot culture* – Pot-up half-hardy species in John Innes potting compost No. 2. Pot on as the roots fill the pots, until 20 to 22.5cm (8 to 9in) pots are reached. *Species* (*Half-hardy annual*) – *L. sinuatum* (mauve, white and rose, June to October, 38 to 75cm (15 to 30in)); *L. suworowii* (rosy purple or white, June to October, 30 to 45cm (12 to 18in)). (*Hardy perennial*) – *L. gmelinii* (purple blue, July to September, 45 to to 60cm (18 to 24in)); *L. incanum* (red or pinky white, July to August, 38cm (15in)).

Linaria (toad flax) – These are mostly hardy annuals and perennials. All species like a light sandy soil and a sunny, dry position; the rock garden species need a gritty soil. *Species* (*Annual*) – *L. bipartita* (red, white or purple, 30cm (12in)); *L. reticulata* (yellow and purple, 30 to 45cm (12 to 18in)). (*Perennial*) – *L. alpina* (violet, blotched orange, 7.5cm (3in)); *L. dalmatica* (orange and yellow, 100cm (40in)). All June to September. Many others.

Linum (flax or linseed-oil plant) – Hardy annuals and perennials which thrive in dry, light soil in a sunny position. The rock garden species need the addition of grit. *Pot culture* – Pot-up in March or April, using 12.5 to 15cm (5 to 6in) pots and John Innes potting compost No. 2. In February or March prune back the previous year's growth to within a 2.5cm (1in) from the base. *Species* (*Annual*) – *L. grandiflorum* (crimson scarlet, black centre, summer, 30cm (12in)); *L. usitatissimum* (blue, July to October, 60cm (24in)). (*Perennial*) – *L. alpinum* (blue, May to June, 15 to 22.5cm (6 to 9in)); *L. flavum* (golden, June to September, 25cm (10in)); *L. narbonense* (deep blue, May to September, 30 to 60cm (12 to 24in)); *L. perenne* (pale blue, May to September, 30 to 60cm (12 to 24in)).

Lippia (sweet verbena) – Only one kind of this sweet-smelling deciduous shrub is grown to any extent. *L. citriodora* (syn. *Aloysia triphylla*) has purple blooms in August. It can be grown in the open or against a wall in the south and west of England and in other parts it is suitable for the cold greenhouse, but requires protection from the frost in winter, even under shelter. *Culture* – Re-pot into a smaller pot in the spring in a rich loam-based compost; when well rooted transfer to a larger pot. It succeeds also in the warm greenhouse. Cut young shoots hard back to the old wood in February. *L. citriodora* has lemon-scented foliage.

Liquidambar styraciflua (sweet gum) – Hardy deciduous trees, growing 12 to 24m (50 to 80ft) high and which like a cool, moist ordinary soil and a sunny position. Propagate by seed or by cuttings. Splendid autumn foliage.

Liriodendron (tulip tree) – Tall deciduous trees, flowering in July and August, and which thrive in well-drained soil in a sunny position. *Culture* – Plant in November; in autumn cut out dead wood. To propagate, sow seed in a frame in March. Clear yellow autumn foliage.

Lithospermum – Hardy trailing evergreen shrubs and perennials, which do well in a mixture of gritty loam and peat in moderately sunny positions, and are excellent for dry walls, rock gardens and for edging. *Species* – *L. diffusum* (syn. *Lithodora diffusa*) (blue); *L. oleifolium* (syn. *Lithodora oleifolia*) (blue). Both June to September.

Lobelia – Genus of half-hardy annuals and perennials, of which the low-growing kinds are suitable for edging, thriving in deep, well manured and moist soil in sunny positions. All varieties of the greenhouse perennial *L. erinus* are valuable for edging and for hanging baskets or vases. Treat all these as half-hardy annuals. The tall perennial species are valuable in the mixed border. *Culture* (*Annuals*) – If required for greenhouse use pot-up singly into 7.5 to 10cm (3 to 4in) pots in John Innes potting compost No. 1. (*Perennials*) – As soon as the foliage is dead in autumn, cut the stems down and lift the roots and store in boxes of dry soil in a frost-proof frame; water in March to re-start growth and late in April divide the roots and plant out. *Pot culture* – (*L. erinus* and vars.) – Pot up in March, using 15 to 20cm (6 to 8in) pots and a compost as above; keep in a frame until about to bloom, then transfer to the cool greenhouse. After blooming, cut down the flower stems, return to the frame in October, and cover with ashes for the winter; give a good watering in February, and a month later divide and re-pot if necessary. *Species and varieties* (*Annual*) – *L. erinus* 'Crystal Palace' (double, dark blue); 'Cambridge Blue' (dark); and 'Sapphire' (trailing). All July to October, 15cm (6in)); *L. tenuior* (blue, white eye, 30cm (12in)). (*Perennial*) – *L. cardinalis* (crimson scarlet, 60 to 90cm (24 to 36in)); *L. fulgens* (scarlet, 75cm (30in)); *L. siphilitica* (blue and white, 60 to 75cm (24 to 30in)). All June to September.

Lonicera (honeysuckle) – Genus comprising all the trailing and climbing hardy and half-hardy deciduous and evergreen plants known as honeysuckles. These thrive in any good, moderately dry garden soil and frequently in shaded positions. *Culture* – Strike cuttings of ripe shoots in the open in late summer; let the cuttings stand in the bed for a year, then plant out from October to April. If preferred, propagate by layering or from seed. After flowering cut away old wood and trim back shoots. *L. periclymenum* 'Belgica' and *L.p.* 'Serotina', the early and late Dutch honeysuckles, are excellent. *L. sempervirens* forms a beautiful greenhouse climber, and *L. standishii* and *L. fragrantissima* (bush honeysuckles) flower outside early in February. *Pot culture* – Pot-up in late autumn in a compost of sandy loam, leaf-mould and rotten manure, and keep in a cold house until February, then move to a sunny position in the cool house; the plants may be stood out from June to October.

Lunaria annua (honesty) – Hardy biennials, 60 to 75cm (24 to 30in) high, carrying purple, mauve or white flowers. They thrive in semi-shaded borders or wild garden in moderately rich soil.

Lupinus (lupin) – Hardy annuals and perennials valuable for borders and wild gardens; the dwarf species are excellent for bedding. They thrive in light, rich and well-drained soil deficient in lime and in sunny positions. Stake the plants early in exposed positions, cut the stems to the ground after blooming and mulch with well-decayed manure. *Species and varieties* (*Annuals*) – *L. hartwegii* (pale blue); *L. nanus* (lilac blue and white). (*Perennials*) – *L. arboreus* (yellow, white and blue); *L. polyphyllus* (Russell hybrids).

Lychnis (catchfly, campion, ragged robin, rose of heaven) – Hardy annuals, biennials and perennials which thrive in any good soil, especially in rich light loam, and like a sunny position; the rock garden species need a gritty loam. *Species and varieties* – *L. chalcedonica* (scarlet and white, June to September, 75cm (30in)); *L. fulgens* (salmon, June to September, 30cm (12in)); *L. haageana* (crimson, July to Agust, 30cm (12in)).

Lysimachia (creeping Jenny, moneywort or loosestrife) – These herbaceous perennials do best in moist, rich, ordinary soil in semi-shade. The low-growing species make excellent subjects for carpeting in the rock garden; the taller kinds for border or wild garden. *Culture* – Propagate by division in April or October, no protection is required during winter. *Species* (*Tall*) – *L. clethroides* (white, 75cm (30in)); *L. punctata* (yellow, 75cm (30in)). (*Dwarf*) – *L. nummularia* 'Aurea' (creeping Jenny) (yellow, trailer). All June to September.

Lythrum (purple loosestrife) – Hardy perennials thriving in rich, sandy soil in shady, moist borders, or in the wild garden. *Species* – *L. salicaria* (purple and rose, 120cm (50in)); *L. virgatum* 'Rose Queen' (rose, 100cm (40in)). All June to September.

Macleaya (*Bocconia*) (plume poppy) – Hardy perennial which thrives in sunny borders and light, rich soil.

Species – *M. cordata* (whitish cream, June to October, 175cm (70in)); *M. microcarpa* (creamy bronze, June to October, 2.2m (90in)).

Magnolia – Hardy and half-hardy deciduous and evergreen shrubs which need a good, deep, well-drained loam and a sunny position. Transplant as little as possible and prune when required (which is but rarely) in summer. *Culture* (*Hardy species*) – *M. denudata*, *M.* x *soulangiana* and *M. stellata*, etc. Plant in April or October. Propagate by grafting under glass in spring, layering, cuttings and seeds. *M. grandiflora* – Plant in

April or September. To propagate, sow seed in a frame, strike cuttings of matured wood of the current year in heat in July, or layer during that period. *Pot culture* – (generally *M. stellata*) – Pot-up in October or November, using 20 to 30cm (8 to 12in) pots and a loam-based potting compost. After flowering prune out weak wood and dead flower shoots, and sink the pots to their rims outdoors from May to December, when the pots should be moved into the house.

Malcolmia maritima (Virginian stock) – Hardy annual which thrives in sunny beds and in fairly light soil and which is useful for edgings. *Varieties* – 'Fairy Queen' (purple and crimson); 'Crimson King'. Both June to October, 15cm (6in).

Malope trifida (mallow) – Tall hardy annuals useful for sunny beds or borders. Flowers are crimson, red and white.

Malus (crab apple) – Genus of hardy deciduous trees at one time included in *Pyrus*. Most species bear delicate blossom and ornamental fruit. *Culture* – Plant in November in sunny position, sheltered from cold winds. *Pot culture* – Pot-up annually (when small) in October, using 20 to 30cm (8 to 12in) pots and a loam-based compost. In December propagate by means of seed, budding or grafting. There are numerous species and varieties.

Malva (marsh mallow) – Hardy and half-hardy annuals and perennials which like a well-drained border of ordinary soil and a sunny position. *Species* (*Hardy annuals*) – *M. verticillata* (white, 150cm (60in)). (*Hardy perennials*) – *M. alcea* (purple red, 120cm (50in)); *M. moschata* (rose and white, 75cm (30in)). All June to September.

Marguerite – *See* **Chrysanthemum frutescens**

Matthiola (stock) – Beautiful annuals and biennials, which thrive in the sun in a rich and not too dry soil with lime in it. Before being set out in their flowering positions, seedlings should be examined to see that they are double, the single-flowered being discarded; seedlings that will produce double-flowered plants generally have long, pale green, concave leaves, while the foliage of the single-flowered is, as a rule, deeper in colour, convex and more rigid.

The ten-weeks' stock (*Matthiola annua*) is a favourite for bedding. This half-hardy annual grows 15 to 60cm (6 to 24in) high, and usually blooms 10 to 12 weeks after being sown.

Intermediate stocks – These provide flowers in the borders from June to October, and are excellent in a cold greenhouse for flowering in late winter and early spring. For spring-flowering, sow thinly in light soil in boxes or pots in a cold frame in August. Thin or transplant singly into small pots when large enough to handle, using a loam-based potting compost. Stand the pots in the open until frost is imminent, then transfer to the cold greenhouse in January and keep near the glass, or if for summer flowering in the open, keep them in a frame until April, when harden off and plant out in May. If preferred, treat as ten-weeks' stocks.

East Lothian stocks – These are half-hardy biennials which bloom from June to September, and are popular for bedding. For early flowering, sow during July in pans of compost in a cold frame. Winter in cold frames and plant out the flowering spring. If preferred these stocks may be treated as half-hardy annuals.

Brompton or Giant stocks – These are half-hardy biennials flowering in May, June and July. The seed should be sown in July, thinly in drills about 15cm (6in) apart in a light, sandy bed. When about 7.5cm(3in) high, thin out the seedlings to 15cm (6in) apart, winter in a cold frame and plant out in March.

Nice or Winter-flowering stocks – For winter-flowering in the cool greenhouse sow in a frame and transfer to the cool house early in December. For spring-flowering, sow in a frame in August, grow as above and take into the house when winter-flowering plants are over.

Night-scented stock (*M. bicornis*) – This most fragrant of hardy annuals likes a fairly rich soil.

Marvel of Peru – *See* **Mirabilis.**

Mazus – Hardy creeping perennials that are excellent for the paved or rock garden, and which thrive in well-drained loam and in sunny positions. *Species* – *M. pumilio* (purple mauve); *M. reptans* (mauve).

Meconopsis – The best of this genus are hardy herbaceous perennials or biennials. They thrive in gritty loam and peat, and in partial shade in borders or rock gardens. *Species* (*Biennial*) – *M. integrifolia* (yellow, 38 to 50cm (15 to 20in)); *M. horridula* (blue purple, 50 to 90cm (20 to 36in)); *M. regia* (yellow, 1 to 1.5m (4 to 5ft)); *M. napaulensis* (blue, 1 to 2m (4 to 7ft)). (*Perennial*) – *M. betonicifolia* (blue, 1m (3 to 4ft)); *M. cambrica* (yellow, orange, double, 30 to 45cm (12 to 18in)); *M. grandis* (blue, 1 to 1.5m (4 to 5ft)). All May to August.

Mentzelia lindleyi (*Bartonia*) – Pretty little hardy annual for the border or rock garden. It grows to a height of 38cm (15in) and bears yellow flowers from June to October.

Menyanthes trifoliata (bog bean) – Hardy perennial which thrives in ordinary soil and a sunny position in bog or in still, shallow water. It bears rosy lilac flowers from March to June. *Culture* – Strike cuttings in mud in summer; plant out in March.

Mesembryanthemum – Useful half-hardy annuals and perennials for rock work, thriving in good soil, in a dry sunny situation.

Michaelmas Daisy – *See* **Aster.**

Mignonette – *See* **Reseda.**

Mimulus (musk or monkey flower) – Hardy and half-hardy annuals and hardy perennials. Seed of the annuals sown in spring makes good bedding plants, and seed sown in autumn produces early flowering plants for the greenhouse. They like a shady site with moist, rich soil. The smaller species are useful for edging and for the rock garden. *Pot culture* – Pot-up in May, using 12.5 to 15cm (5 to 6in) pots and John Innes potting compost No. 2. Pinch back to make bushy, and keep cool in winter. *Species and varieties* (*Half-hardy annual*) – *M.* x *tigrinus* (yellow, spotted, June, 22.5cm (9in)). (*Hardy perennials*) – *M.* x *burnettii* (pale brown, 25cm (10in)); *M. cardinalis* (scarlet, 50cm (20in)); *M. cupreus* (orange, 30cm (12in)); *M. luteus* (yellow, spotted, 22.5cm (9in)); *M. moschatus* (yellow, 15cm (6in)); *M. ringens* (pale blue, 25cm (10in)). All flower from June to August.

Mirabilis jalapa (marvel of Peru) – Greenhouse and hardy perennials which grow best in sunny positions and in a light, rich loam, but do well in any good garden soil. They are best treated in the same manner as dahlias, and can be grown from seeds sown in gentle heat from March to April, hardened off and planted out in May. Flowers red, pink and white.

Miscanthus (zebra-striped grass) – Hardy perennial grass, suitable for borders and cool greenhouses. It thrives in ordinary soil and is propagated by division in March or April.

Mistletoe – *See* **Viscum.**

Monarda (bee's balm, horse mint, Oswego tea, red sage or bergamot) – Useful perennials thriving in deep, moist loam in sunny borders. They will, however, grow anywhere. *Species* – *M. didyma* (red, July to September, 60cm (24in)); *M. fistulosa* (pink, July to September, 60cm (24in)). *Varieties* – 'Melissa' (pink); 'Snow Maiden'.

Montbretia – *See* **Crocosmia.**

Morina (whorl-flower) – Half-hardy and hardy perennials, excellent for the border or rock garden. They like a warm, sunny position and a rich gritty loam. In exposed districts winter in a frame. Sow in March, or propagate by offsets. *Species – M. longifolia* (rose and white); *M. persica* (pink). Both July to August, 75cm (30in).

Morisia monanthos (syn. *M. hypogaea*) (Mediterranean cress) – Hardy little summer-flowering rock plants which thrive in well-drained, deep, gritty loam in an open, fairly sunny spot.

Morus (mulberry) – Hardy deciduous trees which thrive in the sun in deep, moist but well-drained ordinary soil. They grow 7.5 to 9m (25 to 30ft) high and flower in May and June. *Culture* – Plant in October, and do not shorten the long tap roots; little pruning is necessary. Propagate by cuttings or layers in October.

Muscari (grape hyacinth) – Hardy bulbous plants which thrive in good loam in warm, sunny borders or in the rock garden, or in pots. *Culture* – Plant in October from 5 to 7.5cm (2 to 3in) deep and 7.5cm (3in) apart; lift from the ground only when overcrowded. Propagate by offsets in October. *Pot culture* – Pot-up annually in October, 3.5cm (1½in) deep in 12.5cm (5in) pots; dry off in a cold frame after flowering. *Species (Early) – M. botryoides* (blue and white varieties, February to March, 15cm (6in)). *(Late) – M. armeniacum* 'Heavenly Blue' (sky blue, April to May, 20cm (8in)); *M. racemosum* (deep blue, April to May, 15cm (6in)).

Myosotis (forget-me-not) – There are annual and perennial species, some of the latter being grown as biennials. All thrive in the sun in ordinary soil, and are useful for bedding, for the rock garden and for the cool greenhouse. *Pot culture* – Pot in October, using 10 to 12.5cm (4 to 5in) pots and sandy soil and keep in a cold frame through the winter; move into the cool house in early spring. *Species – M. cespitosa* (*M. rehsteineri*) (blue, April to May, 5cm (2in)); *M. dissitiflora* (light blue, April to June, 15 to 22.5cm (6 to 9in)); *M. palustris* (sky blue and yellow, May to September, 15 to 22.5cm (6 to 9in)); *M. sylvatica* (blue, pink and white, June to August, 15cm (6in)).

Myrtus (myrtle) – Beautiful evergreen greenhouse shrubs which will grow out of doors in warm, sunny and sheltered situations. *Culture* – Plant in May or September in loam and leaf-mould; the addition of a little peat is beneficial. Trim in April. *Pot culture* – Pot-up in March using 12.5 to 30cm (5 to 12in) pots and a loamy compost; stand outdoors from July to October, and prune in February. To propagate, strike cuttings in a frame in July, or layer in September.

Narcissus – Beautiful hardy bulbs which are excellent for beds, borders, the rock garden (most species), for naturalizing in grass, and for pots. Most species thrive in well-dug and well-drained ordinary soil, though some few, notably the 'Hooped Petticoat', the 'Cyclamen-flowered' and the 'Angel's Tears', prefer warm, deep and moist sandy loam; the 'Polyanthus narcissi' like a rather stiff soil. Partial shade is desirable, but they will grow well in full sun. *Culture* – Plant from August to October, the sooner the better, 10cm (4in) deep in heavy soil and 17.5cm (7in) deep in light soil, and about 10cm (4in) apart, making exception of small species which should be 5 to 7.5cm (2 to 3in) deep and the May-flowering double white narcissus, which must be not less than 15cm (6in) deep in well-worked moist loam. If used for naturalizing, the bulbs should be left in the ground, but in beds or borders they should be lifted and replanted every 3 years in July. *Greenhouse culture* – Pot-up from August to November, using bulb fibre or compost and place from 3 large to 12 small bulbs in a 10 to 12.5cm (4 to 5in) pot and keep in the open in a cool, shady site under a layer of soil until growth begins, then move into the cool house in batches. Dry off when the foliage dies and plant out in the open in the autumn. The bulbs of the 'Polyanthus narcissus' will need a 12.5cm (5in) pot for a single specimen. Daffodils will not stand forcing, and only gentle heat should be used. Propagate by offsets at lifting time, re-planting the offsets immediately in a nursery bed; seed may also be sown in pans or boxes in August, but they take 4 to 6 years to flower. *See* catalogues for varieties.

Nasturtium – *See* Tropaeolum.

Nemesia – Half-hardy annuals which make excellent bedding, rock garden or pot plants. *Species* – *N. floribunda* (white and yellow); *N. strumosa* (red, pink, orange, yellow, blue and white); *N. versicolor* (white and mauve). All June to September, 30cm (12in).

Nemophila (Californian bluebell) – Dwarf-growing hardy annuals for edgings to sunny beds, or for the rock garden. *Species* – *N. menziesii* (purple, blue, white, blotched black, July to September, 7.5 to 22.5cm (3 to 9in)).

Nepeta (catmint) – Hardy perennials which thrive in sunny positions and in ordinary soil, and are useful for edgings to large borders, or for the rock garden. *Species* – *N.* x *faassenii* (blue, May to September, 45cm (18in)).

Nerine – Beautiful bulbous plants which thrive in the cool greenhouse in John Innes potting compost No. 2. *N. bowdenii* is hardy enough to survive outside in warm corners. *Culture* – Plant singly in August in 10 to 12.5cm (4 to 5in) pots, water well when the flower buds appear and feed with liquid fertilizer. Keep dry from June to August, with the pots exposed to the sun, and when the flower shoots reappear soak the pots and top-dress with fresh soil. Re-pot every fourth year, and propagate by offsets in August, or sow seed when ripe. *Species and varieties* – *N. bowdenii* (pink); *N. pudica* (white); *N. sarniensis* (pale salmon); *N.s. corusca* (orange scarlet); many hybrids. All September to December, 50cm (20in).

Nerium – The best known of this genus of evergreen shrub is *N. oleander*, the common oleander. The blossoms and wood are poisonous. *Culture* – Pot when required in February, using 15 to 30cm (6 to 12in) pots and John Innes potting compost No. 2. Keep in a sunny position in the cool greenhouse, and sponge the leaves frequently. Remove the shoots at the base of the flower buds and prune to within 3 buds of the old wood. Keep fairly dry during winter. To propagate, place cuttings of well-ripened shoots in water, in a sunny frame in summer; when well rooted, pot-up in light soil and stop from time to time.

Nicotiana (tobacco plant) – Although treated as annuals, tobacco plants are perennials, and if the roots are protected from frost they will come up again year after year. Among the sorts usually grown are *N. alata* and *N.* x *sanderae*. The first has white flowers, fragrant in the evening; the second bears red or white flowers, but these are not so fragrant. They thrive in rich soil in sunny beds and borders. For greenhouse use, seed sown in a frame in August will bloom from January to March.

Nigella (love-in-a-mist) – Hardy annuals useful for sunny beds and borders. *Species and varieties* – *N. damascena* (pale blue or white); *N. hispanica* (deep purple); *N.* 'Miss Jekyll' (deep blue, double). All June to September, 45cm (18in).

Nuphar – Genus numbering but a few species, among which is *N. lutea*, the yellow water lily. This is hardy and, like all of its kind, may be grown in a pond or slow stream, and managed in the same way as *Nymphaea*. *Species* – *N. advena* and *N. lutea*. Both yellow, June to August, 30 to 45cm (12 to 18in).

Nymphaea – Genus of water lilies, including the common white water lily. The hardy species have white, rose, orange or yellow flowers. Most species like a sunny, sheltered position in slow-moving water; those from hot countries require a hothouse. *Culture* – Sow seed in spring in rich loam in a basket under water, or propagate by division from April to June and plant in rich loam in weighted openwork baskets sunk so that there is from 30 to 150cm (12 to 60in) of water above the crowns, according to species. Many good species and hybrids.

Nyssa sylvatica (Tupelo tree) – Hardy deciduous tree thriving in moist deep loam, or any good soil in sunny positions. *Culture* – Plant in November (as young as possible). No pruning is necessary. Propagate by seed or layering. It does not transplant well. Leaves brilliant red in autumn.

Oenothera (evening primrose) – Biennials and perennials for bedding, borders or for the rock garden, and also grown in the greenhouse. All the species thrive in rich, sandy loam, or any good soil and in sunny positions. *Species* (*Biennial*) – *O. acaulis* (white, tinted rose, 25cm (10in)); *O. biennis* 'Grandiflora' (pale yellow, 75cm (30in)). (*Perennials*) — *O.* (*Pachylophus*) *caespitosa* (pale yellow or white, 10 to 15cm (4 to 6in)); *O.* (*Kneiffia*) *tetragona fraseri* (golden yellow, 50cm (20in)); *O.* (*Megapterium*) *missouriensis* (yellow, trailer); *O. speciosa* (white to rose, 75cm (30in)). All June to October flowering.

Olearia haastii (New Zealand daisy bush) – Hardy evergreen shrubs from 1 to 3m (4 to 9ft) high bearing white flowers in late summer. They like a sheltered position and well-drained soil. *Culture* – Plant in May or October. Trim to shape when necessary in March, and every 4 or 5 years, cut hard back. *Pot culture of greenhouse species* – In the cool greenhouse they may be had in flower in March. Pot-up when required in October, using 15 to 17.5cm (6 to 7in) pots and John Innes potting compost No. 2. Sink the pots in a sunny spot outdoors from May to December, then take indoors and keep fairly dry until growth starts. To propagate, sow in a frame in March, or strike cuttings in a frame in September.

Omphalodes (creeping or rock forget-me-not, navelwort) – Annual and perennial creeping plants for semi-shade in the border or rock garden and loving a moist, sandy or gritty loam. *Species* (*Annual*) – *O. linifolia* (white, July, 22.5cm (9in)). (*Perennial*) – *O. cappadocica* (porcelain blue, May to June, 22.5cm (9in)); *O. luciliae* (lilac blue, June to September, 15cm (6in)); *O. verna* (porcelain blue, April to May, 10cm (4in)).

Onosma (alpine comfrey) – Hardy perennial and biennial rock plants which thrive in well-drained, gritty loam, peat and sand on hot, sunny ledges. Sow under glass in March, or strike cuttings in summer. *Species* – *O. albo-roseum* (white, tinged rose); *O. stellulatum* (yellow). All June to July.

Orange (citrus – dwarf) – The dwarf fruiting species which are usually grown in the cool greenhouse are grafted plants. They thrive in John Innes potting compost No. 3. In winter they need full sun, but in summer should be shaded from direct sun. Trim to shape only. The trees may be propagated by seed in gentle heat (18°C (65°F)), by budding in July, or by grafting in March; but cuttings struck in spring produce bushes which fruit earlier. The culture of the lemon (*Citrus limonum*) and the lime (*Citrus aurantiifolia*) is identical with that of the orange.

Orchids – Besides the numerous beautiful orchids which may be grown in the greenhouse, there are several hardy species which thrive outdoors in sheltered borders, in the rock garden or bog garden, notably the *Cypripedium* (lady's slipper) and *Habenaria* (butterfly orchid). These thrive in moist loam in semi-shaded positions. Propagate by division in spring or autumn; in some cases by offsets. Greenhouse orchids vary considerably in their requirements and need careful attention. Space does not permit of these being dealt with thoroughly, and the reader is referred to a work devoted to orchid-growing.

Ornithogalum (star of Bethlehem) – Hardy and half-hardy bulbous-rooted plants, for warm borders, for the rock garden and naturalizing in grass, and (chiefly *O. arabicum*) for pots. They thrive in ordinary soil in sun or semi-shade. *Culture* – Plant from September to October, 9cm (3½in) deep and 7.5cm (3in) apart, and protect from frost in winter. *Pot culture* – Pot-up from August to November, placing 3 bulbs in a 15cm (6in) pot, or singly in a smaller pot, and using John Innes potting compost No. 2; grow near the glass in a cold greenhouse. Propagate by means of offsets. *Species* – *O. arabicum* (white with black centre, May and June, 75cm (30in)); *O. nutans* (greenish white, May, 38cm (15in)); *O. umbellatum* (white, green streaks, May, 25 to 38cm (10 to 15in)).

Orontium aquaticum (golden club) – Hardy aquatic plant which thrives in slow-moving water. Propagate by root division in March, and plant with from 15 to 30cm (6 to 12in) of water above the crowns.

Osmanthus – Hardy evergreen shrubs, some of which resemble hollies. *Culture* – Plant in May or September in sandy loam in sun or partial shade. No pruning is necessary, but long straggling shoots should be cut back in June. To propagate, strike cuttings of ripened shoots in a frame in September, or layer in summer. *O. delavayi* (white, March and April, 1 to 2m (4 to 7ft) is the best species. *O. heterophylla* has small, fragrant, white flowers in late autumn.

Osmunda regalis (royal fern) – Tall fern for waterside or other moist situation in rich soil. Rich brown in autumn. Leave dead fronds over crown for winter protection.

Ourisia – Hardy perennial creeping plants which thrive in moist sandy loam in the shade, and are excellent for moist ledges in the rock garden. *Species* – *O. coccinea* (scarlet, May to September, 22.5cm (9in)) is the best known.

Oxalis (Cape shamrock, wood sorrel) – Hardy and half-hardy annuals, perennials, and bulbous plants admirably suited for pots, warm borders, and the rock garden. They succeed in any well-drained, light, sandy soil and leaf-mould; the rock garden species need a gritty loam and a position in semi-shade. *Bulbous species* – Plant from September to November 7.5cm (3in) deep and 25cm (10in) apart. Hardy species should not be lifted from the ground, but half-hardy kinds must. In light warm soils, however, protection from frost by ashes or straw will be sufficient. Propagation is by small bulbs removed from the parent and planted in September. *Pot culture* – Pot-up in March 2cm (¾in) deep to 12.5 to 15cm (5 to 6in) pots of John Innes potting compost No. 1. *Species and varieties* (*Annual*) – *O. corniculata* (yellow, August to October, 10cm (4in)); *O rosea* (rosy, 38cm (15in)). (*Perennial*) – *O. adenophylla* (lilac pink, dark eye, May to July, 12.5cm (5in)); *O. enneaphylla* (white, May to September, 15cm (6in)); *O. bowiei* (carmine, August to September, 20cm (8in)); *O. tuberosa* (rose, October to November, 15cm (6in)).

Oxydendrum arboreum (sorrel tree) – Hardy deciduous tree, which thrives in a loamy or peaty soil and in a sheltered position. It grows some 6m (20ft) high and bears white flowers in July and August. Plant in May or October. To propagate, sow seed in a frame in March.

Paeonia – Paeonies are divided into two classes, the herbaceous and the tree or shrubby. They are mostly hardy and thrive in sun or partial shade in sheltered beds, in well-dug loam enriched with rotten manure, but they will grow in almost any soil. *Culture* (*Herbaceous*) – Propagate by division in April or October and plant out 90cm (3ft) apart with the crowns 7.5cm (3in) deep. Transplant as little as possible, never more often than every 5 years, and if root divisions are wanted, they should be cut out with the plant *in situ*. Mulch with well-decayed manure each spring. (*P. suffruticosa*, the tree or shrubby species) – Plant in September or early October, and protect from frost. If given gentle forcing in pots, they will provide early blooms, but force only in alternate years. Increase by layering or by grafting on *P. officinalis* stock. *Varieties* (*Herbaceous*) – (*Single*) – 'Country Girl' (white); 'Tudor Rose' (white and pink); 'Rose of Delight' (rose pink); 'Kelway's Gorgeous' (deep pink); 'Lord Kitchener' (cherry red); 'Pink Perfection' (crimson). (*Double*) – 'Duchesse de Nemours' (large white); 'Ballerina' (blush white); 'Kelway's Queen' (coral pink); 'Magic Melody' (bright pink); 'President Poincare' (crimson); 'Crimson Banner' (crimson); and 'Dr H. B. Barnsby' (purple). All May to June flowering. *P. suffruticosa* (*moutan*) (tree paeony) – (*Single*) – 'Rock's Variety' (white); 'Countess of Crewe' (salmon pink). (*Double*) – 'Mrs William Kelway' (white); 'Duchess of Marlborough' (flesh pink); 'Montrose' (pale lilac); 'Duchess of Kent' (bright pink). All flower in June.

Palms – Some species require a considerable amount of heat, but such species as the *Areca* (betel nut palm), *Chamaerops* (fan palm), *Corypha* (cabbage palm), *Howea* (curly palm), and *Phoenix* (date palm), may be grown easily in a house merely protected from frost. Palms are usually bought as small plants and should be re-potted in John Innes potting compost No. 2. Spring or early summer is the best time for potting. The roots must not be injured and they must be planted firmly at the same depth as before. Water well both summer and winter, sponge the leaves with warm soft water, and syringe morning and evening in spring and summer. Partial shade is needed in hot weather, and a little liquid manure is beneficial. Propagation is usually by division in April, by suckers in September, or by seed.

Pancratium illyricum and **P. maritimum** (Mediterranean lily, or sea daffodil) – Semi-hardy bulbous plants which thrive in light rich loam and peat in sunny, sheltered positions in warm and well-drained borders. There are also many stove and greenhouse species. Both plants bear white flowers in May and June on stems 45cm (18in) high. *Culture* – Plant in October or March, 12.5cm (5in) deep and 25cm (10in) apart. Do not lift, but protect with straw in winter. *Pot culture* – Re-pot every third or fourth year (in March) in John Innes potting compost No. 3. Dry off gradually after blooming, and stand hardy species in the open from May to September. Propagate by offsets in October or March.

Pansy (heartsease) – *See* **Viola.**

Papaver (poppy) – Hardy annuals, biennials and perennials which thrive in the sun in almost any soil, though a deep, rich soil is best. They are useful for beds, borders and the wild garden. *P. alpinum* is a useful rock species; it needs a gritty loam and is raised from seed sown in autumn. All dead flowers must be picked off, or the season of blooming will be greatly reduced. Perennials should not be lifted more often than every 3 or 4 years. *Species* (*Annual*) – *P. glaucum* (deep scarlet, June to September, (50cm (20in)); *P. somniferum* (opium poppy) (crimson, mauve, rose, violet and white (double and fringed), July to October, 75cm (30in)); *P. rhoeas* (Shirley poppy) (orange, pink, red, lavender, blue and white (single and double), June to September, 60cm (24in)). (*Biennial*) – *P. alpinum* (yellow, salmon, white and orange, May to September, 15 to 22.5cm (6 to 9in)). (*Perennial*) – *P. bracteatum* (scarlet and black, May to September, 90 to 120cm (36 to 48in)); *P. nudicaule* (Iceland poppy) (orange, yellow, buff, salmon and white, May to September, 15 to 60cm (6 to 24in)); *P. orientale* (various, May to June, 75 to 125cm (30 to 50in)). *Named varieties* – (*P. orientale*) 'Perry's White' (white); 'King George' (cerise); 'Goliath' (vermilion); 'Salmon Glow' (orange).

Paradisea liliastrum (St Bruno's lily) – Beautiful bulb which grows about 50cm (20in) high, bears white flowers in May and June and grows in well-drained light soil in sun or partial shade in the border or wild garden. *Culture* – Plant from 22.5 to 30cm (9 to 12in) apart in October or March, and mulch with old manure in March. Propagate by division in September or October.

Parnassia (grass of Parnassus) – Hardy perennials for the bog, marsh or water garden or for the moist shady border. *Culture* – Sow in the open in autumn, or propagate by division in April. *Species* – *P. palustris* (white, June to August, 12.5 to 25cm (5 to 10in)).

Paronychia – Little creeping plants for the paved or rock garden, which thrive in the sun in gritty loam and are propagated by division in March, by cuttings under glass or by seed.

Parrotia persica (Persian witch hazel) – Hardy deciduous trees growing from 9 to 12m (30 to 40ft) high and which flower in March. They like a dry ordinary soil, and a sunny, sheltered position. *Culture* – Plant in November. No pruning is necessary. Propagate by layering in summer. Brilliant autumn foliage.

Parthenocissus (Virginia creeper) – Fast-growing self-clinging climbers tolerant of most soils and situations. Autumn colour is best if plants are in full sun, but *P. henryana* should be grown in shade to intensify the beautiful white markings. No pruning necessary except to keep plants in bounds. *Species* – *P. henryana* (slow, velvet leaves with white veins); *P. quinquefolia* (Virginia creeper) (very vigorous and loose, crimson in autumn); *P. tricuspidata* (Boston ivy) (close clinging to wall, purple red in autumn).

Passiflora (passion flower) – Genus of beautiful climbing shrubs, which grow in almost any well-drained soil, though sandy loam is best, and should be given a position against a sunny wall facing south or west; the root-run should be restricted to encourage flowering. *Culture* – Strike cuttings of young shoots in a frame in summer. Plant out in October or March; cut back shoots to half their length in February or March, and cut out weak wood. *Greenhouse culture* – Plant in March in John Innes potting compost No. 3 and syringe and water well in summer. Prune back to within two buds of the old wood in winter, and cut away all weak shoots in spring. *P. caerulea* (blue, June to September, 7.5m (25ft)) is the most hardy; for the cool greenhouse, the white variety 'Constance Elliott' (June to September, 7.5m (25ft)) is recommended.

Pelargonium – There is frequent confusion over the names geranium and pelargonium. The former term refers correctly to the hardy perennial sorts (*see Geranium*). The term pelargonium includes all half-hardy greenhouse and bedding plants and the show varieties. All pelargoniums need a light airy position, but no draughts and only sufficient artificial heat to keep out frost is needed. *Propagation* – about 6 months after cuttings are struck the plants should come into bloom; June and July are the best months for taking cuttings. The pots are prepared in the usual manner, and filled with John Innes potting compost No. 2. The cuttings should be taken in dry weather when the parent plant has had no water for some days, and they should be kept dry for 24 hours before potting. Place 5 cuttings round the edge of each 10cm (4in) pot and about 2.5cm (1in) deep. If the cuttings are struck in August or September, the protection of a frame is not essential and the pots may be sunk in a sheltered south border, where they will require no shading unless the sun is very hot; if a frame is used, the lights should only be put on as a protection against heavy rain. Gradually harden off the cuttings for potting off into 7.5cm (3in) pots as soon as they are rooted. If they grow too freely before it is time to take them into the house or frames (September), the shoots should be tipped; these may be used to provide another batch of cuttings. Through the winter months, little water and only just sufficient heat (10°C (50°F)) to exclude frost, should be given. Pick off all flower buds as they appear, and as the weather improves give more air. Late in March, or early in April re-pot into 12.5 or 15cm (5 or 6in) pots, so that they may be grown on to be hardened off and planted out late in May or in early June. From April onwards, plants grown for flowering in pots should receive weekly doses of weak liquid fertilizer and should be grown near the glass in a cool greenhouse, being pinched back to make them bushy. Plants stopped not later than February will flower in May; when blooming is to be delayed until July, pinching may be continued until towards the end of April. After flowering, ripen the growth in the sun in the open, then cut the stems back from 7.5 to 10cm (3 to 4in) from the base in August; rest the plants with the pots on their sides in a frame for 2 months. Then pot-up in fresh soil, keep in the frame and remove all buds until the plants are moved into the house early in September.

Plants for autumn and winter flowering – A further batch of cuttings taken from old plants started in gentle heat can be struck in the spring (March) and potted up singly into 7.5cm (3in) pots about May. When these pots are full of roots, move the young plants into 10cm (4in) pots; harden off in a cold frame ready for setting out in the open in June, or into open beds, if for summer bedding. Plants for flowering indoors in autumn and winter should be stopped in July and all flower buds picked off until September. Early in August, move them into 15cm (6in) pots and transfer to a light and airy shelf in the greenhouse at the beginning of September; as the season advances a little heat (13°C (55°F)) will make the plants blossom. Zonal, ivy-leaved and scarlet-leaved pelargoniums, if treated in this way, will flower in autumn and winter; Regals so treated, however, will not come into bloom until March, and will continue to flower until the middle of June. It is very difficult to raise plants from seeds. For varieties, *see* catalogues.

Peltandra (water arrow arum) – Beautiful hardy aquatic plants which thrive in the sun in ordinary soil at the water's edge. They grow from 60 to 90cm (24 to 36in) high, and flower in July. Propagate by division of roots in March. *Species* – *P. virginica*.

Penstemon (beard tongue) – Graceful perennials, both dwarf and tall. The dwarf species are excellent for the rock garden, while the taller species make beautiful bed or border plants if treated as half-hardy biennials. All kinds thrive in the sun in good rich soil. *See also* Chelone. *Species and varieties (rock garden)* – *P. barbatus* (scarlet); *P. bridgesii* (reddish); *P. roezlii* (magenta, 15cm (6in)); *P. hartwegii* and vars. (crimson); and *P. scouleri* and var. 'Alba'. All June to October flowering.

Pernettya mucronata (prickly heath) – Hardy evergreen shrubs which do well in moderate sun in cool and moist, well-drained peaty loam; both male and female forms must be grown to ensure fruits. *Culture* – Plant in March or October; no pruning is necessary. *Pot culture* – Pot-up in October or November, using 15 to 20cm (6 to 8in) pots and a lime-free compost and place in the cold greenhouse. Plant outdoors when the berries fall. To propagate, sow in a frame in March, take cuttings in summer, or divide roots in autumn. *Varieties* – *P.m.* 'Alba' (white berries); *P.m.* 'Atrococcinea' (purple berries); and *P.m.* 'Rosea' (pink). All July, 60 to 150cm (2 to 5ft).

Petunia – Half-hardy soft-wooded perennials, best treated as half-hardy annuals. They like a sunny position and a moderately rich, light soil and may be used for borders, bedding and (double varieties) for pot culture. If pricked off into pots for greenhouse use they should be potted on frequently until in their flowering pots. Double varieties should be propagated by means of cuttings of young wood in a temperature of 15°C (59°F) in the spring, or of mature shoots in a cold frame in August. *Pot culture* – Pot-up in May, using 15 to 25cm (6 to 10in) pots and John Innes potting compost No. 1 and keep in a cool greenhouse. Pinch back to 5 joints from the old stem as soon as established in the flowering pots. Flowering may be retarded by standing the plants in a cold frame or in the open any time after the middle of May. Most petunias are of hybrid origin. Numerous varieties, *see* catalogues. June to October, 30cm (12in).

Phacelia – Dwarf-growing hardy annuals, suitable for edging, for the border, or the rock garden. They like a sunny or semi-shaded position and ordinary soil. *Species* – *P. campanularia* (deep blue, 20cm (8in)); *P. tanacetifolia* (pale mauve, 50cm (20in)); *P. minor* (deep blue, 20cm (8in)). All June to August.

Pharbitis – *See* **Ipomoea.**

Philadelphus (mock orange) – Beautiful hardy deciduous flowering shrubs known under the name of Syringa, a name which rightly belongs to the lilacs. They thrive in any good garden soil and like a sunny position. *Culture* – plant in October or November. Thin out the shoots well immediately after flowering and cut back old and weak wood of the previous year to the young lateral growths at the base. If much overgrown, cut hard back in March. *Pot culture* – In the cool greenhouse, *P.* x *lemoinei* may be had in flower in March, pot-up annually in October, using 20 to 25cm (8 to 10in) pots and John Innes potting compost No. 3. Prune as already described, and sink the pots to their rims outdoors from May to December. To propagate, strike cuttings in a frame in July or August. *Species and hybrids* – *P. coronarius* (white); *P. microphyllus* (white); *P.* 'Avalanche' (white); *P.* 'Belle Etoile' (white); *P.* 'Sybille' (white, single); *P.* 'Virginal' (white, double); *P.* x. *purpureo-maculatus* (white petals, stained purple). All May to July, 1 to 4.5m (3 to 15ft).

Phillyrea (mock privet) – Hardy evergreen shrubs which thrive almost anywhere and in any soil. *Culture* – Plant in May or September. Propagate by cuttings in a frame or by layering in September. *Species* – *P. angustifolia* (white, May to June, 2.7m (9ft)); *P. vilmoriniana* (syn. *decora*) (white, April, 2 to 2.5m (6 to 8ft)); *P. media latifolia* (white, May, 2 to 2.5m (6 to 8ft)).

Phlox – Magnificent genus of annuals and perennials which need a certain amount of sun and enjoy an open position, but one sheltered from strong winds. The *Phlox drummondii* varieties – half-hardy annuals – make splendid bedding and potting plants. *Phlox paniculata* and *P. maculata*, perennials, look fine in borders, while the dwarf perennials or mossy phloxes are excellent for the rock garden. The annual and herbaceous kinds succeed best in deep, rich and moist but well-drained loam. Stake if necessary and thin out all weak growths. *Pot culture* (*Perennials*) – Pot-up in October, using 12.5 to 15cm (5 to 6in) pots and John Innes potting compost No. 2. Stand in a cold greenhouse and water freely from April to October, then decrease the water supply. Give liquid fertilizer from May to September. (*Annuals*) – If seed is sown in a frame in August and the seedlings are potted up and transplanted to the greenhouse, blooms may be had from January to March. *Species* (*Annual*) – *P. drummondii* (various, June to October, 15 to 30cm (6 to 12in)). (*Perennial*) – *P. paniculata* (various, July to October, 100cm (40in)). *Named varieties of P. paniculata* – 'Border Fern' (lavender); 'Brigadier' (orange red); 'Harlequin' (purple, variegated leaves); 'Mother of Pearl' (palest pink); 'White Admiral' (*Alpine*) – *P. adsurgens* (pink, 15cm (6in)); *P. amoena* (carmine pink, May to July, 15cm (6in)); *P. divaricata* (lavender blue, May to July, 15 to 30cm (6 to 12in)); *P. ovata* (red, May to July, 25cm (10in)); *P. subulata* and vars. (pink, mauve, blue and white, May to June, 10cm (4in)); *P. stolonifera* (rose purple, June, 15cm (6in)).

Phormium (New Zealand flax) – Tall foliage perennials which require a fairly sheltered, sunny position in well-drained loam, and flower from June to September. *Culture* – Sow in a frame in March, or propagate by division of roots in April. *P. colensoi* (yellow, 1.5m (60in)) and *P. tenax* (crimson, 2m (70in)) are the best species. *P.t.* 'Variegatum' (green and yellow striped leaves).

Phyllodoce – Race of dwarf, heath-like, evergreen, shrubby plants, rarely exceeding 17.5 or 20cm (7 or 8in) in height, and excellent subjects for the rock garden.

They prefer a well-drained lime-free soil and a moist position in sun or semi-shade. *Culture* – Plant in October or March. No pruning is required. Propagate by cuttings in a frame in October, or layer at that time. *Species* – *P. breweri* (yellowish, May, 20 to to 30cm (8 to 12in)); *P. caerulea* (reddish purple, June, 15 to 20cm (6 to 8in)); *P. empetriformis* (pink, June, 20cm (8in)).

Physalis (winter cherry, Chinese lantern, or Cape gooseberry) – Half-hardy and hardy perennials, growing from 50 to 100cm (20 to 40in) high and flowering from June to October. They like warm, light and rich soil, and a sunny position in a sheltered border.

Physostegia (false dragon's head) – Hardy perennials, growing from 50 to 100cm (20 to 40in) high, and bearing red flowers in late summer. They like partial shade and a rich sandy soil.

Phyteuma (horned rampion) – Hardy perennials. The smaller species thrive in the rock garden in rich, gritty loam; the taller kinds in a deep, rich soil in the border and in a warm, sunny position. *Species* – *P. scheuchzeri* (blue, May to June, 45cm (18in)); *P. ovatum* (violet, May and June, 15cm (6in)); *P. spicatum* (lilac, May and June, 60cm (2ft)).

Picea (spruce) – Hardy evergreen conifers which thrive in well-drained loam and in sunny positions. *Culture* – Plant from October to November or in March and April; no pruning is required. Propagate by seed. *Species* – *P. abies* (*P. excelsa*) (Norway spruce, 15 to 30m (50 to 100ft)); *P. orientalis* (oriental spruce, 18m (60ft)) and named varieties; *P. pungens* 'Glauca' (blue spruce, grey-blue foliage, 6m (20ft)); *P. abies* 'Pumila' (60cm (2ft)).

Pieris (flame of the forest) – Hardy evergreen shrubs, which like a moist peaty loam and a sheltered position in sun or partial shade. *Culture* – Plant from September to October. Do not prune, but keep in shape by means of stopping and removing dead flowers in May. Propagate by layering in autumn. Good kinds are *P. floribunda* (white, April to May, 90 to 180cm (3 to 6ft)) and *P. japonica* (white, March to April, 1 to 3m (4 to 10ft)).

Pinks – *See* Dianthus.

Pinus (pine) – Large family of hardy coniferous trees growing, according to species, from 1 to 60m (4 to 200ft) high. They like a sunny position and prefer light loam, but will grow well in most soil. *Culture* – Plant in May or September when from 60 to 90cm (2 to 3ft) high. No pruning is required. *Species* – *P. cembra* (dark green); *P. contorta*; *P. mugo* (mountain pine) and dwarf forms; *P. nigra* (black pine).

Platanus (plane) – Hardy deciduous trees, which thrive in sunny positions, in any well-drained soil. *Culture* – Plant in November. Prune in winter when the wood is overcrowded. To propagate, sow in March, take cuttings in autumn, or layer.

Platycodon (Chinese bell-flower) – Hardy perennials which thrive in well-drained, deep sandy loam, in open, shady positions, and are excellent for the border or rock garden. They grow from 25 to 63cm (10 to 25in) high and flower in July and August.

Plumbago (leadwort) – Genus comprising 12 species of plants, mostly perennials, suitable only for the greenhouse. The most noteworthy for greenhouse culture is *P. capensis*, an admirable pillar plant, with pale lavender blue flowers in September. *Culture* – Pot-up annually in March in 15 to 20cm (6 to 8in) pots or plant in the cool house border. Use John Innes potting compost No. 3. Water well and syringe in warm weather, but keep dry from October to March. Young pot plants (not climbers) should be pinched back once or twice; with bushes, cut back the shoots to within 25cm (10in) of the previous year's growth in October. Climbers should be trained in a single stem in much the same manner as a vine. Cut back all laterals of climbers to within 12.5cm (5in) of their base after flowering, and prune back again to within 5 to 7.5cm (2 to 3in) from their base early in February, and if grown in the greenhouse border, mulch annually in spring. Propagate by cuttings of semi-matured side shoots in gentle bottom heat in spring or early summer.

Podophyllum (duckfoot or May apple) – Hardy perennials which thrive in partial shade in moist peaty loam and are useful for the bog or rock garden. They grow from 25 to 75cm (10 to 30in) high and carry purple or white flowers in May. Propagate by division in April.

Polemonium (Jacob's ladder or Greek valerian) – Hardy perennials for sunny borders, or the wild garden, and requiring well-drained loam. Rock garden species need partial shade and a compost of gritty loam and leaf-mould. *Species* – *P. caeruleum* and vars. (blue or white, June to September, 45cm (18in)); *P. reptans* (slate blue, March to June, 30cm (12in)).

Polianthes tuberosa (tuberose) – Half-hardy bulbous plants growing from 60 to 90cm (24 to 36in) high and flowering in September. They thrive in sunny positions in sheltered warm borders, in a mixture of sandy loam, leaf-mould, and well-rotted manure, or they may be flowered in pots in the greenhouse. *Culture* – Plant in March, 15cm (6in) deep and 15cm (6in) apart, and do not water until they begin to grow. *Pot culture* – Plant bulbs singly in 10 to 12.5cm (4 to 5in) pots (African kinds) late autumn, (American kinds) early spring, and plunge the pots in a warm frame (bottom heat 18°C (65°F)). When their roots fill the pots, re-pot and repeat the treatment until the buds appear. The bulbs only flower for one season. Propagate by means of offsets.

Polyanthus – *See* **Primula.**

Polygala (milkwort) – Useful little plants, mostly shrubby evergreens or hardy perennials, which thrive in a mixture of cool, moist and gritty loam and peat, or leaf-mould, in partial shade in sheltered positions. They are excellent for the rock garden, border or wild garden. Shrubby species are increased by cuttings or young shoots struck in sand in a propagating case in spring. *Pot culture* (*Shrubby species*) – Pot-up in March in a peaty compost. Shade from direct sun and syringe. Remove all dead flower heads and, after flowering, cut the shoots of the current year back to within 15cm (6in) of the old wood; then syringe and stand in the sun to ripen the wood. Remove to the house in September. *Species* – *P. calcarea* (purple, blue, mauve or rose, May to September, 12.5cm (5in)); *P. chamaebuxus* (purple and yellow, June to July, 7.5cm (3in)).

Polygonatum – Hardy perennials of which the best known is *P. multiflorum* (Solomon's seal or David's harp). They thrive in almost any soil and situation.

Polygonum (knotwort) – Large genus including hardy annuals, hardy and half-hardy perennials, shrubs, climbers and trailers. The tall hardy perennials are useful for the wild garden or border, and grow in any ordinary loam and in partial shade. *P. affine* (pink, July to October, 20cm (8in)) is an alpine species. In the case of shrubby species, do not prune, but cut out old wood from the centre and trim away thin straggly shoots. *Species* (*Annual*) – *P. orientale* (purple rose, June to September, 1 to 1.5m (4 to 5ft)). (*Perennial*) – *P. campanulatum* (pink, July to September, 90cm (3ft) invasive); *P. baldschuanicum* (rampant climber, flowers white, turning pink).

Pontederia cordata (water plantain) – Hardy perennial aquatics bearing blue flowers from June to October, and which like a sheltered position in good loam and still, shallow water. *Culture* – Propagate by division in April.

Poppy – *See* **Papaver.**

Populus (poplar) – Large genus of hardy deciduous trees suitable only for large gardens and which thrive in moist loam in sunny positions. *Culture* – Plant in November. No pruning is required. To propagate, strike cuttings of matured wood in the open in October. *Species* – *P. nigra* 'Italica' is the Lombardy poplar and *P. tremula* is the aspen.

Potentilla (cinquefoil) – Genus of plants, some species of which bear a resemblance to the strawberry in flower, and have a similar manner of propagation. Many species are of a low-growing and shrubby nature, others are hardy perennials. All do well in sun or semi-shade in the border or rock garden (dwarf kinds), in good soil. Sow seed in spring, increase by division in March or October, or strike cuttings of ripened shoots in a frame in autumn. The old and dead wood should be thinned out in September. *Species and varieties (Border)* – *P. astrosan guinea* (crimson); *P.* 'Gibson's Scarlet'; *P. grandiflora* (yellow). All May to September, 30 to 45cm (12 to 18in). (*Allpines*) – *P. alba* (white); *P. nepalensis* 'Minor' (crimson); *P.n.* 'Miss Willmott' (rose); *P* x *tonguei* (orange, spotted crimson). All May to September, 15 to 22.5cm (6 to 9in). (*Shrubby*) – *P. fruticosa* (yellow); *P.f.* 'Red Ace' (crimson); *P.f.* 'Veitchii' (white); *P.f.* 'Vilmoriniana' (sulphur). All July to September, 90 to 120cm (3 to 4ft).

Primrose (*Primula vulgaris*) – *See* **Primula.**

Primula – Large genus, including some of the most popular flowers, the auricula, the cowslip, the polyanthus and the primrose. In the greenhouse, in the rock garden or bog garden, in beds and growing wild in the woods, the primula is one of the most useful genera. The majority thrive in rich deep loam and appreciate leaf-mould and grit with the soil. They are all moisture-lovers, but must have a well-drained soil. The majority like partial shade unless unlimited moisture is available in hot weather. *Culture* – Sow seed in pots or pans under glass in May. Cover thinly with a little sand and keep in a temperature of 16°C (59°F). Prick off 2.5cm (1in) apart into pans as soon as possible and, in about 3 weeks, pot-up singly into 7.5cm (3in) pots; harden off, and plant out hardy types. Keep greenhouse primulas in a shaded frame. Propagate also by division in September or in spring. *Pot culture* – Pot-up firmly in September or October, using 12.5 to 15cm (5 to 6in) pots and keep in a frame until November, pinching off any flower buds that form, then transfer to the cool greenhouse for flowering. A little dilute liquid feed may be given from time to time while the buds are forming. Discard the plants after flowering, except choice varities. Alpine primulas are of great value in the rock garden and the bog garden. The first group thrives among the rocks in rich loam; the second class loves a cool, moist, but well-drained soil. Space does not permit to deal more fully with these, but below the first group is marked with an * and the second †. *Species* – *P. vulgaris* (primrose) (various, April, 15cm (6in)); **P auricula* (golden yellow, March to May, 30 to 45cm (12 to 18in)); †*P. beesiana* (magenta, May to June, 50 to 75cm (20 to 30in)); †*P. bulleyana* (orange scarlet, April to May, 30 to 45cm (12 to 18in)); **P. denticulata* (lilac and white, February to April, 30 to 45cm (12 to 18in)); †*P. farinosa* (rose purple, May, 15cm (6in)); †*P. japonica* vars. (various, May to August, 30 to 60cm (12 to 24in)); †*P. juliae* hybrids (magenta, April and May, 10cm (4in)); *P.* x *kewensis* (pale yellow, April, 38cm (15in)); *P. malacoides* (pale mauve, pink or white, September to May, 30 to 60cm (12 to 24in)); **P. marginata* (lavender blue, margined white, May, 15cm (6in)); †*P. minima* (rose pink, May to June, 5cm (2in)); *P. obconica* vars. (various, spring, 22.5 to 30cm (9 to 12in)); †*P. pulverulenta* (crimson maroon, April to May, 50cm (20in)); *P. sieboldii* vars. (red, purple, lilac, May to June, 30cm (12in)); †*P. sikkimensis* (sulphur yellow, May to June, 50cm (20in)); *P. sinensis* (*P. praenitens*) (various, September to April, 30cm (12in)). Those without distinguishing marks are for the greenhouse.

Prunella (self-heal) – Dwarf-growing hardy perennials, thriving in moist, light and rich soil, in the sunny border or rock garden. *Species* – *P. grandiflora* (purple, red, blue or white, 20cm (8in)); *P.* x *webbiana* 'Alba' (white, 15cm (6in)). All July to September.

Prunus – Large genus of hardy deciduous flowering and fruit-bearing trees, including *P. amygdalus* (*communis*) (almond), *P. armeniaca* (apricot), *P. avium* (gean), *P. cerasifera* (cherry plum), etc. They do best in a deeply dug and well-manured soil rich in lime, or in localities with a chalk subsoil. *P. laurocerasus* (cherry laurel) and *P. lusitanica* (Portugal laurel) are robust everygreen hedge plants to 6m (20ft) or more. Plant young bushes 60cm (2ft) apart in March or September, and cut the vigorous young shoots back below the level of the others. Propagate by cuttings and layering. *P. cistena* makes a low, deciduous, flowering hedge. For named varieties of flowering cherries, almonds and plums, *see* catalogues.

Puschkinia scilloides (striped squill) – Hardy bulbous plant which grows about 15cm (6in) high and flowers in April and May. It thrives in deep, rich sandy soil, in warm sunny borders or in the rock garden. *Culture* – Plant in October, 7.5cm (3in) deep and 7.5cm (3in) apart. Protect with straw in winter and divide every 3 years.

Pyracantha (fire thorn) – Beautiful hardy evergreen bushes or climbing shrubs which thrive in good light loam in sunny positions and against walls. All bear white flowers from May to June, and bright autumn berries. *Culture* – Sow seed when ripe, or strike cuttings in summer. Plant in October or April, trim to shape in early spring, but clip as little as possible.

Pyrethrum (syn. *Chrysanthemum coccineum*) – Hardy perennials, now included under the genus *Chrysanthemum*; they thrive in cool, light, deep and moderately rich soil in sunny, open borders.

Pyrus – Genus of hardy deciduous trees including *P. nivalis* (snowtree), *P. ussuriensis* (sand pear). *Culture* – Plant in November in a sunny position sheltered from cold winds, in deeply dug and well-manured ordinary soil. Thin out the branches when overcrowded and cut out dead wood and weak shoots after flowering. Propagate by seed, grafting or budding in the open.

Quercus (oak) – Large genus of hardy deciduous and evergreen trees, the majority of which are too large for the average garden. There are, however, a few species from Japan, which rarely attain more than bush form here, except in mild districts. *Culture* – Plant young trees in October in a sunny position in deep, good loam; thin out the branches in summer when required. To propagate, sow ripe acorns in the open in September or October, or graft in spring. *Quercus robur* (common oak) and other species.

Ramonda (Pyrenean primrose, rosette mullein) – Small hardy perennial rock plants which thrive in the shade in ordinary soil. *Species* – *R. myconi* (*pyrenaica*) (deep purple blue). *R.m.* 'Rosea'. All May to August, 15cm (6in).

Ranunculus – Large genus of herbaceous perennials and tuberous-rooted plants, including the common buttercup, most species of which thrive in partial shade, in moist, deep, rich soil with ample leaf-mould in it. They are also useful for pot culture, and the dwarf-growing kinds for the rock garden. *Culture* (*Perennials*) – Propagate by division in November or April, the plants should remain in position for several years. (*Tuberous*) – Plant the tubers, claws downward, 5 to 7.5cm (2 to 3in) deep and 10 to 15cm (4 to 6in) apart, early in March. Lift the tubers after flowering. *Species* (*fibrous-rooted*) – *R. aconitifolius* 'Flore-pleno' (white, double, May to July, 60 to 75cm (24 to 30in)); *R. acris* 'Flore-pleno' (yellow, double, May to June, 60cm (24in)); *R. aquatilis* (white, May and June, 5 to 30cm (2 to 12in)); *R. lingua* 'Grandiflora' (yellow, June, 75 to 120cm (30 to 50in)). (*Tuberous-rooted*) – *R.*

asiaticus (various, May to July, 15cm (6in)). (*Alpine*) – *R. alpestris* (white, May to August, 10cm (4in)); *R. amplexicaulis* (white, May to August, 25cm (10in)).

Reseda odorata (mignonette) – Sweet-scented perennial that is commonly grown as an annual; it likes a fairly rich soil with lime in it and a sunny position. Seedlings grown in the open should not be transplanted. *Pot culture* – Sow in pots under glass in March, June, August and September, using John Innes potting compost No. 1, placing several seeds in each 15cm (6in) pot. Thin to 4 plants in each pot and stand near the glass or grow in a frame. Cut off all dead flowers and prune back straggly shoots. *Named varieties* – 'Goliath' and 'Machet' (red). All July to September, 22.5 to 45cm (9 to 18in).

Rhamnus (buckthorn) – These small trees will do well almost anywhere, provided they have shelter from the wind. *Culture* – Plant in the late autumn or early spring and prune in February. Propagate by cuttings in the open in September, by layering in October or March, or sow seed outdoors in September. *Rhamnus alaternus* (evergreen, 3.5m (12ft)) is a good kind.

Rheum (rhubarb) – The ornamental rhubarbs which thrive on moist, sunny banks or in the water garden in deep, rich loam, are grown chiefly for their foliage.

Rhododendron – Among the most handsome and finest of all our flowering shrubs are the hardy rhododendrons. Most species thrive best in a position sheltered from north and east winds and in semi-shade, and prefer well-dug and well-drained moist peaty loam, but will grow in almost any soil deficient in lime or chalk, providing it contains ample humus, and is sufficiently porous. Most flower in May and June, but a few early varieties bloom from Christmas onwards. Rhododendrons bear frequent transplanting as long as the ball of earth round their roots is not broken. They are surface-rooters and will not grow on steep banks, where the roots parch up in summer. Except in the case of such hybrids as 'Bagshot Ruby' or 'Pink Pearl', which will grow in full sun, rhododendrons require light shade. These shade conditions are best supplied by trees and large bushes planted among the rhododendrons. In addition to the hardy and half-hardy species, there are choice greenhouse kinds, which require moist warmth all the year; these are best grown in a cool house during the winter (10°C (50°F)) and kept under glass in summer. When purchasing rhododendrons, care must be taken that the types chosen are suitable for the climate. *Culture* – Plant firmly in October or November or at any time in winter and spring, up to May, providing the soil is not water-logged and that there is no frost. When planting add some well-rotted leaf-mould, and mix it well with the other soil. Fresh manure must not be used. If the weather is dry, soak the hole well before planting, and place a little leaf-mould or peat at the bottom for the roots to rest on. Bushy species should be set 1.8m (6ft) apart and smaller lime-hating subjects, such as azaleas, kalmias, daphnes and heaths, can be used to fill the gaps until the rhododendrons have grown a bit. Do not prune young bushes, merely keep them in shape by means of stopping and removing dead blooms immediately after flowering. When it is necessary to cut back old and straggling plants, do so in April. Top-dress annually in March with good leaf-mould or peat. *Propagation* – To propagate hybrids, graft stock (*R. ponticum*) under glass from January to May, layer well-matured shoots in late summer, or take cuttings. Species may be increased by means of seed sown thinly in March or April in pans, in a peaty seed compost. Most species may be raised from cuttings of semi-matured shoots, struck in a frame with bottom heat, and pratically all species can be layered in summer. For Pot culture, *see* Azalea. Species and varieties are innumerable (*see* growers' catalogues). A few good hybrids are – 'Alice' (deep rose pink); 'Ascot Brilliant' (deep blood red); 'Bagshot Ruby' (ruby red); 'Chanticleer' (scarlet); 'Countess of Derby' (rose);

'Cunningham's White' (white, tinged pink); 'Doncaster' (bright scarlet, spotted dark brown); 'Eldorado' (pale yellow); 'Mother of Pearl' (bluish white, red stamens); 'Pink Pearl' (flesh pink); 'Sappho' (white, heavily spotted maroon); and 'Unknown Warrior' (rose crimson).

Rhus typhina (stag's horn) – Hardy deciduous tree or shrub which likes a sunny position and good loam. *Culture* – Plant in October; cut out all old and dead wood. To propagate, strike cuttings of matured shoots under cloches in September, or layer in September. Greenish flowers in June, orange red foliage in autumn, 3 to 7.5m (10 to 25ft).

Ribes – Hardy deciduous shrubs, akin to the currant and gooseberry, which thrive in the shade in ordinary garden soil, and are treated in the same way as gooseberries and currants, which *see*. *Species* – *R. aureum* (yellow); *R. sanguineum* (flowering currant) with rosy red flowers in April; and *R. speciosum* (fuchsia flowered gooseberry) with red flowers, are best.

Ricinus communis (castor-oil plant) – Half-hardy plant which thrives in rich loam in warm beds or in the cold greenhouse. *Culture* – Sow singly in pots in March under glass (10°C (50°F)); pot on into 12.5cm (5in) pots, harden off and plant out in June, or pot-on into 15 to 20cm (6 to 8in) pots and keep indoors. One of the best varieties is *R. communis* 'Gibsonii'.

Robinia (rose acacia and false acacia) – Hardy deciduous summer-flowering trees, which like a well-drained light soil, and a sunny, sheltered position. *R. pseudoacacia*, the locust tree or false acacia (white, 15m (50ft)) is the most common. The most attractive species for the garden, however, is *R. hispida*, the rose acacia (pink, 3m (9ft)). *Culture* – Plant in November. Do not prune, but merely trim to keep in shape. Propagate by seed or by grafting.

Rodgersia – Hardy perennials growing 1m (4ft) high and bearing pink or white flowers in June or July, and which thrive in partial shade in a moist border or by water's edge in peaty soil. *R. aesculifolia* (pink) and *R. pinnata* (red) are good species.

Romneya (Californian or bush poppy) – Deciduous flowering shrubs or shrubby perennials. They are almost hardy and thrive in the sun in well-drained loam, in a sheltered position or under a south wall. *Culture* – Plant in March; cut out all dead wood in the spring, and cut back any weak growth. In severe winters protect with straw, bracken, or sacking; in the north, these plants should be grown under glass. *Pot culture* – Pot-up annually in April, in a peat-based compost in 15 to 17.5cm (6 to 7in) pots. To propagate, divide the roots in March, or strike root-cuttings in a frame in the autumn. *R. coulteri* (white, June to September, 1.5m (5ft)) is the best known.

Rosa (rose) – *See* Ch. 18, Roses.

Rosmarinus officinalis (rosemary) – Hardy evergreen shrubby perennial, which likes a sunny position and a light, dry soil, but which will grow almost anywhere; it grows 1 to 2m (3 to 6ft) high and flowers in April and May. *R.o. prostratus* is a trailing rock plant. *Culture* – Plant in March or September, trim to shape after flowering. To propagate, sow in a frame in April, or strike cuttings under cloches in July.

Rubus (bramble, raspberry, etc.) – Large genus of hardy deciduous flowering shrubs and climbers, including the cultivated blackberry, loganberry and raspberry. These like a shady position and rich loam. A few, such as *R. deliciosus*, are grown in bush form; many are selected for the beauty of their flowers, such as *R. odoratus* and *R.* x *tridel* 'Benenden'. *Culture* – Plant in October; cut out old and dead wood after flowering. Propagate by suckers in the autumn.

Rudbeckia (cone flower) – Hardy annuals and perennials which like a well-drained ordinary soil and a sunny position. Stake early. *Species* (*Annuals*) – *R. bicolor* (yellow and purple, 60cm (2ft)); *R. hirta* (yellow and purple, 75cm (2½ft)). (*Perennials*) – *R. fulgida* (yellow and purple, July to September, 60cm (2ft)); *R. laciniata* 'Goldquelle' (golden yellow (double), August to September, 90cm (36in); *R. purpurea* (*Echinacea purpurea*) (purple, July to September, 75cm (30in)); *R. nitida* (golden, purple black centre, July to September, 1.8m (6ft).

Sagittaria (arrow head) – Hardy aquatic plants which thrive in a deep, fertile soil. They grow from 25 to 75cm (10 to 30in) high and flower from June to October. *Culture* – Sow seed 6mm (¼in) deep in April, or propagate by division in March. Plant in March in weighted baskets in shallow still water. *Species* – *S. sagittifolia* (white).

Salix (willow) – Genus of hardy deciduous trees and shrubs, excellent for growing near a pond or stream. *S. babylonica* is the common weeping willow. There are a few species with brightly coloured stems; these are usually cut hard back annually in spring. *S. caprea* 'Pendula' and *S. purpurea* 'Pendula' are beautiful small weeping willows, unlike *S. babylonica* which grows to an enormous size. *Culture* – Plant in November in a sunny position and in moist soil at the water's margin or in deep, heavy loam. Pruning, except when the trees are cut hard back annually as mentioned above, is not necessary, but dead wood should be cut out. To propagate, strike cuttings of matured wood in the open in November or March.

Salpiglossis – Half-hardy annuals suitable for a rich soil in sunny beds, or for pot culture. *Species* – *S. sinuata* (purple, etc., July to September, 45cm (18in).

Salvia – There are many species belonging to this genus; annuals, biennials and perennials, which are grown in the greenhouse or in the garden as ornamental bedding plants; all thrive in the sun in rich soil. *Pot culture* – Sow in moderate heat in February, prick off early, and pot on as required, never allowing the plants to become potbound, and using eventually 15 to 20cm (6 to 8in) pots and John Innes potting compost. Grow on in an average temperature of 16°C (59°F), harden off in a cold frame; plunge the pots in the open in summer, and take into the cool house early in October. Pinch back occasionally till August, and syringe often. After blooming, keep the roots fairly dry and cool till March, then give more moisture and slight heat. Rather than raise from seed, however, strike cuttings of young wood in April. *Species* (*Half-hardy annual*) – *S. carduacea* (lilac blue); *S. coccinea* (scarlet); *S. horminum* (various). All June to September, 30 to 45cm (12 to 18in)). (*Hardy perennial*) – *S. argentea* (pale rose); *S. glutinosa* (yellow); *S.* x *superba* (syn. *virgata nemorosa*) (purple blue); *S. uliginosa* (deep blue). All June to September, 60 to 150cm (24in to 60in). (*Half-hardy perennial*) – *S. patens* (deep blue); *S. splendens* (scarlet). Both June to December, 45cm (18in).

Sambucus (elder) – Deciduous shrubs or small trees bearing white flowers in summer. *S. nigra* is the common elder; its two varieties, *S.n.* 'Albovariegata' (silver leaved) and *S.n.* 'Aureomarginata' (golden leaved), are very attractive. *S. racemosa*, the berried elder, flowers a month earlier. The flowers are followed by large clusters of black berries. *Culture* – Plant in October in partial shade, and in moist loam, or in almost any soil and situation; cut well back in spring. To propagate, strike cuttings in the open in October.

Sanguinaria (bloodroot) – Hardy perennials which like sandy loam and a sunny position in the border or rock garden. They grow 15cm (6in) high and flower in spring.

Saponaria (soapwort) – Hardy annuals of tufted habit and perennials, the creeping species of which are excellent for edgings or for the rock garden, and bear cutting back if necessary for a late autumn display.

The taller kinds are useful in the wild garden. All like a sunny position and dry, light loam. *Species* (*Annual*) – *S. calabrica* (rosy red, June to October, 15cm (6in)). (*Perennial*) – *S. caespitosa* (rosy pink, June to September, 10cm (4in)); *S. ocymoides* (rose and white, May to July 15cm (6in)); *S. officinalis* (single and double, rose or white, July and August, 50cm (20in)).

Saxifraga (saxifrage, rockfoil) – Large genus including numerous species of which there are many varieties, and the group is swelled by a seemingly endless number of hybrids.

Euaizoonia (encrusted or silvery saxifrages) are happiest among limestone rocks or in the moraine, but will grow almost anywhere if given a rather gritty soil and a warm, sunny site. Seed can be sown when ripe in pans of light compost in a frame, or the roots can be divided in summer. *Species and varieties* – *S. aizoon* and vars. (creamy white, yellow or rose, 15 to 25cm (6 to 10in)); *S. cotyledon* and vars. (white, 45cm (18in)); *S. hostii* (white, spotted pink, 38cm (15in)); *S. mutata* (orange, 45cm (18in)). All May to July.

Dactyloides (mossy saxifrages) – These plants will grow in almost any well-drained soil, but prefer a compost of gritty loam, leaf-mould and sand, and should be given a cool position in semi-shade. Increase by division of roots in summer, or sow seed in spring in gentle heat. *Species and varieties* – *S. hypnoides* (white, 12.5cm (5in.)); *S. moschata* and vars. (creamy white, rose and red, 5 to 15cm (2 to 6in)); and *S. muscoides* (white or red, 10cm (4in)). All flower from May to June.

Kabschias (cushion or tufted saxifrages) – These plants need an open and cool but fairly sunny site, preferably facing east or west, in the rock garden, and gritty limy soil. Above all, the soil must be well drained, and ample moisture should be available in summer. Plants in the open may be given winter protection. Increase by division of roots after flowering, by cuttings in the spring or autumn, or raise from seed in gentle heat in spring. *Species and hybrids* – *S. burseriana* and vars. (white or yellow, February to April, 10cm (4in)); *S. caesia* (white, May to June, 7.5cm (3in)); *S. luteoviridis* (yellow, April to May, 12.5cm (5in)); *S. grisebachii* (crimson, April to May, 12.5cm (5in)); *S. lilacina* (lavender rose, April to May, 5cm (2in)); *S. marginata* and vars. (white or yellow, March to May, 12.5cm (5in)) and others.

Porphyrions – Give these plants a cool position in partial shade and a well-drained compost of moist, gritty loam and leaf-mould. Increase by division. *Species* – *S. oppositifolia* and vars. (crimson purple, March to May, 5cm (2in)).

Diptera – This section likes a position in the alpine house in light gritty loam, or a sheltered situation in the rock garden. Propagate by means of seed, by division or layering. *Species* – *S. cuscutiformis* (white, June, trailing); *S. sarmentosa* (*S. stolonifera*) (mother of thousands) (yellow or white, June to September, 25cm (10in)).

Robertsonia – These like a shady position in light, gritty loam. Propagate by seed (gentle heat) in the spring, or by division in the summer. *Species* – *S. cuneifolia* (white, 12.5cm (5in)); *S. umbrosa* var. *primuloides* (rose, 12.5cm (5in)); *S.* x *urbicum* and vars. (London pride) (rose and white, 25cm (10in)). All May to June-flowering.

Trachyphyllum – These thrive in semi-shade in moist, gritty loam. Propagate by seed (gentle heat) in the spring, or by division in summer. *Species* – *S. aspera* (yellow, flowering from May to June, 7.5 to 12.5cm (3 to 5in)).

Scabiosa (scabious or pincushion flower) – Annuals, biennials and perennials, which thrive in sunny, open borders and in well-drained rich and light soil. They also make good pot plants for bearing winter blooms if lifted and taken into the greenhouse in September. *Species* (*Annual*) – *S. atropurpurea*. *Named varieties* – 'Cockade Mixed' and 'Tom Thumb'. Both June to October, 60 to 90cm (24 to 36in)). (*Perennial*) – *S. caucasica* and vars. *Named varieties of S. caucasica* – 'Clive Greaves' (mauve); 'Bressingham White'; 'Moonstone' (blue). May to September-flowering and growing 60 to 90cm (24 to 36in).

Schizanthus (butterfly flower, fringe flower, poor man's orchid) – Half-hardy annual which thrives in a light rich soil. The species chiefly grown in the open ground is *S. pinnatus*. *Culture* – Sow thinly in the open in April or under glass with moderate heat in late February for summer bloom; in August for spring flowers. Prick off 7.5cm (3in) apart, harden off and plant out 22.5 to 30cm (9 to 12in) apart in April. *Pot culture* – Sow several seeds in a 12.5cm (5in) pot in September, keep in a temperature of 16°C (59°F) and moderately moist; thin out to 5 seedlings in each pot, and tip the young plants occasionally. Winter on a sunny shelf near the glass in a cold greenhouse, and in February pot up with 3 plants in 15 to 17.5cm (6 to 7in) pots and stake carefully. In 3 weeks' time nip out the tips. Only slight heat is needed to bring the plants into bloom. *Species* – *S. grahamii* (scarlet); *S. pinnatus* (purple and white); *S.p.* 'Monarch Mixed'; *S. retusus* and vars. (salmon rose and orange); *S.* x *wisetonensis* (various). All March to October, 45 to 120cm (18 to 48in), except *S. pinnatus*, which flowers from June to September.

Schizostylis coccinea (Kaffir lily, crimson flag or winter gladiolus) – Half-hardy rhizomatous-rooted plant which grows 50 to 75cm (20 to 30in) high and flowers in October and November. It thrives in sunny, sheltered borders with a south aspect, and moist but well-drained, light, rich soil, and is also useful for pot culture in the cool greenhouse. *Culture* – Plant in March or October; protect with straw in winter. Lift and divide the roots every few years in March, and propagate by offsets during that month. *Pot culture* – Plant in November in John Innes potting compost No. 2 and stand in a cold frame, giving no water until growth commences. Sink pots outdoors in a sunny position in summer, and late in September, when the buds show, transfer to the cold house.

Scilla (squill) – Hardy spring-flowering bulbous plants, which do well in warm, sunny borders, in the rock garden, or in pots. *Culture* – Plant in September or October, 6cm (2½in) deep and 10cm (4in) apart, in good garden or sandy soil. Propagate by offsets in September. *Pot culture* – Pot-up from August to November, placing about 8 bulbs in a 12.5 to 15cm (5 to 6in) pot and using a loam-based compost. Keep the pots in a frame and covered with soil until growth starts, then transfer to the cold greenhouse. Plant out in the open after flowering. *Species* – *S. bifolia* (white, pink, blue, February and March, 15cm (6in)); *S. hispanica* and vars. (Spanish squill) (white, pink, blue, April and May, 38 to 50cm (15 to 20in)); *S. nonscripta* (*nutans*) (bluebell) (blue, rose, or white, May, 38cm (15in)); *S. peruviana* (blue and white, May and June, 30cm (12in)); *S. sibirica* (blue, March, 15cm (6in)).

Scirpus (club rush) – Hardy perennial marsh or aquatic plants of which *S. lacustris*, the common bulrush, is the best known. *Culture* – Propagate by division in March, and plant out in shallow water at the edge of a pond or stream.

Sedum (stonecrop) – Large family of hardy plants, mostly perennials, the low-growing species being chiefly suitable for the rock, paved or wall garden; the taller kinds are useful in the border. Sedums do well in a dry, light soil with lime in it; the summer-flowering kinds like a sunny position; autumn-flowering species do equally well in sun or shade. The smaller kinds require the protection of glass in winter. *Species* (*Perennial*) – *S. acre* 'Aureum' (yellow, May and June, 7.5cm (3in)); *S. dasyphyllum* (pink and white, June to August, 7.5cm (3in)); *S. ewersii* (rose purple, June to August, 15cm (6in)); *S. spectabile* and vars. (rosy pink, July to September, 30 to 45cm (12 to 18in)).

Sempervivum (houseleek) – Large genus of curious succulent plants, mostly hardy perennials, although some require the protection and warmth of a greenhouse. They are well suited to sunny chinks or bare ledges in the rock garden, and thrive in sandy loam. Except for *S. arachnoideum*, the cob-web houseleek, the hardy kinds need no protection in winter. *Species* – *S. arachnoideum* (reddish pink, June to August, 12.5cm (5in)); *S. montanum* (yellow, June, 20cm (8in)); *S. tectorum* (common houseleek) (red, July, 25cm (10in)).

Senecio (groundsel or ragwort) See also *Cineraria* – Large genus of annual and perennial plants, some hardy and others only suitable for the greenhouse. Those in cultivation like a moist, deep and moderately light loam and a sunny position. *Greenhouse culture* – Pot-up in March in a loam-based compost. Propagate by cuttings struck in spring in a frame with slight bottom heat. *Species* (*Hardy annual*) – *S. elegans* and vars. (purple, rose or white, June to October, 30 to 50cm (12 to 20in)). (*Hardy perennial*) – *S. pulcher* (purple, August to October, 50cm (20in)); *S. tanguticus* (yellow, August to October, 1.5m to 1.8m (5 to 6ft)); *S. laxifolius* (hardy grey-leaved shrub, 1 to 1.8m (3 to 6ft)).

Shortia (crimson leaf) – Hardy dwarf-growing perennials which thrive in a moist but well-drained compost of peat. A sheltered, shady position in the rock garden suits them. In spring they carry white or rose flowers on stems 10 to 15cm (4 to 6in) high.

Sidalcea – Hardy perennial plants which do well in sunny borders and in a moist loam. *Species and varieties* – *S. candida* (white); *S. malviflora* 'Rose Queen' (pink); 'William Smith' (salmon pink). All July to September, 90cm (36in).

Silene – Genus containing a considerable number of species, including the plants known as the campion and catchfly. They are for the most part hardy annuals, biennials and perennials, excellent for borders or the rock garden, and like a sunny, open position and a well-drained sandy loam. Most of the alpine species need a moist gritty loam. *Species* (*Annual*) – *S. armeria* (pink, July to August, 60cm (24in)); *S. pendula* 'Compacta' (blue, white, rose, spring to summer, 10 to 15cm (4 to 6in)). (*Perennial*) – *S. acaulis* (pink, June to August, 5cm (2in)); *S. alpestris* (white, May to June, 12.5cm (5in)); *S. maritima* (white, June to August, 15cm (6in)); *S. virginica* (crimson, June to August, 15cm (6in)).

Sisyrinchium (satin flower) – Hardy perennials useful in the border, the rock garden, or the alpine house. A cool fairly moist loam with $\frac{1}{3}$ peat leaf-mould and sand, or sandy peat, suits them best. *Pot culture* – Pot-up annually in September, and place in a sunny position in the cold house. After blooming, keep in a cold frame until re-potting. *Species* – *S. angustifolium* (light blue, May to July, 12.5 to 25cm (5 to 10in)); *S. bermudiana* (deep blue, May to June, 25cm (10in)); *S. douglasii* (*grandiflorum*) (purple, March to May, 25cm (10in)).

Skimmia – Hardy evergreen shrubs which like a sunny, sheltered position and a deep rich loam. They grow about 90cm (3ft) high, flower in April and carry scarlet berries in autumn if both male and female plants are grown. *Culture* – Plant in March or October, grouping 1 male plant with 6 females. No pruning is necessary. To propagate take cuttings, or layer in the summer.

Smilax (greenbriar) – Beautiful evergreen climbing plants which thrive in the cool greenhouse in a mixture of 2 parts of loam to 1 part of leaf-mould and sand. There are also a few hardy species which may be grown in the open. *Culture* – Pot-up in March, using 12.5 to 15cm (5 to 6in) pots, stand in semi-shade, syringe and water well in hot weather. Cut old plants right back each March. Propagate by seed in slight heat (18°C (65°F)) in spring, or by division in March.

Snowdrop – *See* **Galanthus.**

Solanum – Greenhouse or half-hardy shrubs. *S. crispum* and *S. jasminoides* are free-flowering climbers for a south wall. *S. capsicastrum* (winter cherry) is a beautiful evergreen greenhouse shrub which does well in John Innes potting compost No. 2

and in winter bears red cherry-like berries. *Culture* – Sow in March (16°C (59°F)) or strike cuttings of young growths after blooming (February) in moderate heat. Pinch back when 10cm (4in) high, pot-up in June in 12.5cm (5in) pots and stand outdoors in a sunny, sheltered position for the summer. Pinch back again two or three times before July, and early in October move into the house, place near the glass.

Soldanella (moonwort) – Pretty, hardy perennial rock plants thriving in the shade, in moist, gritty loam and peat, and which in winter must be protected with a pane of glass. *Species – S. alpina* (violet blue, May to June, 10cm (4in)); *S. pusilla* (violet, June to July, 7.5cm (3in)).

Solidago (golden rod) – Hardy perennials which thrive in sun or shade in almost any soil. *Species – S. canadensis, S. rigida, S. virgaurea.* All golden yellow, August to October, 60 to 120cm(2 to 4ft).

Sparaxis – Half-hardy bulbous plants which may be grown in the open in sunny positions in warm sheltered borders and in well-drained sandy soil, or in pots in the greenhouse. *Culture* – Plant in September or October, 6cm (2½in) deep and 7.5cm (3in) apart and cover with straw in winter. *Pot culture* – Pot-up in September, placing 6 bulbs in a 12.5cm (5in) pot and stand in a cold frame covered with straw until growth commences. The culture of these plants is very similar to that required for Ixias (*which see*). *Species – S. grandiflora* and vars. (violet, white or crimson, April to May, 45cm (18in)); *S. tricolor* (orange red and purple, May, 50cm (20in)).

Spartium junceum (Spanish broom) – Beautiful evergreen shrubs which thrive in a sunny position in poor, dry or sandy soil. They grow some 2.5 to 3.5m (8 to 12ft) high and carry yellow flowers from July to September. *Culture* – Plant in October. Cut back long shoots in March. To propagate, strike cuttings of young wood in a frame in July, or sow seeds; grow the young plants in pots until ready to be planted out.

Spiraea – Genus of plants, both herbaceous and woody and mostly hardy perennials, which thrive in moist, rich loam and in a semi-shaded position. They are excellent in the border, for forcing indoors, and as room plants. *Culture* – Propagate by division in March or October; cuttings of young wood may also be struck in a frame in autumn. Thin out the older wood of spring-flowering shrubs after flowering if the bushes have become unshapely. Shrubs that flower between July and September should have all weak wood cut right away in February, and all other shoots that have flowered must be cut back by at least one half. *Pot culture* – Pot-up in October, using 20 to 25cm (8 to 10in) pots and a loam-based compost. Keep almost dry in a frost-proof frame till growth starts, then take into the cool house in succession as bloom is required. In a fortnight's time raise the temperature by a few degrees and give bi-weekly doses of weak liquid manure. Prune as advised above, harden off in a frame and sink the pots outdoors from May to October then re-pot if necessary and place in a cold frame. *Species* (*Shrubs*) – *White flowers – S.* x *arguta* (1.8 to 2.5m (6 to 8ft)); *S. nipponica* (1 to 2.5m (4 to 8ft)); *S. canescens* (2 to 3m (6 to 10ft)); *S. prunifolia* 'Flore-pleno' (1.8 to 2.5m (6 to 8ft)); *S. thunbergii* (1 to 1.5m (3 to 5ft)). *Pink – S. douglasii* (1 to 1.8m (4 to 6ft)); *S. japonica* 'Anthony Waterer' (30 to 60cm (1 to 2ft)); *S. menziesii* 'Triumphans' (1 to 2m (4 to 6ft)).

Sprekelia formosissima (Jacobean lily) – Grow in pots in the warm greenhouse in John Innes potting compost No. 3. *Culture* – Plant in February; water well and give liquid fertilizer when the buds appear; and keep dry after flowering. Re-pot every 3 to 4 years and propagate by offsets treated as old bulbs.

Sternbergia (yellow star flower, winter daffodil) – Half-hardy bulbous plants which thrive in sunny positions in warm borders, in the rock garden or greenhouse in well-drained soil. *Culture* – Plant in April, 10cm (4in) deep and 12.5cm (5in) apart; *S. fischeriana*, which flowers in February, should be planted in July or August. Protect from frost with straw and lift from the ground every 3 years; or pot-up in July and grow in the greenhouse. Propagate by offsets in April. *Species* – *S. lutea* (yellow, August to September); *S. fischeriana* (yellow, February to March). All grow about 25cm (10in) high.

Stewartia (*Stuartia*) – Hardy deciduous shrubs requiring a sunny, sheltered site and rich, sandy loam and leaf-mould. Cut away all dead and weak wood every 2 to 3 years. Propagate by cuttings of ripened wood struck under glass in late summer, or by layering. *Species* – *S. monadelpha*, *S. ovata* and *S. pseudocamellia*. All creamy white, June to July, 2 to 3 m (6 to 10ft).

Stock – *See* **Matthiola.**

Stokesia (Stokes' aster) – Hardy perennials which thrive in sunny borders and in light, well-drained soil, grow some 30 to 60cm (1 to 2ft) in height and bear blue or white flowers in eary autumn. *Species* – *S. laevis*.

Streptocarpus (Cape primrose) – Lovely perennials suitable for culture in the warm greenhouse. *Culture* – Pot-up annually in February or March, using 15cm (6in) pots and a peat-based compost. Propagate by seed in gentle heat (16°C (59°F)) in February, by leaf-cuttings or by division in March. If seed is sown, the small plants should be pricked off singly into small pots and gradually re-potted until in 15cm (6in) pots. They must be kept moist and shaded from strong sun. *Species* – *S. caulescens* (pale blue); *S. dunnii* (rose); *S. galpinii* (mauve and white); *S. rexii* (blue); *S. wendlandii* (rose or blue). All May to October, 25 to 50cm (10 to 20in).

Styrax (storax) – Hardy deciduous shrubs or small trees that like a sunny, sheltered position and a moist, rich, sandy loam. *Culture* – Plant in October. In autumn thin out any weak shoots. Propagate by layering in autumn. *Species* – *S. japonica* (2.5m (8ft)); *S. obassia* (2.5m (8ft)). All white, June to July.

Sweet pea – *See* **Lathyrus.**

Sweet rocket – *See* **Hesperis.**

Sweet William – *See* **Dianthus.**

Symphoricarpos (snowberry) – Hardy deciduous shrubs which thrive in sun or shade and in ordinary soil. They grow some 1.5m (5ft) high and flower in July and August. *Culture* – Plant in October or November; cut out dead wood and weak shoots annually in March, and every few years lift the shrubs in autumn, divide the roots and replant the younger and more vigorous parts.

Syringa (lilac) – Hardy deciduous shrubs which thrive in the sun in moist, well-manured, well-drained and rather heavy loam. They grow from 1.5 to 4.5m (5 to 15ft) high and flower in April, May and June. *Culture* – Plant in October or November. Periodically cut away all suckers from the roots of grafted plants, and cut out old and weak wood after flowering, but never trim away the young or half-matured shoots. Propagate by layering in June, by matured cuttings in the open in October, or by suckers in October. *Forcing* – For decoration in the greenhouse, pot-up in October or November, using 15 to 25cm (6 to 10in) pots and John Innes potting compost No. 3. Stand in a sheltered, frost-proof position, and move into the house in succession as bloom is desired. After flowering, remove all dead blooms, syringe and keep up the heat for 3 weeks or so, then harden off and sink the pots outdoors from May until the October of the following year; never force 2 years running. Prune as above. For mock orange or *Philadelphus coronarius*, commonly called syringa, *see Philadelphus*. *Named varieties* – (*Single*) – 'Jan Van Tol' and 'Marie Legraye' (white); 'Congo' (rich red); 'Massena' (crimson purple); 'Souvenir de Louis Spaeth' (purple); 'Charles X' (rich mauve); and 'Hugo Koster' (slate blue). (*Double*) –

'Madame Lemoine' (white); 'Belle de Nancy' (rosy pink); 'General Pershing' (violet); 'Katherine Havemeyer' (soft mauve); 'Charles Joly' (red purple); 'President Grevy' (lilac blue).

Tagetes (African and French marigolds) – Half-hardy annuals for warm, sunny beds and borders. *T. erecta* requires rich soil; *T. patula* thrives in poor soil. *Species – T. erecta* (African marigold), (June to September, 50 to 100cm (20 to 40in)); *T. patula* (French marigold) (June to September, 22.5 to 45cm (9 to 18in)); *T. tenuifolia* (*T. signata*) (yellow flowers and finely cut foliage, 30 to 45cm (12 to 18in)). There are innumerable varieties. *See* seed catalogues.

Tamarix (tamarisk) – Hardy deciduous or evergreen shrubs which do well anywhere in light ordinary soil, growing from 1.5 to 3m (5 to 10ft) high and flowering from May to September. *Culture* – Plant in October or November. Prune summer-flowering species in winter, spring-flowering kinds after flowering. Strike cuttings in the open in October. *Species – T. tetrandra* and *T. pentandra*.

Taxus (yew) – Hardy evergreen coniferous trees or shrubs which thrive in sun or shade and in ordinary soil. *T. baccata* is the common yew, usually used for hedges. *Culture* – Plant in May or September. When necessary trim in May or August. Propagate by means of seed in the open in March, or by cuttings of young wood in a frame in September.

Tecoma (trumpet flower) – Evergreen climbing shrubs which thrive in well-drained, light soil on warm sunny walls or in the greenhouse. *Culture* – Strike cuttings of ripe wood in a frame with bottom heat in autumn. Plant in dry, open weather between October and April. *Species – T. stans* for the cool greenhouse (flowers yellow, salmon and scarlet, leaves pinnate, 1.5 to 2m (5 to 6ft)).

Thalictrum (meadow rue) – Hardy perennials which thrive in well-drained, rich, sandy loam, in sunny or shady borders, or by the side of a stream. Dwarf kinds are useful rock plants. *T. adiantifolium* and *T. dipterocarpum* are excellent for cold greenhouse. *Pot culture* – Lift from the open and pot-up in November, using 12.5 to 15cm (5 to 6in) pots and a loam-based compost. *Species – T. adiantifolium* (yellow, June to September, 50cm (20in)); *T. alpinum* (greenish, May to June, 12.5cm (5in)); *T. dipterocarpum* (rose, purple or white, June to September, 90 to 120cm (36 to 48in)); *T. flavum* (yellow, July to August, 1 to 2m (48 to 72in)).

Thermopsis (false lupin) – Hardy perennials which grow from 30 to 75cm (12 to 30in) high and flower in summer. They do well in sheltered, sunny borders and in rich, sandy soil. Several species.

Thuja (arbor-vitae) – Hardy evergreen coniferous trees often used instead of yew as hedge plants. They succeed in sunny positions in any moist garden soil. *Culture* – Plant in May or September. No pruning is necessary. Trim hedge plants in April and September. Propagate by seeds in a frame, or by cuttings in a frame in September.

Thunbergia alata – Annual climbers carrying pretty flowers from June to September, and much used for hanging baskets and for greenhouse staging. They like a rich, fibrous loam mixed with leaf-mould and sand and are raised from seed in March in sandy soil, in a temperature of 16°C (59°F) or from cuttings subjected to gentle bottom heat. Pot on for flowering into 10 to 12.5cm (4 to 5in) pots or harden off and set out in the open in June in a warm, sheltered bed.

Thymus (thyme) – Hardy trailing plants that are useful for the rock or paved garden, and which thrive in the sun in well-drained, sandy loam. *Species – T. serpyllum* and vars.

Tiarella cordifolia (foam flower) – Hardy perennials which like a shady position in the border or rock garden and a moist, ordinary soil. They grow some 22.5cm (9in) high and carry creamy white flowers from April to June.

Tigridia (tiger iris) – Half-hardy bulbous plants which do best in a light, rich loam and leaf-mould, in a warm, sunny position in a dry border or rock garden, or in the greenhouse. *Culture* – Plant about the middle of April, 10cm (4in) deep and 15cm (6in) apart, letting the bulbs rest on sand. Lift from the ground in November. *Pot culture* – Bulbs may be placed in a 15cm (6in) pot, the latter being kept in a frame or cool house until growth has started. Propagate by offsets in April. *Species* – *T. pavonia* (scarlet, marked yellow and purple); *T.p.* 'Speciosa' (yellow, purple spots); *T.p.* 'Red Giant' (crimson, scarlet). All flower from May to July, 30 to 45cm (12 to 18in).

Tilia (lime) – Hardy deciduous trees, which thrive in sunny, sheltered positions and in moist, rich soil. They bear fragrant yellowish-green flowers from June to August. *Culture* – Plant in October or November.

Torenia – Half-hardy annuals of trailing nature, which flower in August and are suitable for hanging baskets. They need a compost of sandy loam and leaf-mould.

Trachelium caeruleum (throatwort) – Half-hardy biennial which thrives in ordinary soil in sunny beds or borders. It grows about 45cm (18in) high and flowers in July and August. It makes a good pot plant for the cool house.

Tradescantia (spiderwort) – Hardy and half-hardy perennial plants suitable for beds and cool greenhouse. They thrive in sun or shade in any good well-drained soil. *T. canaliculata* (*ohiensis*) (blue, June to September, 50cm (20in)); *T. virginiana* (purple, red, blue or white, June to September, 50cm (20in)).

Trifolium (clover, shamrock, trefoil) – Hardy annuals and perennials which thrive in any light soil and are easily raised from seed or propagated by division of roots.

Trillium (trinity flower) – Hardy tuberous-rooted perennials, which thrive in well-drained, moist, peaty soil, in partial shade in border or rock garden, or in pots in cold greenhouse. *Culture* – Plant in October. Lift from the soil when overcrowded. Propagate by seed sown in a frame in March, or in the open in June, or increase by division of roots in October. *Species* – *T. grandiflorum* (rose or white, June to July, 15 to 30cm (6 to 12in)); *T. erectum* (deep purple, May to June, 12.5 to 25cm (5 to 10in)).

Tritonia – *See* **Crocosmia.**

Trollius (globe flower) – Hardy herbaceous perennials, which thrive in rich, moist loam, in shady borders or in the marsh garden. *Species* – *T. asiaticus* (yellow or orange, May and June, 60cm (24in)); *T. europaeus* (orange, May to June, 75cm (30in)); *T. ledebourii* (golden yellow, April to May, 75 to 100cm (30 to 40in)).

Tropaeolum – Beautiful climbers, mostly half-hardy annuals, invaluable for covering trellises out of doors and for training up pillars and rafters in the cool greenhouse. The best known are *T. peregrinum* (canary creeper) and *T. majus* (nasturtium).

Canary creeper – This well-known creeper flowers best in a rather poor, dry soil and in a sunny position. It is half-hardy. *Culture* – Sow late in April very thinly in the open, or under glass in March in a cool greenhouse. If grown indoors, pot off singly, harden off and plant out 30cm (12in) apart in May, otherwise thin out when large enough to handle.

Nasturtium – Many varieties are well known as climbers; the dwarf varieties are useful for bedding or edging, and for the rock garden. *Culture* – Sow thinly from March to June 1cm (½in) deep in light, poor soil, and thin out to 30 or 45cm (12 or 18in) apart when large enough. The double varieties do not seed, and cuttings must be struck in a cold frame in August or

September. For outdoor use, *T. peregrinum* and *T. majus* are especially good, also the perennial species, *T. polyphyllum* and *T. speciosum* (flame nasturtium). *T. peltophorum* (*lobbianum*) blooms beautifully through the winter in the greenhouse and likes a light, but not too rich soil. Pot-up from March to April in 15 to 25cm (6 to 10in) pots and grow near the glass. Propagate by seed or cuttings in April.

Tulpa – Tulips look best massed in beds or borders, carpeted with other spring flowers. The best tulip for all-round purposes is probably 'Keizerskroon'. For planting permanently, the Cottage and Darwin tulips are best. *Culture* – Tulips require a well-drained, deeply dug, rich loam with a cool, moist subsoil, and a sunny, sheltered position not subjected to draughts and cold winds. Plant early in November, from 10 to 12.5cm (4 to 5in) deep and from 20 to 25cm (8 to 10in) apart. It is best to lift the bulbs and plant them in a different bed each year. If this cannot be done, the soil should be well dug and improved by using bonemeal or well-rotted manure. *Pot culture* – The early single and double dwarf tulips are excellent for this purpose. The former may be planted 6 to 8 bulbs in a good-sized pot; but of the latter, 3 bulbs are sufficient. All tulips require a good supply of water when in flower and should be shaded from the sun; hard forcing will prevent flowering. The soil and treatment necessary for tulips grown in pots are the same as recommended for hyacinths. Propagation is carried out by offsets, separated from the bulbs when lifted in summer, and planted in September or October. Named varieties are innumerable and catalogues should be consulted.

Typha (reed mace, bulrush or cat-o'-nine-tails) – Aquatic plants, which thrive on a swampy bank, in the marsh garden, or at the edge of a sheltered pool with 2.5 to 30cm (1 to 12in) of water above the crowns. They grow some 1.8m (6ft) high and flower in late summer. *Species – T. latifolia.*

Ulex (furze or gorse) – Free flowering spiny shrubs bearing yellow flowers; they like a sunny position and a poor, dry soil. *U. europaeus* 'Plenus' (1.5m (5ft)) flowering from March to June is useful for hedges. *Culture* – Plant out from pots at any time between March and October; cut back when overgrown and propagate by cuttings in a frame in August or sow seed in a frame in March. Single-flowered forms seed too freely.

Ulmus (elm) – Hardy deciduous trees which thrive in almost any soil and in practically any position. *Culture* – Plant in October or November. Thin out the branches in the summer when necessary. Propagate by seeds, grafting or from sucker growths. Several species and vars., but all are more or less susceptible to Dutch Elm Disease.

Ursinia – Half-hardy annuals which can be grown in the open during summer in well-drained soil and a sunny position. Propagate by means of seed sown thinly *in situ*. Thin at seedling stage.

Vaccinium – Large genus of shrubby plants which includes the whortleberry or bilberry (*V. myrtillus*). There are several species grown for the beauty of their flowers, fruit and tinted foliage in autumn; these require a moist, sandy and peaty loam. Propagate by cuttings struck under glass in spring and summer, by root-suckers or by seed sown in autumn when ripe. Plant out in March. *Species – V. corymbosum* (blueberry) (pale pink or white, 2m (5ft)); *V. myrtillus* (whortleberry) (pale pink, 75cm (1½ft)). All May-flowering.

Valeriana – Hardy perennials of which the smaller species are useful for the rock garden. The best known are *V. officinalis* (all heal) and *V. phu*. They thrive in sunny borders and in any ordinary soil. Both flower from June to October.

Vallota speciosa (Scarborough lily) – Half-hardy bulbous plants, which thrive in a loam-based compost. They require the protection of the cool greenhouse or sunny window and flower on stems from 30 to 60cm (1 to 2ft) high in August and September. *Culture* – Plant in July or August singly in 12.5 to 20cm (5 to 8in) pots, with the crowns 15cm (6in) below the surface. Winter near the glass and give liquid manure when the buds form. Water moderately till the leaves die in spring and keep fairly dry and exposed to the sun from May to September. Leave in the same pot for 3 to 4 years. Propagate by seed in spring, or by offsets in August.

Venidium fastuosum –Half-hardy annuals which thrive in sunny, dry, well-drained situations outdoors. Sow in flowering position towards the end of April.

Verbascum (mullein) – Hardy biennials and perennials which may be grown in sunny borders or in the wild garden in light, ordinary soil. *Species* (*Biennial*) – *V. olympicum* (golden yellow, grey foliage, June to September, 1.7m (70in)). (*Perennial*) – *V. chaixii* (yellow, mauve centre, June to September, 1 to 2.5m (50 to 90in)); *V. phoeniceum* (purple, white or rose, June to September, 50 to 65cm (20 to 30in)). Good hybrids, 'Cotswold Beauty', 'Pink Domino'.

Verbena – Half-hardy annuals, biennials and perennials, which do well in rich, sandy loam in sunny beds. (*Perennials*) – Sow in heat (16°F (59°F)) in February and treat as biennials. With named varieties strike cuttings of sturdy shoots that have no flower buds in a frame in spring or early autumn. Autumn-struck verbenas are best left in pots until February; and if sufficient old plants are kept over the winter for stock, spring-struck cuttings are best. Plant out 25cm (10in) apart in June. *Pot culture* – Pot-up in March, using 12.5 to 15cm (5 to 6in) pots and John Innes potting compost No. 1. Stop the young shoots to make bushy plants.

Veronica (speedwell) – Shrubby species – These are now included in the genus *Hebe*, which *see*.

Herbaceous Perennial Species – These thrive in sunny positions and in any fairly good garden soil, especially if it is rather gritty. Every fourth year the plants should be lifted and divided, the younger outer crowns only being replanted. Propagate by division in March or in October. Some of the dwarf-growing species make excellent rock plants. *Species and varieties* – *V. spicata* 'Alba' (white, June to July, 45cm (18in)); *V. incana* (violet blue, silver foliage, June to September, 15 to 22.5cm (6 to 9in)); *V. prostrata* (dark blue, June to July, 5 to 7.5cm (2 to 3in)); *V. longifolia* var. *subsessilis* (deep blue, July to September, 50 to 75cm (20 to 30in)); *V. virginica* (*Leptandra*) (white, July to September, 75 to 90cm (30 to 36in)).

Viburnum – Hardy deciduous trees and shrubs which thrive in any soil, but prefer a moist, well-drained deep loam, and are most useful for shrubberies. The best known shrubby species is *V. opulus* 'Sterile', the guelder rose or snowball tree. *V. tomentosum* 'Plicatum', a splendid border shrub, is also a useful sort for the greenhouse. Pot-up in October, using 17.5 to 25cm (7 to 10in) pots and ordinary loam. Prune after flowering and plant out for 2 years in the open. *V. tinus* (laurustinus) is an evergreen species making a bush 2.5m (8ft) in height and best planted in sun or shade under trees and facing north. It flowers in autumn and all through the winter months. It is also useful for pot culture indoors. In the latter case pot-up in the early autumn using 15 to 25cm (6 to 10in) pots and well-drained sandy loam. Cut well back after flowering and put out in the open in semi-shade from May to October. Other good species are *V. carlesii*, with pinkish-white flowers in April and May; *V. fragrans* (*V. farreri*), pink or white, January to March; and *V. tomentosum* 'Plicatum', creamy white, May and June. *General culture in the open* – Plant in a sunny position, deciduous species in October, November or March; evergreen in May or September. Trim into shape annually and, when necessary, cut out old wood in July (deciduous) and May (evergreen species).

Vinca (periwinkle) – Hardy periwinkles are evergreen trailers, which grow in any well-drained ordinary soil and look well in borders or on rock gardens. *V. major* (50cm (20in)) and *V. minor* (22.5cm (9in)) have purple blue flowers from June to September. There are also mauve and white varieties. *Culture* – Plant from March to October. Cut back straggling shoots in April. Propagate by division in March or October. Invasive.

Viola – The viola and pansy are so similar in their cultural requirements that we treat them under the one heading. Violas, sometimes called tufted pansies, are much used for bedding or as edging plants, where they will flower from May until well into November. Any ordinary, deeply dug, moderately rich loam will suit them. A sprinkling of good compost and a dressing of bonemeal should be scattered on the top. Heavy clay is not good for violas. A cool, but not damp, position in partial shade is best. *Culture* – Violas may be propagated from seed, by cuttings or by division of the roots. Seed intended for spring flowers should be sown in boxes in June, using a seed compost and the box should be covered with a sheet of glass until the seeds are up. When large enough transplant 5cm (2in) apart into other boxes; water liberally and shade from sun. As frosty weather approaches, the boxes should be placed in a cold frame for the winter. At the beginning of April, transplant about 22.5 to 30cm (9 to 12in) apart into partially shaded beds, keeping the balls intact. Cuttings of new, but vigorous growths from the centre of the plant may be struck in September in a shady frame and planted out in March for blooming the following year. Propagation by cuttings may take place any time from April to the end of October, although August and September are the best months. For early flowering, it is best to propagate by division of old roots in September. The hardier kinds can be wintered successfully in the open in any shady nook in the garden, but not under trees. The less hardy kinds should be wintered in cold frames. Pansies bear larger and brighter flowers if raised from seed; violas, however, are more vigorous when propagated by cuttings. All dead blooms should be regularly picked off. *Pot culture* – Strike cuttings in July or August and when rooted, plant in 10cm (4in) pots and plunge in a cold frame, where they should remain until the end of March. Then shift them into 20cm (8in) pots, keep close for a few days, then admit air gradually. *Alpine species* – There are also many delightful alpine species which need similar treatment to that described for the bedding viola, but the soil should be somewhat more loose, gritty and moist. Named varieties are innumerable and catalogues should be consulted.

Viola odorata (violet) – Violets may be grown in pots, by placing 2 to 3 runners or offsets in a pot in April or May and keeping them in a frame, slightly shaded from the hot sun in summer; loam, leaf-mould and sand suit them admirably, but the violet is not particular as to soil. Some flower from September to April, if given the protection of glass; others flower in March and April. There are many varieties, but their culture is so similar that they may all be considered together. Start with good stock from a reliable source, and, although the violet is a perennial, it is best to renew the stock each year. *Cultivation* – The violet should be propagated annually in June; when the plants have flowered, remove them from the soil, divide them into single crowns, cutting off all runners and dead foliage and selecting the finest outside parts only; then plant out the single varieties 38cm (15in) apart each way and the double kinds 25 to 30cm (10 to 12in) apart and press the soil firmly round the roots, but do not bury the crowns. A rich, well-dug and well-drained bed with an east aspect, where they can receive the morning sun, is ideal.

Virginian Stock – *See* **Malcolmia.**

Viscum album (mistletoe) – This parasite is easy to cultivate; an incision should be made in the bark on the underside of a 3-year-old branch of an apple tree – many other trees, such as the pear, plum, ash, birch, etc, are equally suitable – and in February insert some ripe mistletoe berries into this incision, and carefully tie the bark back. Growth is exceedingly slow at first.

Vitis (vine) – Hardy deciduous climbers. They grow well in deeply dug, moist soil with a little lime in it, and should be planted only in sheltered positions. *Culture* – Strike cuttings in a frame in September. Plant in dry and open weather from November to March; trim in winter. *Species* – *V. coignetiae* is known as the crimson glory vine; other good species are *V. davidii* and *V. vinifera* 'Purpurea', the wine grape.

Waltzia (everlasting flowers) – Half-hardy annuals, which can be grown in warm, sunny borders or in the greenhouse. *W. grandiflora* (golden yellow, July to September, 50cm (20in).

Wallflower – *See* **Cheiranthus.**

Watsonia (bugle lily) – Half-hardy bulbous plants which should be grown in sunny positions in warm, sheltered borders and in rich soil or in the cold greenhouse. *Culture* Plant in October or March, 7.5cm (3in) deep and 10cm (4in) apart. Pot plants should be kept dry in winter. Propagate by offsets in October. *Species* – *W. coccinea* (scarlet, 50cm (20in)); *W. densiflora* (pink, 38cm (15in)). All June to August.

Weigela (Diervilla) – Hardy deciduous shrubs which thrive in sun or shade in almost any soil. *Culture* – Plant in October or November, and after flowering cut out old and straggly wood. To propagate strike cuttings of soft wood in June in a frame, or matured cuttings in the open in October. *Species and hybrids* – *W.* 'Abel Carrière' (carmine red, April to May, 1.5m (5ft)); *W.* 'Eva Rathke' (crimson purple, May to September, 1m (3 to 4ft)); *W. florida* (deep rose, 1.5 to 1.8m (5 to 6ft)).

Wisteria – Hardy May-flowering deciduous climbers that do well in any good garden soil, but prefer moist, deep and well-drained sandy loam. *W. sinensis*, of which there are 3 or 4 varieties, is the best known; *W. floribunda* 'Macrobotrys' is a newer form with mauve, rose or white flowers and longer racemes. *Culture* – Propagate by means of layering young wood in the summer, and plant out in permanent positions in dry, open weather from October to April. Both winter and summer pruning are essential to promote flower buds and straggling shoots should be cut away, but sturdy laterals should be encouraged to grow out some 90cm (3ft) from the main stems; once the climbers are trained in this way, the young shoots should, in winter, be cut hard back to within a couple of centimetres (in) of the old wood. *Pot culture* – In the cool greenhouse *W. sinensis* will flower from February to April; pot-up in October, using 20 to 30cm (8 to 12in) pots and John Innes potting compost No. 3. Prune in January or February, cutting back straggly shoots to within a centimetre (in) of the base; sink the pots to their rims outdoors in a sunny spot from May to December.

Wulfenia carinthiaca – Hardy perennial which likes a shady position in the rock garden in loam and peat. It carries purple blue flowers in July and August, on 22.5cm (9in) stems.

Xeranthemum (immortelles) – Showy class of everlasting flowers, all of which are hardy and thrive in sunny beds or borders and in rich soil. The best known is *X. igneum* (purple or white, 30cm (12in); it flowers from July to September).

Xerophyllum asphodeloides (turkey's beard) – Hardy perennials for the border, marsh, or wild garden. They love partial shade, and a moist gritty loam and leaf-mould. They carry spikes of white flowers 60cm (2ft) high in May.

Yucca – These are all practically hardy evergreen plants of quaint appearance, forming striking objects when planted on lawns; they are also suited to maritime gardens. Yuccas do best in sheltered, sunny positions in well-drained ordinary soil. *Culture* – Plant in March or April; cut away dead leaves in March and dead flowers in October. Propagate by means of tops, with the leaves trimmed off, planted in pots of very sandy and porous soil, by rhizomes in spring or by seed. *Y. gloriosa* is known as Adam's needle.

Zantedeschia (arum lily) – The arum lily is easy to cultivate either in the greenhouse or in a room. Re-pot every October in a peat compost or John Innes potting compost No. 2, the offsets having been removed and the old soil shaken out. A 15cm (6in) pot may be used for each plant or 3 may be placed in a 22.5 to 25cm (9 to 10in) pot. From this time till June, or earlier if the plants have flowered, they should have abundance of water and occasional doses of liquid fertilizer. After this, however, they can be planted out in rich soil, or stood in the open in semi-shade, kept moist, and be given occasional doses of liquid fertilizer till October, when the same treatment should be repeated. Propagate by offsets. The yellow species are less hardy and thrive best in the warm greenhouse. Pot-up in February. Withhold water gradually after flowering and keep the pots in a frost-proof frame through the winter.

Species and varieties – *Zantedeschia aethiopica*; *Z.a.* 'Crowborough' is hardier; *Z. rehmannii* (rose); *Z. elliottiana* (yellow, August, 60cm (24in)). The arum (except the yellow varieties) usually flowers in April. In catalogues the arum lily is sometimes listed as *Richardia*.

Zauschneria (Californian fuchsia) – Handsome perennials which thrive in gritty loam in the rock garden. *Z. californica* (scarlet, July to September, 30 to 45cm (12 to 18in) is the best known.

Zea (Indian corn or maize) – Half-hardy foliage annuals which thrive in ordinary soil in warm sunny situations. *Z. mays* 90cm (3ft) is also useful for greenhouse purposes.

Zephyranthes (zephyr flower) – Bulbous-rooted plants, some species of which are sufficiently hardy to thrive in warm, sunny borders and in rich and well-drained peaty loam; the more tender kinds should be grown in pots in the greenhouse. *Culture* – Plant in October, 10cm (4in) deep and 7.5cm (3in) apart, with the bulbs resting in sand, and protect with straw in winter. Lift when overcrowded and propagate by offsets in October. *Pot culture* – Pot-up from August to November, placing 4 to 5 bulbs in a 12.5 (5in) pot in a loam-based compost. Dry off gradually after flowering. *Species* – *Z. candida* (white); *Z. grandiflora* (*carinata*) (pale pink); and *Z. rosea* (rose). All May to September, 15 to 25cm (6 to 10in).

Zinnia – Half-hardy annuals which thrive in light, rich soil. The dwarfer hybrid varieties are valuable for warm, sunny beds; the taller kinds for borders and the cool greenhouse. *Greenhouse plants* – Pot seedlings up singly in small pots of John Innes potting compost No. 1. Give ample light and ventilate freely, but do not let the temperature drop below 16°C (59°F) and avoid draughts. Re-pot before the plants get pot-bound and as soon as the plants are re-established, reduce the temperature by a few degrees and, as the buds appear, water weekly with dilute liquid fertilizer and dress with bonemeal. *Species* – *Z. elegans* (various, 50 to 75cm (20 to 30in)); *Z. angustifolia* (orange, 30cm (1ft)). All July to September.

Index